MW00979754

Shamanic Links
A Comprehensive Foundation For Modern Shamanic Practice

Adam Bear

www.capallbann.co.uk

Shamanic Links

Cover and internal illustrations by Adam Bear
Cover design by HR Design www.hr-design.co.uk

Published by:

Capall Bann Publishing
Auton Farm
Milverton
Somerset
TA4 1NE

'Shamanic Links'

is

Dedicated to:

All the people who have helped me on my Quest, they are too numerous to
mention, but include Marcus, Sara, Cheryl, Cassandra, John, Sarah, Jim,
Ian, Zoe, Conrad, Tan, The Wardens, The Broads Authority, Barbara, Julie,
Margaret, Naomi, George, Jess, Graham, Nicki, Karen, Levannah, Mum,
Louise, Steve, Chris, Val, Georgia, Jon, Brenda, Oddie, Amanda, Terry,
Julia, Dave, Linda, Jo, Darren, Carla, Carol for all her support, &
especially Francesca for doing the proof!
A BIG thank you to you all!

Contents

2

Introduction

The original idea behind this book was to gather my own thoughts about my own Shamanic or Animistic Journey, which for me began consciously 15 years ago. I also realise that the term Shamanism relates to a specific Pagan belief system, however in my experience all Pagan belief systems have much to owe the Animistic/Shamanic systems, so this book will be of as much interest to all Pagans as it will to practitioners of Shamanic systems.

Although as I was raised by what would be classed as an artistic Christian spiritualist family, I grew up believing that most families were aware of unseen beings, spiritual energy and surrounded by poltergeist type activity and that everyone was interested in the many ancient sites of Cornwall; this was my 'norm', so school and 'normal' kids were a bit of a shock to me. From this original form it evolved into a year long foundation course and from there into this book you are reading. At first glance this is yet another book on Shamanism and how to practice it, there are only 13 chapters, an average amount, but where this book differs, you will soon realise is in the volume of useful and practical information contained within it.

I don't use long-winded terms, it is written in much the same manner as I speak, making it very user friendly. Although I use the word Shaman throughout the book, I do so very much in the knowledge that it is in the New Age context of Shamanism, which has far more in common with Animism, than with what a tribal Shaman would consider Shamanism. True Shamanism lives where it has always lived, with the tribes which need it for daily life; a true Shaman in our modern Western culture would at least be a qualified herbalist, doctor, teacher, politician, priest, healer, conservationist, psychologist, hunter, shepherd, tracker, craftsman and medium.

Very few of us are this skilled, nor do we need to be. Today's modern Western Shamen, are more often New Age therapists, with an interest in Native American culture, or Neo Pagans. I personally fall into this category, I am a qualified reiki master, registered spiritual healer, professional relaxation therapist, shiatsu practitioner, crystal healer and I am trained in First Aid, as well as undergoing and completing some introductory courses in counselling. But I have also gained some additional skills; I started and ran a moot in Cornwall for two years, I made and sold magikal tools for five years, I have trained in conservation, worked in zoos and I am qualified to assess National Vocational Qualifications. (The spelling of 'magikal' is used here to differentiate between spell-casting and the magician's slight-of-hand magic show.)

The main difference you will find in this book, is the in-depth information on the meanings, uses and step by step instructions on how to make Shamanic and magikal tools, lots of them. You will also find in-depth information on energy healing; although I am a Reiki Master and also teach it, I am probably one of the few, who might fail someone who is no good at it; actually I'd probably insist on them undergoing additional training and my Reiki courses last a year, not a weekend.

As a Cornishman I have also had the time, interest and opportunity to look at many ancient monuments and related subjects, including information on these subjects here also.

8

As someone who is trained in Conservation, I have often been shocked by the number of Pagans who are unaware of the different types of tree in their countryside. I've even met Pagans who believe that bears still live wild in Britain, so I thought it would be a good idea to include a chapter on the natural world, including such things as a tree identification guide, a basic introduction to ecology, conservation and tracks and signs of animals. In addition to this, I am introducing a new method for interpreting runes, based on an Old Norse Edda (Saga).

I have given the book a largely Norse and Celtic flavour, as these are the main Animistic or Pagan influences on this country (Britain); though I have also included information about Native American, Mongolian and Siberian Animistic beliefs. In other words this book will probably only be of interest to the serious committed Pagan student, not those seeking instant enlightenment. For the same reasons I have also briefly mentioned the darker side of Shamanism and Magik.

I hope what I have created is a down-to-earth practical book with a strong spiritual leaning towards Animism and Shamanic subjects, which will also be interesting to read, educational and useful. I have not seen a single volume book with this type of mixed content before; normally they are either about Shamanic beliefs or nature. In typical Shamanic fashion however, I am attempting to sit on the fence between these two fields and bring them back together again, where they should be; I hope it will be inspirational to you.

Adam Bear 2008

1
THE ROOTS OF SHAMANISM

What is a Shaman?
What is Animism?
What is Shamanism?
Ancient Roots
Links with other Earth Religions
The relevance of Shamanism today

What is a Shaman?

The word 'Shaman' comes from the Tungus tribe of Siberia and roughly translated means 'a state of ecstasy, excitement or agitation'. So a Shaman is an excited person. This is the only tribe to use this word Shaman, although anthropologists use this word to describe a type of tribal priest the world over. Most commonly all these priests have a form of 'trance work' involved in their role. This differentiates them from another type of tribal priest who practices Animism.

A Shaman is many things, a healer, priest, teacher, artist, warrior, medium, leader and guide, to name a few roles. This is not to say all Shamen are all these things, most often they specialize in two or more of these areas, although it is likely they will have some experience and knowledge of most of these areas to some degree. No two SHAMEN (this name applies to both males and females) or SHAMANKAS (to give the modern commonly accepted female terminology) are the same.

PEOPLE USUALLY DON'T CHOOSE TO BE A SHAMAN, THEY
EITHER ARE ONE, OR THEY ARE NOT.

Shamen are usually people who have had a difficult life with many real crises in it. These have forced them to look deeply at who they are and why they are. Shamen rarely want to be a Shaman, they usually just want to live a normal quite life and to be happy. The role of the Shaman is not an easy one. It is said in Tungenese tribes that the spirits call you to be a Shaman and you ignore them at your peril, reluctant Shamen are often reported to die as a result of refusing to follow their vocation. This is a Tungenese belief only, it is very unlikely that anyone will die as a result of refusing to follow a Shamanic path; it is more likely that you would experience something more similar to what I went through when I turned my back on it all. This could be described as a death inside, a void, which grew and could never really be filled by being anything other than being true to myself and to that side of my nature. There is put simply a constant nagging, that there is something missing from yourself and your life.

The art of the Shaman is usually passed down through the generations, as are the spirits and guides with whom they work. This is a relationship more deeply akin to a family bond with all its ups and downs. It is based on love, respect and trust, as well as familiarity. If you are a Shaman (or at least very spiritually aware) you will probably recognize some or all of these experiences:

A constant sense of isolation; never quite fitting in, no matter how hard you try.

Feeling very strong emotions, almost to the point of obsession. When you love you feel it so strongly it feels like your heart will explode. When you are heartbroken it hurts so much you wish you were dead and you suffer excruciating mental anguish.

Never feeling quite settled, you probably move house regularly, change jobs frequently, move to different areas, change your social group or friends, have many different hobbies and interests, maybe even go so far as to try different personalities.

Always feel like you are looking for something, which will make sense of it all.

Probably experienced some form of breakdown, at the very least wondered about your sanity.

Probably had some form of abuse around you, maybe sexual, mental, physical, alcohol or drug related.

You will probably have experienced a number of spiritual revelations, visions, hallucinations, feelings or premonitions. Certainly you will have found yourself drawn to spiritual, religious or psychological interests.

You will also probably find that you are naturally gifted in some way. You may be artistic, you may be someone everyone comes to with their problems, you may be a healer, you may have an affinity with nature, there will be at least one natural talent which everyone recognizes in you.

These are all clues as to whether you are a Shaman/Shamanka or an Animist.

ULTIMATELY THE SPIRITS HAVE TO CALL YOU, TO BE A
SHAMAN

What is Animism?

Animism is a form of spirituality much like Shamanism. The two have much in common, the major difference is that a Shaman travels to meet and interact with the spirit world, while usually in some form of trance state. An example of Animism is the Native American Medicine Wheel teachings. Most of what is called Shamanism today is in fact Animism. Most people can learn to be Animists, in fact all Shamen are Animists. This book will teach you about Animism and where it merges with Shamanism.

Animism is an essential step on the road to becoming a Shaman, it is spiritual ecology. It would be near impossible for most people to live and function as full time Shamen in today's world, it would most likely drive you insane, certainly by normal definitions of sanity. Tribal Shamen usually only perform this role part time. Animism is usually as near to Shamanism as it is possible to go without being born a Shaman. Animism works on the same principles and uses many of the same methods as Shamanism. However it allows you to turn off or tune out when necessary. A Shaman is never fully in this world or the spirit world, but living in a sort of limbo between the two. It is rare, but possible, to become a Shaman after studying Animism. However this would take a total commitment, which most of us would find impossible. It would also take a strong support team in this world and the spirit world.

So the term Shamanism used in this material refers to a mixture between Shamanism and Animism. An example of this would be that all Aboriginals would be Animists, but not all Aboriginal Animists would be Shamen.

What is Shamanism?

Shamanism is literally what a Shaman does. It most often takes the form of healing, although anyone who asks or hires a Shaman to do something for them is more often asking for the help of the spirit world, via the Shaman. So Shamanism could take many forms, for example:

A Shaman may be asked to create an object which links the user to a certain area, animal, time, etc.

A Shaman may be asked to empower an individual for a short term with the energy of something.

A Shaman may be asked to commune with an ancestor, for advice and direction.

A Shaman may be asked to make a ritual magikal tool on behalf of someone.

A Shaman may be asked to find an individuals Totems, Guides, etc.

A Shaman may be asked to give someone training in some form of spiritual development, e.g. a Vision Quest.

A Shaman may be asked to create a Medicine Bundle for someone.

A Shaman may be asked for healing of a variety of types.

A Shaman may be asked to travel to the Other Worlds in order to find an individuals soul, Soul Retrieval.

A Shaman may be asked for protection.

A Shaman may be asked for counselling.

In short a Shaman is usually consulted to do something on behalf of an individual or group that they can't do for himself or herself, usually involving spiritual or magikal energies.

Ancient Roots

Shamanism is the oldest form of 'organised religion' in the world dating back to the Stone Age. I use the term 'organised religion' in its loosest sense. Shamanism is not really a religion as religions need a god or goddess of some type. Shamanism deals with spirits, all spirits. Deities came into being much later in human history than spirits; with the introduction of the Earth Mother or Mother Nature, as she is most often known today. The first deity was probably a goddess, probably because human society was originally governed by women, or was Matriarchal in nature. Spirits have been perceived by humanity ever since the effects of the wind were noticed, or to put it another way, an invisible energy having a physical effect on the mundane world. It is a strange quirk of human nature that even people who have no faith in any form of god, often still believe in ghosts or spirits. This is not to say that Shamans don't believe in gods and goddesses, Shamen evolve in their beliefs as do all of us. However Shamen still most commonly relate to spirits first.

There is a pantheon of spiritual beings, which the Shaman observes, with The One God/dess at its top and the lowest form of individual spirit at its bottom. I will not pretend to know the correct order of these, as it varies from tribe to tribe, not to mention country to country. I will present a guide to these latter however it is down to the Shaman and through his or her spirits, to decide which level of this pantheon is necessary to contact in order to achieve the best results and to some degree what order this pantheon takes for you, it is likely there is no exact order and if there is you will probably never know it all. In this area it is a good idea to remember a little respect and humility can go a long way.

It is easiest to consider this spiritual hierarchy in a manner similar to our own governing bodies. The first port of call when confronting a problem is yourself; only after deciding you can not solve this problem alone do you seek help from others, initially probably from family or friends. Later on you may decide it is necessary to contact strangers in positions of power. At this point you must decide which ones to contact, for example you don't call the Emergency Services, because you are overdrawn at the bank, just as you don't call the Water Authority, because your house is on fire.

To begin with you must take comfort in knowing that you are never presented with an immediate problem you can not deal with, unless, you are being taught a lesson in humility. Another thing you will often notice about Shamen is that they are often quite humble individuals. This is because they have an idea of their role in the great scheme of things and have had contact with Beings of far more importance than themselves. It is also a humbling experience to know that these beings acknowledge you. You may also discover that if you develop an over-inflated sense of importance, they may also knock you down a peg or two, if necessary.

Shamanism is not a religion, although a sense of devotion and faith is inherent within it. It may be more accurate to say it is a philosophy, which will prove or disprove itself to you. You are allowed to question things, in fact it is encouraged, especially things about yourself. Shamanism is an ancient system, which is ingrained within us all, it works on the basis that everything is connected or as the Native Americans would say "everything is your relative". Everything plays its part and has a purpose, there is no good and evil as we commonly think today, there is only that which 'IS'. All things are made of the same electrons, protons, neutrons and atoms, which were all originally parts of stars. Or to put it another way, everything is made of the same stardust.

Good and Evil are the Christian terminology we most commonly apply to things we do not fully understand and as a result fear. It is more accurate to consider things in the terminology of Yin and Yang, Chaos and Order, Night and Day, Winter and Summer. All things are there for a purpose; all things are a part of The One God/dess. I guess ultimately all this, is The One God/dess's way of discovering, learning and coming to understanding itself.

Links with other Earth Religions

Shamanism is as I've already said the world's oldest 'organised religion'. Forms of Shamanism or Animism are found in all cultures the world over. They all vary to a degree, as they are very much influenced by the natural world around them; as are the people who practice these beliefs. However there is a link between them all, which would allow an Innuit Shaman and an Australian Aboriginal Shaman to communicate freely and to understand each other, even if they don't speak the same language. This is because Shamanism is a universal language; it is a language of humanity. It speaks not in numbers or words but in emotions, thoughts, hopes and fears. All

Humans the world over share the same feelings and genetic make up, we all ultimately dream the same dreams.

This genetic code or language is inherent not just in humans but to some degree in all living beings, all things that exist are alive in some way and evolve through their own process. Even things not normally considered to be alive e.g. rocks, metals, plastics, everything. Shamanism takes the next step and the 'leap of faith' that says all things share these feelings, thoughts and dreams with us. As a result it is possible to communicate, to some degree, with all things, as all things are made of the same energy. I guess it is a form of empathy.

All of the imagery and symbolism of Shamanism is found deep within the human mind, within the subconscious. Psychologists are a lot nearer to Shamen than they may realize. Psychology and all medical practices originate in Shamanism, as it was the Shaman who originally began to discover the cures for the ailments of his or her tribe, long before recorded history began. It was also the Shaman who first began to realize how the human animal worked; what motivated it, scared it, empowered it, disempowered it, etc. As a result it was the Shaman who turned to ways of solving these problems and either became aware of the spirit world or created it.

The original Shaman was probably a disabled member of the tribe, who was unable to fend for him or her self, as a result was reliant on the rest of the tribe to take care of their needs. As a result of this disability s/he had more free time to look around at the world in which s/he and the rest of the tribe lived. This disability gave him or her the freedom to ask questions and to find answers. These answers would eventually benefit the tribe and the unproductive individual, would have carved themselves a role of importance and productivity within the tribe. This newfound knowledge would be shared with other tribes and bonds would be forged. As a result it spread and grew with new knowledge being learnt all the time and passed on to these Shamen or record keepers. This in turn would necessitate a more complex language. The first written form of language would evolve in the

18

form of pictures. As this knowledge grew it would eventually lead the Shaman to look within themselves and to try to understand how they worked.

All this would lead eventually to what we know today. It all would have developed from an individuals need to be a worthwhile member of society, from that individuals hopes, dreams and fears. As we are all related way back in time to a small number of individuals I guess we all have within us a part of that original Shaman.

Shamanism has links with all religions. It is most closely linked to what would be classed as Earth Religions; these include Paganism, Wicca, Druidry, Goddess religions, Tao-ism, Buddhism, Nordic traditions, Aboriginal Dreamtime beliefs, Voodoo and Native American Traditions. All of these traditions, beliefs and religions contain strong elements of Animism.

The Shamanic lore, rituals and beliefs contained in this course are not from any one tradition but have been drawn from many of these and other traditions. I have personally studied many of these traditions and beliefs and found so much common ground it would seem wrong not to combine as much relevant knowledge in one place as possible. This may not make sense to some people, especially if their understanding of Shamanism stems from an interest in Native American traditions; however it is important to remember that traditionally the Native Americans are known to have migrated to America from Siberia about 10,000 years ago; so Mongolian and Russian Shamanism is part of their Cultures make up. However what is even more interesting and is recent scientific genetic DNA evidence that they may not have been the first.

It is known that all people originated from Africa, via several migrations at different times. It is believed that the race of people, who migrated from Africa to Australia to become what we know as Aboriginals, actually reached the tip of South America and formed a small colony there about 20,000 years ago. They were eventually nearly wiped out by the later migrations of other tribes, although a few survived and interbred with the newer invaders; as a result there are still a handful of their descendants alive today. Also it is believed that about 15,000 years ago a tribe from France called the Sulutrians also emigrated to America, crossing huge ice sheets and open waters using Innuit-type technology which was available to them; they eventually interbred with a Great Lakes tribe called the Ojibwa; giving them their descendants today, this means they are related distantly to the Celts of France and Britain. As Shamanism is so closely interwoven with the country and wildlife it is practiced in, this course is mainly a combination of Celtic and Nordic traditions as they are who populated this area. In Celtic tradition the Shaman is generally considered to have been called a Vate or Ovate; in Nordic tradition the Shaman would have been called a Vitki (Wildman) or a Thule (Sorcerer).

The Relevance of Shamanism today

Shamanism is an old tradition as is Animism do they or any of the other Earth religions have any relevance in today's world? The answer to this is 'yes'; during the last forty years there has been an enormous growth in the interest of the older traditions. Why is this happening? There are a number of reasons for this resurgence of interest in these old traditions.

1) Since the 1960s there has been a massive explosion of information and communication technologies. This means that everyone is potentially far more informed than they were in the period prior to the 60s.

2) As a result of this information and communication boom the world has metaphorically grown far smaller. Beliefs from half way round the world are no longer that far away. The culture in which we live today is made up of a number of different cultures due to immigration. All of these have a profound effect on the modern cultural views and there is far more choice.

3) As a result of the of the propaganda fed to us by the governments of the world during the Cold War, we have lost faith in the information these governments feed us and we no longer blindly believe what we are told, but rather question everything.

4) As a result of this questioning there have been a lot of changes in society including Women's Lib. We are no longer happy to just let the people in charge make all the decisions for us. This attitude has a profound impact on the Christian Church. Especially when the Church's history is studied in any depth. It doesn't take a lot of research to uncover the thin veneer that the Christian Church laid over the top of the older beliefs.

5) In the same way that we no longer trust the politicians and doctors to do what's best for us, we also no longer trust the priests to the same extent.

6) We are more independent as a species now and as a result of this we feel more able to look after our own spiritual development and well being. The Old Traditions teach that everyone has access to the gods.

7) The environmental concerns we all share, are also another issue, which have strongly influenced this growth in interest in the Old Earth religions.

8) The acceptance of complementary therapies into main stream society have brought with them an increase in information and interest in the old traditions and religions on which many are based.

9) All this is lumped together under the name New Age.

So is Shamanism and Animism of relevance today?

Yes.

Why is it of relevance?

1) Shamanism and Animism see the planet as a living being, an Earth Mother. The plants and animals (including us) as the children of this Earth Mother. This leads to an increased sensitivity about environmental issues, what we will accept being done to the Planet in the name of progress or business. What we will do as individuals, to limit how we live, causing damage to the planet, our Mother and ultimately ourselves.

2) We also care more about what we eat and how it is produced as a result of this environmental awareness. This leads to us eating less meat and more organic fruit and vegetables. It is harder to eat an animal when you see it as a brother or sister. Fruit and vegetables are eaten and it helps to regenerate more fruit and vegetables. If these fruit and vegetables are grown organically they benefit the planet and improve and provide suitable habitats for our wildlife. As a result of this dietary change we become healthier as individuals.

3) Shamanism allows you to contact the gods and spirits, which influence your life, directly. So you are more at peace, than when you ask the local priest to do it for you, if s/he has time. It gives you a sense of more control over your life. Also when you feel you have your own spiritual friends watching out for you it increases your confidence in what you can do and will help to stretch your expectations of your life experience.

4) Shamanism also involves healing and other complementary therapies, as well as encouraging you to get out of the house and back to nature. All of these have a beneficial effect on your health and wellbeing.

5) Shamanism will encourage you to be more creative and to view the world again as you once did as a small child with awe and wonder.

6) Shamanism will teach you more about yourself and how you work. As a result you will learn why you have trouble doing certain things and help you to overcome these limitations, if necessary. It will also help you to understand other people more and be better able to help them when asked.

So in short, Shamanism and Animism is relevant today because it will help the planet, help you and help others. With this in mind I think it is important to learn a little about the natural world around us, before we move deeper into the Shamanic world.

2

THE NATURAL WORLD

Woodlore
Historic Ecology
Global Warming
Walk your Talk
Carbon Footprint
Basic Ecology
Conservation
Tree Identification & Tree Lore
Other Plants relevant to Shamanism
Direction Sense
Animal Tracks and Signs

Woodlore

This chapter will cover things like folklore connected with trees, tree identification, traditional shamanic plants, conservation, basic ecology, food chains, food webs, tracking and animal signs, coppicing techniques, ancient woodland, direction sense, etc.

I do not know of a lot of Shamanic or Animistic courses or books which deal with these subjects; however as a long-practising Pagan who has led and organised a number of Pagan Moots and open celebrations, I have spoken to lots of Pagans, young and old. I have also spent a lot of time making magikal tools, often to order, with people asking for specific requirements and materials.

Sadly, I am often amazed at just how little about nature these 'Pagans' actually know. I am trained in countryside management, I have spent a couple of years doing practical conservation and briefly worked in Zoos and wildlife parks. I find it amusing and sad, when I am talking to someone about this wonderful staff they have made, they tell me all about it, because I am always interested in such things, I look at it and then they tell me its made of cherry or apple or something else and I think to myself, actually it's hazel. So I am going to make sure, that anyone who reads my book, at least knows the basics about nature.

Historic Ecology

Ecology is a fairly new science, it has only been taught since the 1960's; conservation is one of its results, however ecology has been around forever, it is basically the study of 'how everything inter relates to everything else'. Our ancestors used ecology and understood it, although they called it by different names and understood it in a largely instinctive manner.

However the idea of ecology and conservation has been around a long time, the Native American Indians have often been forwarded as the symbol of conservation and living in harmony with nature; the 'Crying Indian' from famous American advertisements for conservation, is well known, the Noble Savage of the American West, is an even more famous idea. Sadly it isn't quite true, the Native Americans' image of the Noble Savage was largely created by their European conquerors. It is true that they lived in a form of harmony with nature and never stripped the land bare, they always left something for the seventh generation, for their children's children. They also buried the kidneys of the buffalo they killed, so that it would grow another one. The truth is the Native Americans Plains Indians lived in a simple hunter/gatherer fashion for many centuries before we messed it up for them. The whole human race has lived in this simple manner for the majority of its history. The hunter/gatherer lifestyle is the most environmentally friendly way of living, it does less damage than any other system of living, living in harmony with and dependent upon the natural world for all our resources, keeps damage to a minimum (due to the harsh, dangerous, constantly moving lifestyle) and population numbers low (due to the lack of suitable partners for breeding). For one and a half million years, our ancestors lived in this fashion, the natural world thrived around them; but in the last fifteen thousand years, especially the last 5000 of these, we have altered and tamed the natural world, almost beyond recognition to our distant ancestors. The Native Americans also changed when they came in contact with the white people, especially when introduced to the horse.

It was not uncommon for whole herds of buffalo to be driven over cliffs, to their deaths, which mainly went to waste. This is a far cry, from using every scrap of the buffalo and wasting none. They also burnt down areas of Forest to allow for planting of crops, just as the Celts did. Prior to the Horse being introduced to America by the Spanish, the Native Americans walked everywhere, using dogs to pull their equipment. They simply weren't fast enough to pose a major threat to the huge buffalo herds. It is true, that no matter how bad they were, they were never as bad for the buffalo as the white man, who shot them from passing trains to relieve boredom, or hunted them for only their skins or tongues.

In Russia and Mongolia, there are a lot of people still living hunter/gatherer type lifestyles; there are many the world over, Australian Aboriginals, tribes in South America, Africa and Thailand.

Sadly even Shamanic beliefs cause problems. In Russia, hunters shoot whole herds of reindeer as they cross rivers; it is a very good place to set an ambush, the hunt is very bountiful; but sadly much of the meat is wasted and simply rots. This sort of wastefulness is why I became a vegetarian.

The reason all the reindeer are killed is because they believe any surviving reindeer will tell the other reindeer they meet, not to cross there.

Global Warming

Conservation and ecology are very important issues today, not simply because of Global Warming. Firstly, global warming is something that no scientists have yet proven is not just a natural occurrence, I've attended lectures at one of the most influential universities in Britain when it comes to Environmental Research. What I gathered from these lectures was that there were several theories but no one could decide which one was the most accurate. The 'predictions' for what will happen globally with regards to global warming are based on the calculations and data fed into a computer which then 'predicts' the most likely outcome using a global model. However like most statistics programmed into a computer, they can be manipulated to prove almost anything. So to try and make sense of the global warming issues, I will stick to what is known:

1) It is getting hotter.

2) A hotter environment will have profound effects on the glaciers.

3) The glaciers will melt more quickly.

4) The ocean level will rise.

5) Salt levels within the oceans will decrease.

6) These effects combined will have an effect on what is perceived as normal weather.

7) This will have big effects on agriculture.

You can see from this that things will change, for some areas of the planet things may improve for humans, for other areas things will get worse. The same is true for the plants and animals, the biodiversity as it is known. However, the most normal state of being for this planet, taking into account its long history, prior to humanity, is an ice age. Humanity, as a race has developed during a mainly warm spell.

Humanity has only existed very briefly in relation to the planet. We are still coming out of the last great ice age which saw the demise of many species, including our cousins the Neanderthals. As a result it is bound to get warmer. England used to be a tropical environment when the dinosaurs walked the planet, even in the Dark Ages it was considerably warmer on average each year than it is now. What global warming is really about, is the question 'are we making it warmer quicker?'. The answer is simple 'YES'. The next question is 'can we have an influence on how quickly it gets warmer?' Again the answer is 'YES'. The question becomes 'are we doing enough to slow down global warming?' The answer sadly is 'NO'.

Why?

Technology causes most of the problems, the buffalos were almost wiped out for one main reason: the gun. The trouble with modern technology and society is, we use it before we understand it. We are like children playing with guns, we are not as developed as a species as our technology implies. We are all still hunter/gatherers underneath the modern trappings. Man's place on the planet is an interesting one, though ecologically speaking not an important one. The human animal has had more influence of the condition of the planet we see around us than any other animal. yet, if mankind died overnight, the planet/nature would forget us very quickly, without having a drastic effect on the natural balance. Yet if all the Insects died overnight, the planet/nature would be virtually destroyed.

Our decision to settle and live an agricultural pattern, has caused no end of trouble. It was a good idea, for our species; but settling in large groups means we need to create space for us to live, there are more potential breeding partners, hence a bigger population, hence we need more resources to support us, there is nothing awful here, but it is these simple life facts that lead to the problem.

The White Man, has created nearly all the problems we are potentially looking at environmentally; so perhaps it is appropriate that the 'Crying Indian', turns out to be a white actor; or that 'Grey Owl', a famous Native American environmentalist of the 1920's and 30's, turns out to be an white Englishman, playing Injun.

Wiccans have a basic rule: 'if it harms none, do as you will'; a good idea, impossible, but a good idea. The truth is a simple and harsh one; 'if you live you harm', there is no way around it. What we need to do is limit the damage we cause; that will not happen quickly, because it would cause hardship and a fall in profits. That is the world we live in, apparently, in the 1960's someone invented a car that ran on water and caused no pollution or toxic substances. The oil companies bought it outright and lost the plans; it was not good for their business. Although Vauxhall/GM have created a similar new version now, that runs on a nuclear power plant and only produces water as a bi-product, though it is still years from being economically viable.

It is fossil fuel (petrol, oil, coal, gas) which is one of the main contributions to global warming and acid rain. The effects of the 1960's caused a massive changes to people's attitudes, with its 'free love' attitude; the 'Pill', liberated women from their unwanted pregnancy fears, sex became fun and safe; it also allowed them to become liberated from the role of housewives and mothers, to pursue careers of their own. This is all good, but it creates other problems, there is more competition for work between the sexes, modern technology, computers allowed industry to drastically reduce their staff needs, so there is today a world with more people than there is work. People's attitudes to marriage have also changed, we think nothing of marrying several times during our lives, instead of just once; often this means at least one new child for each marriage, leading to more people, which means, more housing, less wilderness, more resources needed, less wilderness, less nature, less trees which nature designed to remove CO_2 emissions.

Global warming does not mean we will just have warmer weather all year; it means we will have more of a tropical weather pattern. We are experiencing the results of this on a small scale now. The flash floods we are experiencing can be attributed to these changes, as can the mini tornadoes of a couple of years ago. Rising sea levels will mean more permanent flooding, loss of land and some low level countries are at risk of disappearing.

The dispersal of salt levels in the ocean, could also mean that the oceans are more liable to freeze, which could bring on an ice age. Especially as the Great Ocean Conveyor, an underwater river on two layers, warm and cold water, which flows through the oceans has a large influence on weather, could be effected.

We also have improved health, people live to their hundreds quite often today, this also means more strain on housing and resources, hence on the wilderness. There are now in excess of seven billion people living on the planet; it has been estimated that the planet can only successfully sustain six billion; we are in trouble.

It is our attitudes that need to change though; technology is good, if used with forethought and wisdom, not wealth as its aim. We tend to forget, or not even consider, the damage we cause the environment, our Earth Mother. We all love animals, there are millions of cats living in this country; they kill in excess of four million birds, mice, rats, voles, etc each year. We kill millions of sheep, cows, pigs, etc each year, to feed us; yet millions of tons of this meat is wasted, yet millions of people starve on a daily basis.

Nature is made up of many interesting animals, living, breathing, feeling, aware beings, they are not simply resources. But then again humans are often referred to as simply consumers, like a plague of locusts. Human life is often undervalued, however we do need to be more aware of the whole, not just ourselves. Probably the biggest overall contribution to global warming and other environmental issues is human population growth.

Our farming practices kill huge numbers of insects, the birds starve, the forests are cut down to produce millions of tons of newspaper, which we throw away. Waste is our main problem, not simply wasted resources, but wasted lives, human and animal. I recently saw on the news, two stories within minutes of each other, one spoke of famine in Ethiopia, and the other spoke of a massive tomato fight in Spain. I thought 'that sums life up, you either have or have not'; that isn't the way it should be.

Walk your Talk

Ecology teaches us that all things are living in an interdependent relationship; everything is connected. Shamanism/Animism teach us that all things are self aware and living in an interdependent relationship, what affects one being, eventually affects us all, to some degree. These two philosophies are closely connected, but one is a science and listened to, if grudgingly, by governments; the other is an ancient belief system to which our ancestors paid tribute, so ignored today, by the ruling bodies.

It is the people, the citizens who elect the governments, so don't waste your votes, if you don't have any specific, political parties you believe strongly in, then don't waste your vote, by not voting, vote for the Green Party, it's unlikely they will win, but large numbers voting for them helps to gain them seats, that helps to get their voices heard, which helps to influence the major political party policies. This will help the planet our mother, which in turn will help you. It is, even when it doesn't feel like it, your individual thoughts and feelings, positive and negative, which shape the world you live in, our actions and our inactions, determine this. Things take time to change, things also often get worse, due to the chaos of change, before they get better.

Positive thought, on its own, changes little, but positive thought, backed up by positive action, will make a difference; the Native Americans say "don't just talk your talk, walk your talk". I said earlier, if you want to follow this path, then there is a lot more to it, than simply thinking nice thoughts; going to an ancient site, to 'OM', (talk your talk,) for world peace or Earth

Healing, is okay, but it is infinitely better to 'OM' and then go and join 'Friends of the Earth' or 'CND'; it is better still, to then go out and do something more individual, like some practical conservation with the BTCV, (walk your talk).

If we want to change the world we can, or at least contribute to it; we all have money, no matter how much or how little; money is not simply a token that can be exchanged for something else; money is a VOTE. When you buy something you are saying that you want that thing and you accept how it got to you, how it was made, who made it, what they were paid, what their working conditions are, etc, etc. Very few of us ever seem to realize this; we are so desperate simply trying to get more of the stuff, we don't think what it really means.

'Money makes the world go around', the song goes, it's a light trivial song, yet it is performed in a dark, sinister, sort of way. Money influences everything; it is ultimately why wars are fought, why governments come and go, what's acceptable and what's not. The Native Americans say 'only when all the animals are gone, only when all the plants are gone, will man realize you can't eat money'.

If you want to be a force for positive change, you have to evaluate your life, what's important to you, you may have to make sacrifices; the old definition of the word sacrifice is 'to make sacred', not to kill, although this often was a part of it in the dim and distant past. The point of Macrocosm and Microcosm is that the two are connected, influence one, change one and you will have a subtle effect on the other; consciously change yourself (Microcosm) and you will have a subtle effect on the World (Macrocosm), this is 'Walking your Talk'.

Carbon Footprints

We have all heard this term by now, we all have one, put simply 'Carbon Footprints are how you walk your talk'. I suggest you look at the web site www.direct.gov.uk/ActOnCo$_2$. There are many other web sites too, which talk about Carbon Footprints and reducing CO_2 emissions, 'Offsetting' as it is commonly known. It is why more tax is charged on air travel, it is why the congestion charge is in place in London. It is here to stay and you need to know, at least roughly what your 'Carbon Footprint' is, then you can think of practical ways to reduce it.

Sadly, it is also being used to generate money e.g. 'pay this and we will plant 'X' number of trees for you to offset your Carbon Footprint and make you 'Carbon Neutral'. In other words chuck some money at it and the problem will go away. But it's not that simple. Basic problems include things like 'sustainable forestry', in essence you buy something and the trees used to make it are replaced by new trees. It's a good idea, but sadly a fully grown mature tree can not be replaced by several saplings. The saplings will take the best part of a century to grow and then repair more than the damage done by removing that one full grown mature tree. Time is the problem, no one knows how little time is left before things get to bad to be able to stop the damage, some estimates are as little as 10 - 20 years! Using hemp or something else that is more sustainable and quicker growing, would be a far better idea. But it's a start.

How do you work out your Carbon Footprint? Obviously the easiest way is to visit an appropriate and trustable web site and use their CO_2 calculator, many take different things into account, so it is up to you how hard you want to be on yourself, but mainly they are about reducing your annual fossil fuel usage.

We all use electricity, most of us use gas too, some use coal, lots use petrol or diesel. Obviously reducing this annual usage will reduce your CO_2 emissions. Many of the suppliers of these fossil fuels use this to sell you a higher tariffed 'green alternative'. Again a nice idea, but most of the fuel companies nowadays are only billing companies; they don't produce anything in reality. There is not enough energy being produced in an environmentally friendly way (wind farms, hydro electric, solar power, bio fuels, etc) to actually supply everyone who signs up for it, with any viable electricity from these sources.

Nuclear power, which terrified us all only a few years ago and was due to be scrapped, is the nearest, cheapest option we currently have, which is why the government is pushing for it. But we all know the problems that could cause, remember Chernobyl or Long Island, not to mention the nuclear waste, which we still don't know how to dispose of safely. Again time is a factor. The only real way to make a major difference is to generate your own power, install solar panels if you can or a small wind turbine, generate your own hydro electricity with a stream. Unfortunately many of us can't do these things, we don't have the land or couldn't get the planning permission if we did.

So, we need to buy more efficient energy saving devices, such as boilers, fridges and freezers, energy saving light bulbs, smaller cars that ideally run on bio diesel. Use more public transport, walk or cycle. Take fewer holidays abroad, take a train instead of a plane. Buy fewer televisions with smaller screens, then turn them off instead of having them on standby, which uses 80% as much energy as if it was on. In other words if you are not using it, turn it off and recycle all you can.

You could also join a conservation group and do some conservation work, like planting trees or coppicing trees. Each new tree planted will reduce CO_2 emissions by 7.3 kg per year on average, so plant 10 and you have reduced your Carbon Footprint by 73kg per year, plant 200 and you have reduced it by 1460kgs nearly 1.5 tonnes, this is easier than it sounds, I've planted over a 100 in a day before now. Believe it or not, more trees are planted due to the building of new roads, than any other planting schemes. Other things also come into these equations like whether you are a vegetarian or not. This is because if you eat meat, you are supporting cattle farming. Cows have several stomachs and a very complicated digestive system, which produces a huge amount of methane each year; another greenhouse gas, which heavily contributes to global warming.

As I said carbon footprints are more complicated than we are led to believe, but at least having a rough idea of your own will allow you to make changes to reduce it. Britain currently produces 153 million tonnes of CO_2 per year (this doesn't include emissions from landfill sites, forestry and other agricultural land use; so it's probably nearer 200 million tonnes per year.) The government aims to reduce this 153 million tonnes by 20% by the year 2010, but this is unlikely to happen.

Individually, the government would like us all to reduce our CO_2 emissions to 5.82 tonnes per year. On the plus side this will save us all money in the long term. It must also be remembered that the USA and China produce the most greenhouse gases and are doing the least to reduce this. Plus the developing countries, like India are racing to improve their standards of living, nothing wrong with that; but sadly this means they are trying to produce more greenhouse gases as a by product. Sadly, globally Britain's contributions to reducing greenhouse gases (these cause global warming) will only make a tiny difference anyway. But this doesn't mean we shouldn't do our bit.

Basic Ecology

As I mentioned earlier all things are interconnected, in ecology this is shown in a number of ways, the most simple of which is the food chain:

Sun - Plants - Herbivores - Carnivores

In this simple food chain, we can see that the sun feeds the plants, through photosynthesis, turning light, water and carbon dioxide into glucose; the herbivores then eat the plants, which in turn are eaten by the carnivores. A more accurate version of the food chain is the food web, which shows the interconnection of species:

Sun - Evaporates Water, Creates Weather and Carbon Dioxide

Moon - influences Oceans Tides - Tides produce Weather

Earth stores Water - Water creates Oceans - Water Evaporates - Rain produced feeds Plants and Animals

Weather - Fertilises Seeds - Seeds Germinate and grow- Produce waste in the form of Oxygen and Water, which is absorbed by all Animals

and Insects - Plants pollinated by Insects and Animals - Fruit/seeds produced- Plants eaten or die off

Plants and Fruit eaten by Insects, Herbivores and Omnivores - Creatures Defecate spreading Plant Seeds and feeding Insects, also produce waste via breathe (Oxygen) which is absorbed by Plants - Animals Breed - Animals die and are eaten by Carnivores, Omnivores and decaying remains are eaten by Insects

Insects eat decaying organic matter and plants - insects defecate, fertilise the Earth and pollinate plants - Insects are eaten by Arachnids and Omnivores - Insects breed - Insects pollinate Plants

Plants die off and fertilise the Earth - Plants grow and produce Water, Oxygen and Food.

As you can see the process works in cycles of growth, harvest, decay and death, this is the basis for all ecology and life. The food web is a simplified version of the patterns of nature; it can be viewed in far more complicated ways showing the specific life cycles of individual species and their direct interactions with other species. But at the end of the day it is the sun which makes it all possible, from there the plants are the most important as they produce oxygen, water and food, followed by the insects and animals; in order of importance humans, are the least important, despite being top of the food chain, we are the one species which, if we vanished, would be of benefit to all the other species.

Having said that, humans are the only species on the planet who have a hope of completing the cycle and benefiting the sun. We know the Sun will eventually die out as it burns up all its fuel, when that happens the Earth will die, though it still, thankfully, has millions of years of life left in it yet. We as humans produce a waste product which we could feed the Sun with, we don't produce enough to extend its life a lot, but we do produce more than we know what to do with. Nuclear fuel produces the waste I am talking of; nuclear fuel produces waste that we do not know what to do with, it is lethal to nearly all life and its life-span lasts thousands of years.

Currently we bury it deep in the ground or at sea, sealed in lead containers, we cant do anything else with it, we do not have the technology; we have tried recycling it, sadly that produces waste which is ten times more dangerous than the original waste. The only safe thing to do with it is to load it on rockets and shoot it at the Sun, it is unlikely to ever happen due to the enormous cost involved, we are more likely to send it to the Moon, or ignore it and hope it goes away.

Conservation

You have probably guessed by now that I believe conservation is important, also that many green issues concern me. I have talked about 'Walking your Talk', this is something I try to do, but it isn't always easy. One of the things I always find difficult is when I go out to do conservation work, it often involves cutting trees down and burning them. If any of you have done the same and felt horrified by it, I will explain why it is done now. Conservation is about preservation of species diversity, the term biodiversity is often used nowadays to describe this process.

Conservation, does not aim to preserve all flora (plant species) and fauna (animal species), what it tries to do, is recognise that human population growth and all that goes with it, makes conservation very difficult. So it attempts to preserve the largest number of flora and fauna species it can, in the space available to it. It also attempts to maintain each country's native species (the oldest or original established species of the country) and reduce non native species. In many ways conservation is quite racist in its approach to flora and fauna; a good example of this is that sycamore trees (*Acer pseudoplatanus*) are always cut down, burned and prevented from re-growing whenever they are come across. This is because they thrive so well in our British climate, it is a native species of the central and northern European mountains, they are a member of th maple family (*Acer*), where they are native they are an intricate part of the food web, providing food and shelter for many species of insects and animals. However in Britain, this is not the case, they do not play an important role at all; but since they are very well adapted they have spread over the entire country, since they were introduced to gardens by the Edwardians and Victorians. What they do though is establish and outgrow our own native species (which do benefit our native fauna), which reduces the light available to them, so they grow stunted or die off.

Many of the most endangered species in conservation are what are termed as 'Specialists'. 'Specialists' are vulnerable as they only feed, breed, or live in/on specific conditions. Humans are classed as 'generalists', this means we have evolved to live virtually anywhere, on anything. As a result 'generalists' thrive and 'specialists' die out, as they are unable to success-fully compete for the limited resources available.

As a result of this, conservation always will take the side of the weakest species; this often means modifying the natural environment to give these rare species the best chance of survival. This can often mean what looks to the untrained eye as very destructive behaviour, cutting down trees and burning, sometimes shooting other animals, or fencing off areas from other animals and humans. One way in which this is done is to create a layered effect in the natural environment. This means cutting down or back on areas of land flora, to create an area which has a variety of differing habitats, some flora and fauna prefer short grass, some prefer large mature (standard) trees, whilst there are others that prefer all the conditions in between.

Shown overleaf is a diagram of the woodland structure, showing the differing layers of flora growth, which is healthy and varied, providing the best sort of conditions for the most species possible, showing the differing layers:

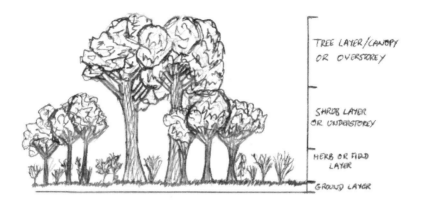

TREE LAYER/CANOPY OR OVERSTOREY

SHRUB LAYER OR UNDERSTOREY

HERB OR FIELD LAYER

GROUND LAYER

Woodland Structure

The most common place this is done is in coppiced woods (see Hazel), combined with the ride (large machinery access roads and footpaths, often with stone foundation) system:

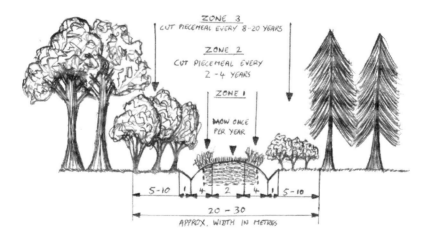

ZONE 3
CUT PIECEMEAL EVERY 8-20 YEARS

ZONE 2
CUT PIECEMEAL EVERY 2-4 YEARS

ZONE 1
MOW ONCE PER YEAR

5-10 | 4 | 2 | 4 | 5-10

20 - 30
APPROX. WIDTH IN METRES

Ride Layer Effect

These cross the woodland, allowing easy access for conservation workers, the public and creating many differing habitats, which serve to attract more wildlife, than if the wood was left to its own natural regeneration:

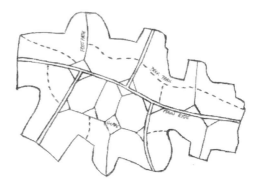

Typical Rides and Glade System

The ride system often incorporates glades, which are larger open areas, allowing for practical things like large machinery to turn and allowing additional sunlight to reach the ground, which encourages the growth of rarer, more specialist flora species, from the seed bank (a natural store of seeds contained within the soil, which can be several hundred years old and still active). The next diagram illustrates the differing manners, in which different woodland regenerates itself, showing managed and unmanaged woodland; the main difference in unmanaged woodland is that the dominant species of flora, are most abundant, things like ferns and brambles, whereas species such as orchids wouldn't get a look in.

Natural Regeneration

There are conservation sites around the country, which are given special titles such as ESA (Environmentally Sensitive Area) and SSSI (Site of Special Scientific Interest), these are the most important to conservation, it means things like the local farmers are not allowed to use various chemicals on their crops in the area, as it would damage the area wildlife,

Planted High Forest

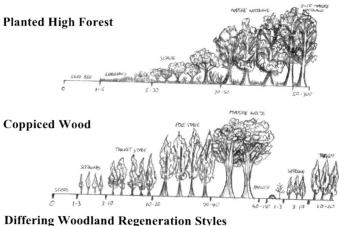

Coppiced Wood

Differing Woodland Regeneration Styles

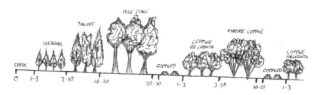

huge fines and even prison sentences can be imposed on people, who damage the area. It also means that rare and interesting species of fauna or flora, live there. Often these areas include ancient woodland (woodland over 200 years old), if this is the case they can usually be easily identified by the old boundary ditch, which encircles them. Needless to say, conservation is not all about planting trees, often it involves what looks like very destructive behaviour, but there is always a good reason for it.

Tree Identification & Tree Lore

This section will give brief details about trees, including an illustration, interesting facts and the common and Latin names. The reason Latin names are given is because the common names change from country to country and often county to county; the Latin name does not, the first part of the

Latin name refers to the family species, the second part is the genus. This is not a complete guide to trees, it simply gives some of the most common native species.

I claim no responsibilty for any harm caused by anyone, to themselves or others, trying any of the natural remedies menioned in this book. I suggest you seek professional training prior to experimenting with any herbal or natural remedies.

Alder (*Alnus glutinosa*)

The Alder is a tree which is native to Britain, growing to up to 60' in height. It is often found close to water and on boggy ground, this is because it drinks about 45 gallons a day. In the past it was used for making water troughs and sluices, the bark was used for dyeing and tanning leather. It has been grown as coppice for charcoal and gunpowder. Its leaves can be put in shoes to soothe tired feet, it has also been used to dress cuts and wounds, preventing gangrene. Its bark can be made into a tea to stop diarrhoea, it can also be used to gargle with for sore throats, as a lotion for cuts, bruises, burns, scalds, varicose veins, boils and abscesses. It is the letter 'F', from the Irish name of Fearn, in the Celtic Ogham Tree Alphabet. Its bark is grey or brown in colour, with a fine network of shallow fissures; its leaves are very rounded, resembling Hazel.

Ash (*Fraxinus excelsior*)

This is the only native British tree of the Olive family. The leaves form in horizontal rows, looking much like a Rowan tree's leaves, the black buds on twigs' ends are very sticky, the bark is smooth and grey, splitting in older trees. It is the letter 'N' in the Ogham Tree Alphabet, after its Irish name, Nuinn. This is the Norse Tree of Life, the Yggdrasil Tree, it was used to make their spear shafts, as it was so straight and strong. It was believed to protect from witchcraft, spells and evil, so sprigs were kept in the house. It was also associated with love; if a tree with an even number of leaves was found, a young girl would pluck a leaf, put it in her left shoe and say "Even, even Ash, I pluck thee off the tree, the first young man that I do meet, my lover he shall be".

It was believed to ward off snake bites, the leaves and seeds are used for their diuretic and laxative effects, they are also good for treating gout and rheumatism. The bark is used for a bitter tonic, which aids digestion, diarrhoea, dysentery and stemming bleeding. It is good for reducing fever including malaria. An infusion (tea) of the leaves taken every 4 weeks is said to improve general health and prolong life. It was also used as a charm for a wide range of ills, including ague, rickets, whooping cough, hernia, warts, snake bites, earache, ringworm, toothache and impotence, this involved leaving locks of hair or nail clippings attached to the tree. A common practice was to merge a young Ash tree's Spirit with a young child's, to act as a guardian through their life, or to cure the child or adult of illness. This was done by splitting a young sapling and passing the child or adult through it, the sapling was then rebound carefully together so that it would heal and continue to grow.

Aspen (*Populus tremula*)

The Aspen is a member of the Poplar family, growing up to 70' tall; it has smooth silvery green bark, which turns brown or grey as it ages. It has gently scalloped circular leaves, which flutter in the lightest of breezes. It is the letters 'EA' in the Ogham Alphabet after its Irish name of Edhadh. In folklore a person suffering from a fever, was to tie a lock of their hair to an Aspen and say "Aspen Tree, Aspen Tree, I pray thee to shake and shiver instead of me".

The leaves of the Aspen are very pale on the underside and dark on the upper, which they are believed to turn upright, so that the pale sides show when rain is due. Twigs and branches of the Aspen are used for making arrow shafts and were believed to possess divinatory properties. Their buds and leaves were carried to attract wealth and were said to be an ingredient in flying ointment.

The leaves, buds and bark are known to stimulate appetite and aid digestion, wind, acidity, colic, diarrhoea and liver problems. Its bark also contains salicin, which acts like asprin, making it good for headaches, pain, inflammation and fever.

Crab Apple (*Malus sylvestris*)

This is the original Apple tree, which was later cultivated and harvested, becoming the orchard apple (*Malus domestica*). The Apple has always been revered as a sacred fruit, as it was easily gathered in the Autumn, forming a good food source. It is the Apple which Adam eats in the Garden of Eden, taken from the tree of Wisdom. It is Apples that are eaten by the Norse Gods to keep them young, Apples are in the Celtic paradise and King Arthur is taken to Avalon (the Apple Vale) to heal. The Apple is associated with the Underworld and unconscious knowledge, hence Apple bobbing at Halloween. Apples are often associated with magic and romance, cutting an apple will reveal a pentacle, the five pointed star which symbolises witchcraft. They are the letter 'Q' in the Ogham Alphabet, named after their Irish name Quert.

An old game played by single people involved tying a piece of string to an Apple and twirling it around near a fire; the person whose apple fell off first was believed to be the one who would marry first; another version, involves peeling an apple, throwing the peel over their left shoulder; this would then form into the initial of the person they would eventually marry. In Cornwall, girls would sleep with an apple under their pillow to ensure fertility and a good husband; Apple blossom has also been worn by brides for many centuries for good fortune. To find out if lovers would work out, an apple pip was thrown into the fire with the words, "If you love me, bounce and fly, if you hate me lie and die".

The old saying of "an Apple a day, keeps the doctor away"; indicates its healing properties. Not only can it be made into an alcoholic drink, to bring visions, etc, but it is an excellent detoxifier, helping to break down fats and binding toxic metals such as mercury and lead, so they can be expelled via the bowels. They are good for a number of illnesses including gout, fluid retention, arthritis, skin problems, headaches and lethargy.

Beech (*Fagus sylvatica*)

The Beech is one of my favourite trees, I consider them very magikal and like a Beach is the space between two worlds, the sea and the land, I believe the Beech tree is a possible bridge between the Other Worlds; I have certainly had Sidhe encounters near them. They are the letters 'AE' in the Ogham Alphabet, named after their Irish name of Phagos. Lovers commonly carve their initials into their bark, as they are long-lived and keep their leaves during the winter, in a beautiful rusty shade of red. Beech masts are tasty nuts, which form around Beltaine. It is said that carving your greatest wish into a Beech stick will make it come true. Medicinally their leaves are valued for the cooling effect they have on the blood, they are also good for hot swellings, skin conditions, inflammations and as general antiseptic. They are also one of the first broad leaved trees to evolve and Britain was once covered by a huge forest of them.

Birch (*Betula pendula*)

Birch is a fairly small tree, rarely growing above 20 metres; its life span is similar in length to that of a human. It is easily recognised by its silver bark. Birch is the letter 'B' in the Ogham Alphabet, named after its Irish name of Beith, it also symbolises the Bard, the first level of Druidry training, which focuses on creativity. The Maypoles of Beltaine were often made of Birch, so it is associated with fertility, catkins are both male and female, a bundle of Birch twigs was often given to newly weds to ensure fertility. Birch is also believed to protect against evil, babies' cradles were often made of it, for this reason. The Birch is often the first tree you will find when approaching woodland, this is because it is fast growing and spreads easily, making it the most common tree in scrubland. It is also good at preparing the ground for longer lived trees to succeed. As a result it is often sadly cut down by conservationists, as the scrubland often intrudes onto other habitats. In the Spring a flood of sap fills the tree, which can be tapped and is very good for dissolving kidney and bladder stones as a tea; it is also very antiseptic, so is good for all manner of cuts, grazes and skin infections. The oil from the buds and bark is used as a liniment for arthritis and rheumatism; the leaves in tea form are also used to aid these conditions as they are good at eliminating toxins and lowering blood cholesterol levels, this tea will also help to keep colds and fevers at bay.

Blackthorn (*Prunus spinosa*)

Blackthorn is easily identified by its long sharp black thorns, blueberry-like berries and shiny black bark. It is normally fairly small, growing up to 4 metres tall, it is most commonly found in hedgerows as its thorns make it good for keeping livestock in the fields. It is important for wildlife, supplying both food and safety.

It is the letters 'STR' in the Ogham alphabet, named after its Irish name of Straif. It is considered a holy tree capable of warding off evil, spells and witchcraft. This is because Christ's crown of thorns was believed to be Blackthorn. However an older tradition is that it is bad luck and can bring trouble, this may be because witches often used to make their cursing wands from it. The Black Stick is the emblem of the town mayor, which was often a Blackthorn walking stick. The leaves and flowers are used to make tea which helps to clear away toxins and excess fluids, it also has a mild laxative effect. Its sloe berries are used to make a syrup, by adding sugar and brandy, leaving this in a sealed jar from October - Christmas. The wood, bark and leaves have been used homeopathically for eye pain and inflammation of the eye. The Blackthorn is a tree with a mixture of associations, both good and bad, but it is a truly beautiful wood for walking sticks, its bark shines wonderfully when polished. It is good for nature, makes a good hedge and was used by the Celts as a part of their village defences.

Wild Cherry (*Prunus avium*)

Wild Cherry is a beautiful tree, often growing to 20 metres amongst Beech woods, it has a purple grey, shiny, often peeling horizontally banded bark, it also, of course, has cherries.

The Cherry's blossom is the sign of the Chinese New Year, its beautiful but brief blossom, is a warning that life is beautiful but short. The Cherry has associations with fertility, in Japan on the 3rd May, young girls tie a strand of their hair to a Cherry tree as a love spell. Cherries are good at removing toxins from the body and have a slight laxative effect. Cherry stalk tea is well known for lowering uric acid levels and relieving gout, but it is good for most forms of digestive problems.

Cherries are known to be good for stress and soothing the nervous system, the sugar within them is safe for diabetics and they help the body to fight infections, they are a good food for people who are recovering from illness and run down; which is probably why they are so often found in hospital wards.

Elder (*Sambucus nigra*)

Elder is easily spotted, with Ash-like leaves, bedecked with white flowers and berries; it has a hollow nature with a pithy core. Elder is the letter 'R' in the Ogham alphabet, named after its Irish name of Ruis.

The Elder has much folklore attached to it; it is believed to be bad luck, especially if cut down, without seeking the permission of the Dryad, brought into the house or burnt. It is also believed that cribs made of Elder will leave the child pinched black and blue, if it doesn't simply die. It is believed to be the tree that Judas hung himself from, it is also the 13th letter of the Ogham alphabet; it is these such superstitions which give the Elder its negative reputation. Personally, I think the Elder is a wonderful tree, if a small one. You should always ask permission of the Dryad before cutting down any tree, in my opinion. The Elder is a hard tree to kill though it is often beneficial to cut it down, as it will come back the following year, even healthier. Its hollow stems have been used for centuries to make pipes and flutes, its name *Sambucus* is derived from an ancient Greek bagpipe type instrument called a Sambuca. It is of great benefit to nature supplying large quantities of food to wildlife and us. It is used to make elderflower and elderberry wine and cordial. Its flowers are often fried in a sweet batter to eat and its berries make good ingredients in a variety of pies, tarts, chutneys and jams.

If you stand under an Elder at Midsummer's Eve, it is believed you will see the King of the Fairy Folk and his retinue pass by.

It is believed that you must ask permission of the Dryad by saying 'Hyldmoer, Hyldmoer, permit me to cut thy branches', Hyldmoer is the Elder Dryad or Mother Dryad of the tree in Norse Mythology, it is also believed to protect from lightning.

As a medicinal plant it has been described as the 'medicine chest of country folk'. The roots and bark are a powerful laxative, the fresh leaves can be held on the temples to cure nervous headaches, bruised leaves rubbed on your face or worn in a hat, keep insects away. An infusion of leaves will keep mosquitoes away, as well as stem bleeding, speed-healing of wounds, bruises, sprains, burns and swollen joints. The flowers make a good tea to drive away colds, sore throats, fevers and flu. They also help you to relax, release tension, allay anxiety and lift depression. They have a good detox effect, helping to relieve toxins in the body via the kidneys. Lotions and creams can also be made out of the flowers for various rashes, haemorrhoids, sunburn, inflammation and ulcers. Distilled Elder water is an excellent toning and cleansing lotion for the face and was even believed to stop freckles.

The German name for the tree is Holdre, which means hollow, but it is also believed to be derived from the Goddess of Love, Hulda, this connects it with fertility rites and Beltaine, when it is in bloom. It is also said to drive away all evil, spells and witchcraft and sprigs of it are carried for this purpose.

Elm (*Ulmus procera*)

Before Dutch Elm Disease, this was a very common hedgerow tree, it has small rounded beech-like leaves, dark finely ridged bark and slim, hairy twigs, its leaves are slightly longer on one side than the other, they can grow quite tall - 30 metres or more. It is the letter 'E' in the Ogham alphabet, after the Norse name Embla. When Odin created man he made him from the Ash tree, when he created woman, he made her from the Elm. Elm is a wonderfully pliable wood, and can be shaped as a sapling for later use, bending it to the shape of a plough for example. People used to pin strands of hair or nail to the tree to rid themselves of ague. The inner bark was often chewed or boiled up in water to relieve sore throats and colds,  this mixture could also be applied to scalds and burns, or it could be boiled in milk as a cure for jaundice. The bark of the Elm was often made into an infusion to treat bowel problems, diarrhoea and infections, or it could be applied externally for ringworm, sores, ulcers and other skin problems to stop bleeding.

Hawthorn (*Crataegus monogyna*)

Hawthorn is a common tree often seen in hedgerows, as its thorns are good for keeping livestock in their fields. It is often fairly small in size, but left to its own devices can grow up to 12 metres tall. It is a member of the rose family and displays wonderful white blossom in early May, it is also known as the May thorn, as it is associated with  Beltaine and fertility, the May Queen is crowned with Hawthorn and represents the Greek Goddess Maia, whom the month is named after; an old verse says "The fair maid who is the first of May, goes to the fields at the break of day, and walks in dew from the Hawthorn tree, will ever handsome be".

It has been associated with the crown of thorns that Christ wore, but unlike the Blackthorn has never been considered unlucky. It is worn to protect against evil and lift the spirits, though was considered to be unlucky if brought indoors. It is commonly believed to be the meeting place of spirits and fairies, sitting under the Hawthorn at Beltaine, Summer Solstice or Samhain you could become enchanted by the fairy folk. Sprigs and garlands of it were attached to the May Pole and brides were often given a sprig of it at their wedding, to indicate the trials of marriage (thorns) as well as the beauty (flowers). The Glastonbury Thorn is a member of the Hawthorn family; Hawthorn has been dedicated to the Virgin Mary by the Christian Church.

Medicinally the Hawthorn's flowers, leaves and berries all aid the heart and circulation, by opening the arteries and increasing the blood flow, making it good for high blood pressure. It can also slow an overly fast heart rate, by working on the vagus nerve. The berries are good to help diarrhoea, in Russia they are used for amoebic dysentery. The leaves, flowers and berries are all good at relaxing the nervous system, relieving stress and anxiety, restlessness and nervous palpitations, inducing sleep. They can be eaten in salads and have a diuretic action, relieving fluid retention, dissolving stones and can be used for night sweats with the menopause. Externally the flowers and berries can be used as a decoction for skin problems such as acne rosacea, a gargle for sore throats can also be made from the berries. In addition to all this they are an excellent food source for wildlife.

Hawthorn is the Ogham Letter ŒH, and means Huathe in Irish.

Hazel (*Corylus avellana*)

Hazel is not really a tree, as it does not produce a single trunk, rather a mass of branches, this is due to it being coppiced so often. It can produce a trunk though and grow to a height of 10 metres. It is most easily identified in the autumn by its bunches of 1-4 nuts. Hazel is one of the most commonly coppiced woods, but Ash is also often coppiced as is Willow.

Coppicing means the branches are cut down in a cycle of 1-30 years; this is most commonly done during the autumn when the sap has returned to the roots, so that the tree is not damaged. The cuts are made low to the ground at an angle of 45 degrees, other angles do not work as well, allowing rot to set in due to the damp, nor does cutting the branches higher up. When the branches grow back a mass of small twigs and branches grow

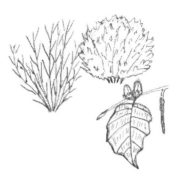

from the stumps left by the old branches, these grow larger over time, until they are ready to be coppiced at about 5 - 10 years. This far from damages the tree, in fact it can extend a Hazel's lifespan by 3 times. The coppiced wood is used to make fences, charcoal, baskets, furniture, brooms and a number of other products. The diagram below shows how a coppice wood is managed and the sort of growth cycles you would find in a coppiced wood:

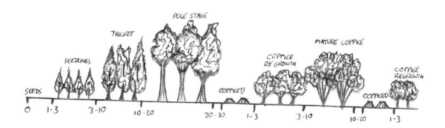

Wildlife responds to coppicing in stages as well, with a wide variety of benefits for both Flora and Fauna.

1) Ground Vegetation - in the 2nd and 3rd years of coppicing most ground Flora is at a peak, with spring flowering species benefiting most, this is due to the extra light from the opened tree canopy.

2) Invertebrates (Insects) - the highest density of insects is recorded in the 2 - 5 years after cutting; the majority of Butterflies and their larvae live in open sunny woodland areas, Beetles also benefit strongly from these conditions.

3) Birds - unlike butterflies, birds are not restricted to specific trees, but respond to the overall habitat structure, as a result 3 main groups of birds respond favourably to different stages of Coppice re-growth:

a) Open Coppice - Tree Pipits, Yellow Hammers, Linnets and White Throats prefer the first 3-4 years after Coppicing.

b) Canopy Closure Period - Willow Warblers, Chiff Chaff, Nightingales and Dunnocks prefer the low very dense vegetation created after 3 - 4 years of re growth. The Dunnocks prefer the 4- 10 years of growth.

c) Old coppice/derelict coppice - Blackbird, Chaffinch, Robin, Great and Blue Tit, prefer the conditions of 10 years re growth plus.

Mature trees or standards as they are called, attract Woodpeckers, Nut hatches and Tree Creepers, but too many standards keep Warblers away. Coppice woodland always maintains a suitable number of native standards in the area.

4) Small Mammals - freshly cut coppice is only used by Woodmice, by 2 years of regrowth Common Shrews and Bank Voles appear, but the 3rd year, sees the most small mammals, double any other stage of re-growth. The rare Dormouse needs Honeysuckle and coppiced conditions for it to survive.

A well maintained coppiced wood is divided into large blocks each coppiced at different times, so that all the stages of re-growth are present at all times; this creates a haven for wildlife. In Norfolk Ashwellthorpe and Foxley Woods are both ancient woodland and coppiced regularly in the past; both of these are owned and managed by the Norfolk Wildlife Trust and are being restored to working coppice woodland, from their derelict state.

The Hazel itself is the letter 'C' in the Ogham alphabet, named after its Irish name of Coll. The Hazel is a wonderful tree traditionally used for making many magikal tools by Witches, Druids and Shamen. It is often found in close proximity to Honeysuckle which has a beautiful twisting effect on the wood, when the two join.

Holly (*Ilex aquifolium*)

Holly is easily identified, it has hard, sharp, dark green spiky leaves and red berries in the winter, it grows up to 20 metres, but is usually smaller. It is also a hedgerow tree, good for keeping livestock in their fields. In the Ogham alphabet it is the letter 'T', named after its Irish name of Tinne. Holly is considered to be good luck, if growing near a house, it will protect against thunder and lightning, if taken inside and hung over the door, it will defend against evil spirits and witchcraft; it can also be carried for good luck.

Holly water was sprinkled on new babies for protection and good fortune, but it is bad luck to burn it, or bring it inside when it is in flower. Holly leaves are used to make a tea, which was a common substitute for normal tea in the Black Forest. Holly leaves have a diaphoretic effect, bringing blood to the surface and causing sweating; this makes them good for bringing down fevers, they also act as an expectorant useful for persistent coughs, bronchitis, pleurisy and pneumonia; as well as for colds, flu and sinusitis. It is also good for eliminating toxins from the body, so is beneficial for fluid retention, arthritis, gout and rheumatism.

The berries are very popular with birds, but cause diarrhoea and vomiting in humans.

Hornbeam (*Carpinus betulus*)

Hornbeam is an attractive tree growing up to 30 metres tall with steeply ascending branches, often producing a crown widest at the top. They have smooth grey bark, fissured at times, but always buttressed. Young trees may look conical, but short trees are likely to have been pollarded. The leaves are very similar to the Beech, which it can be mistaken for, though they are more jagged at the edges. The male's flowers are short, green, feathery catkins; the female's are short and green, but with elongated fruit on a three-lobed wing.

Pollarding was a practice which was popular in medieval times, it is a form of coppicing, the difference being that the coppicing was done at the top of the main trunk, known as the bole. This produces a thick trunk with many short thick branches growing from it, looking a little like a large ornamental tree. It was done as large trees became rarer, due to excessive wood use and felling. The results were an ample supply of wood, while keeping the tree alive. This helped in lengthening the tree's lifespan. Pollarding is rarely done today, although there are still a number of pollarded trees around, they are usually ancient (200+ years old), as such they are rare and provide a mini specialist eco system, which is important to many forms of rare lichen and fungi, as well as animals and insects. Conservationists are gently re-pollarding these trees, to ensure their survival and many have preservation orders on them, making it a crime to cut them down.

Ancient trees are quite rare, they are often named and have folklore attached to them. It can be difficult to recognise an ancient tree, many are large anyway, but a tree with a diameter of over 1.5 metres (4.7 metre girth) is a rare and valuable tree, a tree with a diameter of over 2 metres (6.25 metre girth) is certainly an ancient tree, which has survived from the 'Wildwood' which used to cover this country, they are most often found in surviving medieval forests and parklands, such as Nottingham Forest; though they can also be found in old village greens and churchyards. The genetic material from these trees is very important and they act as important indicators of environmental change over the centuries.

Horse Chestnut (*Aesculus hippocastanum*)

The Horse Chestnut is a well known attractive tree often planted along roads in residential areas. This is not a native tree, but was introduced in the 17th Century. It forms candle-like flowers in May; it also produces inedible nuts, which children play 'Conkers' with. Its name is derived from its nuts which are used to make flour from, which is mixed with horses' oats in Turkey; horseshoe-shaped scars are also left on its small branches after the leaves fall in autumn. The conkers are rich in saponins which when mixed with water forms a lather, so they have been used in soap making. They have also been used as a bitter tasting coffee substitute. The buds of the flowers, bark and conkers are all used in the making of ointments, creams and lotions for strengthening the veins, good for treating varicose veins, ulcers and haemorrhoids.

Juniper (*Juniperus communis*)

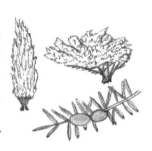

Juniper is the most widespread tree or shrub in Europe and one of the most variable; ranging from dwarf species, to columnar and pencil shaped forms; usually only 2-3 metres in height, it can reach 15 metres. It is most commonly found in gardens in Britain, though does grow wild too. It has a long association of driving away evil and protecting humans and animals.Sprigs of it hung over doors are used to drive away demons, thunderbolts, the evil eye, ghosts, hexes and curses. It was grown near to houses for its aromatic scent and antiseptic qualities. The leaves and wood are burnt to drive away infections, Hippocrates used it in Athens to keep the plague at bay. The berries are used in Shamanic smudge mixes in Mongolia, to purify the area; they also give gin its unique flavour. A tea made from the berries was used to prevent unwanted pregnancies, being drunk after a period was missed, earning it the name 'bastard killer', in some areas. The fragrant tops and berries can be used to make a powerful antiseptic, which is good for stimulating and disinfecting the urinary system, remedying fluid retention and bladder infections, though they should be avoided with kidney disease.

Juniper berries are good for the digestive system, increasing appetite and enhancing digestion. In the respiratory system they are good for coughs, colds, catarrh and bronchial phlegm, especially when used as inhalations. They can be used to bring on childbirth, as they stimulate menstruation in the reproductive system.

Larch (*Larix decidua*)

Larch is not an evergreen pine, its needles die off in the winter, fresh needles reapp-earing in the spring. It was introduced to Britain in the 17th century, for its value in house and ship building. The larch has very strong wood, stronger than most conifers and it also has the benefit of being almost immune to fire. As a result it has long been associated with purity and incorruptibility. It was carried to protect against evil, spells and fire. The whole tree is scented and its resin is known as turpentine, which is collected from full grown trees and used in making medicines and varnish. Resin and sap are regarded as the soul of a tree, a source of fire and regeneration, resin represents immortality and the undying spirit.

Medicinally Larch's new twigs and bark can be boiled and used as an expectorant, to clear phlegm from the chest in catarrhal coughs and bronchitis. Its astringent qualities can be useful in treating heavy periods, diarrhoea and bleeding. As a diuretic, it can help relieve fluid retention and cystitis, aiding the kidneys in eliminating toxins, this makes it a good remedy for arthritis, rheumatism and gout. A weak decoction makes a useful eyewash for inflammatory eye problems and a lotion for skin problems such as eczema, psoriasis, haemorrhoids and varicose veins. Larch has a reputation for its ability to lift the spirits and dispel melancholy.

Small Leaved Lime (*Tilia cordata*)

The Small Leaved Lime is an ancient woodland indicator, it grows to 30 metres, with an uneven crown, which grows irregularly. Its bark is greyish,finely cracked and broken by prominent ridges. It has an abundance of flowers, each with 5 petals growing in clusters of 4 - 12. It is commonly planted along roads, gardens and parks, growing well in most conditions. It is very resilient, it can be cut and trained with little trouble. It used to be planted as a mark tree; a tree which is planted at significant sites of importance, such as crossroads and village greens, to symbolise the cosmic axis, or Yggdrasil Tree. In German traditions it was the tree under which justice was carried out.

The Lime has much mythology connected with it, in Lithuania women made sacrifices to them to ensure good harvests. In Greek mythology Philyra, daughter of Oceanus, who was in love with Cronos, gave birth to Chiron, the learned centaur, ashamed she asked to be turned into a tree, the gods made her a Lime.

Good luck charms are often carved from Lime, as it is an easy wood to work with. It is a tree associated with feminine beauty, happiness, conjugal love, sweetness and peace.

Medicinally the Lime's blossoms make a wonderful tea, which has a relaxing effect, it is good for all conditions of stress, working well on excitable children as well. Lime flowers are good for most conditions of the heart, being used to treat high blood pressure and arteriosclerosis, as

57

they relax and strengthen the arterial walls. Not only do they prevent blood clots, but they also heal the heart emotionally, unblocking problems from painful past experiences, increasing openness and warmth in relationships. Lime flower tea, if combined with elderflowers, is very good at clearing fevers and catarrh. On its own, it is good at detoxing the system and applied externally is good for inflammatory skin problems.

English Oak (*Quercus robur*)

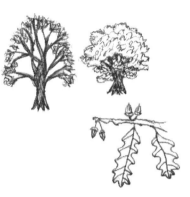

The Oak has many different varieties in its family. Though I believe the English Oak, or Common Oak, is known to everyone, at least when it has its acorns, which is every 2 years. The most unusual form of Oak is the Holm Oak, which is an evergreen Oak whose leaves look more like Holly, than an Oak, though its Acorns and bark show it to be an Oak. The Oak is the letter 'D' in the Ogham Alphabet, named after its Irish name of Duir, from which the word Druid is derived, which means 'One with the wisdom of the Oak'. It makes sense that it is also the symbol of the Druid grade in their training, which is connected with teaching, wisdom, law and leadership.

The Oak has always been one of the most sacred of trees, its lifespan is measured in hundreds of years, it is capable of reaching enormous proportions and has always been associated with the gods. In Norse traditions it is connected with Thor, probably as it was commonly hit by lightning, which has always been a sign that it is blessed. Laws and oaths were spoken beneath its mighty boughs, to give them more weight and meaning. It is also a highly practical tree, the acorns are harvested to make a flour, from which bread was made, its timber was used for making fire, buildings, boats and roads, its acorns fed livestock as well as people.

The Oak has long been associated with prosperity and bountiful crops, an acorn planted at the New Moon meant money was on its way; couples would drop acorns into a bowl of water, to see if they should marry, if the acorns floated towards each other, they would. Then the marriage would often be held beneath an Oak; if they had trouble conceiving children an Oak was embraced between them, to improve their fertility.

Large Oaks often marked boundaries of land, in latter times they became Gospel Oaks, under which the Christian Gospels were preached. The Oak is seen as a symbol of protection, fertility, longevity, abundance, law and order.

Medicinally a decoction of acorns, bark and milk was an old remedy taken to resist poisons and infections in the digestive and urinary tract. The bark due to its astringent action is good at relieving catarrhal congestion, sinusitis, heavy menstrual flow and has a toning effect on muscles throughout the body, it can also be used as a lotion to tone varicose veins and haemorrhoids. A decoction of bark can be used to make a gargle for sore throats, mouthwash for ulcers and inflamed gums, as well as a lotion for cuts and grazes.

The centre of a branch of Oak usually has a pentacle in it, a 5 pointed star, in the Holm Oak this is surrounded by the rose-like formation of the wood.

Pine, Scots (*Pinus sylvestris*)

Norwegian Spruce is probably the most common form of Pine or Fir tree you will come across today, as they are often planted in huge plantations, such as Thetford Forest, in Norfolk. This is because they grow quickly, tall and straight, making them ideal, along with Larch, for timber production. They are the traditional Christmas Tree and are grown in large numbers purely for that market.

However the true native Pine to Britain is the Scots Pine, this has a red coloured bark and is often grown alongside the other pines, in smaller numbers, for its wildlife value and to add variety to the woods.

The Scots Pine is the letter 'A' in the Ogham alphabet, named after its Irish name of Ailm.

The Scots Pine symbolises uprightness, vitality and strength of character; it also represents the connection between Heaven and Earth, due to its great heights, it grows to.

Pines were the first species of tree to evolve and for thousands of years, huge forests of them covered the globe, many trapping insects in their sap, which eventually turned to amber, under the right conditions, preserving the ancient insect inside. The Pine tree forests usually have very little ground flora, other than the ferns, which are even older than the Pines. This is because they actually produce a high quantity of acid which filters into the ground around them, killing off any weaker plant growth, which is in competition with them, for the light. They are known as the Peace Tree to the Native Americans and are chiefs among the Standing People (tree) Tribes.

The red squirrel feeds on the Scots Pine, but doesn't do so well with the other non native Pines, which is why the grey squirrel, who is more of a generalist feeder, is so common today, despite being a non native, later introduction, itself. Pine kernels are a wonderful-tasting nut, which as well as being nutritional is a good medicine. They are recommended to eat after illness such as tuberculosis, they can also be mixed with barley water for urinary problems; Native Americans make an antiseptic from extracts from them.

The Pine resin makes a good medicine as well, especially for respiratory problems, used as an expectorant it helps to liquefy and expel phlegm from the bronchial tubes, clears the head of congestion and its antispasmodic action in the chest helps to relieve asthma. The gum can also be chewed for toothache and headaches. A tonic made from Pine has an invigorating effect, at the same time as being calming and refreshing, making it good for stress related problems.

Rowan (*Sorbus aucuparia*)

The Rowan, or Mountain Ash as it is often known, is actually a member of the Rose family. It does have leaves which are very similar to the Ash, as are its uses in the past, often used for coppice and as tool handles. It has a profusion of red berries growing on it in the winter, which the birds gorge themselves on. They do not grow very big and are often found growing around houses and along streets, this is because they are considered to be very lucky and very good at driving away evil spirits and witches, acting as a guardian of the dwelling. They are the letter 'L' in the Ogham alphabet, named after their Irish name of Luis.

If incorporated into the house, such as over a fireplace or doorway, they are thought to keep witches from entering the house, cattle were often even dressed with sprigs of it between their horns, to keep them safe.

In Wales it is found in all the churchyards, considered to be as sacred as Yew is in English churchyards. It is possible the name Witch or Wicca comes form the Welsh name for the Rowan of Witchen. The Druids held it in high regard and used to burn fires of it during battles, to invoke the powerful guardian spirits of the tree, to fight for their side. Stakes of it were also hammered through corpses to prevent their ghosts from wandering, this is probably also connected to the vampire myths.

The Rowan as well as being steeped in magikal lore, also had very practical uses, being coppiced and used to make tool handles, spinning wheels, stakes and pegs. In addition to this, in the Highlands it was used to trap birds for the cooking pot, using horse hair nooses among berry-laden trees, it has even been used to make a form of Welsh and Scottish cider or spirit.

The name Rowan comes from the Norse Runa or Rune, meaning a charm, in some areas it was known as the Witch or Wicken Tree as runes and other esoteric symbols were carved into its trunks in Scandinavia and Britain. The red berries were made into necklaces to protect the wearer from the evil eye and Sidhe. Many of these trees are thought to protect against witches, spells and other evils, this is as a result of Christianity, but also it is taken to mean black magic, curses and evil cast against you, by witches, hired by your enemies. The unknown has always been scary to our Ancestors, the people who worked with these occult forces were also feared and seen as being able to work good or bad spells.

Medicinally the berries are rich in vitamin C and are often made into a jellied sauce to accompany game meats. The berries were fed to animals to help they with their birthing; unripe berries are astringent as well as antiseptic, being made into gargles for sore throats, tonsillitis etc. Externally as lotions they are good for skin problems and haemorrhoids; internally they are good for diarrhoea, stomach and bowel infections. The bark has been used as a gargle for bleeding gums, mouth ulcers and sore throats.

Sweet Chestnut (*Castanea sativa*)

Sweet Chestnut looks a little like a Horse Chestnut from a distance, but close up the leaves are very different, as are the nuts, which look more like Beech masts, than conkers. The bark of the Sweet Chestnut is also very distinguishing, forming prominent almost lattice-like ridges. It was introduced to this country by the Romans, who relied heavily on its nuts. The nuts are rich in vitamins C and E, calcium, magnesium, phosphorus and iron. They also contain less than half the fat of normal nuts. They are easy to digest, their slight bitter-ness is reduced by cooking, they are commonly sold as roast chestnuts, made into chestnut stuffing and make a good flour.

Gypsies used to wear chestnuts in a bag around their necks to prevent haemorrhoids and they were also used as love charms, having slight aphrodisiac qualities. Medicinally the leaves are used to relax spasms, particularly in the chest. They are also used to bring down fevers and to stop bleeding, especially menstrual. Powdered nuts were used as a remedy for haemorrhoids.

Crack Willow (*Salix fragilis*)

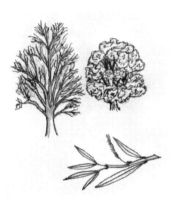

Willow is well known to us all, especially Weeping Willow (*Salix chrysocoma*). Mainly found near water, or on damp ground. There are several species of Willow, found throughout Britain, however there are 250 species world-wide. Willow is the letter 'S' in the Ogham alphabet, named after its Irish name of Saille. Willow is an amazing tree, often used for coppicing, as it regenerates so easily, it is used for fencing, weaving, cricket bats and a number of other crafts requiring supple wood. In conservation, especially around the Norfolk Broads it is necessary to cut it down, as it upsets the water table, this is difficult though, as it will grow back from almost nothing.

Willow is associated with the loss of love, hence the weeping, People used to wear Willow sprigs as a sign of their mourning, not only for loved ones who had died, but for others who had simply left. Yet a girl seeking her true love is said to be able to a hold Willow stick in her left hand and while turning clockwise 3 times reciting 'He that's to be my good man, come and grip the end of thee'; by the third turn the desired partner is said to be at stick's length.

In Greek mythology, the Willow is dedicated to Artemis, the Moon Goddess, who rules fertility, pregnancy, childbirth, crops and running water; in Pagan traditions Willow wands are used for lunar magik.

Branches of Willow were also used to 'Beat the Bounds', a Spring purification ritual, in which villagers walk around their village's boundaries beating the floor with the Willow, to drive away ill fortune and negative spirits.

Medicinally Willow, mainly White and Black, are used for healing. The most famous thing about White Willow is that it contains salicylic acid, which is the active ingredient in Asprin, which was created from the observations of Rev. Edward Stone in 1763 using Willow bark, to cure all that we use Asprin for today.

Yew (*Taxus baccata*)

Yew is a squat, but large, evergreen tree with dark green flattened needles are red berries in winter. It was red peeling bark and is most commonly found in graveyards. Yew is ancient, it has a lifespan of 2,000 years, when the main trunk dies it redirects a large root out of the ground to replace the former trunk. It is well known for being used to make the British long bow, it is also poisonous, the juice from the Yew acts as a nerve poison, which the Celts used to use to coat their arrow tips. It is also poisonous to cattle and horses. The wood itself has two main properties;being hard and elastic, making it ideal for bows.

The Yew is the letter 'I' in the Ogham alphabet, named after its Irish name of Ido. It is also the symbol of the Vate or Ovate grade of Druidry, which focuses on the more Shamanic side of Druidry, the wilderness, nature, animals, death, rebirth, animism, herbalism, divination and the healing arts.

Yew was planted by the Druids at their places of worship, when Christianity took over these sites and built churches, the Yews remained. In Christian beliefs the Yew represents immortality, its red heartwood represents the blood of Christ, whilst its white sapwood represents Christ's body. It has been said it keeps evil spirits away and guards against storms, it is also said that a young maiden, wanting to know the face of her future husband, should pick a sprig of Yew from a graveyard she has never been to before and sleep with it under her pillow, when he shall appear in her dreams.

Medicinally, despite being poisonous, the juice from the berries was used for chronic bronchitis, the leaves are used homeopathically for epilepsy, nausea, dizziness, Menieres disease, rheumatism, arthritis, liver and urinary problems. It has also been found to be effective against some forms of cancer.

Other Plants relevant to Shamanism

All plants and animals, flora and fauna are relevant to Shamanism, though there are a number of other plants which are connected to Shamanism, via history, culture, effects and environment. Some of these are other plants, which are not classed as trees, some are fungi. Given below are brief details of them:

Deadly Nightshade (*Atropa belladonna*)

Belladonna, is a member of the potato family, it is fairly rare nowadays, but it used to grow quite commonly in hedgerows; it was decided to be too poisonous though and as a result, it was largely killed off in the 60's.

Belladonna, is the main ingredient in the infamous 'Flying Ointment' of the medieval Witches. It is true they did ride their broomsticks, but they covered them in Flying Ointment first, then rode them naked, allowing the hallucinogenic drug to enter their bloodstream via their vaginal lips.

I do not recommend you try this; it is included, along with all the other hallucinogenic plants, simply out of historical interest.

Woody Nightshade (*Solanum dulcamara*)

Woody Nightshade or Bittersweet, is another member of the Nightshade family; it is far more commonly found than Belladonna; though not as potent, it is still poisonous. It is most often mistaken for Belladonna.

Henbane (*Hyoscyamus niger*)

Henbane is yet another famous member of the potato and Belladonna family.It is likely that this was another of the ingredients in the Flying Ointment, as it is supposed to bring on flying hallucinations. Again it is poisonous and rare and should not be used.

Liberty Cap Fungus (*Psilocybe semilanceata*)

The Liberty Cap Mushroom, or Magic Mushroom, as it is more commonly called, was used by Shamen the world over, to encourage ease of travel within the Otherworlds. Often brewed up as an infusion and the liquid drunk. It was a commonly used as a training aid, for novice Shaman; as they progressed it was no longer needed to help them into the Otherworlds, the Drum was enough. This is a poisonous plant and should not be taken, it is also quite a rare fungi.

Fly Agaric (*Amanita muscaria*)

Fly Agaric, is a very well-known Shamanic aid, used in a similar way to Magic Mushrooms, though it is considerably more potent and poisonous. It was picked, dried and then used sparingly, sometimes with other ingredients as an infusion, the liquid being drunk. It has similar effects to the Magic Mushroom. It is a dangerous drug and should not be used, it is believed this is what created the Norse berserkers' rage, making them lethal foes.

Honeysuckle (*Lonicera periclymenum*)

Honeysuckle is a beautiful climbing vine, which is essential habitat for the rare Dormouse. It is also what creates the wonderful spiralling patterns on the wood often found in coppice woods, such as Hazel, Ash and Rowan. Despite not being a tree, but a vine, it is the letters 'UI' in the Ogham alphabet, named after its Irish name of Uileand.

Ivy (*Hedera helix*)

Ivy is well known to us all, it is another vine, like Honeysuckle; again it is capable of creating wonderful patterns in the wood it climbs, though this is much rarer as it climbs using tendrils, rather than wrapping itself around the other trees. Again despite being a Vine and not a tree, it is the letter 'G' in the Ogham alphabet, named after its Irish name of Gort. It is also a traditional Winter decoration, considered to be sacred to the Moon Goddess and Earth Mother. It is also believed to have been possible to make a lethal form of beer from it, which the Celtic equivalent of the Norse Berserkers, consumed prior to battle, it put them into a lethal rage, but it also often killed them.

Mistletoe (*Viscum album*)

Mistletoe is a parasitic plant which forms on trees, it is most strongly connected with Oak, but forms on most trees. It is most strongly connected with Druidry, especially when it grows on an Oak. Fertility and healing of poisons is what the Mistletoe represented to the Druids, this was due to its berries' similarity to male sperm; it was considered to be sacred because it never touched the ground, still growing while in descent or ascent to the Heavens. Traditionally it was cut by a white robed Druid, with a golden (Male) sickle (Moon crescent Female); it is still associated with fertility in its Christmas role today.

Wood Sage (*Teucrium scorodonia*)

Sage is strongly connected with Shamanic traditions, being the main herb used in smudging ceremonies, it is a purifying herb, burnt in Smudge mixes in all Shamanic Cultures to clear people, objects and areas of all negative energy, in preparation for other ritual activity. It is a popular food ingredient as well, so is easily available fro all New Age shops as smudge sticks, or as a dried herb from supermarkets, which is considerably cheaper and just as effective. Shown here is Wood Sage, a wild-growing relation of the commonly used herb. Cedar, Pine and Lavender can also be burnt for they serve a similar purpose, when used as an incense.

Sweet Grass (*Glyceria declinata*)

Sweet Grass is found growing in wet marshy areas. It is mostly used in the Native American tradition, where it is braided and burnt, it is burnt to attract beneficial energies and ask for support from the spirits. It is sometimes mixed with Sage in the smudge stick. Juniper and Thyme another Herb available in super-markets can also be burnt for similar reasons.

The remaining letters in the Ogham alphabet are not trees: ŒNG, is Broom (or Fern), named after its Irish name of Ngetal ŒU, is Heather, named after its Irish name of Ur ŒIO, is Gooseberry, named after its Irish name of Iphin.

ŒM, relates to Vine or Muinn in Irish, ŒO, relates to Gorse or Onm in Irish, ŒOI, relates to Spindle which is Oir in Irish.

It is important to remember that all plants, trees and fungi are living beings with spirits, which are capable of communicating and working with you on a Shamanic level, if I have not mentioned one of your plant allies or favourite plants here, it is because there simply isn't room. These are obviously not all the flora in Britain, it is simply the tip of the iceberg, I strongly recommend you continue to research and look into nature, there are many fascinating TV programmes about wildlife, thousands of books and dozens of college courses available locally. Shamanism is a uniquely personal journey and what you experience about the natural world about you is more valid than anything that you will read about.

However, don't be fooled into thinking that the esoteric knowledge of the natural world is the only valid view; much of the esoteric knowledge is very old in its nature, from periods vastly different from our own. Shamanism, if it is to survive and flourish, needs to evolve also, hand in hand with science, would be nice, but I suspect we have a long way to go before that vision is realised, but we can learn from science, just as science can learn from us.

Direction Sense

Our ancestors probably had a more acute sense of natural directions, than we do today. In the modern world, we rarely need to think about what direction we are facing, we simply follow the road signs to our destination. This is not because we have lost that sense, we simply don't use it. There are people I know who work in conservation, often in the middle of nowhere, who simply seem to know where North is, at least most of the time; this is because they need this sense to find their way about. Animals still use their own inner compasses to find their way about, we are animals and we simply need to know how to reawaken our own instinctive inner compass.

There are clues all around us, to what the time is, what direction is what, day and night. In this chapter I will tell you what to look out for, as a result your inner compass, will become more active, then it simply takes practice, like most things.

The first thing to remember is that there are 3 Norths:

True North - the celestial North; which is gained from Sun and Star readings, this is the one we will be dealing with mostly.
Grid North - this is the North to which maps are aligned.
Magnetic North - this is the North to which a compass points and from which all magnetic land bearings are taken.

Clues to True North

The natural world around us is constantly giving us clues and signs about where North is in relation to us at all times. However it isn't always fool - proof, so when seeking North we must always double and sometimes triple check, to ensure we are getting it right. Obviously this is more important when we are lost in a huge forest, rather than walking through the local park. These rules, tend to apply to the Northern Hemisphere, they may need to be reversed if you are in the Southern Hemisphere.

Clues to finding your way include:

a) Moss normally grows on the darkest side of a tree or rock, this is normally North, but it can depend on the environment you are in.

b) Ants' nests are normally located on the Southern side of a tree; again this can vary as they are building it in the lightest area, which again can be influenced by the environment.

c) Flowers and leaves, will usually follow the sun's path through the sky, so if you are wearing a watch you should be able to estimate the direction the sun is in. Again this can depend on the environment in which you are in, as the flowers are aiming at the greatest light source.

d) Watches - if you are wearing a working watch (not digital), with a face, then you are wearing a compass. To find South in the Northern Hemisphere, point the hour hand at the Sun; South lies halfway between the Hour Hand and 12 o clock, so North is behind you.

In the Southern Hemisphere, point the 12 o clock at the sun, half way between there and the hour hand is North, as long as your watch is set for local time.

Finding South (Northern Hemisphere)

e) Felled trees - the tree rings are normally widest on the Northern Side.

f) Birds - they tend to fly South in the Winter, Geese in large V formations are the most accurate, but this only works once a year.

g) Conifers and Willows - usually lean to their sunny side, which will be South in Northern Hemispheres, North in Southern Hemispheres.

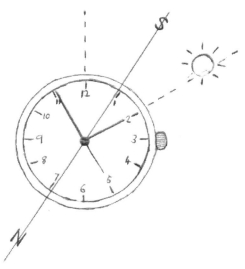

h) Moon - if the Moon rises before the Sun sets, it will be illuminated on its Western Side, if it rises after the Sun has set, it will be illuminated on its Eastern side.

i) Sun - the Sun rises in the East, is in the South at Noon and sets in the West, in the Northern Hemisphere. If you are facing North, East is on your right side and West on your left side, South is behind you. In the Southern Hemisphere Noon is in the North, as the Sun travels anticlockwise.

j) Shadows - these can be used to determine time and direction.

To find the direction using a shadow, place a stick vertical in level open ground, mark where the shadow's tip is with a stone; wait about half an hour and mark the shadow's new tip with a stone. Now draw a straight line between the 2 stones to give a rough East - West direction (the shadow moves in the opposite direction of the Sun, a shadow will be cast Westwards by a rising (East) Sun. Now draw a line at 90 degrees to the first line, to give you an approximate North - South line. The diagram below also shows you how to make a sundial, to discover the time, at least during the day, using this method, the East - West line is at 6am in the West and 6pm in the East, North is 12 pm. Obviously this doesn't take into account, seasonal variations in time.

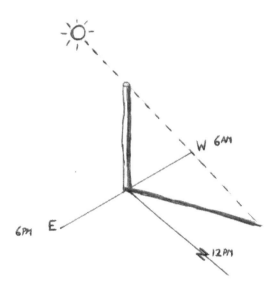

Using Shadows

k) Stars - at night it is still possible to tell what direction you are travelling in, providing you can see the stars.

This is due to the Northern or Pole Star; all you need to do to find North is look for The Plough (Big Dipper, Great Bear) constellation. Once you have found this, look for Cassiopeia, this looks like a big W on its side:

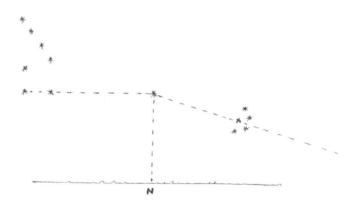

The Northern Star

Orion

l) Orion - this is a useful star system which everyone knows; it also rises above the Horizon (Equator) on its side, due East and sets due West, regardless of your position on the Planet, so it also points North:

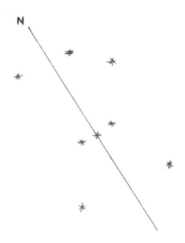

Animal Tracks and Signs

I am not going to pretend to be an expert tracker, tracking is a skill which takes a lifetime to acquire, with regular practice. I do have some basic knowledge though, enough for you to be able to get a rough idea of what's going on around you in the woods. This section will show you tracks of a number of British wildlife and give you other hints which show their presence; I will include a Lynx track in this section, as although the Lynx is no longer a native resident, the last having been killed for its fur, at least 200 years ago, there are a lot of stories about big cats living in the wild, in this country. I have never seen one, or one's tracks, outside of a zoo, but I have worked in zoos and know how to tell the difference, between a big cat and most other suitable candidate animal tracks. This doesn't mean there aren't any though, I'd like to think there are; I would also like to see the other former native species, our recent ancestors have hunted to extinction in this country, returned to the wild. We have made a start, the otter's numbers have been vastly increased and the European beaver has also been 're-introduced' to the Scottish Highlands; there have also been tests to find out how a wolf pack (the last wolf was killed in the mid 18th Century, near the source of the River Findhorn in Scotland) would respond to being 're-introduced' to the Scottish Highlands; so there is hope yet for the return of the lynx and bear also.

Tracks and Signs

When you are walking through the woods, there are various clues all around you of what animals have also passed by, when and what they were doing. I am not a good enough tracker to tell you all about this, I doubt there would be room in this book anyway, so I will simply present some images of animal tracks and tell you a little about them. I recommend you buy some good books on tracking and animals, also that you practice trying to identify such signs.

Many animals use well-used paths, some of these are highly visible as the animals who make them are large or travel in groups, some consist of very few visible indications, relying more on scent and being made by rarer or smaller animals; but there are clues such as droppings, nibbled twigs, broken undergrowth, etc. The easiest way of identifying an animal is to see it, but often, they see, hear or smell us first and stay hidden.

Clear animal tracks are not all that common, depending largely on the terrain, weather conditions, animal weight and movement, if you are able to find some then you are in luck. Many tracks are distorted, by age, weathering, other tracks, etc; this can obscure them, or make them appear larger than original. When you do find tracks, you want to look for others, as one print may help you to identify an animal, but several will tell a little about what it was up to. There are also other things which may help to identify local wildlife, such as latrines, boundary marking spots, burrow entrances, decomposing prey, rotting food, smell, sounds and calls, etc. It is always best to look for as many signs as possible. This means you will often be looking at the ground, it is important to remember to look up regularly, as while you are tracking it, the animal will occasionally run past.

Below are some tracks of the commonest animals in Britain, you may come across, if you do find some animal tracks and identify them as badgers or foxes, don't tell everyone you know, as badger baiting still goes on and fox hunting is a horrible sport. Also be careful if you come across rare animals, such as dormice, as they can be greatly distressed by hordes of human visitors. If you come across any burrows, do not be tempted to look for young animals, if there are any and you touch them, often their parents will desert or kill them. If their parents are with them, they may respond to your presence violently.

Badger (*meles meles*)

Here are 2 badger prints in the snow, often the best time to go tracking, as virtually everything leaves a track. Because of their stocky build, they are surprisingly heavy, they tend to walk at a slow leisurely pace, which is indicated by this one after the other track, this picture shows a front and back paw; a fast moving track would be indicated by the tracks being nearly side by side. You can also see the claw prints in this picture, in the front set; many animals can't retract their claws, so they are visible in tracks. If you have found a badger track you are lucky, in some areas of the country, like Norfolk, they are quite rare, I only know of 12 sets in Norfolk, in other areas, like Cornwall, they are quite common. If you have found the

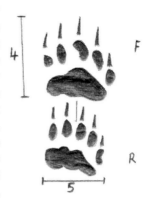

tracks of a badger, you may be able to find its sett. You will recognise this easily, by the size of it; they are quite large with many entrances, often in a small hill. It will also have a pile of dirty straw nearby, as badgers change their bedding daily.

You are most likely to see them at night, or at twilight, as they are mainly nocturnal in nature, if you are lucky enough to see them, stay quiet, as they are easily startled; do not try to touch any, as they are very powerful and could hurt you badly.

Cat (*Felis catus / F. silvestris silvestris*)

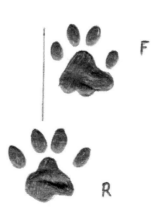

The domestic cat is a common enough print to find, the Wild Cat is a lot rarer; you are likely to only find it in Scotland, its name '*silvestris*' means 'forest loving'. The easiest way to observe this animal is to watch your own, the two species are very similar. The Wild Cat's print is slightly larger than the domestic cat's. The important thing to note here, is that the cat will always retract its claws when walking, this keeps them sharp. This is also true of its larger cousins, such as the Lynx (*Lynx lynx*), whose tracks are shown.

Cat tracks, while walking through the woods, check to see if they have claw marks, if they do, it is not a cat, big or small. If you come across, a cave that looks like a possible big cat lair, you will know if it is, it would stink of ammonia; a tom cat's spray is nasty, but it is nothing compared to a big cat's. If you come across any dead sheep or deer, with their throats ripped out, it is a dog kill; big cats are very efficient, there would be only four large puncture wounds on the throat, as they suffocate their prey. I hope I don't need to tell you, but if you do see a big cat, don't approach it, it could easily kill you.

Dog (canis familiaris)

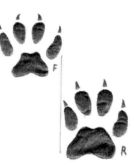

We have all seen dog tracks, I include it here more as a method of eliminating it from potential big cat mistaken tracks. A dog's print is usually slightly larger than a fox's, but it really depends on the breed of dog. A wolf track you are very unlikely to come across, but it is a lot larger than the other two's. You will also note that they all have their claws out, as they walk.

Deer

There are 6 types of deer living in Britain, in surprisingly large numbers, I have heard it said that there are in the region of 40,000 deer in Thetford Forest alone.

Red Deer (*Cervus elaphus*)

The Monarch of the Glen image, is a famous painting of this majestic creature. The trails of this deer are very easy to follow, you may mistake them for well used footpaths. These are big animals, the stag (male) can easy reach 80 kg in weight, without its antlers, they are surprisingly common, living in often large herds of 30 plus. They are most easily seen around woodland at twilight, where they sleep for the night. October is the start of their rutting season, the stags roar during the rut. they are native to Britain.

Roe Deer (*Capreolus caprelus*)

Roe Deer are another native of Britain, they are about a third of the size of a Red Deer, reaching about 16kg in weight, very common. They make a loud barking noise, which could be mistaken for a dog. They are active day and night, either solitary or living in small groups of 3 - 6 in woodland.

Fallow Deer (Cervus dama)

Fallow Deer are about the same size as Red Deer, the stags sport palmate antlers during the rut, these are flatten in look, spade-like. The bucks emit a loud belching noise during the rut. Fallow Deer were introduced to Britain by the Normans, Sherwood is a good place to see them, again they live in large herds, sheltering in woods at night.

Muntjac (*Muntiacus reevesi*)

Muntjac were introduced to Britain in the 20th Century, they originate from China. They are quite small, about knee height, living in woodland, they are easily missed unless carefully looked for. The bucks have a small set of antlers and fang-like canines. They do not rut, their young are born throughout the year. They live solitary in dense woodland or in small groups of 3-6 in less dense cover.

Sika Deer (*Cervus nippon*)

The Sika Deer were introduced from Japan about 100 years ago; they are similar to Red Deer in many ways, also interbreeding with them, which is resulting in less pure blood Red Deer.

Chinese Water Deer (*Hydropotes inermis*)

Chinese Water Deer were introduced from China, as the name implies, in the last century. They are doing very well and spreading fast, as the name implies they tend to live solitary in wet woods and reed beds, quite common in the Norfolk Broads area. Unlike other male deer, they have no antlers, only long fang-like tusks. They are slightly smaller than Muntjac.

Rutting season for deer, is in late autumn, around October, the males become quite aggressive during this period and are prone to attack almost anything which looks like a threat, including cars in the case of Red Deer. The smaller deer, Roe, Muntjac and Water, are fairly safe; but the larger deer should be avoided if possible.

Antlers are usually shed around late March - early April, they often gnaw on them, as they are full of protein. Given below are the tracks and droppings of these deer, they are all fairly similar in shape, though the size varies considerably:

Deer Tracks

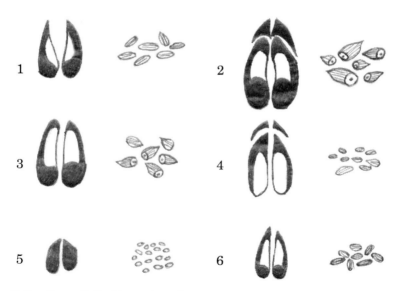

1) Roe Deer, 2) Red Deer, 3) Fallow Deer, 4) Sika Deer, 5) Muntjac Deer, 6) Chinese Water Deer.

Fox (*Vulpes vulpes*)

The Red Fox is quite a common sight in this country, it is a highly adaptable animal, which lives as often in town, as it does in the country. As we saw earlier its track is very similar to that of a dog, with the claws showing. If you come across a fox's briar you will know it, it is similar to the badger's sett to look at, though not as big, it will probably only have two entrances, there are likely to be a number of small bones and other small meal remains outside its entrance; Foxes are not as clean as badgers. Occasionally foxes will take over abandoned badger setts. Foxes can often be heard at night during the winter, especially the vixen (female) who makes a horrible screaming sound which sounds like 'Help'. The dog (male) fox is larger than the female, reaching collie type sizes.

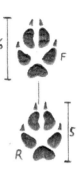

Hare (*Lepus europaeus*)

The hare is a large rabbit-like animal, it does not walk or trot, it only bounds, in short or long leaps, as you can see from the picture, despite having large rear feet, only the tips and toes of the feet make contact with the ground. It has long claws, which make a deep impression in soft ground, in hard ground they are all that shows as tracks. Hares unlike rabbits, don't make burrows, simply scrapping out a shallow hole for cover, when needed, called a scrap. Their speed is what they rely upon.

Hedgehog (*Erinaceus europaeus*)

The Hedgehog is a wonderful creature, known as the 'gardeners' friend' for eating all the slugs. They make nests of leaf litter, often in flowerpots or similar abandoned objects.

Hedgehogs rely upon their spikes for protection, so are not fast, when they walk, it is with a slow shuffle leaving separate prints. However they can lift themselves higher, revealing surprisingly long legs and move at a sort of trot, producing overlapping tracks.

Otter (*Lutra lutra*)

The otter is becoming more common once again around our watercourses; the otter has a home range of up to 35 miles, this is a large area for a small mammal, showing how much space is actually needed for an animal of its size to live successfully. It is an amphibious animal nearly as happy on land as in the water. Its holt has its entrance below the water level, so will rarely be seen, the remains of meals, fish scales and foot prints are the main clues to its presence around water ways. The otter can move in three main ways on land depending how fast it is moving. The tracks can be one after the other in a slow gait, or when bounding in sets of 2 side by side and over lapping or when flat out running they will appear as 4 tracks forming a diagonal line. Otter tracks are occasionally mistaken for a big cat, as water can swell them to a larger size, but again, the claws show they are not.

Rabbit (*Oryctolagus cuniculus*)

The rabbit was introduced to Britain by the Romans as a good food source, it was farmed in large warrens, such as can be found at Thetford in Norfolk, this consisted of a fenced off area, patrolled by a gamekeeper. The rabbits were so plentiful a simple club was all it took to harvest them.

Rabbits live in large groups in burrows called warrens, they feed on plants and grass.

Wild Boar (*Sus scrofa*)

The wild boar is native to Britain, though it became extinct a long time ago, numbers of them have escaped from wildlife parks and re-established themselves in areas of the country, Dorset particularly has a good number of them. The wild boar is the ancestor of the domestic pig, having been domesticated over several centuries. They are mainly solitary in nature, though females sows do form small family groups of 2 - 10. They are large and dangerous animals, a full-grown male boar can weigh up to 175Kg, with tusks and an attitude to match. Their hoofs or trotters are deer-like in appearance, save for the 2 prominent spikes at the rear.

Opposite are a number of other hoof prints you may come across:

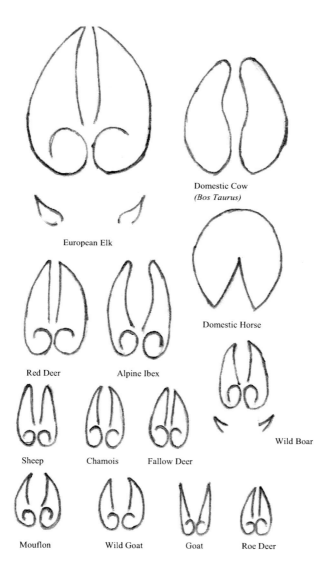

Domestic Cow
(Bos Taurus)

European Elk

Domestic Horse

Red Deer

Alpine Ibex

Wild Boar

Sheep

Chamois

Fallow Deer

Mouflon

Wild Goat

Goat

Roe Deer

84

Mammal Droppings

In addition to tracks there are also droppings which may help you to identify the animals living around you and how recently they were in your area, given below are some examples of these:

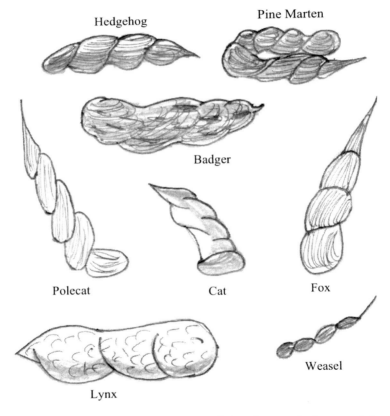

Hedgehog

Pine Marten

Badger

Polecat

Cat

Fox

Weasel

Lynx

Pine Martens (*Martes martes*), Polecats (*Mustela putorius*) are mainly found in the Scottish Highlands; Weasels (*Mustela nivalis*), as well as Stoats or Ermines (*Mustela erminea*) are also found in our country.

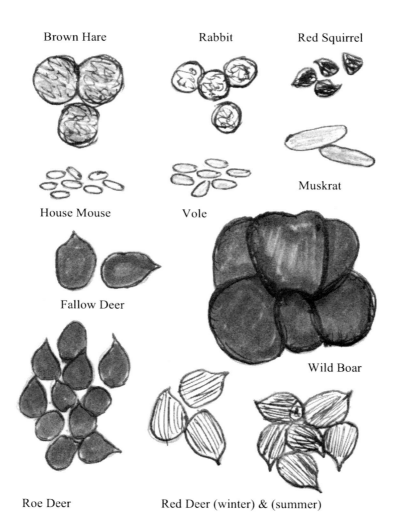

Brown Hare

Rabbit

Red Squirrel

Muskrat

House Mouse

Vole

Fallow Deer

Wild Boar

Roe Deer

Red Deer (winter) & (summer)

Bird Pellets

Pellets are what the birds, mainly raptors (birds of prey), can not digest; they are normally dry to the touch and consist of bones, fur and feathers of their prey, they can be very interesting to pull apart and examine, often containing whole tiny shrew skulls and similar items.

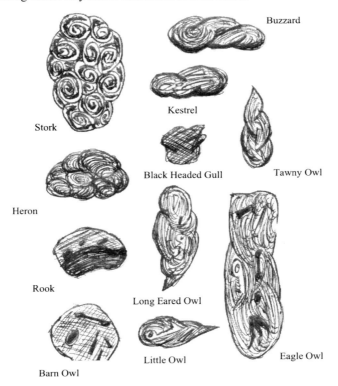

Buzzard

Stork

Kestrel

Black Headed Gull

Tawny Owl

Heron

Rook

Long Eared Owl

Little Owl

Eagle Owl

Barn Owl

This book does not cover all the wildlife and signs in Britain, there are many more animals, signs, trees, plants, insects, reptiles, amphibians, etc and much more to learn about conservation and ecology. This is simply a taste of it all, which I hope will encourage you to delve deeper.

3

THE SHAMANIC REALITY

The Shamanic Self

The Shamanic body or Self is made in exactly the same way as everyone else. It is a good idea to study basic anatomy to find out where all the major organs are, what they do and what the skeleton looks like, etc. What we will be looking at in this section is the subtle body or the energy/ spiritual body.

The spiritual body is made up of energy, which is invisible the vast majority of the time. This consists of many subtle levels or bodies including the astral body and the physical Body. I will be focusing on the aura, the chakras or energy centres and the meridians. These are the spiritual aspects of the body, there is no scientific proof for the existence of any of these, however there is proof that energy is created by the body, which radiates around the body, in the form of electricity, most often seen as static electricity.

In Shamanism the individual is viewed as a being of energy, power or medicine. Before I start to focus on these energies it is important to explain some aspects about energy and its effects on you and your world.

Energy in your Life and its Effects

We are all affected by energies around us, positive and negative. In turn we have affects on these surrounding energies, via our personal powers, positive and negative. These effects happen whether we are conscious of them or not. It is assumed that someone who is ill or diseased is being affected by excessive negative energy, often they are considered to be under attack by negative spirits.

Energy is neither positive nor negative; it is neutral. Electricity can be used to generate warmth, light and a host of other positive effects, however it can also be used to power an electric chair, launch nuclear missiles and a host of negative effects, but it is still electricity. The energies around you and within you can only act in a negative or positive manner, once you have decided what effect they are having on you.

In this sort of work you will discover a lot of change will take place within your life. Change is often perceived as a negative effect and certainly many of the changes you will experience within your life will initially be perceived of as negative in nature. However in time you may come to realize that what you initially perceived of as negative had a very positive effect in your life.

A very important fact to be aware of in this work is that "your mind creates the world in which you live, or at least your perception of it". If you are at a point in your life when everything seems to be going wrong, then it is more likely that you have outgrown what you once perceived of as positive within your life. This negativity will focus on specific areas of your life; relationships, work, interests and it will be these areas that need change. This doesn't always mean you must end your relationship, or give up your job etc; it may just be that you need to make changes within these areas of your life. Only you can ultimately decide what is for the best for you.

You will already have probably gone through a number of changes, which may even have felt forced on you, to be in this place now doing this course, with the people around you. When you change, those people closest to you will also have to change. It will seem like a natural process a shift in the balance of power around you. Some friendships may end or simply drift away from you as a result of you new found interests. You will also find yourself in new situations, surrounded by new people, making new friends.

Long-term relationships may also be drawing to a close, these will be harder to deal with and more painful. If this is the case you will be well aware of it already, especially if it affects children, family and friends. It could be that the relationship is entering a new stage and the people most strongly affected, need to discuss what is happening and what they feel they now want from the relationship. This sort of work will affect you and as a result, will affect everyone in your life. Eventually as everyone is connected, it will affect the whole world, just as the ripples on the water, will eventually touch all the banks of the pond, after you throw a pebble into it. This is why the energies involved are called subtle energies. It's the old story of the butterfly beating its wings in Japan causing a hurricane in America.

90

These energies affect us all and would happen whatever you were doing, if you had decided to learn accountancy, rather than Shamanism, then energies would also be affected, with similar results. The main difference is that in Shamanism you are conscious that there will be changes. In fact you may be doing this course in order to initiate these changes, this helps you to avoid any unnecessary confusion and pain, for yourself and others. These effects are known in Norse traditions as the way of 'Wyrd' (pronounced 'weird'), it is also called karma or fate.

The energy itself also has a variety of names to the Chinese it is called 'Chi', to the Japanese it is called 'Ki', in India it is known as 'Prana'. The Shaman and other spiritually aware people know these energies can be manipulated to create change. This often called magic, or magik as it is often spelt today to differentiate it from conjuring tricks.

Chakras or Energy Centres

There are traditionally seven main Chakras or energy centres within the body, these are located at the Crown, Forehead (3rd eye), Throat, Heart, Solar plexus, Tanden (2" below the Navel) and the Genitals (Base Chakra). In addition to these Major Chakras there is one hovering about 6" above the head and one about 6" below your feet. In addition to these, minor Chakras are located at all the main joints, e.g. wrists, elbows, knees, shoulders, ankles, hips, also at the centre of the palm and ball of the foot (see fig.1). These Chakras, are not all the Energy Centres and it is believed we are still developing new ones. The Meridians are covered in energy centres called Tsubos, or acupressure points approximately 600 of these exist, on the 12 Meridian lines of the body.

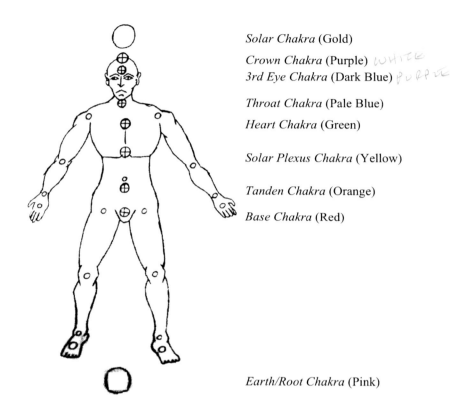

Solar Chakra (Gold)

Crown Chakra (Purple) WHITE
3rd Eye Chakra (Dark Blue) PURPLE

Throat Chakra (Pale Blue)

Heart Chakra (Green)

Solar Plexus Chakra (Yellow)

Tanden Chakra (Orange)

Base Chakra (Red)

Earth/Root Chakra (Pink)

The minor Chakras shown are in approximate places. The major Chakras are the most important when it comes to healing. The major Chakras are shown with their corresponding colours. The minor Chakras are more useful for healing with, than for doing healing on. The major Chakras go all the way through the body like a funnel with vortex-like energy at their furthest point from the body on both front and rear. This is not the case for the Chakras shown in italics, which are connected in an up and down action. This creates a grid-like pattern over the body. A healthy happy person who is well balanced will have strong unblocked Chakras and a good energy flow.

92

The Aura

The Aura is the energy around the body. It looks a little like a sliced onion with layers. The state of the Aura is a reflection of an individual's personality and health. Each layer of the Aura is a different colour. These correspond to the Chakras' colours. The distance a person's Aura is away from the body will reflect how open and outgoing a person is. The Aura is constructed in a similar fashion to a feather; this is why a feather or wing is used in the cleansing ritual known as smudging. The aura often gets negative energy trapped in it and this can lead to minor health problems. It is the job of the Aura to protect the individual from any negative energy, which is floating around from others. It equates to an individual's personal space or territory around their body.

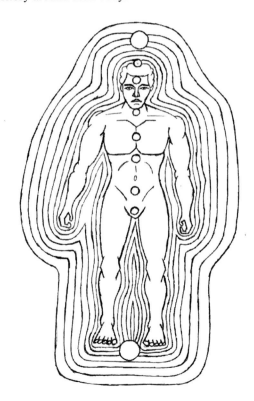

The Meridians

The Meridians are Chinese in their origins, the Samurai discovered them by accident, when after battle it was discovered that wounds to the body in certain places, cured other physical ailments. The Meridians are like roads, which the body's energies travel along. At regular intervals along these roads (about every 2") is an energy centre called a Tsubo. These pressure points are closely associated with the body's nervous system running along almost identical routes. Each of these 600 or so pressure points can be worked, either individually or as a group, using acupuncture, moxibustion (applied heat or vacuum) or acupressure, to relieve symptoms of illness, pain or dis-ease.

It is also these points, which can be used to inflict pain, paralysis, etc with the Martial Arts (Do not attempt to use them unless you have received special training). These 12 Meridians are closely associated with the 5 Chinese Elements of Wood, Fire, Metal, Water and Earth. The energy flowing through these Meridians can become blocked which can result in too much energy in some Meridians and not enough in others. This leads to illness etc. The blockages often occur at the pressure points, which then needs to be unblocked. The Meridians of the body are very similar to the ley lines or dragon lines of the planet, with the sacred sites indicating a pressure point.

Other Subtle Bodies

The body is present on three planes or in the three worlds. These are all related to the Chakras.

1) The 'Spiritual Plane' (Asgard), is connected to the body via the Crown Chakra and the Ketheric Body (mental aspect), the 3rd Eye Chakra and the Celestial Body (emotional aspect), the Throat Chakra and the Etheric Body.

2) The 'Astral Plane' (Bifrost rainbow bridge), is the link between the 'Spiritual Plane' and the 'Physical Plane', this is connected to the Heart Chakra and the Astral Body.

3) The 'Physical Plane' (Midgard), is connected to the body via the Solar Plexus Chakra and the Mental Body (lower mental

aspect), the Taindan Chakra and the Emotional Body (lower emotional aspect) and the Base Chakra and the Etheric Body (lower Etheric aspect).

There are more bodies than this connected too, the Instinctual Body (emotional aspect) or Animal Body (etheric aspect) or Reptilian Body (mental aspect), which are connected to the Underworld (Nifleheim). These are also connected to the Base Chakra and to the Root Chakra. The Christian Church classes this area as Hell. It is said to be a fiery inferno ruled over by the Devil. However this is a realm in Norse mythology, which is said to be a frozen wasteland ruled over by the Giantess/Goddess Hel, who is portrayed as a beautiful woman who is rotting from the waist down. It is an area in which it is often necessary to travel in spirit, in which to perform soul retrieval, which is a common Shamanic process.

The 3 Souls

The last section may have been confusing to some, especially if you are used to thinking in terms of a body and a spirit, some of you are probably aware of the concept of a Higher Self. A common belief in a wide-ranging selection of Shamanic cultures is that we all have at least 3 souls; a soul is a smaller part of a spirit. In Siberia and Mongolia these are known as:

Suld

Ami

Suns

The roles of these Souls will be explored fully in the chapter on Shamanic Journeying.

The Shamanic Reality

The Shamanic universe is very different to the world we know and function within most of the time. The world we call 'Reality' is in fact only a small part of what the Shaman would call 'Reality'. The Reality we live in is a reflection of a greater 'Reality'; as I sit here typing on a computer, in a centrally heated, double-glazed flat, the stereo playing music in the background, the electric oven cooking my evening meal, while I work; surrounded by the simple comforts of Western civilization; simple, huh. In the same world, my reality, at the same time, there are people at war and dying for what they believe, or for what has been thrust upon them. There are people dying of starvation or dehydration, illness, disease; there are people living in mud huts, skinning the animal they have killed, preparing it to feed their families, feeling very lucky, people who would look at my 'simple comforts' with awe and wonder; there are people talking to researchers about their alien abduction scenarios. There are people shooting up drugs and drinking themselves into a stupor out of the despair at the horrors of their lives, due to child abuse, poverty, ignorance, fear, etc. There are other people robbing, stealing, mugging, raping, killing their innocent victims and there are people falling in love. This is just another day in my 'Reality' my 'World', your 'Reality', your 'World'.

Is it really so hard to believe in the other realities of the world around us? Don't forget this is also the same world in which the deer are currently in rut; the stag fighting off all contenders for his herd of does. The birds are migrating to warmer climates for the winter, the trees are withdrawing their sap into their roots in preparation for winter and new growth in spring; the bears are beginning their hibernation. This doesn't even touch on what is happening in other galaxies, among other alien races; is there an alien equivalent of me writing the same things in an equivalent situation in a distance universe?

The Shaman says there are 3 Worlds; in Norse Mythology these are split into 9 Realms. These worlds are inhabited by gods, goddesses, powerful spirits, nature spirits, fairy folk (sidhe), aliens, ghosts, demons and all sorts of other mythical creatures, as well as Humans, is it really nonsense as many believe?

Macrocosm and Microcosm

The Shamanic Universe/Reality also effects time, in our everyday world time is measured as a straight line from point A - B. In the Shamanic reality, time works in a spiralling or circular fashion, as does reality. When in deep meditation you will experience a sensation of this reality, in this state as you feel yourself become smaller and smaller, you enter the Microcosm, you become aware of the vastness of yourself, yet at the same time the inconsequential scale of yourself in relation to all that is, the Macrocosm; at this point you are standing on the boundary of where the two sides of reality meet, where your own vast potential meets with the vastness of true potential.

If you could travel as fast as is imaginable out into the vastness of space, I believe you would come out on the other side, within yourself; I believe this is what it means, when it states in the Bible we are created in God's image. We are ultimately all gods and goddesses; it is our perception which creates our reality. Perception is based on what we feel is real to us, it is not always the case, our perception can be wrong. There are events in our lives we do not understand, the future can be scary or bright, mostly a bit of both. Perception is mainly based on our concept of Self; it is this concept which often needs to changed; when we do change it for the better, we will have a knock on effect, the people we come into contact with will be altered subtly by our changes in our Self, in order to continue to fit in, it may be that they will leave our circle of friends, normally simply drifting away. This will affect them, hopefully for the better.

We tend to forget, or never realize our own personal power, we can all change our immediate worlds (family, friends and workmates) simply by changing ourselves into someone we would sooner be; this is usually a simple case of recognition, of what we don't like about ourselves, facing our fears. They usually are not as scary as we think, this is because most of our fears were developed as children, so when we encounter them, we do so from a child's point of view, not from that of a full-grown adult. It is usually emotional pain that needs to be dealt with.

If we want to change the world we can, or at least contribute to it; We all have money, no matter how much or how little; money is not simply a token that can be exchanged for something else; money is a VOTE. When you buy something you are saying that you want that thing and you accept how it got to you, how it was made, who made it, what they were paid, what their working conditions are, etc, etc. Very few of us ever seem to realize this; we are so desperate simply trying to get more of the stuff, we don't think what it really means.

'Money makes the world go around', the song goes, it's a light trivial song, yet it's performed in a dark, sinister, sort of way. Money influences everything; it is ultimately why wars are fought, why governments come and go, what's acceptable and what's not. The Native Americans say 'only when all the animals are gone, only when all the plants are gone, will man realize you can't eat money'. If you want to be a force for positive change, you have to evaluate your life, what's important to you, you may have to make sacrifices; the old definition of the word sacrifice is 'to make sacred', not to kill, although this often was a part of it in the dim and distant past. The point of Macrocosm and Microcosm is that the two are connected, influence one, change one and you will have a subtle effect on the other; consciously change yourself (Microcosm) and you will have a subtle effect on the world (Macrocosm).

The Earth Mother

As I've mentioned before, I have trained in conservation and looked into ecology; so this is as much about these issues as about the Earth Mother herself. We all understand the concept of the world as our mother; from a child-like perspective of the being that inspires, clothes, homes, feeds and takes care of our needs. In the Shamanic tradition she is very much a living being, who we spend most of our time relating to and trying to improve our relations with.

We are all her children, the Native Americans say 'all my relations', in their prayers and blessings; they are not simply talking about Aunt Nelly, in Australia, etc, they are talking about EVERYTHING they share the planet with and the planet herself, they are also talking about the universe, extra terrestrials, other planets, etc, but for this section it is more important to focus on what we KNOW is; not what we believe is.

The planet has her own cycles, ones we simply haven't existed long enough to fully understand or even recognize yet. Ecology is a young science, having started in the early 60's, although its roots are much older than this, going back to when man first started to try and make sense of the world around him. I would class Moses as a good ecologist, having an understanding of the world's cycles, enabling him to be able to predict some of the plagues which attacked the pharaohs. The River Nile is affected regularly by floods which travel across red clay, staining the Nile red, the locusts swarm every 7 years; I can't explain it all, but he certainly knew more about these sort of events than the Pharaohs did; I would also call Moses a Shaman.

Ecology is such a new science it didn't know about the El Nenio cycle which causes so much damage, especially to the fishing industry, yet is a natural cycle, they have now learnt. It is also understood that the world's normal cycle is to be in an Ice Age, this warm spell we are going through is an exception to the norm, not the norm. So as we are still at the tail end of the last Great Ice Age, it is no wonder we are experiencing global warming. This however doesn't mean we are not influencing this global warming, or that it is good for the planet; the effects of global warming take 30 years to materialize, so what we are experiencing now is from the industries of the 70's, or to put it another way, it will get worse before it gets better.

It is important to remember that Britain used to be a tropical climate, when the dinosaurs roamed, as such it may become so again. This will mean increased storm weather and torrential downpours, much like America's weather. The fierce gales of the autumn, which are now a regular event, but we didn't always experience, will increase and stay with us, for the future.

Going back to the money issues, as Shamanic practitioners or Animists, people who follow an Earth religion, it is important, essential, for us to do all we can to improve our Earth Mother's conditions; many of us go to the ancient circles to 'OM' for a better world or similar, but next time you do, pick up some litter as well. It is about balance, do something spiritual, but back it up with something practical; study conservation, go out with the BTCV on a regular basis to do some Conservation work; donate to the nature charities; be more conscious of what you do spend your money on; if you worry about conditions in the Third World, buy Fair Trade products, if you don't like the way animals are exploited for food, buy RSPCA approved meats or become vegetarian. If you know that companies use exploitive child labour, don't buy their products, no matter how much of a 'bargain' it is. If you are worried about your bank's investments, change to a co-op bank; don't buy GM foods, buy organic.

The world's markets are influenced by your decisions, on what you spend your money on; remember you are 'voting' when you buy; vote sensibly, for what you want. I know a lot of these things cost more, that is because they are more hassle for the companies to produce, because they are positive alternatives and we are being exploited over them; but if everyone only buys these environmentally friendly products, they will become the norm, prices will come down and the less friendly products, will become the expensive alternative.

The Earth Mother still has many exciting and interesting things to be learnt about her.

Cycles

The circle is a sacred shape in all cultures, the world over; in Britain we have still got literally hundreds of ancient stone circles; in the past there would have been thousands; at least one wherever mankind lived as a group. It is a shape without end; it is the reflection of the seasons of the year, the times of the day, the stages of life, Nature works in circles or cycles.

This shape is one of the most important things you will ever learn, it is this shape around which Shamanism and all Earth religions are based. It is not just a metaphor it is a map, a guide to life and existence. When we are feeling down and depressed, all our problems seem insurmountable; yet when we are feeling happy and 'up', our problems seem insignificant. The problems haven't changed, only our perception has. It is very important at this time to remember we are in control of our own feelings, our own perception, I know it doesn't feel like it at times, but it is true, we decide how we feel; we can change it if we don't like it, although like most things it does take practice.

We are very used to an instant world, if we want to eat, we zap it in a microwave or order fast food, we undervalue everything and accept the disposable world we live in. This attitude is filtering down into everything, including friendships and relationships. Everything is fast and easy. But worthwhile things take time to grow and develop, like an acorn, it doesn't become an oak tree overnight, yet that acorn contains within it the potential to become an ancient majestic oak.

This means what goes around, comes around, it is based on the observation of the seasons, the moon, the day and sun. It is saying that there is a cycle in your life, which repeats itself, in me it appears to be every 7 years; I have not studied astrology, but I am sure there is an explanation within that system, which also works on the cycle of the planets. This means when you say 'I wish, I could do it all again, knowing what I do now'; we do. True, it's never exactly the same, that's because we are not and we have travelled another cycle of the spiral; but the situations are similar, as our reactions to them will be. This indicates that in life there are a set of lessons we are expected to learn, only when we have passed the lessons do we move on to the next ones. Sometimes these cycles are positive ones, sometimes they are negative ones which need to be broken; as in the case of the battered wife; who despite getting divorced form her original tormentor, ends up with a completely new one; or ends up battering her new husband. Child abuse works in a similar way; often the child who was abused, becomes an abuser; or the child of alcoholic parents ends up an alcoholic. These are extreme cases, but they serve to illustrate the point. It could be that the cycle you need to break is that you always end up in something as simple as a dead-end job. In all these cases there is something that needs to be changed on an inner level, this can often be very emotionally painful, requiring the assistance of a good counsellor. In most cases it is about breaking our victim consciousness. At the end of the day it is only really you that can change, as a result everything else will also change; this is not always pleasant, often you will find yourself at odds with the people you were once close to, then you will seek out new friends and lovers who are more compatible for you.

That is the negative side, sometimes we can get carried away, as a result of our need to change, we can end up throwing everything away, going back to basics; in this case it is necessary to be able to swallow your pride and admit when you are wrong; then you can pick up those things which you still want in your life once again, although they will often feel different, as you do.

The circle allows us to see the cycle of the Seasons as they progress through the year moving in a clockwise or sun-wise direction; to this cycle of the sun through its solstices and equinoxes other associations were added, such as progress through life, the elements, times of the day, times of the month, etc; this circle of existence will be looked at more fully in the section on 'ritual and the sacred circle'.

The cycle of the year was considered as an aspect of our life cycle; which was also seen as a circle, spiral or maze. Within this cycle of the year there were smaller cycles, such as the moon's cycle, which was originally used to measure the length of the year giving us 13 months, not the 12 we use today; this month was divided into the cycle of the phases of the moon, waxing moon, full moon, waning moon and dark moon; so it was possible to enact a representation of the year within a month, or even within a day, as the day can be separated into an even smaller representation of the year, by its times of the day, dawn, noon, twilight and midnight.

So you can see how the circle of the year became a spiral, circles within circles. The year was a smaller aspect of the larger cycles of the sun and moon, in Cornwall the stone circles are representatives of the moon cycle with 19 stones in each to represent the 18.7 year cycle of the moon. The Shamen of the past were also very aware of the cycles of the animals, especially the common prey ones; this would also have been fitted into the circle of the year, showing the times of their birth, maturity, mating and rut/death. Such things were important to our ancestors as the Shamanic cultures were more often nomadic cultures, hunter/gatherers; rather than agricultural people, which the majority of modern Earth religions were based on. To the Shamanic culture (we are talking about Stone Age Man mainly) travel was important through life, as they followed the migrating deer, etc, travelling in their own form of migration, from summer to winter camps. Most shamen were strongly connected with a tribal identity, staying with the tribe as it moved; but others were known as travelling Shaman, they wandered through out the length and breadth of their world, seeking new ideas and knowledge from many different tribes, before returning to their own tribe; this may well have been an aspect of their training, which would have benefited all the tribes via shared experiences. It is known that our ancestors gathered in huge inter tribal gatherings on a regular basis, this would have allowed for additional sharing of knowledge, trade, mating opportunities (reducing interbreeding), etc.

The Other Worlds

Most Earth religions and Shamanic traditions have an shared concept of 3 Worlds, these are the Upper World, Middle World and the Under World; sometimes a fourth World is referred to called the Lower World, which is related to our Subconscious aspects in the everyday world; these are related to our Spiritual Bodies as mentioned in 'Other Subtle Bodies', they are also strongly connected to our brain functions and levels of Consciousness.

In our everyday world the Middle World, known as Midgard, we tend to function in a waking state known as Beta Consciousness or an Alpha State. In a Theta State we are able to travel to the Under World, known as

Niflheim and Muspell, which is related strongly to our Subconscious (Lower World) and Unconscious (Under World) this is normally done during sleep, though it is also possible to travel to the Upper World of Asgard, our Super-unconscious.

The Theta state of Consciousness, a lucid dream-like state of deep meditation, is what we would normally use to travel to all these Worlds, after we have learnt to meditate to a sufficient level; we can also travel to all these worlds in a Delta state of consciousness, which is related to our Super-unconscious, higher brain functions, which allow for those 'Eureka' moments, which is more of a collective human consciousness, though it takes many years of practice to attain these states of consciousness in a wakened state. The traditional descriptions of these three Worlds are given below:

The Lower World is described as very Earth-like, though a lot less developed, think of Canada and you are about right, though it is slightly darker there, the Sun isn't as intense. The Middle World is the world you know (conscious), it is also a place you can travel within spiritually, or physically, though there are many places within it which merge with the other two worlds, which are neither here nor there (subconscious). The Upper World is described as very bright, sometimes with two suns, it is more ethereal there, the landscape can change; to almost anything imaginable, is very dream-like it in its structure, when meeting a spiritual being there it is likely the landscape will alter, to fit him or her as is appropriate to them and in which they are most comfortable. These Worlds do change according to the Cultural Perspective from which you view them. Given below are the descriptions of the Norse Otherworlds, which are formed from 3 Worlds, but divided into 9 Realms:

Niflheim - Reached by travelling 9 days down and North; ruled over by the Goddess Hel and is a barren frozen wasteland where the dead live; also known as the Land of the Dead. (STAGNATION & DEATH)

Muspell - Separated from Niflheim by a wall of fire, it is ruled over by the Fire Giant Surt, it is a volcanic wasteland of lava, ash and smoke, populated by Fire Giants and the Fears of Man, known as Muspell's Children. (SUB CONSCIOUS FEARS & LIMITS)

Midgard - This is the Human World. (LIFE & LEARNING)
(NORSE PLACING)

Jotunheim - This is in the East of Midgard, were the other Giant Races live in their mountain stronghold Utgard. (OBSTACLES & CHALLENGES)

Nidavellir - This is in the North of Midgard, in a hilly region; it is the home of the Dwarves, who live in their underground cave cities making beautiful, magikal items. (CREATIVITY & INSPIRATION FROM THE SUB CONSCIOUS)

Svartalfheim - This region is also in the North of Midgard, near the Dwarves, this is the home of the Dark Elves, who practice Occult Magik. (UNKNOWN POTENTIAL & POWER)

Midgard - This is the Human World. (LIFE & LEARNING)
(CELTIC PLACING)

Asgard - This is reached from Midgard via the Bifrost Rainbow Bridge, a Rainbow of only 3 colours, the red of fire, the blue of air and the green of the deep sea. It is here that the Aesir (warrior Gods) live ruled over by Odin. (FREE WILL & ACTION)

Alfheim - This is the classical Otherworld, lived in by Faery (Sidhe, Fairies) Folk and the Light Elves. The Elves were known as Alfar to the Norse, which means The Shining or Golden Ones. (HOPES & DREAMS)

Vanaheim - This is the land of the Vanir (fertility Gods) ruled over by Njord, these are an older pantheon of gods than the Aesir; although they were conquered by them and now also live peacefully under the rule of Odin; these are the gods in charge of peace, abundance, love and beauty. (SPIRIT & LOVE)

In the Celtic world it is seen slightly differently; there are still 3 Worlds; the Upper World, the Middle World and the Under World; but they are not quite as dark and sinister; The landscapes in which the Celts lived lacked the frozen wastelands of the glaciers and the volcanic aspects of Greenland, which the Norse lived in; so the realms of Muspell and Niflheim are missing. It is the combination of these two realms and the Goddess Hel, a beautiful woman from the waist up and a rotting corpse from the waist down which gave rise to the idea of the Christian Hell.

In the details of the three Worlds given above, I have placed Midgard in two positions, giving a rough guide to the differences between these Celtic and Norse Traditions. I have also indicated the sort of Lessons or Energies, which are likely to be drawn from each of these Worlds. The Celts tended to view the three Worlds in the traditional manner mentioned earlier. If any of this sounds familiar it may well be because you have read or seen the film 'The Lord of the Rings', much of what is mentioned in this course may remind you of J.R.R.Tolkien's work, this is because he borrowed directly and strongly from Norse Mythology.

In all these Traditions, there was always a link between these three Worlds, which connected them all and allowed the Shaman to travel between these different Worlds; this was sometimes seen in the form of a Great River (as in Mongolia), but most often it was seen as a Tree as in both the Norse and Celtic Traditions, this was known as the World Tree; the Norse called it the Yggdrasil World Ash Tree; to the Celts it was an Oak Tree.

The point of the Tree is that it exists in all three Worlds at once, the Branches and Leaves stretch up to the Upper World, the Trunk is firmly rooted in the Middle World and the Root system, which is as big as the Branches above, burrows deep down into the Under World.

The World Tree

The World Tree is common to nearly all Shamanic Cultures; anywhere there are lots of Trees. The Shaman is often said to travel through a tunnel on the way to the Other Worlds, as do people who have had NDEs (Near Death Experiences). It is the World Tree that they are travelling through; or its root system it is most commonly believed.

In the Norse Tradition the Yggdrasil Ash Tree is depicted as having three Roots, each one terminates in one of the three Worlds. The World Tree is closely related to the Tree of Life, a Hebrew Magikal System adopted by Western Mystical Societies such as the 'Golden Dawn'.

Yggdrasil means 'the steed of Yggr', Yggr is another name for Odin, his Steed was the magikal horse Sleipnir, an eight legged horse who could run like the wind and through the air. Sleipnir's eight legs are representations of the 8 major Pagan festivals of the year, so the Yggdrasil Tree in a sense is a representative of time, with each of the three roots representing the Past (Under World), Present (Middle World) and Future (Upper World). The God Odin was also the God of the Shaman and the reference to the 'steed of Odin', closely relates to the Shaman's Drum, the essential Shamans Tool, which is often called the 'Shaman's Horse'. The Drum induces a mind altering state in the Shaman, inducing a state of Ecstasy or Trance, in which the Shaman is freed to travel to the Otherworlds. The Drum beat also acts as a Lifeline for the Shaman to follow to the Otherworlds and back again, as the Heart will often synchronises with the Drums beat.

Another common way of travelling to the Otherworlds, especially the Under World, which is the most common destination of the Shaman, was via water. In Mongolia, the Great World River is followed to the Under World, in Celtic and Norse Traditions a Sacred Spring was often followed. The Yggdrasil Tree was also almost an Otherworld in itself, with its own inhabitants; in Norse Tradition two Giant Deer gnaws at the Tree's base, an Eagle plays 'Flyting (a game of insults) with Nidhogg (a Dragon who chews at the Under World Root)', a Hawk (messenger of the Gods) sits between the Eagle's eyes and the Squirrel Ratatosk (the Gossiper), who carries insults between the Eagle and Nidhogg. In Mongolian Shamanism the World Tree is the home of the Ami souls.

The World Tree is said to 'Grow from the Past, Lives in the Present and Reaches for the Future', just as we do.

To further indicate the World Tree's connection with time, in addition to the three roots, it has 13 Branches, which relate to months of the year; Our Shamanic ancestors observed a lunar calendar, not a solar one as we do; so there are 13 months in the year, their days also began and ended at dusk, the months are about two weeks out, compared to our modern calendar; so the months given below start about the 14th of the previous month and end on the 14th of the mentioned month; they start at the Norse New Year, which is the Full Moon, nearest the Winter Solstice December 21st - 22nd:

December - Wolf Moon
January - Snow Moon
February - Horning Moon
March - Plough Moon
April - Seed / Planting / Lenting Moon
May - Hare Moon / Ostara (Easter)
June - Mead / Merry Moon
July - Fallow Moon
August - Corn / Hay Moon
September - Harvest Moon
October - Shedding Moon
November - Hunting Moon
December - Fog Moon

The World Tree's Roots

As I said earlier the Roots of the World Tree are related to the Past, Present and Future. As with all things in the Shamanic Reality, there are powerful

108

spiritual beings in charge of time; in the Norse Tradition these are the Norns. The three Norns are aspects of the Triple Goddess, a very Celtic concept, related to the Moon, the Maiden (Waxing Moon), Mother (Full Moon) and the Crone (Waning Moon); The three Norns control everything, even the Gods are unable to escape their decisions. It is the Norns who weave the 'Web Of Wyrd (Fate)', which governs all things, including themselves and teaches us of personal responsibility, allowing us to see that our actions and inactions, ultimately have an effect on all things. The 3 Norns are:

Urd (Maiden) - The Past- Fate shaped by what has been, full of nostalgia, she weaves the Web of Wyrd. (Experience)

Verdandi (Mother) - The Present - Present circumstances of your own creation, she only looks to the present as she carefully weaves the Web. (Necessity)

Skuld (Crone) - The Future - What must be if you follow your current path, she only sees the future, as she carefully unpicks the Web of Wyrd-unset; subject to change- freewill governs. (Being)

The Under World Root comes out in the Seething Cauldron of Hvergelmir (a Spring from which 12 major rivers stem); this is guarded by the dragon Nidhogg, who constantly tries to chew away the Root, destroying the Tree; this will bring about the Battle of Ragnarok; the downfall of the gods, the end of the Worlds and a new beginning, as everything travels in cycles.

The Middle World Root comes out in the Fountain of Mimir, guarded by the God Mimir, or at least his Head, (God of all Knowledge and Wisdom). This is the water the World Tree drank from, the source of all Wisdom and was also known as the Fountain of Knowledge or Life.

The Upper World Root comes out in the Well of Urd (Past Experience / Memory), where the 3 Norns sit weaving the Web of Wyrd and tending to the World Tree, which is under constant attack from two giant deer, the dragon Nidhogg and Rot (Corruption).

Pictorial View

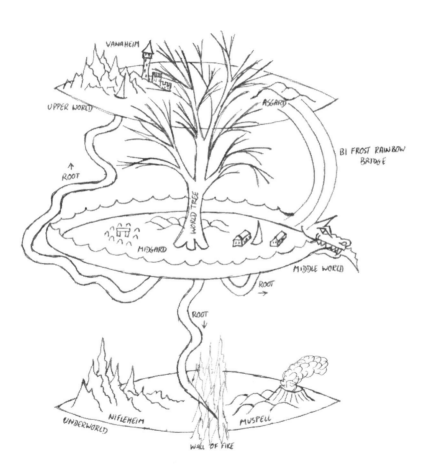

4

THE WHEEL OF LIFE

The Wheel of the Year
The 8 Celtic Festivals
The Norse Festivals
Mongolian Shamanic Festivals
The Wheel of Life

The Wheel of the Year

The circle was very important to our ancestors for a number of reasons and they expressed this in a number of ways. Our Neolithic ancestors built impressive lunar circle complexes; later they built, or modified existing circles, into even more complex solar orientated henges. We know from their alignments they had something to do with the seasons and time. We also know from history that they celebrated a number of festivals. The first festivals of our hunter/gatherer ancestors would no doubt have been celebrated at the Full Moon, which is how they counted time and what they aligned their stone circles to, this is what modern-day Witches or Wiccans as they are often called, do. We also know that later in history the orientation of these circles changed to solar events, which was very important to our now agricultural ancestors, modern-day Druids hold these festivals in high esteem.

As Shamanism is the forerunner of both of these traditional Animism religions or philosophies it makes sense that our Shamanic ancestors worshipped when the Moon was full; as it is the most obvious sign of the turning of time. However modern-day Shamanism holds both of these cycles in high regard, as such I would suggest you do some sort of ceremony on the Full Moon (Note: a Blue Moon occurs every 2 and a half years, this is when there are two Full Moons in a single month) to acknowledge your roots and observe the eight solar festivals of the year:

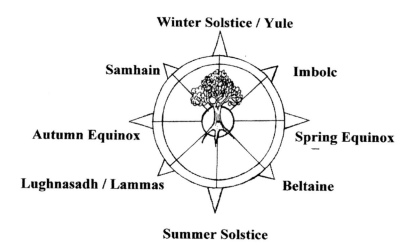

Four of the festivals are the solstices and equinoxes; this cycle was probably observed by our hunter/gatherer ancestors prior to them becoming agricultural, at least the solstices would have been, simply due to observation of the daylight hours changing. It is likely that rather than using predetermined dates as we do today, due to our calendars that certain festivals would have held as the result of some form of natural indication, e.g. Imbolc is naturally marked as when the first Snowdrop plants appear. In Mongolia the Shamanic Tradition also holds eight festivals, although their landscape and weather patterns are not the same as ours they give an indication of how the Shamanic year of our Hunter/Gatherer Ancestors may have looked. Their festivals are marked by the Moon and the Sun, as well as natural indications. It is important to remember that due to our modern solar calendar being adjusted several times over the Centuries, including an event in 1752 that almost caused a civil war, when twelve days were removed from the old Julian calendar in one go; many believed that they had actually lost twelve days of their lives and demanded them back. The adjustment was to make up for the earlier calendar ignoring what we call leap year adjustments to the Sun's cycle. As a result of this adjustment, four of our festivals are probably about twelve days earlier than they would have been for our ancestors. The solstices and equinoxes are accurate as they are indicated by solar observation, rather than predetermined dates. The four fire festivals (Imbolc, Beltaine, Lughnasadh and Samhain) are likely to be earlier today, than they would have been.

The 8 Celtic Festivals

The Wheel of the Year has eight main festivals on it, there are additional smaller festivals or celebrations performed at the Full Moon each month, called in Wicca Esbats, these tend to be working meetings, in which a coven gathers to perform or train in their magikal skills. Other Animistic belief systems often do similar things on a monthly basis, so although the Wheel of the Year is a solar wheel with solar festivals, the lunar cycle is far from ignored or forgotten; often these solar festivals are celebrated at the Full Moon nearest the festival date, sadly they are more often celebrated, due to work and family commitments, when it is practical, often at the weekends. However, Shamanism is a practical and adaptable belief system; our ancestors would understand these things. Given below is information about the eight festivals, in order of the Celtic year. I said earlier all the calendars were out by about twelve days, as a result, I have included the most appropriate lunar phase, in relation to the four fire festivals and suggest they should be celebrated on the appropriate phase of the Moon, nearest to the usual Festival dates, this will help to compensate for this:

Samhain

Samhain (pronounced Sow-hain), is the Celtic New Year, so this is the first and last festival of the year, it is one of the four fire festivals. Samhain is better known as Halloween nowadays; it is an ancient festival lasting three days, October 31st 'All Souls Eve', November 1st 'All Hallows Eve' and November 2nd 'All Saints Day', as they are called today, or 'The night of Spectres', 'Ancestors' Night' and 'Feast of the Dead' as they were known to the Norse.

Samhain was the first harvest of the new year. It was the time when the Celts brought their livestock down from the pastures; the Celts for very practical reasons kept their best livestock with them in their Roundhouses over winter, this helped to generate extra heating, through body heat within the roundhouse, to supply easily gathered fuel for the fire, in the form of dried droppings, to supply fresh milk and it ensured their best breeding stock survived the winter and didn't fall foul of the elements, wolves or cattle thieves. The roundhouses were not huge though, so to ensure the Celts survived the winter months, all but the best breeding stock was slaughtered; following the Samhain Feast, all spare meat was dried and stored for the coming months, along with all the other spare crops saved for the winter. From this time on, any fresh food would have to be hunted, if the weather permitted such excursions. The winter months were hard on everyone, many died of the cold or starvation, especially if they had had poor harvests, or the winter dragged on later than usual.

Samhain was also a strange time, or non time, this was the thirteenth month of the solar year, a time, out of time. This on a practical level resolved the problems of the time difference between the lunar and solar calendars. However, it was also a time when the nights got longer, people stayed in round the fires and told stories. It was the time when the Veil between the three Worlds was believed to be thinnest and that the ancestors of the Celts also drew nearer the camp fires to listen to the, often scary, stories.

The Lords of Mischief and Chaos (mischievous Sidhe and other Spirits) ruled, this was a time when even the smallest of accidents could have dire consequences, a time when a hard life became harder and death was never far away. As a result the ancestor spirits were called upon to stay close and lend their aid, a feast was held in honour of them, libations of food and drink were left out for them. It was also a good idea to be on the good side of the Lords of Mischief and so libations were also left out for them, to buy their favour, a tradition that remains, if only on a subconscious level, in the form of 'Trick or Treat' games.

Samhain should be celebrated at the New Moon (Dark Moon) nearest to the Samhain Festival, or after it.

Winter Solstice or Yule

Winter Solstice on the 21st or 22nd December, is the longest night of the year; the darkest and scariest night; yet at the same time it is a turning point, from this night on the nights get shorter, spring is on route, the worst is over. The Sun is reborn renewed; this is why the birth of Christ is celebrated at this time.

This is the time of the Norse New Year, a feast of twelve days was held at this point, it was for many similar reasons as the Celts' Samhain Festival was held, this twelve day feast gives us the twelve days of Christmas we now celebrate. A Yule log held an important role in this, this was the largest log of the wood pile and was lit with the remains of the previous years Yule Log; it's ashes were gathered up and sown on the soil when it was time to plough, to ensure a good harvest.

Imbolc

Imbolc (im - olk), or Maidens Day, Candlemas, is celebrated on the eve of 1st February or 2nd of February, it is the second of the Fire Festivals. Imbolc marks the beginning of spring, the first Snowdrops appear and the ewes give birth to their new lambs and begin to produce milk again. It is a time of new beginnings, of birth, dedicated to the maiden goddesses; it is a time of celebration, simply for still being alive, surviving the long winter.

115

It is especially dedicated to the Goddess Bride, (Goddess of Midwives, Healing, Arts and Crafts, her symbol is the Eternal Flame), as many human babies were also born at this point, having been conceived on Beltaine the previous year, many young minds would also be turning to the 'cuming' Beltaine.

This Fire Festival should be celebrated on the Waxing Moon nearest or after the normal Festival dates.

Ostara or Spring Equinox

Spring Equinox is celebrated on the 21st March, it is the time when the Sun is becoming stronger, spring is upon us, the natural world around us is coming into bloom and the trees are beginning to show new leaves. It is a period when the day and night are equal in length, but we know winter is over, now we can start preparing for the summer, ploughing the fields, sowing the seeds of wheat, barley and rye for the summer harvest and returning the livestock to their pastures, now the fresh grass is there.

Another important festival of this period, which incorporates the essence of the Spring Equinox, is Eostre, or Easter as it is better known now. This is a very old festival, despite the thin Christian veneer, it is still an obviously much older festival dedicated to the Norse Goddess Eostre or Ostara, Goddess of Fertility, Spring and Dancing, whose symbols are the Serpents Egg (Easter Eggs) and the Hare (Easter Bunny). The Serpents (Adder: Common Viper) representing the Earth, via the Ley or Serpent Lines are emerging from their underground burrows, performing their mating rituals, which involves the males' test of strength, which looks like a dance and the females are laying Eggs. The Hare, is 'mad as a March Hare', because they also are in their mating season, hence their boxing matches and other strange behaviour.

Even the date of Easter, the first Sunday (Christian influence), nearest the Full Moon, after the Spring Equinox, is an obvious sign of Pagan origins. Ostara should be celebrated on the first Full Moon after Spring Equinox.

116

Beltaine

Beltaine (Bell-tane) is the third Fire Festival, it is celebrated on the Eve of 30th April or 1st May, we have a bank holiday at this time as a reminder of the importance of this festival. This is the opposite of Samhain; it is the time of long, warm Summer nights, when our thoughts turn to the opposite sex and to sex in general, to new life, future generations, joy, fun, celebration, holidays and sowing our own seeds.

This festival is still strongly indicated, even in today's fast moving modern world. In Padstow in Cornwall, there is the 'Obby Oss' celebration, in Helston in Cornwall there is the 'Floral Dance' or 'Furry Dance', whose tune was made famous by Terry Wogan on Radio 2, in the mid 70's, when it reached Number One in the charts, these are fertility and mating dances; as well as a host of other fertility dances, under the guise of morris dancing, etc, all over the country. This festival is dedicated to Bel, the Celtic Sun, Livestock and Fertility God, this is probably the origin of the term 'Bell End', referring to a certain part of the male anatomy. Another famous symbol of this period is the Maypole, which is yet another fertility dance, the Maypole's original form was a huge penis, but the dance was the same.

The livestock kept in the round houses over Winter, are all now in the pastures again, with their new born young and once again their mating Season is in full swing. It was also traditional to drive the livestock through a gap between two bonfires, this blessed them and helped to de lice them, another tradition is to jump over the bonfire, to encourage the crops to grow high and purify yourself.

This should be celebrated at the Full Moon, nearest or after the Festival date.

Summer Solstice

This is celebrated on the 21st or 22nd of June; this ritual is most commonly associated with the Druids and Stonehenge in today's world, despite the

Druids not making Stonehenge, it is likely the modern-day Druids' ancestors did indeed worship there.

This is the time of the longest day, when the Sun is at its peak, yet despite this, we know that after today, the nights will be getting longer and the days shorter, as Winter once again shows its first signs of approach.

It is traditional to perform an all night vigil at this period to celebrate the Sun's rising on the dawn of the Solstice. It is also quite common for huge bonfires to be lit on the Beacon Hills, all over the country, to mark this occasion and to sympathetically encourage the Sun, to rise to its peak of power, this can also be done at Winter Solstice, when it is probably more necessary and the sense of warmth and security provided by it, would be more strongly appreciated. Another tradition is tree dressing, when a Hawthorn tree was bedecked in ribbons and sung to, this originally took place on 5th July, the Old Midsummers Day, in the Julian Calendar.

Lughnasadh

Lughnasadh (Loo-nus-uh), Lammas, Hloaf, is the last of the four fire festivals, celebrated on 1st August. This festival is dedicated to Lugh, the Celtic God of Sun, Harvest, Arts, Crafts, Warriors and Poets. This is the second harvest of the year, the Harvest of Wheat, Barley and Rye, of Crops. It was (hopefully) a time of Celebration and abundance.

This was also a time of business and markets, of horse fairs and Tribal Gatherings. It was also a time for trial marriages, when the couples who had gotten together at Beltaine, could enter into a years trial marriage which could be null and voided the following Lughnasadh, if it didn't work out. This is were the term 'jumping the Broomstick', in relation to marriage comes from, as this was part of the ritual. In Ireland there was a thirty day feast and festival held.

Lughnasadh should be celebrated on the Waning Moon nearest or after the Festival Date.

Autumn Equinox

This is celebrated on the 21st of September; the day and night are once again equally balanced, but from this point on, the nights get longer and Winter is drawing closer. This is the thirrd harvest of the year; in our modern agriculture using GM chemicals and science, we are able to force more crops to grow, than the Earth would naturally allow, and so we do indeed have a second crop harvest at this point of the year. However that is not the harvest of the natural world, which is referred to here; it is the harvest of the gatherer, of berries, fruit, nuts and fungi that I am referring to. For the wild animals this is the most abundant season of the year, with many wild harvests, that we have forgotten about today. So the cycle is complete and is reborn anew:

Norse Cycle

Yule Start/Mother Night/Festival of Light/Yule/Winter Sunstead/ Solstice/Yule End

The eight main Norse festivals were very similar to the Celtic Ones and held for very similar reasons, which was highly influenced by the agricultural culture the Norse lived by. The Norse were often farmers

Yule Start/Mother Night/ Festival of Light/Yule/ Winter Sunstead / Solstice/ Yule End

Night of Spectres/ Ancestor Night / Feast of the Dead /Hero's Day

Valas Vision Maidens Day

Fall Eve (Equinox) /Mabon

Spring Eve Equinox

Hloaf Festival

Walpurgia Feast

Lither / Summer Sunstead (Solstice)

during the Summer months and then transformed into the feared Vikings, during the Winter months, simply to subsidise their income, scraped from the harsh environment in which they lived. Given below are the Ceremonies the Norse observed during the Year:

December 20th - Yule begins
December 21st - Family day / Mother night/ New Year
December 24th - Festival of Light
December 25th - Yule
January 1st - Winter Sunstead / Winter Solstice
January 12th - Yule ends
February 2nd - The Valas Vision (Maidens Day)
March 20th - Spring Eve
March 21st - Ostara
April 30th - May Eve
May 1st - Walpurgia Feast
June 21st / 22nd - Lither / Summer Sunstead / Summer Solstice
August 1st - Hloaf Festival
September 20th - Fall Eve / Autumn Equinox
September 21st - Mabon
October 31st - The night of Spectres / Samhain
November 1st - Ancestors Night
November 2nd - Feast of the Dead
November 11th - Hero's day

In addition to these there were also larger inter tribal gatherings at various yearly periods. It is easy to see that many of these have been adopted into our modern calendar as public holidays, etc; this is as a result of the Norse in the guise of the Angles and Saxons (Anglo-Saxons) and the Normans (meaning Norse Men) having invaded and settled in Britain. However to give you an idea of a more Shamanic / nomadic culture, I have included the next section, which is based on the Mongolian culture:

Mongolian Shamanic Festivals

In Mongolian Buryat Shamanic traditions there is a festival to mark the beginning of Spring called the White Moon Festival (Sagaalgan), this is held in mid February, it starts with the New Moon (Dark) of the month and usually falls close to the beginning of Lent. In their system it is believed that the Shamanic and nature spirits withdraw back to the Upper World for Cleansing and return on the sunrise of this day. It is a time of forgiveness and reconciliation, all conflict is avoided during this period. The Spirits are welcomed back with fire, incense, food and drink. This is also the New Year Festival and lasts for two weeks, until the Moon is Full. The New Year Festival used to be held on the third Full Moon following Ulaan Tergel, but was moved during the Medieval period.

On April 20th - 21st, the Great Spring Festival is held, this is indicated when the Migratory Birds arrive and the Mushrooms start to appear. It welcomes the Birds and celebrates the Spring. A Shamanic Journey is customary at this time to ask for blessings on the community, animals and Earth. Offerings of dairy products are made.

Around June 5th or 6th the Great Summer Ceremony is held honouring the Earth Mother.

Summer Solstice is celebrated at the Day of Suns Return (Naran Butsah Odor) or day of Red Round (Ulaan Tergel), this is held on the Full Moon closest to the Summer Solstice, around June 20th. This starts a period of three months when the Spirits are most powerful and Shamanic work can be done during the day or night until the third Full Moon following the festival; normally it is reserved to the night time. Traditional games are played, food and drink offered and water is thrown upon a shrine (Oboo), which symbolises the World Tree to ensure fertility and good rainfall. Food and candy is also thrown about for the children to gather, a little like Trick or Treat here, where the children are representing the Sidhe and nature spirits.

July 3rd or 4th is a day dedicated to Shamanic Rituals in honour of the Water Spirits and the Spirits of the Lower World, Ancestors etc.

September 11th or 12th is a day dedicated to the honouring of the Upper World Spirits and the Spirits of Sacred Places.

The Harvest Festival was the original New Year Festival, held on the Full Moon nearest the Autumn Equinox. This is a celebration of the Harvest and marks the end of the peak period of Shamanic activity. The Shamanic and Nature Spirits, now begin to return to the Upper World, to cleanse and refresh themselves. Food offerings and feasting play a major component in this celebration. Shamanic activity now slows down until the New Year, apart from the following Festival.

October 16th or 17th is the Hunting Festival, it honours the Spirits of the Forest and Natural World; marking the beginning of the Hunting Season, it helps to establish a good relationship between the community and Bayan Hangai (Spirit of the Natural World, an environmentally friendly Spirit, Shrines are made by carving his face into a tree, offerings of drink are made to him, will sometimes appear as a large white deer called Orboli Sagaan Noyon (Prince White Deer) provider of the Game Animals and Natural Harvests, we call him Cernunnos or Herne. This also marks the beginning of Winter and the first snow begins to fall in Siberia.

I included this section as it gives a more accurate idea of how our Celtic and Nordic Shamanic Ancestors may have worked out their festivals' dates using a largely lunar calendar; the Mongolian and Siberian people also live a more hunter/gatherer lifestyle than we do; their main form of agriculture is herds of Horses, Sheep and Reindeer. From which they also derive their dairy products and meat, vegetables, fungi and nuts are gathered rather than grown. Their environment and weather is a lot harsher than ours though, they also have bears, wolves and tigers living in their forests. This would have been more like the environment our Ice Age ancestors had to endure.

Winter Solstice
Hunting Festival

White Moon Festival
Current New Year

Harvest Festival
Old New Year

Great Spring Festival
Spring Equinox

Upper World Festival
Autumn Equinox

Great Summer Ceremony

Lower World Festival

Day of Suns Return
Summer Solstice

The Wheel of Life

The Wheel of the Year, is a simple diagram of a crossed Circle, it can be more complex, like the one on the cover of this book, which is based on a Wheel of the Year partly also; or it can be even simpler, like the one below:

Solar Wheel

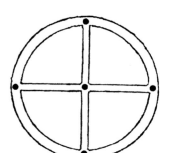

This Wheel could be taken to mean the Solstices and Equinoxes; however the Wheel of the Year and the Circles in general also have a far deeper meaning than this. So far we have been looking only at the Outer Circles, the reflections of the natural world around us and how our ancestors tried to interpret the cycles of life around them, to understand and work with it. The Circle is the basis of all Animistic Philosophies and Traditions, the Stone Circles of our Neolithic Ancestors, the Wheel of the Year of our Celtic and Norse Ancestors, the Oak Groves of the Druids, the Native American Medicine Wheel, the Magikal Circle of Protection and Containment, our journeys through life, the Earth herself, the Cycle of the Sun and Moon, all of these and more are the Circle, all at the same time. The simplest shape and a very complex shape, when Michael Angelo was asked to prove his worth as an artist prior to painting the Sistine Chapel, did he send the Pope a masterpiece? No, he sent him a perfect circle, drawn freehand, try it.

The circle is very important, you will learn to think, feel and act in a circle; you will become a circle and a part of the ONE CIRCLE of existence. Given below is another example of the simple circle, this time expressing our life path, don't look at this as a separate cycle or circle, look at it in relation to the Wheel of the Year, see the similarities between, your own life and the 8 Festivals, remember that everything is connected:

Life Cycle

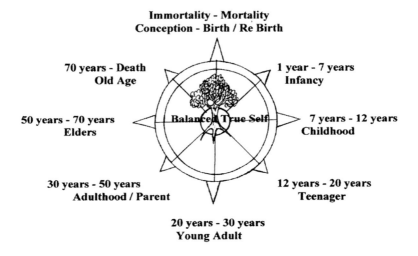

Emotional Cycle

Even our Emotions follow a Cycle, being free to move around the Wheel, changing from one to another in a pattern similar to this:

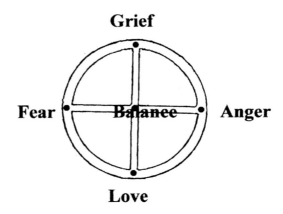

5

THE SACRED CIRCLE

Ley Lines
Ancient Sites
Stone Circles
Balance, the Circles Centre
The Medicine Wheel
Working with the Medicine Wheel
The Circle in Ritual
The Magik Circle

Ley Lines

Our hunter/gatherer Mesolithic ancestors built the first wooden monuments and later simple stone monuments. Eventually more complex stone circles and henges were built by our agricultural Neolithic ancestors. Both groups lived in harmony with the natural world around them, they had to, even then it was necessary to understand things like where to find water, their crops depended on it, as did their lives.

When our hunter/gatherer ancestors went out hunting and tracking deer and other herd animals, they would have noticed that theses animals tended to follow well defined paths across the landscape, just as they still do today. Scientists today are still trying to figure out how migratory animals know where to travel to. Many travel thousands of miles, to other continents. They have begun to realise that these animals, birds especially, have a strong sensitivity to the magnetic fault lines within the Earth's surface and it must have something to do with these. Apparently, it is believed that mobile phones are beginning to affect homing pigeons and more are getting lost.

Our distant ancestors would also have been more attuned, to these same fault lines. It is also known that some animals, like deer, often tend to follow underground water courses. Our ancestors would have also observed this, they may have even attempted to map these, or mark them. It has long been believed that many of the ancient monuments, like the menhirs (standing stones), served dual purposes, sometimes as spiritual centres, sometimes as fertility symbols, sometimes as sign posts (e.g. 'this way for food and water'), tribal boundaries or meeting places. It makes sense to me.

Our distant ancestors probably wouldn't have had the luxury, or the time needed, to put up such huge and heavy objects, unless they served a very practical function. In Cornwall it is still possible to see how these menhirs, etc, could have served as signposts, although some have been lost, there are still enough left, that you can usually see them from each other, not always easily, but if you know what to look for they are there, some are natural rock formations. Dowsers today, have often been able to detect the energy of these watercourses, mineral deposits and fault lines; our ancestors would have had their dowsers, within their tribes, although this was probably another role of the Shaman.

As a Shiatsu practitioner I have always been interested in the connection between the Ley Lines and the body's meridians; in Shamanism the way that everything reflects everything else has always been observed and recognised as how things manifest themselves; it appears that our distant ancestors also knew about the Meridians as the frozen mummy found in Italy, known as the Oetzi Ice Man, proves. He was from the period known as the late Stone Age/early Copper Age and had tattoos on his body to indicate pressure points, which would relieve arthritis, which he was known to suffer from due to scientific study. If our Ancestors were aware of the Meridians in the Body, they must also have known about the Ley Lines, or Serpent / Dragon Lines as they are also called.

It may have even been that some of the ancient monuments were literally attempts to effect positive change or healing, within the Earth Mother herself, well, it makes more sense to me than UFO landing strips. Whatever the reason for these ancient monuments, the facts are that there are very long and straight paths marked out in our landscape by these ancient monuments, which would have been very difficult to map out by our ancestors, they certainly would have taken a lot of effort and time, over many generations, to plan and build them; as I said before I don't believe our ancestors would have done such things unless they served a very practical purpose, or they at least believed they did.

The Ley Lines are not limited to Britain, they spread out across, Europe; I've not heard of them everywhere, but all countries have sacred sites, which would form their version of them, the Aboriginals have their Song Lines, the Native Americans have medicine wheels and mounds and the Mongolians have many cairns.

These Ley Lines are usually dowsed for, this is a simple process, which involves the use of two 'L' shaped pieces of wire (often a cut coat hanger), inserted into 2 Bic pen handles, so that they are free moving, a 'Y' shaped hazel twig or a pendulum, usually a crystal is used, but any evenly balanced and weighted object will do, held loosely but firmly, sometimes nothing is needed but your hands. To dowse, then all you have to do, is ensure you are not influencing the dowsing equipment you are using, so a stiff arm is needed. Then you simply concentrate on what it is you are dowsing for and move slowly and steadily over the area you are searching.

128

In the case of the metal dowsing rods when they cross you have located something, move over this area again at least three times to confirm it is a positive reading. A hazel twig will tug downwards for a positive reading, basically point at it. A pendulum needs programming first, this simply means telling it how to respond to a positive reading, usually this is to spin in the direction of the energy flow. Always double-check the readings, be very careful not to subconsciously influence the readings by involuntary movement. It is important to remain as emotionally detached as possible from any indications for the readings to be more accurate.

In the case of pendulums, it is possible to dowse over a map, using the same process, though this often needs the use of several maps, getting progressively larger in scale; this then needs a site visit to clarify finally. It is easier to learn to dowse for water or electricity to begin with, as there are maps for such things, plus they are tangible and real, so can be confirmed by metal detectors, etc. ley lines are also mapped, but as there is no solid evidence of their existence, you can't dig them up and look at them, or detect them with electrical equipment so it is harder to prove accurate readings. This doesn't mean they are not real, just that we don't fully understand them. There are maps of the body's meridians too, but you don't see them when you operate on someone, they are an energy phenomenon, but their effects are still recognised by many in the medical profession.

It is also believed to be possible to communicate with the spirit world using a pendulum, or the spirit of the pendulum at least; although, I often feel it is communicating with your subconscious self. This involves the pendulum being programmed to react in different ways to 'Yes' and 'No' answers, e.g. spin clockwise for yes, anticlockwise for no. Then again remaining as emotionally detached as possible and being careful not to move it unconsciously, asking it yes and no questions; check it first with questions you know the answers to, just to ensure it is working.

You don't have to be a dowser to see the effects of these ley lines. I remember when it snowed quite heavily in Cornwall, a rare occurrence in

Cornwall; there was snow everywhere, not deep, but enough to cover the ground, that is except around the menhirs and circles, they must have a higher heat radiation level than the surrounding country, as all I walked to were clear of snow, for several meters, all around them.

Ancient Sites

Ancient sites come in a variety of forms, they were constructed in the late Mesolithic (5000-4000BC) and Neolithic (4000-2000BC) periods, most have a plaque of some type nearby to tell you what they are; although some are still not fully understood by archaeologists. Stone circles are a good example of this, it is known that many of them have alignments to the heavens, to groups of stars, the moon and sun, usually indicating their points on the horizon, where they rise and set.

Some are understood as simply burial remains, such as quoits, chambered tombs and burial mounds; although it is less understood why they are where they are. What is also not understood is the carvings on the rocks and the cup marks. These are indentations, usually round or oval in shape, which are found on the tops of the cap stone most often, sometimes in large numbers. It is thought they are for offerings, such as water, alcohol or food, though this is still not proven.

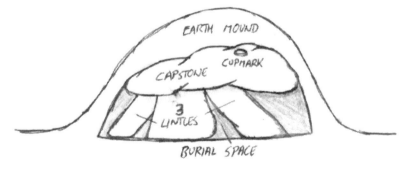

Chun Quoit (burial mound as it once looked)

Lanyon Quoit (remains of a Burial Mound)

The most interesting and mysterious ancient sites, certainly in Cornwall are the fogous; these are rare outside of Cornwall, there are a couple in Ireland and France, but they haven't been found anywhere else I am aware of. They consist of an underground passage made of stones, with a side passage, often dug directly into the Earth, with no other support; archaeologists describe them as possible storage chambers. This they are most definitely not, they are if anything underground initiation /rebirth chambers, dug into the Mother Womb. They are all accurately aligned to sunrise and sunset of summer and winter solstice; only at these times is the side passage illuminated. They are quite common in Cornwall; given opposite are diagrams of their layouts:

Cornwall also boasts a profusion of holy wells; most of these have mineral waters which are supposed to have a variety of healing properties, although one I know of is famous for its leeches. Most have clouties trees; trees bedecked with colourful rags, an ancient tradition which claims that as the rag decays, the illness that was associated with the rag will also decay, healing the person it was intended for. Some of these holy wells are near ancient Celtic chapels, which are still used regularly by Pagans. Christians also use them annually around springtime, as they are often associated with saints and many are under the care of local churches. All of them have a beautifully calm and refreshing atmosphere.

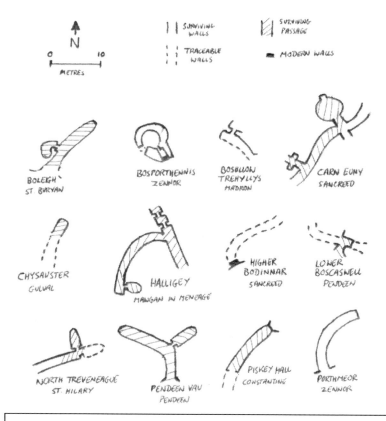

Thanks to Cheryl Straffon of Meyn Mamvro and Craig Weatherhill for these Fogou illustrations, from the book the '*The Earth Mysteries Guide to Ancient Sites of West Penwith*'.

All of these ancient sites are connected to the sacredness of the land, our Earth Mother, a reverence which our ancestors held for the area in which they lived and to nature as a whole. To them nature was a daily miracle, not simply a relaxing walk as it so often is now, it was life and death, it fed them and it healed them, occasionally it also killed them. It was respected and loved, it was their cathedral where they lived and worshipped.

132

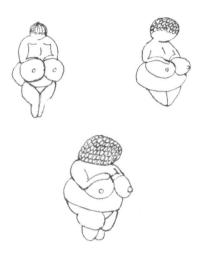

Ice Age Earth Mother Figures

Stone Circles

Probably the best known of these is Stonehenge; however a henge is different to a stone circle; henge refers to the earthworks surrounding the circle, usually at least one ditch with two raised banks on either side. A henge is a far more complex structure than a simple stone circle, it's a little like comparing a small rural village to a city. Henges tend to have a lot more to them than just the circle, for example at Avebury there is a huge circle, with Avebury village in it, there are also two smaller circles within the main one, at least two processional avenues, one ends at two menhirs called Adam and Eve, the other ending at the Sanctum, another smaller circle, with another smaller still circle within it, plus nearby there is Silbury Hill, a man-made hill and West Kennett Long Barrow, a large chamber grave.

A stone circle, is also often more complex than it sounds; often there are three circles, not one, built in close proximity; unfortunately usually only one remains, the others have been dug up and built into walls or buildings in the area, unfortunately they tend to get in the way of farmers, sometimes there is a small processional way to this group of circles and occasionally there are graves nearby. Tregeseal Circle, near St. Just in Cornwall, is a good example of this and also boasts a holed stone row and Carn Kenidjack, the Hooting Carn (when the wind is in the right direction it creates a hooting sound), a natural rock formation, through which the Winter Solstice sun sets, when viewed from Chun Quoit, all in all, a very impressive complex, but there are no Earth Works. So what were these circles for? In truth no one is sure why they were constructed, as I've said earlier, it is unlikely that our ancestors had the time to undertake such enormous projects, unless they were highly functional, in some manner, be it practical or religious; though the two were probably, one in the same in Neolithic times. I can't speak about all circles, but I lived within half a mile of Tregeseal for several years and there is an enormous concentration of Neolithic sites in the area, I used to jokingly call it Megalith Central.

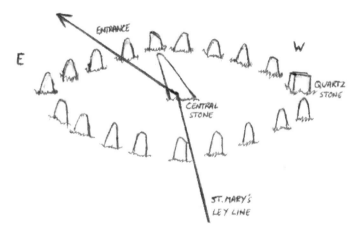

Boscawen-Un Stone Circle (showing major Ley Line Flow)

So I would guess, that the area was an important one to our ancestors, I believe the circles formed a central point of possibly three tribes, which formed a bigger extended tribe, hence three circles, although they could also represent the three worlds; the circles each had nineteen stones in them, which is a lunar cycle (18.7 years), so we had three lunar years, maybe there was a big festival held there every three years?

It has been said that the stones themselves may have been like tombstones to the ancient ancestors of the time, maybe chiefs or other important individuals like shamen, this is possible, as the graves of the time often contained multiple burials rather than one individual. I've no doubt that the circle complexes had an important ceremonial role for the inhabitants of the area, they also worked as calendars, which to the average person back then would seem magikal. I also suspect they were areas used for markets, gatherings and to resolve tribal disputes, etc. From Tregeseal Circle the Isles of Scilly are also visible on a clear day, maybe that symbolised the Otherworld? Or maybe large bonfires could be used to signal the isle's inhabitants, certainly the hilltops in the area are used every year and on special occasions as signal beacons, which is a very old local tradition. So to me, and many others, the stone circles were multifunctional, acting as a hub of activity to the area.

The circles themselves are also more common than you may realise at first and were used for many years as places of worship for the local people. When the country was first Christianised, which when it happened simply meant the king was converted to Christianity, the country's inhabitants were slowly converted over many years after that happened. One thing that was common was to build a church on the site of a stone circle, often it can still be seen incorporated into the church's surrounding wall. This was because the local inhabitants would simply continue to go to the same place to worship, regardless of their faith. The local inhabitants would build the church; as a result they would also incorporate many of their old gods into it, which is why there are so many Green Man images in the old churches. In later churches they became gargoyles, used to frighten off evil spirits, which is what the Green Man image was also for, Sheelanagig was another commonly carved image, of a scarier Earth Mother:

Green Man   Sheelanagig

There are also a lot of stone Celtic crosses in Cornwall, often in church-yards, which isn't surprising, but many were former giant phalluses; the cross part was a latter alteration, to make it less offensive, these Stones were reputed to be able to make Women pregnant; who used to sit on them, or make love below them.

The circle was an important symbol to our ancestors, even their houses were circular; round houses; the Romans introduced square houses to us. Other versions of the circle were spirals, webs and mazes like the ones found at Rocky Valley, near Tintagel:

Emotional Cycle

Given below is a very simplistic cycle of our 4 main emotional states:

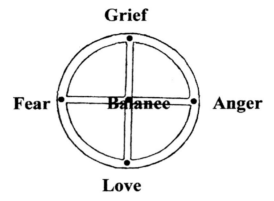

Balance, the Circle's Centre

In the overly simplified cycle of the emotions, you can see that it is our normal balanced/contented state, which is influenced by outside forces, to generate within us our strongest emotional states, be they positive or negative. It looks a bit unbalanced, this cycle, what would commonly be considered three negative emotions and only one positive emotion. This is not the case; all of these emotional states are both positive and negative.

We have probably all experienced unrequited love. It's not very positive, no matter how strongly we love the person, they seem totally unmoved by our overwhelming feelings. Anger is often considered a negative emotion, but it is anger which leads to courage, action and motivation, true these can also be negative depending on what the actions are. Fear is seen as a negative emotion also, yet fear saves our lives all the time, it is fear that stops you walking under a passing lorry, fear that stops you jumping off a skyscraper. There are a few people in the world who experience a rare condition which means they are literally without fear. As a result, they need constant supervision and to be trained to constantly evaluate the consequences of all their actions, otherwise they would be dead. Fear can be a terrible thing to live under, but many of us love going to the latest horror movie or the biggest roller coaster ride. Grief is another terrible emotion, which has a well observed cycle of its own, but it is grief which allows us to feel guilt, compassion, empathy and love for others.

So as you can see, things are not always as black and white as they may first appear. It is when you can experience all of these emotions as fully as possible, that you become a well balanced individual. Women don't seem to have problems with most of these; anger is usually the hardest one for them. With men, it is often grief; though I think we all have trouble experiencing love, at least often enough. Obviously the emotions are a complex subject and there are far more than these four; but they do light the way and illustrate how they interact with each other.

In the New Age movement of today, there is far too much emphasis put on positive thinking. Positive thinking is good, provided you are using it and acting on it in a constructive manner; however if you are simply walking around, brainwashing yourself into being happy, whatever is going on around you, you are benefiting no-one, you are simply becoming delusional. Positive energy is always shown as being the best way. Love and white light, is always being said is the best way. this is delusion, this is false and this is not how the universe works, this is certainly not Shamanism. Balance is the way; balance is what Shamanism is all about. The best example I know of to show this is another circle and cycle:

Yang

Yin

The Tai Ji Symbol

The Tai Ji Symbol

The Tai Ji symbol is familiar to us all, it is Chinese in its origins, evolving out of Taoism, a later form of Shamanism in the East. It is based on nature and expresses the powers of Yin and Yang; they are not seen as opposing opposites or two separate entities, but as complementary opposites, symbiotic in nature. Neither exists without the other, neither is viewed as good or bad, they are simply the opposite of each other. Yin is feminine in nature, cold, empty, dark, wet, soft and yielding; Yang is masculine in nature, hot, full, light, dry, hard and forceful. Each contains the seed of the other; it makes more sense to see this symbol as a ball, with each of the seeds as a tunnel entrance, leading to the other. When something becomes excessively Yin, it becomes Yang and vice versa. This symbol is rotating constantly. It is not static, as the diagram looks, but not by moving round, simply by changing from Yin to Yang and back again.

The Shaman strives to stand at the centre of their own world, at the centre of their circle, in a balanced and true expression of themselves. It is at the centre of the circle that all the compass points meet and it is from there that you must learn to meet the challenges of life. When you place an object at the centre of a circle and stand 4 people around it, they will each have their own unique view of the object at the circle's centre. If you do not allow these people to move, given time, they will begin to believe that their view of the object is the only true one. It is this conditioning, brought on by our own genetic code, parental behaviour, peer pressure, social expectations, media, national culture, flawed perceptions, instinctive fear of the unknown, religious upbringing, past experiences, psychology, etc, which the Shaman must overcome, only then can he break free and learn to fly around the entire circle, getting a complete view of the object at its centre, then having decided what it is, he can fly to the centre and ask the object what it is, it will probably tell him, "I am you".

When you are facing a problem, look at it from as many different angles as possible, find out what it is teaching you; then only when you have all the information you need, can you overcome it and grow from the experience. Shamanism is about self-empowerment, not about being able to control or request help from the gods or spirits; if you spend your entire life looking to others to sort out your problems for you, you will not grow, you will not become empowered, you will only become less than you were to start with, no amount of positive thinking can change this, only you can. Shamanism is not about what you do to solve a problem when the spirits are there to help; it is about what you do to solve a problem, when they are not helping. The spirits are always present, they have their own agenda, to which we are not always privy; they tend to do what is best for all concerned in the long run, they have a clearer view of the big picture; this does not always fit in with your expectations of what is best for the now.

If you have a long-term friend who is constantly causing you problems, constantly asking for your help, constantly playing the victim and never trying to solve anything themselves, never offering you help with your problems, what do you do? Do you allow it to continue and sort out all their problems for them, or do you walk away and tell them they are on their own? Which is the more empowering for the people involved?

Shamanism is not one of the fluffy New Age positive brainwashing traditions, it is quite a tough discipline, it knows how to be cruel to be kind and often is. True most of the time it is fairly positive, even outwardly fluffy, but not all the time; Shamen are feared as much as they are respected in tribal societies. Shamanism is the forerunner of psychology, which can be very difficult to practice or have practiced on you at times, but does get the job done.

The gods are often seen as parent figures, in the sense we perceived our parents in when we were children. As we grow we begin to realise our parents are not all-powerful or all-knowing, they have their own limit-ations, they have their own faults, problems, hopes and dreams, their own lives. Eventually we want to strike out on our own, do things our own way, live by our own rules, become their equals, perhaps even surpass them.

It is, I believe, the same with the gods; or at least the One True God, the Creator, the First Being. In my opinion, in the beginning there was nothing,

140

a void, then for some reason nothing, or No thing, became self aware and conscious, in this state, this Being asked "Who am I?"; as a result there was what we call the Big Bang. I think of it as more of a 'Eureka' moment, in that instant, the Being's mind, sent the first electrical impulses of thought, out into the Void (Being). From the Void thoughts and feelings were formed and these began to express themselves, they became the gods and goddesses. Next the Creator asked "Where have I come from?"

These gods and goddesses then began to create the universe and all its inhabitants. Everything that is, was and shall be, began to take form, all that exists is here only in order to answer this original question, all our lives are simply one small part of a huge equation, smaller reflections of the original question, amounting to self exploration and a need for meaning. Wakan Tanka means 'One in whom everything that is made exists'. In this context, the creator is probably only still in its Infancy stage, in my mind the next questions become, "Where am I now?" "Why am I here?" and "Where am I going?":

The Cycle of Meaning

These are the big questions we all ask in one form or another; at various stages throughout our lives. The Native Americans use a circle called a medicine wheel to help to find clarity in their lives when it is needed.

The Medicine Wheel

All Shamanic traditions have a similar idea or map, to use in order to do the same. The solar wheel of the Celts is their equivalent of the Medicine Wheel, and is also the basis for all magikal work, Shamanic or otherwise. This course is about Celtic and Norse Shamanism/Animism, so the associations I will be using for the four quarters will have more of a Celtic or Norse feel to them, as we are in Britain, not America. If you look into Shamanic cultures and magikal circles from other animistic traditions are the world, you will see they are all very similar, there are differences though; such as at what quarter you would start to cast a magikal circle, which element or animal is associated with which quarter; little things like that. Some make more sense than others, but it is dependant mainly on the culture you are in. The Native American medicine wheel is usually aligned in an X formation cross, equating to the north east, south east, south west and north west, rather than the cardinal directions of north, east, south and west that the Celts used, in our solar cross. The other compass points are indicated with the moon phases, appropriate to the fire festivals. A medicine wheel is usually made with stones, preferably appropriate to the colours associated with the direction. Personal Native American Medicine Wheels usually consist of 24 stones, they can have less, although they can have many more in a Tribal one, however they always have a multiple of 4 as their basis, personally I tend to use 16 (4X4), the Celtic wheel or circle usually also has a multiple of 4 as its basis:

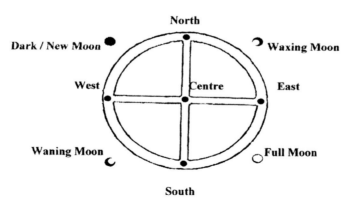

Associations with the Quarters

Each Quarter has a lot of associations connected with it, such as Power Animals, Elements, Aspects of a Person, Seasons, Colours, Times, Kingdoms of Control, Guardians, etc, etc:

East – Dawn – Spring – Birth / Childhood – Red / Yellow – Mind – Past – Air – Birds (Eagle, Hawk) – Waxing Moon – Plant Kingdom - Place of Illumination, Inspiration, Creativity, Enlightenment and Clarity - Tool: Wand and Fan - Sex: Male - Negative aspect: Spiritual Pride / Space Cadet Syndrome

"Where am I now?"

South – Noon – Summer – Youth / Adulthood – Yellow / Red – Will/ Drive / Motivation – Present – Fire – Reptiles (Snake, Adder, Lizard) or Stag / Horse / Mouse - Full Moon – Human Kingdom - Place of Innocence, Faith, Trust, Expression, Power, Goals and Humility - Tool: Knife and Sword - Sex: Male - Negative aspect: Continual pain games and Sadness / Victim Consciousness

"Why am I here?"

West – Dusk- Fall–Maturity /Old Age – (*White / Blue – Emotions –Future – Ice / Water – Cetaceans / Fish (Whales, Dolphins, Salmon, Shark) –Dark / New Moon - Animal Kingdom - Place of Introspection, Dreams, Intuition and Transformation - Tool: Chalice, Cauldron and Drinking Horn - Sex: Female)* ** - Negative Aspect: Self absorption and Depression

"Where am I going?"

North – Night – Winter – Death / Spirit World / Re Birth – (*Green / Brown – Body – No Time / Dreamtime – Earth – Mammals (preferably which live below ground) Bear / Badger – Waning Moon -Mineral Kingdom - Place of Wisdom, Knowledge and Gratitude - Tool: Pentacle, Altar and Shield - Sex: Female*) ** - Negative Aspect: Arrogance and Knowledge unguided by Wisdom

"Where have I come from?"

Centre – Life – Integration – Balance – Soul / Spirit – Universe – Oneness – Great Mystery – Self - Mythical Creatures (Unicorns, Griffin, Dragon) Otherworldly Kingdoms- Place of Balance - Tool: Staff and Medicine Objects - Sex: Both / Yours

"Who am I?"

In addition to the associations given, there are many others, you can add these as you discover them. The Native Americans believe when you create a Medicine Wheel the last stone to be put down should be the one in the East, after the Spirits have been invited to enter first. All others are laid first starting in the South and working around Clockwise, until you end up with something like this:

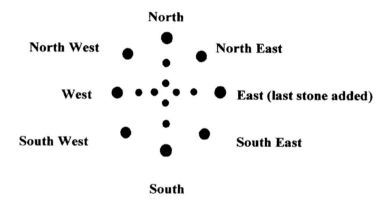

This Medicine Wheel has only 16 stones in it, but as you can see, it is basically a circle with a cross in its centre, a stone is never placed at the centre of the wheel, this is usually reserved for a buffalo skull, in Native American traditions, to represent Wakan Tunka; a suitable Celtic equivalent would be an antlered deer skull, which would represent

Cernunnos. This central cross could also be interpreted as 2 smaller circles, of 4 stones each, indicating the 3 Worlds.

It is essential to remember in Shamanism, there is no right or wrong way of doing things, the best way of doing things is to gather information from a variety of sources, compare them and do what you feel is correct or ask your guides, what to do if you are still unsure. Shamanism is very much an individual path, no two Shamen are the same, they may have a lot of similarities, but all are unique and it is this which gives them their Medicine or Power. In the section on Associations I have used italics ** for the West and North, this is because I often swap the associations in italics with each other, placing the Earth in the West and the Water (or more accurately Ice) in the North, I often feel this is more appropriate for me, though not always. Most Native Americans associate the colours and associations of East as Yellow, South as Red, West as Black and North as White; but Black Elk didn't, he saw the same colours, but in different places, so he used the colours in the order, he saw them in. In reality many of the elemental associations are inter changeable as the four elements reside in all the quarters, not just one.

Working with the Medicine Wheel

The idea of the Medicine Wheel is to work our way around it, learning its lessons for each quarter; which involves meditating or Journeying in the appropriate quarter of the Wheel and asking for the guidance of that quarter's guardians. As with all Shamanic practices, it must be done on a regular basis and at a regular time, to derive the full benefits from the exercise.

The Native Americans believe we are all born into one of the four quarters, a little like astrology sun signs; the energy of the quarter then gives us a basis for our personalities. It is our task in life to work our way around the Medicine Wheel, learning all the lessons of each quarter. it is believed that we master the lessons of the quarter we are born into almost instinctively, we then usually learn to master the lessons of 2 of the other quarters, we can move to any quarter we like, so are not limited by directions. however the last quarter is one we will often avoid, as its lessons are difficult, even painful, for us to master. It is also important that we do not get stuck in the energy of any one of the quarters, as they each have a darker side to them. It is important to learn all the lessons, which are repeated over and over, throughout our lives on deeper and deeper levels. We aim to be comfortable in each of the quarters and to move to the centre of the wheel, the point of balance, where we can move to all the quarters with ease, when we choose to. If you look at the associations above, look at the negative aspects and see if any of them apply to you, if so that is the quarter you need to work most on. It is necessary to deal with all these aspects as their energy becomes more powerful, the more/longer we try to suppress it, until it can be contained no more and we find ourselves facing real problems in all areas of our lives. This is basic psychology, dealing with unfinished business, emotional pain and traumatic incidents from our lives, which have tainted our perception on a subconscious level, which in turn has negative effects on our lives; in a sense we subconsciously sabotage our lives. This is also known as our stress level, this is the amount of stress we subconsciously feel we need in our lives to indicate that all is okay, or our individual perception of our norm; which isn't always very good for us.

This is not the sort of problem that any amount of positive thinking or white light will cure. These are issues that need deep level counselling, the breaking of negative cycles, which requires we face up to and overcome our deepest fears; I do not recommend you go to a 'Shamanic Counsellor' for major problems, unless they are also a fully qualified and registered BACP member. If you feel you have this sort of deep-rooted problem, it is important to remember you are not alone. Most of us have some sort of issues that need dealing with. It is also important to remember that you have already experienced and lived through the worst of these problems; what you would be dealing with in a counselling scenario are only the memories and reflections of these events, the Shadows.

It is also important to remember that you probably had to deal with these problems from the position of a small powerless child; it is this inner hurt child who now controls your emotional and mental reactions to the scenarios in life, which remind you of these past events. However you are not a child anymore, as a result you are no longer powerless and need to take control of those areas of your life and look after the inner hurt child; act as parent to yourself on a conscious level.

When you have overcome all this, you will derive power or medicine from it, which will often lead you to be able to help others who have experienced similar problems to you and are also working through them. In Mongolia and Siberia, this process would be called overcoming the 'Spirits of Trauma', in our tradition it is often called the 'Dark night of the Soul', an inner Samhain or Winter experience.

A strong belief system, such as Shamanism, will often benefit you in this process. I say often because sometimes the belief system we were raised with is a part of our problems; sometimes in this situation, it is necessary to take on the role of an atheist, prior to involving yourself in any other belief system; the benefit of Shamanism is that it is not, a blind faith system, it has to prove itself to be of benefit to you. I know, I've been through this process and counselling.

The Circle in Ritual

The circle has been used in rituals for centuries by all traditions and cultures the world over. It probably originated in the sense of comfort and security, generated by the first camp fires, which also tend to light an area which is circular.

When we talk about the circle, we are in fact talking about a sphere, the circle contains the area it is affecting in all directions, including up, down and within. This Sphere is in effect a miniature Temporary world, generated in limbo space.

The use of the Circle in Ritual is threefold:

PROTECTION: The circle acts as an invisible barrier to all negative energy outside of it, protecting all within it from spiritual harm. It is in effect sacred or hallowed ground. The circle will stay in existence for approximately a day, if it is not banished after use; this is occasionally useful.

CONTAINMENT: The circle acts as a container for all energy raised within it, helping to multiply and focus this energy, whatever its purpose. The energy will be stored and contained until the circle is banished, when all the raised energy will leave in a fashion a little like breaking a bottle of wine, this energy therefore needs to have been consciously directed, prior to banishing the circle and all the people within the circle, need to act in unison, to this end.

BRIDGE: The circle acts as a bridge between realities and the other worlds; this is a 2 way bridge, the spiritual beings you are asking for the help of, can enter the circle if they are invited, allowing them to cross from their world to a point between worlds, in a sort of limbo space, whilst also allowing you to do the same. The events that occur in the circle do not take place within this world; they take place in a limbo space, which joins 2 worlds.

The Magik Circle

You have a fairly good idea of what the circle is all about now, so now I will tell you how to cast one:

Space and Personal Preparation

The area where the circle is to be cast needs to be prepared, whether it is inside or out, it needs to be cleaned. In the case of a room, give it a hoover and dust; if it is outside a symbolic sweep with a broom (besom) is sufficient. It is also advisable for yourself and anyone else involved to at least have a symbolic wash, wash your hands, face, and dab some water on your chakras. It is also a good idea to smudge all the people involved.

148

Circle Casting Preparation

In order to cast a circle you will need representations of the four elements of earth, air, fire and water; the fifth element of spirit is being supplied by the person casting the circle.

For the element of Earth, sea salt is usually used, although sand or earth would also be good to use. Air is usually supplied by the use of incense or joss sticks. Fire is candles, if outside a lantern or a flaming torch could be used. Water is obviously water though spring water is far more preferable to tap water; if this must be used it should have been left on a windowsill for at least 24 hours, to absorb the energy of the Sun and Moon.

Each of the elemental representations (except salt, which is the purest substance we know of) needs to be cleansed and purified prior to use, if you know how to heal, then simply channelling some healing energy through them and asking for them to be purified works well. Everything and everyone who is to be involved in the circle needs to be within the space where the circle is to be cast.

If it is indoors it is common to include any areas which will be needed during the time the circle is in effect, e.g. bathroom. If only one person is casting, or working within the circle, they will perform all of the actions needed. If more than one person is involved, it is a good idea to decide who will do what in advance, five people is a good number, as each can perform one action. Remembering the associations for the circle and medicine wheel from earlier, you will see that each quarter has an element associated with it. if the circle will have five people involved, each person should take up a position around the circle at the quarters associated with the element they will be invoking (calling):

The altar, if used, is usually positioned in the north, occasionally in the centre of the circle. The altar is the focus of attention within the rituals, it should be used to store all the tools used during the ritual, it is elemental in its nature and should reflect this with representations of the elements e.g. candles for fire, incense for air, etc; it is also usually decorated to look both

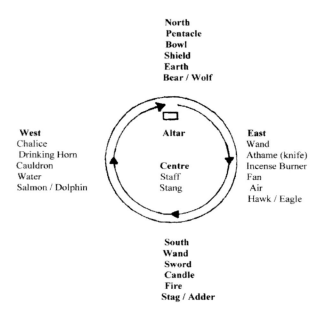

North
Pentacle
Bowl
Shield
Earth
Bear / Wolf

West
Chalice
Drinking Horn
Cauldron
Water
Salmon / Dolphin

Altar

Centre
Staff
Stang

East
Wand
Athame (knife)
Incense Burner
Fan
Air
Hawk / Eagle

South
Wand
Sword
Candle
Fire
Stag / Adder

pleasing and to remind those present of the season and the ritual's meaning.

The diagram above gives you all the basic information needed to cast a circle. It is essential you know where the directions are, a compass is very handy for this, or east is where the sun rises, west is where it sets; facing east, south is on your right side, north on the left.

Now you must decide where to start casting the circle from; the Druids start in the east, Wiccans start in the North, Mongolian Shaman and some Native Americans start in the south, other Native Americans start in the west. All are valid and all work, I suggest as you have been working with the Celtic/Norse Wheel of the Year and coming to terms with the new year starting at Samhain (North West) that you either start in the North. This is because you are starting to cast the circle from the Earth, which is where you are, it is also nearest to Samhain in the Circle and the New Sun's Cycle

150

of Winter Solstice, but it is up to you, when you are on your own. Try them all, see which feels the best to you, letting the seasons guide you is a good idea, e.g. nearest Spring Equinox, start in the East, nearest Summer Solstice, start in the South.

The circle is always cast in a clockwise (sun wise) direction and banished in an anti-clockwise (Earth Wise) direction; unless you live in the Southern Hemisphere, where things are all back to front of the Northern Hemisphere.

Assuming you are starting in the North:
Northern quarter; pick up the bowl of salt, etc, focus for a moment on what the Earth means to you, hold it down to the Earth, in front of you and then up to the Sky, as if in offering or salute. Then facing the North, invoke the spirit of the bear or wolf, the element of earth, or all of these, to be with you all in this circle and to guard and guide those within it. This should be done out loud, the words should come from your heart and not be excess-ively rehearsed.

Walking clockwise (right), sprinkle the salt, around the perimeter of the circle, asking that the element of earth, bless and purify this sacred space, as you do so. You can walk round once, or 3 or 4 times, whatever you do everyone else must do the same.

When you walk around, you can visualise a large bear, brown or black, and a wolf, walking around the outside of the circle with you. When you reach the north again for the last time, put the bowl of salt down and visualise the bear and wolf sitting down comfortably outside of the circle in the north. Lastly turn and face into the circle again, if someone else is doing the air element, if not move to the eastern quarter and repeat the process, using the air symbols. This process is repeated with the southern and western quarters also, until the circle has been purified and blessed, by each element and the circles guardians are in their places.

The person at the circle's centre will now cast the circle; to do this a staff, wand, sword or athame, can be used. The idea is similar to the other quarters, firstly the tool is asked for its assistance in casting the circle;. take a deep breath and then exhale as the tool is pointed down at the ground in salute, as this is done imagine a line of white light is descending down into the earth several feet. As you raise the tool, imagine the line is drawn up into the sky as you salute that, creating a pillar of white light from the ground up into the sky.

Pillar of Light

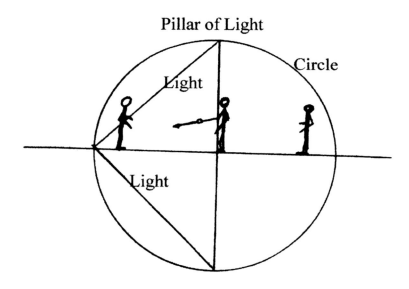

Take another deep breath and bring the tool down fluidly, to point in the direction of the north, as you exhale, keep on imagining a line of white light attached to the pillar at the circle's centre, coming from the bottom and top of the pillar and ending beyond the person in the northern quarter, forming a triangle. Holding the tool at arm's length (this may not be possible with a staff) walk slowly clockwise in a small circle at the circle's centre, as you trace a larger circle around the area being used. When you

152

are back at your starting point hold the tool to your chest, so it is upright, close your eyes and imagine the circle forming into a shimmering sphere around everyone as you ask for the circle to be formed around you. Thank the tool and put it down.

Some groups have a collective totem for the group, which is associated with the centre of the circle, for example a celtic group, working in East Anglia, may have a white (grey) horse, as the local Celtic Iceni tribe was famous for its horses, this would be Invoked now. The altar is common in most Shamanic cultures, it usually consists of elemental representations, i.e. earth, air, fire and water, such as candles, incense, water, earth or salt; it is also where magikal tools used for the ritual are placed when not in use, it may have images of gods or other sacred items as well as being decorated in an attractive manner, relevant to the season.

The Circle is now Cast

6

TOOLS OF THE TRADE

Futhork Runes
Pebble Runes
Variations on Runes / Ogham
Pendants / Talismans
Wooden handled smudge feather
Poppy seed head rattle
Seaweed knife handle
Candlestick holders for the Quarters
Wooden Pentacle
Bullroarer / Windroarer
Flaming torches
Brazil nut bowl
Staff
Stang
Tomahawk pendant
Simple Wand
Crystal tipped Wand
Copper cored & crystal tipped Wand
Tomahawk / Warclub
Talking Stick

Cloth bag
Altar Cloth
Banner
Cape
Medicine Wheel
Medicine Shield
Rawhide Rattle
Goat horned headdress
Married persons: Peace (Medicine) Pipe
Single persons: Peace (Medicine) Pipe
Small Pipe
Decorating Techniques
Attaching feathers
Relief Carving
Bark carving
Handle carving
Shamanic / Magikal Tool Consecration Advice

Magikal Tool Making

The name I have always used to describe the process of magikal and shamanic tool making is:

CraftWeaving

CraftWeaving is what first got me hooked on the Shamanic/Animism path, as such this process taught me a lot about Shamanism, Animism, other Pagan traditions, healing, myself and led me to form a moot in Cornwall, as well as many other related things. The tools are not essential to any magikal tradition, often when you need to do something of this nature, it is an emergency and you are nowhere near your tools, so have to adlib with what is at hand; the real power comes from within yourself.

However the tools are present in all the magikal traditions. The tools also have their own lives, purpose, paths, power and personalities; they are very much alive. In creating them and breathing life into them, you are acting as their parent or guardian, not their owner. There is much more to the process of making a tool than simply assembling it, you will learn how to hunt for the raw materials, much of this will be covered in 'Wood Lore'. In these tools you will be able to see how most of the information in this course links together. This book supplies not only practical information , but I have also included information about each tool and the development process:

The Shamanic / Magikal Tool Cycle

The cycle begins in the east of the wheel and follows a clockwise cycle of the seasons:

East: Dawn, Spring, new beginnings - Inspiration and knowledge first received, in my case via meditations, visions and trance on how to make the new tool.

South: Noon, Summer, maturity - The prototype for the new tool is created, during which I found the tools meanings and associations became clear.

West: Dusk, Autumn, decay - The prototype for the new tool has been created, but there is usually a flaw within it which needs to be learnt from and rectified; so the prototype is destroyed/sacrificed so that it can be re-created anew without its flaws.

North: Midnight, Winter, death/re-birth - The new tool is finally created; If you've followed the cycle in harmony , with the right intentions and balance you may be lucky enough to experience a Shamanic / Magikal Tool creating itself. If it happens you'll know; I've made hundreds of tools and only experienced this 10 times.

Centre: Hub of the Wheel , the Cosmic Axis, the Now, Balance, Oneness - The creation of the Shamanic/Magikal Tool will have an affect on you the creator, because you have been affected, you will effect the world outside of you. The effect may be small or large, but you will notice it in time. This is also the place of consecration.

I recently came upon a quote which sums up this cycle of creation better than I could. Be warned you may only think you are making an interesting object, but the following quote could be re-titled 'In making a fine person' or 'As above, so below':

In making a fine sword

"In making a fine sword, the iron is continually stressed, forged in flames,
it is softened by the heat of aggression, so that shaping and refinement may
take place. It is beaten, pounded, folded back upon itself, heated and
pounded until all the impurities are driven away.
When it is plunged into water, the temper is set, the fires are controlled and
wisdom prepares to sharpen its edge. The process is very complicated and
no part can be omitted. Its hidden layers number more than a million, but
the finished product is simple and pure of line. It is strong, yet flexible and
its surface reflects all that is around it. "

By Mitsugi Saotome - *"Aikido and the harmony of Nature"*

Many of you will recognise the initiation process within this passage; I too underwent various initiations during my path including nervous breakdowns of various degrees and most recently an elemental initiation by the Invisible Ones. I've not found this path easy, especially as it is often hidden behind fears and self delusion generated by ego, but I've also found I couldn't help but follow it. Each cycle/tool is intense, although it may only take a short period to initiate, its effects are felt on a more Seasonal level. You may live under the illusion that it is you who are making the tools, but don't be surprised if one day you realise the tools turn around and create/recreate you.

157

I also realised I was subject to a "Geist" (taboo), which caused some initial difficulties. This was because I was only able to cut willow as a living wood, for which I paid in blood. All other wood had to be supplied by windfall, other people or rescued from the back of tree surgeons' lorries. Cutting a limb from a living tree hurts the tree, even when it allows you to take it. Trees have given more than enough over the years and they are still being abused now. The traditional laws for cutting a wand from a living tree were written when the vast majority of this country was covered by forest; this is no longer the case. If you need wood, go to a tree and ask it for some, explain to it why you won't cut it; It will usually supply the wood via windfall within a couple of days, they take a little longer to react than we do.

Note: It was due to this Geist (I am no longer subject to this) that I didn't cut living wood; however since then I have learnt that if you use proper coppicing techniques you will not harm the tree and can even extend the tree's lifespan, by up to 3 times in the case of hazel.

Also remember to thank the tree that supplies the wood. Do this by first cutting the tree in the Autumn and in the correct manner, doing some conservation work, planting a new tree, or making a donation to a nature charity. Leaving a coin for the tree really doesn't benefit it in any way. The human race has abused the natural laws of balance for far too long and it is time we all took personal responsibility instead of endlessly passing the blame. If you want to make a positive change to the world then look at yourself and change yourself and your attitudes; Don't just say " I ought to do more re-cycling, be less wasteful, be more ecologically aware , etc.", do so; "WALK YOUR TALK ", don't just talk your talk . Everyone can do something, even if it's just picking up rubbish, when you go for a walk .Pagans can be just as bad at this as others, don't just go to an ancient site to "OM" for the healing of the Earth, pick up some litter as well.

The tools are not necessary for Shamanic work. Often when you need them, it is unexpected and they are miles away at home. It is certainly possible to perform simple Shamanic work without them, however it is a good idea to be prepared, carry a small bag in your car, with the essentials in it; I always say its better to have something and not need it, than to need it and not have it. The size of the tools is also not essential, many Eastern forms of Shamanism use miniature versions of the real things. This is because in Shamanism, as in dreams, things are not limited to their normal values; a miniature item can grow huge with the power flowing through it. There is a legend of a great beast being Shamanically destroyed, by a bow and arrow, made from a twig, silk thread and a splinter.

Anyway that's enough from me, so good luck with your CraftWeaving. The instructions are laid out in an Easiest - Hardest - Easiest sequence. Don't doubt your ability to make all of the tools contained here, after all I failed my woodwork C.S.E. and I didn't even do art, so if I can make them anyone can. The "CraftWeaving Path" isn't compulsory, you'll know if it has picked you to follow it or not.

Futhork Runes

"Odin" (Woden, Wotan, Allfather) Norse Chief God of the "Aesir" gods & goddesses; god of war, poetry, dead warriors, hanged men, Shamanic knowledge, discovered the Runes when he sacrificed himself to himself, by hanging himself from the "Yggdrasil Ash Tree" (Cosmic Axis World Tree), for 9 Days and Nights, pierced by a spear, with no food or drink. Eventually he received a vision of the Runes and their wisdom and fell back down to the Earth screaming and clutching them to his breast.

The runes have been used as a powerful divination system for thousands of years however they are also a magikal alphabet and self discovery system. I will not go into the meanings of the runes as there are already many good books available on their uses and meanings but as with all occult (hidden) knowledge be aware that they work on many levels, so none of these books are 100% right or wrong, they are all valid and you will get out of them what you put in, so be aware of your true motivations.

Wooden Runes

Equipment Needed:

A branch of Ash about 18" long x 1"- 2" thick, with its bark in good
condition

Hacksaw

Electric sander or several sheets of sand paper

Burning iron with a " V " shaped tip

Wood polish / wax

Pencil and eraser

Polishing cloth

Instructions:

1) Carefully cut the branch into 25 discs all roughly the same size, shape
and thickness. Try not to damage the bark around each disc.

2) If the wood is damp leave them in a warm dry place to dry out.

3) Sand each side of each disc until the grain shows through and they are
smooth to the touch. Take your time in this to avoid raw and bloody
fingertips!

4) Now draw the runes shown in Fig.1 onto the discs; one will be blank.

5) Heat the burning iron and using a "V" shaped tip smoothly burn a Rune
onto each disc, using the pencilled Rune as a guide. If you haven't used a
burning iron before spend some time practising with it on some spare wood
until you are satisfied with the results. If you don't have a burning iron you
could use a chisel or sharp knife to cut the Runes into the discs.

6) Now cover each Rune in the wax/polish; leave them to dry for a while,
then polish each disc until it is shiny.

Pebble Runes

Equipment Needed:

25 x flat pebbles of roughly the same size, shape and colour.

1 x tin of enamel modelling paint (red, green, blue are ideal but
don't use metallic colours)

1 x tin of hard wearing shiny varnish, yacht varnish is ideal

1 x very finely tipped modelling paint brush
tissue
tray or biscuit tin lid

Instructions:

1) Wash the pebbles thoroughly in fresh water to remove any salt which will react to the varnish. Dry the pebbles thoroughly.

2) Carefully paint a different Rune onto each pebble. It's a good idea to practice on some spare pebbles first.

3) Leave the painted pebbles to dry on the tray.

4 When they are all dry use the tissue or a spare brush to apply an even coat of varnish to one side/face of each pebble. When finished, leave the pebbles on the tray to dry.

5) When the pebbles are all dry turn them over and varnish the other side/face. Leave the pebbles to dry again.

Some variations on wooden / pebble Runes

Ogham

Now you know how to make wooden and pebble Runes you could also use the same techniques to make Celtic Ogham; or to make double-sided Runes with Ogham on the opposite face. I use Oak to make separate wooden Ogham discs. You could even make a larger wooden disc set in which you could burn two holes through at their tops. This would enable you to attach them, one at a time, to a piece of cord or thong, so that you could wear them as talismans or cast them for readings. I use alphabetical connections to decide which Runes go with which Ogham; but you could use any associations that make sense to you.

Ogham are probably easiest to describe as being the Celtic equivalent to the Norse Runes. This is because they are also a powerful divination system, self discovery system and magikal alphabet. They were discovered by the Celtic God of inspiration and poetry " Ogma Sun - Face ", which no doubt meant he was also a Solar God. The Ogham (Oh - Am) are most closely associated with trees, birds, flowers and animals. There are not as many books available about Ogham as there are on Runes, as they have managed to keep their secrets hidden far longer than the Runes, but there are far more books available now than there were five years ago.

Wooden Talismans & Pendants

Pendants and talismans have been worn for many thousands of years, as decoration, religious symbols, magikal protection devices etc. . . . . There are many books available on the subject of talismans, amulets etc. and on how to magikally empower them.

Equipment Needed:

A wooden disc with about a 2" diameter
A drill with a small bit
A variety of enamel or acrylic paints
A few fine tipped modelling paint brushes
A pencil and eraser
Tissue
A tin of gloss varnish
2 feet of thong or cord
Drawing paper
Sandpaper

Instructions:

1) Prepare the wooden disc by sanding it until it is smooth to the touch and its grain shows through.

2) Design the 2 sides of your pendant on the drawing paper to save messing up the disc

3) Lightly draw your designs on both sides of the disc.

4) Now carefully paint your design on one side, using the pencil lines as a guide; leave this to dry.

5) When this is dry, turn the disc over and repeat step 4 on this side.

6) Now drill or burn two small holes at the top of the pendant about 1cm apart, do this where they won't mess up the designs.

7) Now varnish one side of the disc at a time, leave to dry before varnishing the other side.

8) When the disc is dry you can thread some cord or thong through the holes so the pendant can be worn

Wooden Handled Smudge Feather

Smudge feathers are used to purify yourself, others, objects, ritual areas, e.t.c. by fanning consecrated and blessed incense smoke up through the aura. The feather is constructed in a similar way to the aura and as a result acts like a comb to brush away negative energy.

Equipment Needed:

A large feather, ideally a bird of prey's secondary feather

A piece of elder wood about 4" - 5 " long, with a foamy core, about the same size as the feather's nib.

Hacksaw

Sandpaper

Polish or varnish

Other equipment may be needed depending on how you want to decorate the handle

Instructions:

1) Cut the elder to the size required this should be slightly longer than your hands width.

2) Push the feathers nib into the elder's foamy core, until it fits securely.

3) Remove the feather and clean up the handle by removing any unwanted bark, twigs, e.t.c.

4) If you want to decorate your handle further see the Chapter on 'Decorating your Tools "for further suggestions.

5) Now polish or varnish the handle; this once the feather has been securely replaced completes a very simple handled smudge feather.

Poppy Seed Head Rattle

See the Chapter entitled "Gourd Rattle" for details about the meanings and uses of rattles.

Instructions:

This is made in exactly the same way as the "Wooden handled Smudge Feather"; the only difference is that the feather is swapped for a dried poppy seed head. These can be picked and dried by yourself, or bought as a bunch from most dried flower shops.

Combined Wood Handled Smudge Feather & Poppy Rattle

Yes, you've guessed it. This is simply made in exactly the same way as the wooden handled smudge feather and the poppy seed headed rattle .You simply make the handle, push a feather in one end and then push the poppy seed head in the other end as well. You will soon realise that most of the tools contained in this book work on a simple theme ; well I said you'd be able to make them . It may take a little practice, but I've already made most of the mistakes so hopefully you won't have to; I hope this book will be "user friendly " to use a modern quote.

Seaweed Knife Handle

It's difficult to make a complete knife and I'm not a blacksmith so I can't tell you how, but it is very simple to make an interesting knife handle if you already have the blade.

Equipment Needed:
A knife blade shaped like this
Seaweed
Polish

Instructions:
1) Visit the beach and find a piece of seaweed that looks a little like a bullwhip.
2) Use the knife blade to cut a thick piece of seaweed to the required length for your handle. It is important to remember that when the seaweed has

dried out it will have shrunk in thickness by about 75% ; so it will look far too thick to start with in relation to the blade.

3) Thoroughly rinse the seaweed in fresh water.

4) Now push the blunt end of the knife blade into the seaweed until only the blade is showing. Now leave this somewhere to dry for about 3 weeks.

5) If you want the handle to look more interesting you can push a small crystal or similar, into the handle's other end. You could also use a sharp knife to cut or carve symbols into the handle; do this while the seaweed is still wet and remember the symbols will shrink considerably.

6) If, during the drying process, the seaweed becomes sticky, rinse it thoroughly in fresh water; you may have to do this more than once.

7) When the seaweed has dried out it will be very strong, like wood, and will hold the knife blade very firmly. You can now polish the handle to give it a slight shine.

Candlestick Holders for the Quarters

If you work indoors ritually, you may like to decorate the ritual area in which you work with these candle stick holder ideas; which will not only help to set the ritual mood but will also help you to remember which of the 4 quarters you are facing.

Equipment Needed:

4 x pieces of wood 4" long x 6" wide x 1/2 " thick, an old plank or similar

4 x pieces of wood 12" long x 6 " wide x 1/2 " thick, an old plank or similar

Hacksaw or Jigsaw

Drill

8 x 3 " wood screws

166

Screwdriver
Pencil and eraser
Sandpaper
A variety of enamel or acrylic paints
A few modelling paintbrushes with various tips
Tissue
Varnish

Instructions:
1) Cut the pieces of wood to the required size and shape; Fig.1 gives some examples.
2) Sand these pieces of wood to smooth the edges e.t.c. and to bring out the grain.
3) Drill 2 holes in the back piece (largest) near its top. These can then be used to hang on nails or hooks in the wall.

FIG.2

4) Draw an appropriate design on each back piece to represent their elemental associations e.g. elemental triangles or pentacles e.t.c.
5) Now paint these designs in their appropriate colours and leave them to dry.
6) Now connect the base to the back, as shown in Fig.2, using the screws.
7) Now varnish the completed candle stick holder (if you wish to). When its dry you can them on the appropriate walls, add a candlestick and coloured candle.

Wooden Pentacle

A pentacle is a magikal tool which is used as a representative of the Earth element; it also represents the 5 elements in perfect balance (in Chinese traditions it represents these elements in a balanced creation/destruction cycle) and a person standing with their arms and legs outstretched. It is a representation of what we should all be aiming for a perfectly balanced self, living in a perfectly balanced world. Its more mundane use is as a ritual plate on which things can be blessed, consecrated and served e.g. salt, cakes, bread etc. but they are served on the pentacle to remind us of where all things come from and ultimately where all things must return to, at least on a physical level; but then this is a physical world, which we often choose to forget in our search for higher things.

Equipment Needed:

> Rip saw
> Large wooden log, with at least a 5" diameter or a wooden bread board
> Burning iron or Stanley knife (you could use paints instead)
> Sand paper
> Pencil and eraser
> Drawing paper
> Sharp metal point
> Polish or varnish
> Metal ruler

Instructions:

1) Cut a large wooden disc from the log at least 1/2" thick.
2) Remove the bark if you wish.
3) Sand both faces of this disc until the grain shows through and it is smooth to the touch.
4) If you removed the bark, sand the edges of the disc until round and smooth.
5) Place this disc on the drawing paper and draw around it.
6) Draw your Pentacle design within this circle on the paper.
7) When you've finished cut out the circle and place it on the wooden disc

so that it fits well. Now take the metal point (compass, nail, e.t.c.) and make small holes through the paper into the wood at the pentacle's points.

8) Remove the paper and using the pencil and ruler, join up these small holes in the wood to form the pentacle on the wood.

9) Heat the burning iron and use the metal ruler as a guide to burn along these pencil lines to burn a pentacle design onto the wood. Alternatively you could cut out the pentacle using a Stanley knife or a hammer and chisel or if you want a really easy life simply paint the pentacle design onto the wood.

10) You can now polish the pentacle or varnish it one side at a time.

Bullroarer

A bullroarer is a simple wooden device used by Aboriginals, Native Americans and Witches (who call it a windroarer) to call their totems, spirits, elementals, guides, ancestors etc. It can also be used to generate rain, communicate over distance or as a simple instrument. The bullroarer generates a rhythmic, haunting, roaring sound, which can be varied slightly, by lengthening and shortening the cord and adjusting the speed at which it is twirled at your side. Be careful not to smash it into the ground or someone's face!

Equipment Needed:

A piece of wild hard wood or an off cut from a plank or similar at least 1/4" thick x 3" wide x 8" long

6` of cord or thong

Stanley knife

Sandpaper

Drill and small bit

Burning iron or usual paints e.t.c.

Wax polish or varnish

Strong thread

Instructions:

1) Using the Stanley knife and sandpaper (if you own a band saw and sander it makes life a lot easier for most of these projects) shape the wood into the shape of the illustration below, its edges should look like Fig.1. The overall effect should look a bit like a surfboard or aeroplane wing; Always remember to work with the grain.

2) Now pick one end of the bullroarer and drill a small hole through the wood's thickness, this is to attach the cord by; see Fig.2.

3) Now cut a groove into the bullroarer's edge near the hole, this is to keep the cord in place during use; see Fig. 2.

FIG.1

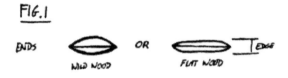

ENDS   WILD WOOD   OR   FLAT WOOD   EDGE

FIG: 2

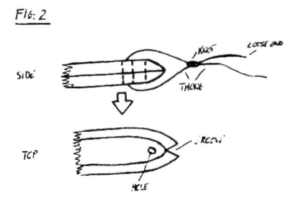

SIDE   KNOT   LOOSE END   THICK

TOP   GROOVE   HOLE

4) Now ensure the bullroarer is smooth; pay special attention to its edges.

5) Now thread the cord through the hole leaving about 2" of cord loose. Tie a knot tightly in this cord; as in Fig.2.

170

6) Now use the thread to tightly bind the cord from its knot - the groove in the bullroarer's edge. This strengthens the connection between the bullroarer and the cord. Study the illustration to ensure you understand these instructions.

7) You can now decorate the bullroarer using the burning iron or paints; then polish or varnish it in the usual way. You can also decorate the cord using beads e.t.c.

Warning

Always ensure the bullroarer is tightly connected to the cord and that the cord is not damaged; as it can be dangerous if it hits someone! Don't swing the bullroarer above your head as this can result in it hitting you. Always maintain a firm grip on the cord with one hand and swing it round at your side using the other hand . Be careful not to smash it into the ground, walls etc. or it will break.

Flaming Torches

Flaming torches have been used for thousands of years, to generate heat, light and a magikal atmosphere.

Equipment Needed:

6" rough piece of hardwood with flat ends
1 x large clean tin can e.g. baked bean can
1 x straight wooden pole about 4` long x 2" thick
Stanley knife
Hammer
Flat headed nail e.g. roofing nail about 3" long
Sandpaper
Burning iron
Wax polish or varnish
Saw

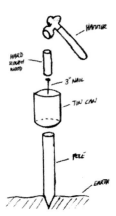

Instructions:

1) Clean off any excess bark or twigs from the pole and sand it until it is smooth. If you live near a pine plantation, you could collect some long straight pine as this is usually discarded by the plantation workers as to small for their uses; or you could buy some broom handles.

2) Level off the top end of the pole so it is flat.

3) It is easiest to decorate the pole now e.g. by painting it or burning designs on it, but don't varnish it yet if you intend to.

4) Now place the tin can on the centre of the pole and hammer the nail through the tin cans bottom into the pole; use the rough wood as an extension of the hammer see Fig. 1

5) Once the tin can is securely attached to the pole, use the knife to sharpen the other end of the pole to a point.

6) You can now varnish the pole

Instructions for use:

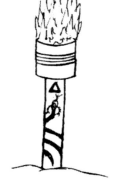

1) Use a hammer and the rough wood to knock the torch firmly into the ground.

2) Take some old newspaper screw it up loosely and put it in the can, then place a large fire lighter into the can's centre.

3) Spray a little lighter fuel into the can.

4) Light the torch with a taper or similar from arm's length and up wind.

Alternative Central Bonfire

I find it is a good idea to buy an old wok or something similar to use as a central fire. The benefits of this are that you don't end up burning the ground, leaving evidence of your rituals, or leaving a mess at an ancient site or beauty spot. You can keep the fire under control and when it is finished with, you can put it out; wait for the container to cool and then pick it up and take it home with you, to be disposed of responsibly. You can also always be sure that there will be a suitable place for the bonfire, wherever you hold your rituals.

Warning

Fire is dangerous, especially if you're wearing robes. Take safety precautions; always have some water or sand standing by just in case, if a robe does catch fire wrap the person in a blanket or another robe to smother the flames and make them roll on the ground to help the smothering. Of course if you have time, before doing any of the above, get the burning robe off the person , before extinguishing the fire.

Brazil Nut Bowl

Shamen and Earth Religion followers always prefer to use natural tools if possible, borrowed from nature. A good example is a brazil nut bowl. Brazil nuts grow within a large coconut-like nut, which is very strong. The hardest part to making a brazil nut bowl is finding one of these outer casings, but there are some interesting alternative dried flower shops which sell such things. A good alternative would be a coconut.

Equipment Needed:

    Large brazil nut outer casing
    Candle
    Matches
    Hacksaw
    Sandpaper
    Wax polish

Instructions:

1) Saw the rounded base off the nut to create a flat surface, on which the bowl can sit.
2) Sand down this surface until it is smooth.
3) In the middle of this flat base will be a number of small holes. Light the candle and drip the hot wax into these holes to seal them; Push the cooling wax into the holes to ensure they are sealed properly.
4) Remove any excess wax, so that the bowl's base is flat again.
5) Now lavishly coat the outside of the bowl with wax polish to smooth up the outside of the bowl and to fill any other holes.

6) When the bowl has had time to absorb the wax and dry, give it a good polish to remove any excess wax. The bowl should now be watertight.

Staff

Staffs have been used within magikal traditions since time began; firstly as a simple weapon and walking aid. Later they became associated with the World Tree (in Norse mythology the Yggdrasil Ash Tree, which connects the 9 Worlds, within the 3 Spiritual levels of consciousness). The World Tree, Tree of Life or Cosmic Axis is at the centre of the Shaman's Circle, Medicine Wheel or Wheel of the Year. It is this that the Shaman climbs or descends into the Nagual, Dreamtime or Otherworlds. This journey often takes the form of a tunnel, as the Shaman travels within the World Tree's trunk, branch and root system to his or hers destination. Another symbol of the World Tree is the May Pole. Staffs are used in the same way as a wand, which is a small staff. By walking with a staff you are consciously moving within the centre of your own circle, world, and life while also staying connected to the World Tree.

Equipment Needed:
A sturdy straight length of wood / branch about 5` long is a good length; the thickness depends on what's comfortable for you to grip, the type of wood depends on your choice, but oak is a good wood to use.

> Hacksaw
> Sandpaper
> Stanley knife
> Wax polish

Instructions:
1) Cut the staff to the appropriate length.
2) Remove any excess twigs and bark.
3) Round off the ends of the staff using the knife.
4) Sand the whole staff until its grain shows through and it is smooth to the touch.

5) This is a simple staff finished except for the polishing; If you want a more decorative staff see the chapter on "Decorating Your Tools" for instructions on carving e.t.c.

6) Polish the staff

Stang

A stang is similar to a staff in its construction; except it should be "Y" shaped.

A stang is a mobile altar dedicated to the Horned God Cernunnos or Herne. It is made the same way as a staff except its ends should be slightly sharpened. It should also be shod in iron to contain its energy; this means hammering a nail into its base. A staff can also be shod in iron, this also helps to strengthen the stang's/staff's end.

Tomahawk Pendant

I'll explain the tomahawk's/warclub's meanings when I tell you how to make a full-sized warclub.

Equipment Needed:

A fresh twig about 3" long and about 5mm thick
A small piece of slate about 2cm long x 1cm wide; or a small thin axe blade shaped pebble
Stanley knife
Reel of strong brown cotton thread
Scissors
Enamel paints or acrylic paints
2` of cord or thong
3" of copper wire (gardening wire)
Varnish
File

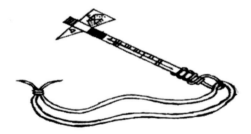

Instructions:

1) Split the twig at one end about an inch in length with the Stanley knife.
2) Wrap the cotton around the twig tightly, at the end of the split.
3) File the slate into an axe blade shape.
4) Slot the slate/pebble into the split in the twig.
5) Bind the top of the mini axe with some more thread tightly, joining the twigs split ends together.
6) Force one end of the copper wire into the twig's centre at the other end, to a depth of about 2cm.

7) Bend the remaining wire over, so it is close to the twig, to form a hoop at the twig's end; now wrap the remaining wire around the twig, like you did with the cotton thread.

8) Carefully paint designs on the axe's blade and shaft; leave to dry.

9) Varnish the entire tomahawk; simply dip it in the tin of varnish; allow the excess varnish to drip off, then hang it up to dry.

10) When it is dry, attach the cord/thong to the pendant by threading it through the hoop and tying the cords two ends together.

Wands

Wands have been used as a magikal tool for directing concentrated bursts of willpower (energy), to alter or influence events, since mankind first awoke to the subtle invisible forces at work around and within them. The wand is commonly associated with the element of fire, although it is also often associated with the element of air. The wand is masculine in its energy, being a phallic symbol, it is also associated with the athame, sword, staff, stang, maypole e.t.c.

The materials used to make a wand vary considerably, e.g. wood, horn, silver, gold, etc., as do their designs. From the humble twig to a golden sceptre bejewelled with precious stones and inlaid with esoteric symbols. The materials used have an influence over the wand's primary power e.g. healing, cursing, protection, e.t.c. So many Pagans use a number of wands, although Hazel remains the all round general purpose favourite.

Given below are the instructions to construct 3 types of wand, all fairly simple in design:

Simple Wand

A simple wooden wand with a tapered point.

Equipment Needed:

> 1 x straight branch about 2 1/2` long x 1/2" - 3/4" thick
> Stanley knife
> Saw
> Sandpaper
> Drill
> Burning iron
> Wax polish or varnish
> 8" cord or thong
> File

Instructions:

1) Clean up the branch removing any excess twigs and bark.

2) Cut the branch to the length from the base of your elbow - the tip of your forefinger; this is the first traditional measure of the wand, which creates an intimate relationship between you and the wand.

3) Decide which end of the wand will be the tip, and which will be the handle/grip; I'd suggest thinnest for the tip, thickest for the grip.

4) Round off the grips end of the branch using the knife, to create a neat finish.

5) Cut a groove about 1" up from the rounded end of the wand, around the circumference of the wand using the file; see Fig. 1.

6) Now place your hand's edge on this groove, grip the wand and mark where your hand reaches to, when you grip the wand how you would if you were using it .This is the wand's second measure and strengthens further the bond between you and the wand; See Fig. 1. Cut a second groove around the wand at this point.

7) Now begin to taper off the wand using the knife and sandpaper, so that the wand is pointed at its tip; see Fig. 1.

8) Drill a small hole through the wand at the rounded end; see Fig.1.

9) Decide how you are going to decorate the wand; see the appropriate chapter; decorate the wand. Now polish or varnish it.

10) Thread the cord or thong through the hole, tie a knot in it and decorate the cord / thong; see Fig. 1.

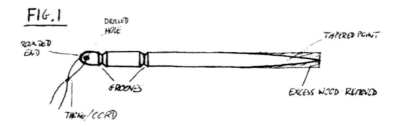

FIG.1

DRILLED HOLE

ROUNDED END

TAPERED POINT

GROOVES

EXCESS WOOD REMOVED

THONG/CORD

Crystal Tipped Wand

This is very similar to the simple wand but is tipped with a crystal.

Equipment Needed:

This is the same as for the simple wand plus:-
A crystal about 3" long and thin enough to fit into the wand's end
Wood glue

Instructions:

1) Follow steps 1- 6 in "how to make a simple wand"

7) Drill a hole just large enough for the crystal to fit into tightly at the wand's tip, about 1 1/2" deep; see Fig. 1.

8) Taper the wand's tip slightly around this hole; see Fig.1.

9) Glue the crystal securely and neatly into the hole; see Fig.1.

10) Follow steps 8-10 in "how to make a simple wand".

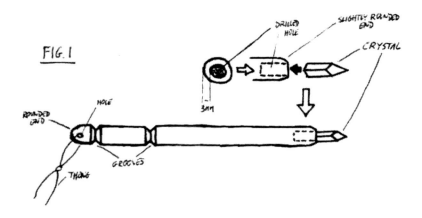

FIG. 1

Copper Cored & Crystal Tipped Wand

This is very similar in looks to the crystal tipped wand, but with a copper core and grip connected to the crystal.

Equipment Needed:

This is the same as for the crystal tipped wand, plus:-
A slightly thicker branch
A metal coat hanger or welding rod
About 5` of 2mm thick copper gardening wire

Instructions:

1) Follow steps 1-6 in "how to make a simple wand"
7) Take the coat hanger and cut it into an "L" shaped length of wire.
NOTE: This can be done with 2 coat hangers to make dowsing rods!
8) Begin to force the coat hanger/welding rod through the wand's core, this is usually fairly soft in wild wood. If you have some trouble try heating the end of the wire. Continue doing this until the wire appears out of the wand's other end; see Fig. 1. Now continue to do this until the wire travels fairly easily through the wand from either end, then remove the coat hanger /welding rod.

180

9) Follow steps 7+ 8 in "how to make a crystal tipped wand", except make the hole for the crystal slightly larger than the crystal.

10) Thread the copper wire through the wand.

11) Wrap one end of the copper wire tightly around about half of the crystal's length; see Fig.2.

12) Put some wood glue into the crystal's hole and pull the crystal wrapped in the wire tightly into the hole; (you may possibly have to re-drill the hole to do this, if so, remove the copper wire, re-drill and replace the copper wire); wipe off any excess glue.

13) Form the surplus copper wire at the end of the wand's grip into a small hoop.

14) Now (except for the small hoop) wrap all the excess copper wire tightly around the wand's grip, until it is covered neatly. Cut off any excess wire; it is a good idea to bind the last 2 coils of the wire together, to stop the wire coming undone. See Fig. 2

15) Follow steps 9 + 10 in "how to make a simple wand"; except thread the cord/thong through the small copper hoop at the wand's end.

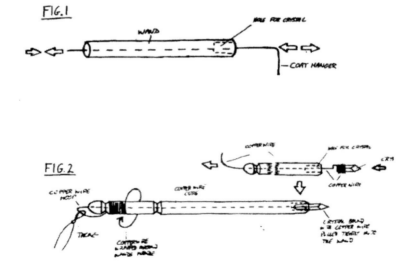

Tomahawk / Warclub

The tomahawk is a metal bladed throwing axe. This is in truth not a tomahawk but its predecessor the warclub and complementary opposite of the peace pipe. The warclub is masculine in its energy, although it contains an equal balance of feminine and masculine (yin/yang) energy. It is less spoken of, as peace is always preferred to war. A true peace pipe is a combination of a peace pipe and warclub and it is from the peace pipe that the term "to bury the hatchet" originates.

The handle of the warclub represents the life path or red road, from south to north on the medicine wheel. It is symbolic of the male and the energy of necessary action. The blade of the warclub represents the spirit life or blue road, from west to east on the medicine wheel. It is symbolic of the female and the energy of receptivity to spiritual guidance and destiny. The warclub is material and earthy in its energy, being often motivated by passion rather than spiritual ideals. However it is a necessary energy and one that is to be learnt from and balanced by the spiritual energy of the peace pipe, for neither can exist in harmony without the other.

Equipment Needed:

    1 x straight fresh (still with sap in it) flexible/strong branch; about 2 1/2 ` long x 2" thick.

    1 x flat thin blade shaped beach pebble; about 7" long x 4" wide

Ball of strong brown string
Hacksaw
Stanley knife
Sharp old knife
Hammer
Variety of Enamel / Acrylic Paints
Fine tipped modelling paintbrush (I usually buy a cheap one and trim it with scissors)
Varnish
Tissue

Instructions:
Basically the warclub is made in the same way as the tomahawk pendant, it's just a lot bigger!

1) Take the branch, remove any excess twigs and bark you don't want.

2) Position the old knife in the centre of the upright branch and hit it with the hammer to split the branch; see Fig. 1; The split needs to be about 1` long and as straight as possible.

3) Very Important: Now tightly bind the end of the split using the string; see Fig. 2; this will prevent the branch splitting any further.

4) Wash the pebble in fresh water, to remove any salt.

5) Force the pebble between the split in the branch; see Fig. 3; Push it down so it is at least 3" below the top of the branch and forms an axe shape.

6) Now tightly bind the top of the branch together; you may need some help or a vice to do this properly. The split ends should touch if possible, but this isn't essential; see Fig. 4.

7) The warclub is now constructed; you may now paint the pebble, carve the handle etc.; until it is decorated as you want it. See the chapter on decorating tools. When you are satisfied with it and it is dry, varnish the whole thing

Warning: This is not a toy!! Do not allow children to play with it!!

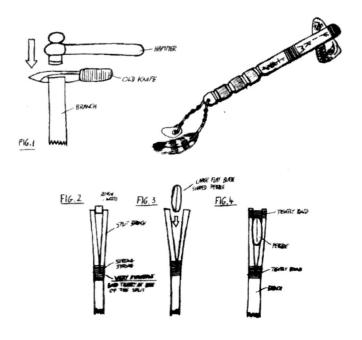

FIG.1 — HAMMER, OLD KNIFE, BRANCH

FIG.2 FIG.3 FIG.4 — LARGE FLAT BLADE SHAPED PEBBLE, TIGHTLY BOUND, PEBBLE, TIGHTLY BOUND, BRANCH, SPLIT BRANCH, STRONG STRING, VERY IMPORTANT BIND TIGHTLY AT BASE OF THE SPLIT

Gourd Rattle

Rattles have been used in Shamanic cultures for thousands of years. As a tool they are closely associated to the Shaman's horse (drum). The rattle is used in the same way as the drum, to induce an altered state of consciousness (ecstasy), in which the Shaman is totally relaxed and yet totally aware and hence receptive to guidance. The drum and rattle's rhythm also acts like a lifeline during Shamanic journeying; This the Shaman follows into the Otherworlds and back again.

The rattle produces a higher sound frequency than the drum and is very soothing (which is probably why babies like them). The rattle can also be used to purify ritual areas of any negative energy and also as a diagnostic tool in extraction healing. It is used to locate energy imbalances, in a similar way to that of a pendulum; apparently the sound becomes dulled when you find an imbalance.

Equipment Needed:
1 x large dried gourd, shaped like a pear (make sure it has no cracks in it)
1 x branch about 12" long x 1" thick
A variety of meaningful seeds, small pebbles, crystals, herbs, e.t.c. to use as the rattle's filling.
Wood glue
Hacksaw
Stanley knife
Variety of enamel/acrylic paints
Modelling paintbrush
Sand paper
Varnish
Wax polish

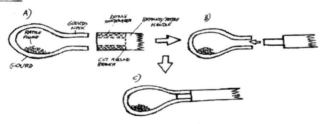

Instructions:

1) Very carefully saw off about 1" - 2" of the pointed end of the gourd. This will reveal a hollow neck, it will vary depending on the gourd. If you crack the gourd at this point you will need to start again with a new gourd as it will have very little structural strength.

2) Take the branch and shape one end so that it will fit snugly into the gourd's neck, do not force it; see Fig. 1; This will probably involve cutting into the branch all around to a length equal to the gourd's neck. Then shaving away the excess wood to reduce the branch's thickness at one end, so that it will fit snugly into the gourd.

3) Use a small twig or a knitting needle to scrap out the gourd's contents and leave it hollow. It is usually full of seeds and flaky fibre

4) When the handle fits securely into the gourd's neck; fill the gourd with your symbolic seeds etc. Shake it with the hole in the neck covered and continue to experiment with the filling until it produces a sound you like.

5) You may now want to decorate the handle by carving or burning it.

6) When you have finished the handle, you can glue it into place in the gourd. Before doing this make sure the gourd still contains its filling, otherwise it may be a little too soothing!

7) You may now paint the gourd with your designs. when it has dried you can then varnish it.

8) As with all the tools you can now finish it off by adding additional decorations e.g. shells, feathers, beads, stones, bells, e.t.c. or dangly bits to use my technical term for them.

Talking Stick

Talking sticks have been used to conduct respectful discussions in group situations, by Shamanic cultures worldwide for thousands of years. The judge's hammer evolved from a talking stick (with a little help from Thor, the Norse god of justice and protection). The Black Rod used to open Parliament, was once a talking staff. The principle is a simple one, the person holding the talking stick is the only person allowed to speak. When they've had their say the talking stick is passed on to the next person, until everyone has had their say.

An answering feather is also often used with the talking stick. The person holding the talking stick may need to ask someone else a question, without giving up their right to the talking stick. When this is the case an answering feather is employed. This is handed to the person who's been asked a question, this person then has the right to speak out of turn and so answer the question. It is then handed back to the holder of the talking stick, so they can finish their say; it is then passed on with the talking stick.

Equipment Needed:

1 x interestingly shaped piece of wood
Sandpaper
Stanley knife
Wax polish / varnish
Decorating tools (e.g. burning iron, paints, e.t.c.)

Instructions:

1) There are no real instructions! You may remove any excess twigs and bark from the wood, sand it until smooth and polish it. Or you could carve the wood and decorate it in any way you wish.

2) The real making of a talking stick is in teaching others to treat it with respect; this really means learning to treat others with the respect they deserve; so that in turn they will learn to respect you and what you have to say. It also means learning to wait until you have something worth hearing to say and learning to listen.

3) An answering feather is made in the same way as a smudge feather.

Cloth Bag

Cloth bags have been used for a long time to store things in e.g. crystals, runes, ogham, money, etc. No, I wouldn't consider this a Shamanic tool, it could be if you decided to make it into a crane bag or medicine pouch/ bundle; but it *is* a useful tool!

Equipment Needed:

> Calico material; the size depends on how big you want the bag to
> be; I'd suggest 16" long x 8" wide
> Strong White thread
> Sewing machine or needle
> Steam iron
> Drawing paper
> Soft pencil and white eraser
> Black felt tip pen
> Modelling paintbrush
> Spare material
> Variety of Dylon colour fun fabric paints
> 1 1/2' of cord
> Scissors

Instructions:

1) Iron a 1cm hem around the material

2) Sew along this hem to tidy up the material

3) Fold the top edge of the material over onto itself about 1 1/2" wide and iron this in place. Then sew along line "A" in Fig. 1

4) Fold the material in half widthways and iron this crease in place; you should now have a piece of material that looks like Fig.1

5) Now fold the material in half again and sew along the edges marked "B"; so you end up with Fig. 2 ; I suggest you always backstitch as well to add extra strength to the seams.

6) Now tie a knot in one end of the cord and thread it through the tunnel like hoop, at the top of the bag. When it comes out again, untie the original knot and tie the two ends of the cord together to form a drawstring.

7) Now fold the bag inside out to remove all the stitching from sight and iron the bag

8) To decorate this bag, take the piece of paper and fold it to a size that fits snugly inside the bag.

9) Remove the paper and draw a design on it that you want on the bag; draw it first in pencil and then, when you're happy with it, go over it in the felt tip.

10) Put the paper back inside the bag and you will be able to see the design through the material; now trace the design onto the bag in pencil.

11) Remove the template so that you can use it again. Now put some spare plain paper into the bag; this will prevent the paint soaking through onto the bags other side.

12) Now paint the design onto the bag. I'd suggest you paint in the designs outline in black first and then fill in the colours. Next leave the bag to dry.

13) When the paint is dry, leave the paper in place. Cover the bag with some spare material and iron over the design for about 3 minutes. The design will now be permanently fixed in place. If you wash the bag (do it separately the first time as the paint will run) you will find the design remains but it will have become the texture of the material.

Note: The method just used to decorate the bag is also very good for painting drum skins with, although I'd use acrylic/enamel paints instead. It can also be used to paint T- Shirts etc.

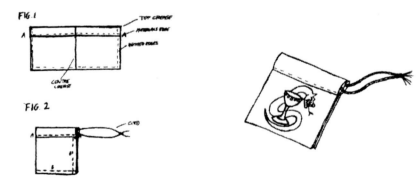

FIG 1

FIG 2

Altar Cloth

Once you have made a cloth bag you can use the same methods to make a cloth on which to cast runes, ogham, tarot, or a variety of other cards e.t.c.; you could even make an altar cloth or wall hanging.

Equipment Needed:
The equipment is the same as for the cloth bag, just make sure you have enough material for your requirements.

Instructions:
1) Hem the material all around, do this twice to produce a neat finish.
2) Iron the material.
3) Follow steps 9 - 14 to decorate the cloth in the same way as you did with the cloth bag

Banner

Banners placed at the 4 quarters or around the altar, combined with the flaming torches and bonfire e.t.c. can create a truly magikal atmosphere within your ritual circle.

Equipment Needed:
     1 x straight pole about 6` long x 2" thick
     2 x straight poles about 1 1/2` long x 2" thick
     1 x 6" long piece of dowelling about 3/4" - 1" thick
     1 x 2` wide x 3` long piece of calico material
     Drill
     Saw
     Stanley knife
     Sand paper
     Variety of fabric paints
     3 x 6" pieces of cord / thong
     Modelling paintbrushes
     Soft pencil and white eraser
     Iron

Sewing machine
Strong White thread
Hole punching kit (for fabric)
Black felt tip pen
Drawing paper

Instructions:

1) Clean up all the poles, removing any excess bark or twigs, sand them down until smooth to the touch.

2) Decide which end of the longer pole will be the top. Flatten 2 of its edges slightly about 1` down from the top and drill a hole through the pole the same size as the thickness of the doweling; see Fig. 1

3) Slot the doweling through this hole, so that it forms a cross with very short arms.

4) Now take the other 2 shorter poles, flatten off their ends and drill a hole about 2 1/2" deep into one end of each pole; the same size as the doweling's thickness; see Fig.1

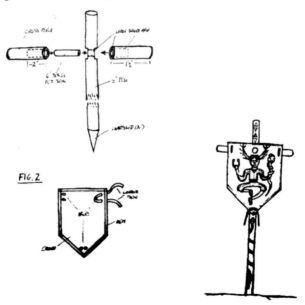

FIG. 2

5) Now sharpen the end of the banner pole which will go into the ground.

6) You can now decorate the poles if you wish; I suggest you take the banner apart first.

7) Assemble the Banner as in Fig.1.

8) Make a Banner cloth similar to Fig.2; Use the hole punching kit to make and re-enforce the holes.

9) To decorate the cloth follow the instructions on how to decorate your cloth bag; steps 8 - 13.

10) Thread the 3 pieces of cord / thong through the holes and tie it onto the Banner poles. You can disassemble the whole thing for easy storage; you can also make a variety of different cloths to fit onto the Banner.

Cape

A cape is a simple garment to make and wearing it will help to put you in a more appropriate frame of mind to perform ritual; as do all magikal garments as you will subconsciously associate them with this state of mind. Capes can be very simple or more complex, such as the feathered cloak, traditionally worn by many Shamans.

Equipment Needed:

> 1 x large heavy piece of material at least 6` square
> 1 x tack
> 2 1/2 ` string
> Piece of chalk
> Sewing machine
> Scissors
> Thread
> 4" strip of Velcro
> Long straight edge, e.g. plank, meter rule.

Instructions:

1) Lay the material flat; find its centre (an easy way to do this is to fold the material corner - corner; then iron the middle to leave an 'X' shaped crease).

2) Tack one end of the string in the centre of the material into the floor; pull the tight and tie the chalk to the other end, so that it is about an inch in from the outer edge of the material.

3) Now pulling the string tight, use the chalk to draw a large circle on the material.

4) Now undo the chalk and string and use the chalk and ruler to mark out a quarter section of the circle; use the crease at the centre of the material as a guide.

5) Now draw a dinner plate sized circle around the centre of the material, use the chalk and string again or draw around a dinner plate. You should now have a piece of material marked like Fig.1.

6) Now cut out the large circle, the quarter section and the small circle. You should now have a piece of material that looks like Fig.2

7) Now strongly and neatly hem the edge of this material.

8) Stick the velcro halves at points "A" and "B" in Fig. 2

9) The cape is worn with your head at the centre and one edge thrown over a shoulder. The velcro should hold it in place, but you may have to adjust the position of one half of the velcro. It looks better if a large brooch is worn on the wrapped over shoulder, this creates the illusion that it is the brooch holding the cape in place.

FIG.I

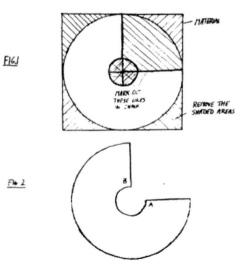

193

Medicine Wheel

The Native American medicine wheel is very similar to the Western traditions' wheel of the year. It is the solar cross found in the Celtic cross and expresses the equinoxes and solstices, the 4 seasons. But it also expresses the seasons and elements within each of us. You may have heard of the Native American tradition of balancing the shields, this relates to using the medicine wheel as a guide to work with the 5 energies/elements within you e.g. emotional, physical, mental, motivational and at the centre the point of equal balance or spiritual. These 5 energies are often seen as guardians of the quarters or totem animals. There are actually more than four points on the medicine wheel, because each quarter is a medicine wheel in its own right, so there are at least 20 points within the wheel, the 8 spoked wheel of the year shows this more clearly. Except in the western tradition you balance the elements within; This doesn't just mean earth, air, fire and water; but means earth of earth, air of earth, fire of earth, water of earth, spirit of earth, air of air, fire of air, etc; the overall exercise is to be able to live with all your shields/elements balanced, within the one point at the very centre of the wheel of the self, or your god/dess self.

This is a very hard exercise as it involves looking into an inner mirror with no preconceived perceptions of the self and seeing the true self. This is very difficult, because we all carry within us many hopes and fears, of who we would or wouldn't want to be and all these hopes and fears have to be faced, accepted and overcome. In a less spiritual sense it is an intense long term psychotherapy session, but you have a degree of choice, about how much or little work you do on yourself and what form or trigger it takes to set the ball rolling. This is because the medicine wheel is life and beyond this medicine wheel there is another and another and another etc., because there is only one and every turn of the wheel takes us closer to the original source. You also have a choice in what you decide you are, as you are a reflection of the one, you can choose to be as pure or as impure as you want, as happy or as sad as you want, as rich or as poor as you want, etc., because ultimately it is only you who really ever judges you; you are what you decide you are and if you're not happy with your choice, you can always change.

194

Equipment Needed:

2 x thin flexible fresh pieces of Willow; about 18" long (although the size depends on how big you want the Medicine Wheel to be)
Stanley knife
Strong Brown thread
4" of copper wire
Enamel / Acrylic Paints
Modelling paintbrush

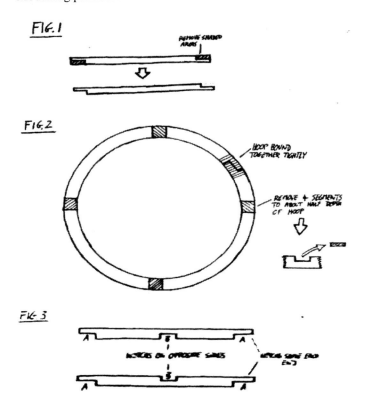

FIG.1

REMOVE SHADED AREAS

FIG.2

HOOP BOUND TOGETHER TIGHTLY

REMOVE 4 SEGMENTS TO ABOUT HALF DEPTH OF HOOP

FIG. 3

NOTCHES ON OPPOSITE SIDES

NOTCH SAME END END

Instructions:

1) Cut the 2 pieces of willow to the same length.

2) Cut one of the pieces of willow in half, to form 2 equal lengths.

3) Cut the long piece of willow at each end so it looks like Fig. 1

4) Very carefully and slowly begin to bend the long piece of willow round into a hoop, until its two ends slot together.

5) Bind these 2 ends tightly together to keep it a hoop.

6) Now cut 4 notches/segments out of this hoop in a cross shape. The notches should be the same width as the remaining 2 pieces of willow and half their thickness. See Fig.2

7) You now need to form the cross for the hoop's centre. To do this cut 3 notches from the remaining willow sticks, see Fig. 3; the 4 notches marked "A" should be half the thickness of the hoop. The 2 notches marked "B" should be the same width as the 2 pieces of willow and half their thickness.

8) Now join the 2 pieces of willow together at their centres, by binding them into an equal armed cross. See Fig. 4

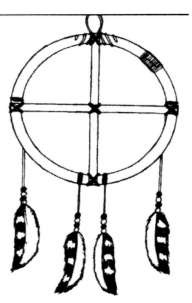

9) Now lay the cross onto the hoop, they should fit tightly into the hoops notches. Then bind them to the hoop tightly.

10) Now form a small hoop with the copper wire and attach this to the of the medicine wheel to hang it up by.

11) The string at each quarter should be painted in appropriate elemental colours.

12) To finish it off you could bind a crystal, shell, e.t.c. to the cross` centre and hang some feathers from the medicine wheel's bottom.

Medicine Shield

Medicine in Native American terms means an acknowledged skill, ability, power, e.t.c. A medicine shield is a little like a badge of office, it is a magikal tool used to express the owner's medicine and to inform others of its owner's empowerment and what protects, guards and guides the shield's owner. They were not designed to act as a shield in the Western sense of the word, they were more talismans to ward off negative energy. The shields changed as the owner did, they were not static objects; symbols and power objects were added, and sometimes lost, as the owner continued their life. Sometimes after a really big change the shield was destroyed and a new one made or it was kept and a new one also made. We all change and grow as we live our lives and as a result the energies that work with us, our medicine, changes and grows also. The same is true of our totems and guides, they either change and grow as we do, or they leave to help someone else.

The shields were not idle boasts, a Native American would not express a medicine on their shield that they did not actually possess. This is because by expressing your medicine you could be called upon to use it by other members of your tribe. It would be the same as someone hanging a sign outside their door here, telling the world that they were a dentist, when they were only really trained as a butcher! It is dishonourable and irresponsible to tell lies, especially if others need the help you are advertising that you possess. The shield is a lesson in responsibility and honesty.

So if you are going to make a medicine shield don't paint an eagle on it, if you are not working with eagle medicine etc; otherwise you may get caught out! All energies arrive when we decide we are ready for them, but if you're not actually ready you may be given a taste of your own medicine, so to speak! It may be that you are able to handle this new medicine, but you may not, in which case be honest with yourself and save yourself a lot of pain! If you still want to make a medicine shield, but don't know what sort of medicine you have, then make it and leave it blank so that others will at least know you are truthful, which is a very strong medicine in its own right!

Equipment Needed:
1 x large dog chew (rawhide) Made in large sections e.g. shin bone dog chew
1 x long thin piece of willow, which is fresh and flexible; the size depends on the size of the dog chew, about 18" long is probably about right.
Stanley knife
Strong brown thread
3` of strong brown string or thong
A variety of enamel / acrylic paints
Modelling paintbrush
Scissors
Sandpaper
Burning iron or nail
Pencil and eraser

Instructions:
1) Soak the dog chew thoroughly until it is pliable and can be taken apart.
2) Select the biggest piece of rawhide and cut out of it the biggest circle possible.

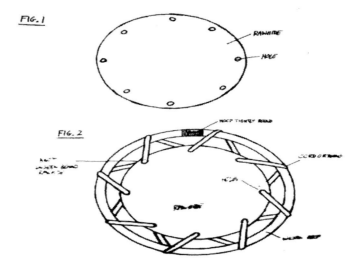

Soak this until it is soft, place a heavy flat object on it to keep it flat.

3) Construct a hoop from the Willow using steps 3 - 5 in "how to make a medicine wheel".

4) Now lightly dry the rawhide with some tissue.

5) Take the rawhide circle (it should be slightly smaller than the hoop, there should be at least a 5mm gap between the rawhide and the hoop all round). Now either use the burning iron with a pointed tip or a nail, make 8 - 16 small holes around the circumference of the rawhide; see Fig. 1

6) Now place the hoop around the rawhide and begin threading the string / thong through the holes (tie a small knot at one end of the string, to keep it in place) and around the hoop; so you end up with Fig.2; The string / thong should have a little play left in it as the rawhide will shrink as it dries and pull the string / thong tight.

7) Place a heavy flat object on the rawhide as it dries, to prevent it from buckling. You can adjust the string as the rawhide dries to keep the pattern even.

8 When the rawhide has dried it will be very tough and the hoop will be firmly attached. You can now lightly scrape or sandpaper the rawhide to smooth it.

9) You can now lightly draw your design on the shield in pencil and when your happy with it paint it on.

10) The medicine shield can have some copper wire or similar attached to it to hang it up. You can also hang feathers, beads, stones, etc. from it to decorate it like the medicine wheel.

Rawhide Rattle

See Gourd Rattle for meanings.

Equipment Needed:

A large dog chew (a shin bone one is ideal)
1 x branch about 12" long x 1 1/2 " thick
Saw
Stanley knife
3` of thong
Burning iron / nail
Pencil and eraser
Paper
Scissors
Variety of enamel / acrylic paints
Modelling paint brush
Wax polish
A bucket of dry sand
Wood glue
Rattle fillings (see Gourd Rattle)

Instructions:

1) Soak the dog chew until it is soft and pliable; flatten it out, weigh it down and continue soaking it.

2) Take the paper, fold it in half widthways; then draw the shape in Fig.1 on it.

3) Cut out this shape and unfold the paper, you should have a template like Fig.2.

4) Dry the rawhide lightly, lay it out flat; place the template on it and cut out this shape from the rawhide.

5) Now either using a burning iron or a sharp point e.g. nail; make holes around the dog chew; as shown in Fig.3.

6) Cut the thong in half. Tie a knot in one end of each piece of thong. Now using the thong begin to sew the rattle head together, by bending the rawhide in half and threading the thong through the holes. Points " A " and " B " should be pulled tight (the knots should prevent the thong coming

through). The further along you stitch the looser the stitches should get.

7) When you have finished, you should have a purse-like object. Now turn this inside out, so that most of the stitches vanish.

8) Now tighten the stitches, so that all the stitches virtually vanish.

9) Now very tightly pack this object with sand, so that it begins to look like a gourd. When the neck is half filled put the biggest end of the branch into the neck, it should fit tightly.

10) Shape the rattle head until you are happy with it, now leaving the handle in place put it away to dry, it will take about a day.

11) When the Rattle is solid and dry, remove the handle and empty out the sand.

12) Decorate the handle, as you want it.

13) Fill the rattle head, in the same way you did with the Gourd Rattle.

14) Glue the handle into place, leave to dry.

15) You may now paint the rattle head and decorate the rattle further.

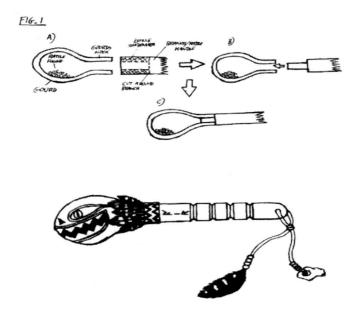

Goat Horned Headdress

Horned headdresses have been worn by Shamen and other Pagans for thousands of years to recognise the sacred spirit within all humans and to help in channelling the Horned Lord (Cernunnos, Herne) into his priest.

Equipment Needed:
2 x Goat horns, preferably from the same goat or sheep, left and right.
A " Y " shaped branch , about 4 " long with as wide and flatter bottom as possible about, 3" wide is ideal .
A flexible metal strip, like a packing case strip, preferably 1/2" - 1" thick and 2` long.
An old belt, made of 2 pieces and stitched together top and bottom.
Hacksaw
Stanley knife
Sand paper
Drill
2 small screws
Selotape
Screwdriver
Needle and thread
Burning iron or paints e.t.c.
Varnish

Instructions:
1) Clean the horns.
2) Take the 'Y' shaped branch and using the saw, knife and sandpaper; shape the bottom until it looks like Fig. 1
3) Adjust the top 'V' part, so that the 2 horns slot onto the wood tightly.
4) Wrap the metal strip around your head and cut it to a size slightly longer than you need
5) Now drill 2 holes about an inch apart at the front of the metal band.
6) Position the wooden bit in front of these 2 holes and screw it in place.
7) Unscrew the wooden bit.
8) Thread the metal strip through the belt, cut the belt to the correct size.
9) Now selotape the metal band into a hoop the size of your head. Now sew

the 2 ends of the belt together, (this should all be done while the band is still inside the belt).

10) Now use the needle to locate the 2 holes at the front off the headband. When you have found them both, push the 2 screws through the head band and screw the wooden piece in place.

11) Now slot the 2 horns in place; Fig 2 explains most of these instructions.

12) Decorate the wooden piece and varnish.

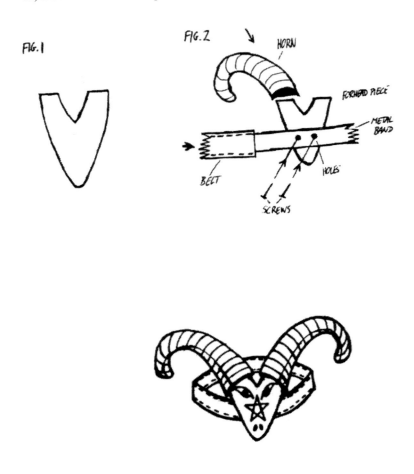

FIG. I

FIG. 2   HORN

FORMED PIECE

METAL BAND

BELT

HOLES

SCREWS

A variation of this can also be made using roe deer antlers, instead of attaching goat horns to the wooden face plate, drill a small hole in the centre of each of the wooden horns and in the middle of each antler, now fix them together using a double-ended screw and a pair of pliers.

Married Person's Peace (Medicine) Pipe

The peace pipe that the daughter of the Great White Buffalo, Wakan Tanka, gave the Lakota is their most sacred artefact; the Western equivalent would probably be the Holy Grail!

The peace pipe is feminine in its energy, although it contains an equal balance of Yin/Yang energy. It is the complementary opposite of the warclub. Its energy is considered to be more refined, spiritual, than the warclubs. All medicine pipes are representatives of the ancient originals, and as such should be treated with the utmost respect. For this reason it is forbidden to lie when you are holding the pipe. The pipe represents the West - East path on the medicine wheel, the Blue Road or Spirit Road. The pipe's stem represents the male; the bowl represents the female. When the two are joined as one, they represent creative union. Each pinch of tobacco placed in the bowl represents one of our relations e.g. animals, fish, humans, aliens, etc. all the Mother's children. As a result, all of the tobacco must be smoked otherwise it is considered an insult to that relation left unsmoked. The bowl of the pipe is round to remind us of the sacred hoop of life. The flame in the bowl represents the life giving sun, the smoke from the pipe represents spirit and carries our prayers to the spirit world to be answered.

The first six puffs on the pipe are never inhaled as they are an offering to the sacred directions of West, North, East, South, Above and Below. You may inhale the seventh puff as this represents the seventh sacred direction of Within.

There are two types of Pipe given here; the Single person's is roughly L shaped; the married person's is roughly T shaped, but upside down. The additional bit on the end of the married person's pipe represents man and woman united as one and creating life (children, the future) so the pipe continues on after the flames of passion (creation). A single person upon marriage should have their pipe adapted into a married person's.

The pipe should always be treated with respect and should be rested on 2 "Y" shaped sticks stuck in the ground when not in use ritually. When not in use, it should be wrapped in cloth or hung up safely. The pipes made here are not peace pipes but medicine pipes, a real peace pipe was described in the chapter on warclubs. I would not and could not make a real peace pipe as I am not a Native American and the real peace pipe's bowl is made of a special red stone (occasionally Black) found only in America, The Turtle Isles.

Equipment Needed:
A variety of Elder wood of various sizes
A long piece of Elder at least 2` long x 2" thick
Hacksaw
Stanley knife
Drill
Variety of drill bits; preferably one at least 12" long x 1/4" thick
Some additional small solid branches of various thickness, but short
Sandpaper
Sharp pointed knife
Long length of wire e.g. coat hanger, knitting needle, welding rod
Burning iron
Gauze
Varnish
Wood glue

Instructions:

1) The Elder has a foamy core which can easily be pushed or drilled out leaving a hollow stick.
2) Select a length of Elder about 1 1/2 ` long x 1 1/2 " thick. If possible

push out its core with the wire. If not possible drill out its core using the longest 'bit' at both ends. The maximum length of the stem is the bits length while in the drill x 2.

3) If there's enough of this stick, cut off a section at least 4" long, to make the bowl from.

4) Now if you have a thicker drill bit, drill out the bowl further as in Fig. 1 cross - section. If you don't use the sharp pointed knife to scrape out a bigger hole in the bowl, by rotating the knife, so that it ends up like 'C' in Fig. 1

5) Now choose a point on the stem and drill down into its hollow core, through its hard outer surface.

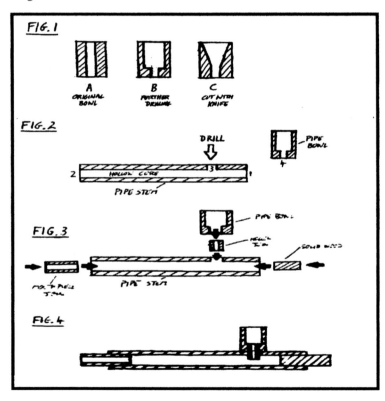

206

6) Now find a piece of smaller elder which will fit tightly into holes 2 -4 in Fig. 2.Hollow this out. The wood needs to be fairly strong as this wood will form the pipe's main joints.

7) Now find a solid piece of wood that will fit tightly into hole 1 on Fig.2; it should be about 4 " long.

8) Now assemble the pipe as in Fig. 3

9) When it's assembled it should resemble Fig. 4 as a cross-section.

10) This is the basic pipe; the pipe is built up in the same way so it can be further lengthened and shaped . An example is given in Fig. 5

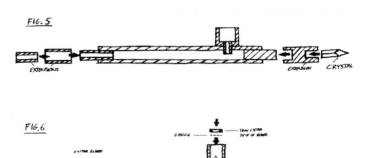

FIG. 5

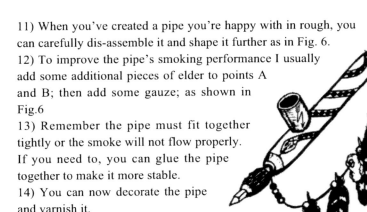

FIG.6

11) When you've created a pipe you're happy with in rough, you can carefully dis-assemble it and shape it further as in Fig. 6.

12) To improve the pipe's smoking performance I usually add some additional pieces of elder to points A and B; then add some gauze; as shown in Fig.6

13) Remember the pipe must fit together tightly or the smoke will not flow properly. If you need to, you can glue the pipe together to make it more stable.

14) You can now decorate the pipe and varnish it.

Single Person's Peace (Medicine) Pipe

Equipment Needed:

The same as for a Married Person's Pipe

Instructions:

1) The pipe is made in exactly the same way, except you don't do step 5; this step should be done on the bowl instead, See Fig.1

2) The rest of the pipe is assembled in the same manner except use Fig. 2 as a guide to the changes.

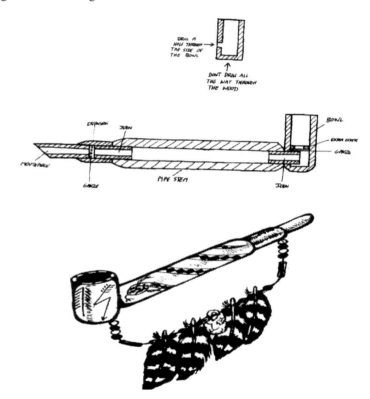

Small Pipe

This is just a small pipe for smoking.

Equipment Needed:
The same as for a Married Person's Pipe.

Instructions:

1) This is made in a very similar way to the Single Person's Pipe, except it is a lot smaller and requires a lot less wood or work. Simply use Fig. 1 as a guide.

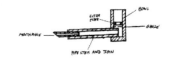

Decorating Your Tools

After or during the assembly of your tools, you will no doubt want to decorate them. Given below are some ideas and tips for doing so.

Useful Equipment and Decorative Items:

Electric drill	Coloured wooden beads
Scissors	Sea shells
Wood glue	Small plain wooden beads
Needle and thread	Stones with a hole
Enamel/ crylic paints	Small crystals
Modelling paintbrushes	Selection of feathers
Stanley knife	Small bells
File	Small bones and skulls
Sandpaper	Animal teeth, fur, claws
Burning iron	Leather thong/cord
Wax polish/Varnish	Use your imagination!

Attaching Feathers

1) A simple method is to drill a small hole through the handle's end; this should be done prior to varnishing.

2) Thread a length of cord/thong through this hole; the two halves should hang down from either side of the wood.

3) Tie a knot in the cord, on either side of the hole to keep it in place.

4) Now you can thread some beads, stones, shells, bells, e.t.c. onto each length of cord/thong.

5) To attach feathers you will need the needle and thread. Simply stitch through the feather's quill a couple of times. Now bind the quill with the thread and tie a few small knots. The other end of the cotton with the needle should be hanging from the quills tip. Sew the needle and thread through the end of the cord / thong.

Bind the thong/cord with some thread and fix with a couple of knots. See Fig.1.

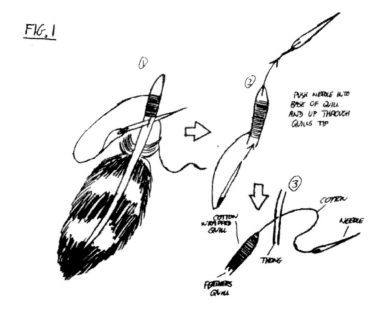

FIG. 1

Relief Carving

This is the simplest form of carving, but it is very versatile. I'll give instructions on how to carve a snake, as this is probably the easiest thing to carve.

1) Take a branch and strip off any twigs or bark, sand this down.

2) Draw a snake around the branch; simply draw a head on one edge and taper this off into a body that coils around and around the branch, until it is long enough, then taper the body into a pointed tail. See Fig. 1.

3) Now repeat this process over the pencil line using a Stanley knife. You want to cut down into the wood about 5mm, do this all along the pencil lines.

4) Now carefully cut away the wood around these cut lines, use the knife blade laid flat against the wood; so you cut away thin slivers of wood. They should break off when you reach a cut line.

5) Taper the wood up at the end of the carved area, so that the finished results look like Fig.2

6) Now sand the snake's edges and the rough wood, so it is all smooth to the touch.

7) Alternatively, you could cut out the snake's body, so you have a snake-like groove cut into the branch.

FIG.1

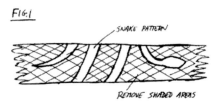

FIG.2

Bark Carving

This is done the same way as relief carving, but it is a lot easier. Provided the bark is in good condition and still firmly attached to the wood. You simply do the same as you did to carve the snake out of the wood, except you only cut the bark. You will end up with a snake of bark wrapped around the branch; See Fig 1.

FIG. 1

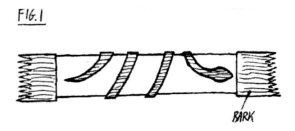

BARK

General Carving

The easiest way to carve is to find a branch with something, already nearly there, e.g. a notch that resembles a face. Then simply enhance what's already there by carving, cutting and sanding the wood.

If you look in ancient woodland (woodland over 200 years old) you will often come across some interesting pieces of wood. Don't cut down wood from conservation areas though, such as SSSI sites or ESA sites. Coppice woodland is very good for wood and it is often already cut and stacked; this wood is largely destined for charcoal, which can be a waste. Look for ancient coppice woodland with lots of honeysuckle and you are on a winner, the wood is usually hazel or ash and the honeysuckle will often create some wonderful serpentine patterns in the wood, then very little work is needed to produce a beautiful piece of work. Coppicing is good for the trees, if done correctly, it can extend the tree's life by three times. Make sure you don't cut down wood until the autumn as the sap has then returned to the roots and you will not hurt the tree's life force. If you are unsure how to coppice read a book on the subject or attend a day course with the BTCV.

Handle Carving

A very simple handle can be made by using a file, to form a simple grip.

1) Simply strip off any excess bark and round the handle's end using the Stanley knife and sandpaper.
2) Then make a width-ways mark, across the wood's grain using the file's edge. Now keeping the file's edge on the mark, keep the file still and roll the wood so that the file traces a shallow groove around the branch. Now use this groove as a guide as you cut this groove deeper with the file, until it is about 5mm deep.
3) Now lay the file flat on the wood and make another mark a file width away from the last one. Now repeat step 2
4) Now repeat steps 2 and 3 until you've done about 8 grooves, this makes an effective and simple handle. See Fig. 1

FIG. 1

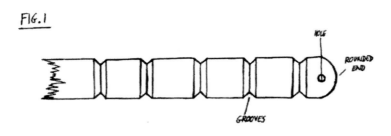

Shamanic Tool Consecration Advice

Consecration is a method of dedicating your magikal tool to the service of the God and Goddess. But it is more than this, it is also a birth, it confirms a new creation, which is presented to the God and Goddess for their recognition and blessings. If you consider the tool you've made a new baby, then this is its baptism.

There are many good preset rituals available in many books for consecration of magikal tools; so I won't write another preset ritual as this book is intended to inspire you. Therefore I will simply provide you with the basic elements of the consecration ritual, use your own words etc., speak from your heart.

The Elements of Consecration

1) Choose the area in which the consecration will be held. Physically clean this area and lay out all the equipment necessary for the consecration.

2) The elemental representatives e.g. incense, candles, water, salt, are blessed and purified to remove any negativity. These are then used to psychically clean the ritual area.

3) A magikal circle is now cast around this area and your guardians, guides, gods, goddesses, totem, etc. are called to bear witness and support.

4) The tool to be consecrated is then blessed and purified by all the elemental representatives.

5) The tool is now held up to be presented to your gods, guardians, etc. Tell them the purpose of the tool and what uses you intend it to be used for in their service. Ask that they bless and recognise it.

6) Now cradle the tool in your arms as you would a child, love it, talk to it, give it your proud parental attention.

7) Now breath onto the tool, to give it the Breath of Life and then kiss the tool.

8) Give the tool a name; If possible let the tool tell you its name; baptise the tool with this name using water or all the elemental representatives. Announce the tool's name to your gods, goddess, etc. and ask that it be blessed and empowered.

9) Now thank your gods, goddess, etc. and bid them farewell, uncast the circle.

10) From now on refer to your tool by its name, treat it with respect, don't let it be ridiculed by yourself or others. In time you will become more aware of the tool's personality and also that it grows as you do.

The Mongolian and other Shamanic cultures believe that a master spirit called an Ezen, will enter the Tonog (Tool) upon its completion, this makes the Tool's Amitai (alive) or Ezetei (having its own Master Spirit). The task of the Shaman is to then form a link, bond or rapport with this Ezen, this will make the tool far more effective as the Ezen will add its own power to the tool's and your's. Without contacting the Ezen the tool will still work, but not as effectively.

As a result of having this Ezen within it, it is a good idea to handle the tools with the respect they deserve; as a Shamanic/animistic practitioner and hopefully the tool's creator, this is no problem for you, but be careful about who else handles them, the Ezen may not like it. Once you have contacted the Ezen it is a good idea to ask, whether it wants to be stored out of sight or not; many of mine seem to enjoy the attention of others, like me I guess; everyone I know, tends to be very respectful of them anyway.

How you contact the Ezen I leave up to you, meditating with the tool, or going on a journey to meet it, are good methods.

7

TOTEMS & POWER ANIMALS

Jay / Kestrel
Ladybird / Lynx
Mouse
Otter / Owl
Rabbit
Rat /Raven
Robin
Salmon / Seal
Shark
Spider / Squirrel
Swan
Toad / Frog
Wasp / Weasel
Whale
Wolf

Totem Animals

Totem animals are not the personal animal guides that they are most commonly expressed as in New Age literature. What most people commonly refer to as their totem is in fact a power animal. When we think of totem animals we also often think about the totem poles of the Native Americans, these are the most well-known totem poles, but they are common to most Shamanic cultures, although often much smaller in size or sometimes called a tribal fetish.

The totem poles of the Native Americans show a history of the tribe, clans and the ancestors, all are topped by an eagle, as he flies closest to the sun and heavens. The Native American tribes which erected the large totem poles we think of, used to live in the same area all year round, they were not nomadic like the plains Indians, but lived in villages and towns, often formed from more than one tribe. When circumstances, such as war, natural disasters, shared enemies, marriages and famine made different tribes band together, the totems of those tribes went with them, eventually being included in a joint totem pole of the whole tribe.

Other figures represent the clan totems, such as warrior clans, hunter clans, women's clans and medicine clans. So totems are not individual animal guardians, but tribal or clan guardians. This doesn't mean an individual within the tribe wouldn't have contact with the tribal totem, or that the tribal totem wouldn't look after an individual in need, it was also possible for an individual to have the same power animal as the tribal totem, but it would express itself in a more personal manner. The Celts and Norse also had similar ideas about totems, often they were referred to as 'Spirits of Place' or 'Landvaetti' as the Norse called them. These were powerful nature spirits which acted as guardians of areas of land, often where tribes lived. They were usually associated with a prominent natural feature, such as a river, rock outcrop, lake, cave, etc; often eventually becoming a tribal god or goddess. The Celts and the Norse also had their versions of the clan systems often with animal totems as their symbol of power, such as the wild boar of the Celtic warriors or the bear of the Norse berserkers (meaning 'Bear Shirt') warriors.

In Shamanic practice a group, circle or council of Shamen would be likely to have a clan totem, which would make itself known to them; as would a coven of witches or a grove of druids, in addition to their own individual totems or power animals. Totems share the same qualities and characteristics as their power animal counterparts, but are usually more powerful, older and wiser, concerned mainly with the needs of the group, rather than the individual.

Power Animals

Power animals are what we are talking about, when we are usually discussing totems. A power animal is a guardian spirit, which assumes an animal form when we encounter them in meditations and on journeys. Power animals have characteristics which are associated with their animal species, which we also share in our personalities; they are similar to us, as a result we are drawn to them, as they are drawn to us, like attracting like. There is a bond, a kinship between us, this is usually lifelong with at least one of them.

The number of power animals we have varies from time to time, depending on our activities. When we are healing, for example, there will be far more around us, or at least making themselves known to us, than when we are shopping in the supermarket. Power animals will be more strongly drawn to us during some activities, than at other times, when we are expressing the energies, characteristics or traits most closely associated with them.

As human beings we tend to forget we are animals ourselves, we are mammal fauna of the Earth's eco system, just as much as is the wolf or worm. As such we are all ruled by the same base urges and needs, these energies allow us to link with our animal counterparts. Shamen have specific power animals which are connected to them more strongly than others, in many northern Shamanic cultures they are viewed as the original ancestors of shamen, these tend to be the owl, eagle and bear. The snake, deer and wolf, are also very commonly associated with the Shaman, as their spiritual energies are also considered to be very compatible with Shamanism. It is likely that you will have noticed some, or all, of these power animals around you already. These are not the only power animals you will attract, but at least one of your permanent power animals is likely to be from this group.

It is commonly believed that we all have two permanent power animals, which stay with us at all times, during our life, one walks on our left (female) the other on our right (male). These are the most important power animals or allies we have, all other power animals will be attracted to us via them. It is commonly believed among the Native Americans that we have up to nine power animals with us at any one time, including our two permanent guardians. The other seven are attracted by our needs and actions during life, changing as our lives do, some may stay with us a very long time, almost adopting the role of a permanent guardian.

The nomadic Shamanic cultures, instead of having totem poles, often have a spirit pole. This is a staff which depicts the power animals we feel walk with us most commonly.

Shapeshifting is the most commonly used way of working with power animals. This process doesn't involve actually physically transforming into a power animal; that is lycanthropy. Shapeshifting is an inner transformation, which involves channelling the spirit or energy, of the power animal, to various degrees. It is possible to shapeshift to the extent that you are able to make use of the power animal's heightened senses, but it would not be a good idea to allow total possession by a spirit, you should always remain in control.

This shapeshifting process is of the most use during Shamanic journeys, although it can happen in normal states of consciousness, usually this happens when a strong survival need arises, you may not even be aware of why it happens, or conscious of it happening. I have experienced this:

'One sports day, while at school, I saw a javelin, which was flying through the air, off course, towards a friend running towards me, (this would have been easy, except I normally wear glasses, being very short-sighted. However on this occasion I wasn't wearing them, fearing they might have fallen off whilst I was running the 100 metres) however I looked up and for a split second, saw the javelin perfectly. I realised the danger and ran into my friend, knocking him back, enough for the javelin to just miss us.'

This would be a small shapeshifting from my natural eyesight, to that of a power animal, such as an eagle. This sort of thing probably happens all the time, we are just not aware of it; perhaps a terrible smell makes you change direction and walk down another alley, possibly avoiding a mugger. This could be explained as your power animal the rat, warning you of approaching danger, in its own special way, by heightening your sense of smell.

The truth is, many eons ago, our ancestors would have probably needed their power animals to survive all the time, but in the modern near sterile world, in comparison to theirs, we probably don't need their help as often; or maybe we need it more, but the dangers are not as obvious.

Power animals can be fun as well, animals like to play, it can be fun to let the power animal in you out for a walk, you could use the wolf to track deer for instance as our ancestors would have, or use the deer to track deer. In Shamanic journeys, pathworkings and meditations your power animals excel in their abilities, don't be surprised to discover they can talk to you, or you to them, communication is via thoughts and feelings.

It is fairly easy to contact at least one of your power animals simply by going on an intentional journey to meet them. We all have them, whether we recognise it or not. You probably have a fairly good idea of what species they are anyway, simply by thinking about your favourite animals, or the animals you would most like to be or respect. I personally found their enthusiasm almost overwhelming when I first met my power animals. I have also found that a strong kinship between you and your power animals will often lead to some interesting physical encounters, with wild animals of their species, if they are native to the country you live in. But it must always be remembered that if you do have a close encounter with a physical wild animal, whether they are one of your power animals or not, they are also wild animals, they can be startled easily and hurt you, sometimes worse, if you do not treat them with the cautious respect due to all of the Earth's wild children.

I have had some very enjoyable experiences chasing wild deer, going for a long walk with a fox, playing tag with a badger, watching fox cubs playing close by, meditated in a field with a hedgehog between my legs and I was even given an eagle feather by a bald eagle, (although that was in a bird sanctuary). The first animal I saw when I visited Scotland was a golden eagle, sitting beside me, on a branch, in a layby.

I have also found that I seem to be given animal skins by people, as they feel uncomfortable with them, having such things as leopard skin, bear skin, fox skin and wolf skin, in my possession; to me this is my power animals saying 'Hello'.

I also believe this 'kinship' is as a result of the magikal tools I make, I often find dead owls, buzzards and deer on the side of roads; I hate to think of any animals being killed so needlessly, so I have always stopped to pick them up. I then use what I can, to make magikal tools with, promising the animal's spirit I will make something beautiful from its remains, so that its death was not in vain and it will be honoured. I also drag the bodies clear of the road, I used to bury them, but now I realise that other animals will find life from their death, in the form of a safe meal. I also always leave a tobacco offering and say a short prayer. I've always felt this is appreciated.

Thankfully, in addition to finding dead animals, I occasionally find injured ones which I help in the best way I can. They also seem to know I will not hurt them and I have never been bitten or scratched. I feel I have been very lucky and truly blessed, by my encounters with animals.

Although power animals are wonderful when they turn up in meditations and journeys, it can't beat the physical encounters, the only way to have these, is to spend time alone among Nature.

Power Animal Characteristics

Given over the next few pages are the characteristics which are associated with power animals from the Northern Hemisphere. This is not a complete list of all the wild animals in our hemisphere and is focused on British and European species, there are many books available with more information about American species. Don't forget when you read this, that power animals may express different characteristics or parts of their nature, to different people, your own feelings about the animals are just as valid, as is the information from wildlife books and TV documentaries.

It is also important to remember that, like people, there are the wilder sides to all these animals, which are not always pleasant to think about, a bear power animal, may let you sleep curled up with it in a meditation, but it can also rip your head off, (and will, if that's the best way to teach you something you need to know) just as its wild physical counterpart could.

Never take a wild animal for granted, even in your meditations. Power animals like all true spiritual beings, as opposed to the ones your ego creates, are there to teach you important lessons about yourself and life, even the lessons you don't want to learn. They have their own wild power, which must be respected. Given below is a picture made up of a variety of commonly very pleasant power animals, which together are forming a scarier image of a lynx, to illustrate this point:

Adder

The adder, or common viper is the
only venomous serpent in Britain,
it is a small snake growing up to 25
inches long, its distinguishing features
are browny green scales, the black
'zig zag' pattern down its back and the
'V' on its head.

The adder or snake has been associated with negative energy, even evil, since the Christian Church rose to power. In the Garden of Eden it was the snake which tempted Eve to eat the apple, so gaining the powers of free will and wisdom. Christ cast out the serpents, which represented the devil's evil acts, the snake was said to have lost its legs and been made to crawl on its belly in the sight of God, in repentance for its evil acts.

St. George slew the serpent, dragon or snake, to symbolise the victory of Christianity over Paganism. The adder started the battle in which King Arthur died, when his and Mordred's forces met to negotiate a truce, both armies were warned not to draw their swords, or betrayal would be suspected and war would begin. Whilst Arthur and Mordred were in debate, a knight saw an adder ready to strike; instinctively he drew his sword and slew it, inadvertently starting the war, which resulted in Arthur's victory, but also his death.

The adder is not evil, though it is very powerful. The adder, more than most serpents is a representation of the dragon and a living representation of the ley / serpent / dragon lines which criss cross the Earth. The adder is a representation of Earth energy. It is associated with the kundalini life energy contained within us all, which flows in a zig zag pattern between the chakras. It is the same energy used in healing which is why the snake is shown on the caduceus, the symbol on our ambulances and hospitals. Snake venom has been used to make many powerful life-saving drugs, especially associated with heart attacks. It is also a representation of the lightning, with its lightning-fast strike and forked tongue. The adder is a symbol of earth power, which is why it is associated with Paganism.

The adder is also associated with fertility, due to its phallic shape, and eggs, from where our Easter egg tradition arises. The serpent's egg has always been a symbol of power and new life associated with the Druids. The dance of life, is also associated with the male adders, wrestling match for the right to mate, which looks like a dance.

The adder appears weak and slimy to look at, yet it is incredibly strong and very dry to the touch, proving that looks can be deceptive. The adder is also associated with transformation and rebirth, due to its ability to shed its skin and grow. The snake is associated with the element of fire, due to its need to heat its cold blood, at the start of each day it greets the sun each morning, drawing energy directly from its warmth. The snake can also be associated with the elements of earth, like the bear and other animals the adder hibernates within the Earth over the winter months. The adder is also at home in the water, as it is an excellent swimmer, often looking more graceful in the water than out of it.

The adder is held by Cernunnos on the Gundestrup Cauldron, depicted with goat's horns to indicate its power and his, acting in this image almost as a sceptre. Cernunnos is also shown with antlers, to indicate his own power.

The adder is a powerful ally for change, growth, empowerment, healing and transformation.

Badger

The badger is known to us all by its striking black and white face. A shy, virtually nocturnal animal, the badger like the bear, hibernates through the cold winter months. The badger is a clean animal, changing its bedding on a daily basis, being careful not to make a mess and storing the soiled bedding in a compost heap, away from their extensive underground burrow or sett. They have established routines, territories and pathways, which are marked on a daily basis. These often cross the boundaries of other badgers, where a communal marking post, often a tree will be found. They are tolerant of their close neighbours entering their territory, who are usually closely related anyway, at least up to a point. Badgers do not have good eyesight, so they mark other family members with a unique scent, their sense of smell and hearing being their most reliable senses.

Badgers have a reputation for spreading TB amongst cattle, which often leads to them being persecuted, where they are common, such as in

Cornwall. This is a fact which, despite extensive research, is still to be proven. Badgers are also known as being vicious and aggressive creatures, which is a reputation which also gets them illegally persecuted by badger baiters. This reputation is an undeserved one. Badgers can be extremely dangerous, being deceptively strong and armed with powerful jaws and claws, when being threatened and trapped; but given the option they will run away. I've seen badgers who are tame, wild badgers who sit and wait with foxes and hedgehogs for an evening meal from some human friends; I've also played tag with a wild badger. They can be extremely playful creatures, who usually only attack when there is no other choice.

The badger has no natural predators in Britain, except man. Their numbers are recovering from previous 'culls', due to TB scares and they are an endangered and protected species. There are a few setts now in Norfolk, which is a good sign of their recovery. Badgers eat most things, including hedgehogs (being the only predator which can in Britain), their main diet is roots.

As a power animal, they are methodical, clean and efficient, being excellent healers, due to their determination and 'get the job done' attitude, as well as their knowledge of roots and herbs. They are good guides in the Underworld and in the dark, spending all their time below ground or under the cover of darkness, they, like the bear, are also good dream and subconscious guides, spending months of the year in hibernation, they are also very protective and loyal.

Bat
Bats are the largest single group of species in the world, there are many species, some eat fruit, some eat moths and some drink blood. There are at least 27 different types of bat in Europe alone, surprising little is known about them, they are very difficult to identify when flying, but 'bat detector' equipment can make it easier. Their numbers are also on the decline, due mainly to loss of habitat. There are bats who are literally 'blind as bats', relying instead on a complex sonar system and their hearing, there are also bats with excellent vision, who don't use sonar.

Bats are very adaptable, their presence on nearly every continent attests to this and they come in a variety of sizes. They usually live in the dark of caves, mineshafts, abandoned houses, hollow trees or empty lofts. This association with the dark has earned them a fearful reputation in the past, latched onto by Hollywood and used in horror films, most notably Dracula and vampires. The bat is able to enter an instant hibernation stage upon contact with freezing conditions and then revive unharmed months later, this is very rare in mammals. The bat is a protected species and should not be disturbed if come across, as they are highly sensitive.

The bat as a power animal speaks of the ability and need to be adaptable, to learn to fit in, with wherever you may find yourself. It also speaks of the ability to find your way in the dark, be that at night or when you are simply 'in the dark' about what to do next. The bat is also a powerful dream and underworld guide, its ability to suddenly revive after extended periods of dormancy also speak of its rebirth attributes, about initiation and new life paths, its habitat deep within the Earth Mother's womb, also indicate this gift of change and adaptability, of light at the end of the dark tunnel.

Bear

There are a number of species of bear in the world including Black, Grizzly, Kodiak, Polar. They have omnivorous characteristics, can stand on two legs and can be very good parents. Basically we share similarities, this may be why the bear has always been held in such high esteem by the Shamanic cultures, which come in contact with them. Or it could be that they are the most dangerous animal in the woods and it's a good idea to get on its good side. In Siberia the bear is viewed as the Master of the Animals and revered as an ancestor, the bear is one of the power animals that all Shamen are supposed to share. The bear is associated with the Earth element as it hibernates deep in the ground for much of the winter, only occasionally venturing out when a break in the weather allows it to hunt.

In Norse traditions the bear was believed to announce the spring, and a ceremony was held outside a known bear's den, to hear the bear 'pass wind'. The gases which build up in the bear after gorging itself and then not eating for months, are apparently capable of producing a lot of noise, when the bear stirs.

The bear is often associated with the Earth Mother herself, in the guise of Artemis. A female bear is capable of putting her pregnancy on hold for a season; simply retaining the male bear's semen inside of her, until she chooses to become pregnant, no other species can do this. The bear's association with dreams stems from its hibernation, it is believed to be an excellent guide for the subconscious. Its main power is that of looking within, seeing through the inner darkness, it is also good for guidance and support in all forms of meditation and Shamanic journeying.

As a healer, the bear is second to none, an excellent herbalist, knowing the plants to pick and what parts to use to cure ailments, as well as being well versed in all the other healing arts. The bear is also a powerful ally, with enormous strength, always handy if in a Shamanic punch up.

The bear has inspired many legendary Heroes, including King Arthur, whose name is derived from Artos, the Celtic for bear, making him the Bear of Britain. As well as the Norse berserkers, who wore bear skin shirts into battle, these fierce warriors put the fear of the Gods into their enemy, often being carried onto the battleground in a cage.

Beaver
The beaver became extinct in England in the 12th Century and Scotland in the 16th Century, hunted for its pelt and the medicinal properties secreted from its castoreum gland. It was reintroduced to Scotland in 1999, thanks to the Scottish Natural Heritage and since then has been doing well. There are plans to release additional beavers into the Riparian (riverside) woodland. Their presence assists other wildlife as they alter the environment, creating 'beaver ponds', which act as sediment traps, reduce

flooding, help in neutralising acid rainfall, provide extra food and pools for fish, which in turn benefits other aquatic animals, like the otter. The beaver's foraging behaviour helps to prevent scrub invasion of the rare wetland habitats, creates deadwood which insects live in and are fed on by birds.

When the beaver lodge is abandoned, it will eventually decay; this creates a fertile water meadow, which is an increasingly rare habitat of Britain.

Beavers mate for life and have large extended families, their young are produced in litters of 2-4 each year; as the young do not become independent until their 3rd year, there can be up to 14 beavers living in one beaver lodge.

The beaver's medicine or power is about building, the beaver is constantly active, building and repairing its lodge and dam, mending leaks and storing young roots for the coming winter. Beavers are very much homemakers, focusing on their home and offspring, they work as a team, looking after the young, carrying out repairs and building extensions. Their energy teaches the need to be creative and doing something, this may mean the house needs decorating or some DIY done, or perhaps you have more creative talents that you dream about turning into a small business. Beaver says 'don't just dream, do it'. The beaver is also very much about team work and the extended family, so if in building your dream and making it concrete, you can help others on the way, then even better.

Bee

There are many different types of bee, including Leaf Cutter Bees, African Killer Bees, Bumble Bees and the Common Honey Bee. The common honey bee lives in large colonies, with a queen leading it, they fly over huge distances relative to their size, collecting flower pollen to turn into honey. They are all female, except for the few males which born when the colony creates a new queen and expands the colony, by hiving off. A large swarm of bees leaves the hive and seeks a new home to build a colony. The males fight over the right to mate with the queen, the king bee has a short life, as he is unable to separate from the queen after mating, unless he loses his tackle, which results in his death. However his tackle continues to fertilise the queen throughout her long life, about 3-4 years, the average infertile worker bee, only lives for about 2 months.

Bees are amazing navigators. They fly huge distances to find flowers in bloom, upon their return they perform a complex dance, which is watched closely by the other bees. This acts as a map for these bees, to find the flowers just visited by the scout.

Bees are totally dedicated to the hive, their only defence is to sting, which due to the barbs on it, is ripped out of the bee, complete with venom sack, this results in the bee's painful death. However the bees will willingly sacrifice themselves in huge numbers to defend their hive from predators.

The bumble bee, lives in small groups, with only a few daughters sharing the small burrow in which they live again making honey. Many other small groups of bumble bees will also often live nearby, but they act as neighbours rather than as a large colony.

Bees are about total dedication to the whole, they do not act as individuals, although they are, they do what is best for the whole community. They serve, they create many things much loved by humans and other animals, their honey is the sweet treat of the gods and used to make mead, a sweet alcoholic drink much loved by our ancestors. The wax they produce is used to make the finest candles and their royal jelly is reputed to do countless wonderful things for our health.

Bees' power is in their dedication to the larger community. The bee talks of doing community and charity work, of looking after the home, also about creating opportunities to experience the honey sweetness of life, about exploring the world around you more and about weekend trips away from home.

230

Blackbird

Blackbirds are well-known to us all; the distinctive black plumage and bright yellow eyes and beaks of the male are in complete contrast to the rather bland-looking camouflaged browns of the female. Their sweet songs, heard most often at dawn and dusk, are their grateful songs of surviving another day and night.

They have long been associated with the Otherworld and Magick, their Gaelic name 'Druid-dhubh' links them with the Celtic Druids. They are also believed to be the 'Birds of Cliodhna', whose magikal songs lulled people into a deep healing Otherworldly sleep.

The blackbirds' medicine is the power to bring messages, via dreams, from the Otherworld to you during sleep. Their sweet song is also able to act as a guide on otherworldly journeys during meditation.

Wild Boar

The wild boar was once a very common species in Britain, but now has been bred into extinction. Although in the last decade several escaped from wildlife parks and have successfully re established themselves in areas of the country such as Dorset. They are still common in their tame bred form of the pig, they were one of the first wild animals domesticated by our ancestors, used in the same way we use pigs today.

The intelligence of the pig is well known, they are considerably smarter than dogs. The wild boar incorporates this intelligence with a ferocious nature, a full grown male boar is a powerful animal, growing up to 1.5 metres in length and 3 feet at the shoulder, weighing up to 175Kg, with long tusks and a powerful bite.

The wild boar was much admired by our Celtic and Norse ancestors, often they are associated with the gods and tribes were named after them such as the 'Orci' meaning the 'People of the Boar', they featured prominently as tribal totems and on battle standards, their fierce natures gaining them reputations as battle pigs, they also inspired the Orcs of Tolkein's *'Lord of the Rings'*.

Their wisdom is also spoken of in legend. Merlin, during his wilderness exile, is said to have spent a lot of his time in the company of a small pig or boar.

The pig's sense of smell is also well renowned, with them still being commonly used in France for truffle hunting.

The wild boar's medicine is that of balance, in the same way the Celts viewed themselves, as warrior bards, the boar balances great strength and power with great intelligence and sensitivity to their environment.

Bull

The bull has always had the respect of our ancestors, inspiring the Minotaur legends of Greek mythology and their Bull Dancers, who performed acrobatics from the backs of wild bulls.

In Celtic and Norse life the bull, cow or aurochs or wild oxen, were beheld as sacred, as were all horned animals, and associated with wealth and prosperity. In Celtic mythology there are many tales relating to cattle raids, which were performed in much the same way as the Native Americans performed horse raids on neighbouring tribes. The young men of the Norse tribes, had to prove themselves worthy of being considered men, by hunting the wild aurochs of their land. The buffalo would be the Native American equivalent of the bull.

The medicine of the bull talks about growing up and taking responsibility for your life, about proving yourself and not talking 'bull'. About proving you have the strength and stamina to prosper and maybe start your own family.

Butterfly

The butterfly comes in many forms, they are widely distributed in most areas of the world, some only live for a brief season, some hibernate over winter and can live 3- 4 years. Their caterpillars are as varied as the adults, often living in this stage longer than in their adult form. They eat the nectar of flowers and the beautiful patterning on their wings is usually in a form of masks to scare off predators.

The butterfly is highly sensitive to the health of the environment, as such many of their species are quite rare, conservationists closely monitor the number of butterflies in the environment and adapt many of their management plans to increase their numbers.

The butterfly is a beautiful and delicate creature, whose medicine speaks of the courage to transform and express yourself. The butterfly begins life as an egg, this hatches into a caterpillar. The caterpillar then cocoons itself, to transform into the adult butterfly, who expresses itself with its beauty, it also speaks of sensitivity to Nature, about living in balance with the natural world.

Buzzard

The buzzard is the largest most common wild raptor or bird of prey in Britain. Mostly present on the western side of the country, preferring the more rugged moorland, they are now slowly spreading across into the eastern counties.

The buzzard is a large raptor, which hunts rodents and snakes, as well as carrion. Eagle-like in many ways, but not as big, it relies upon its talons for the kill. Its beak is much smaller than an eagle's, so it favours smaller prey. The buzzard, like all large raptors needs air thermals to gain altitude, which is why it favours the hilly moorland regions.

Buzzards are usually one of the first birds used when training in falconry, as they are more tolerant to weight change than many of the smaller, faster falcons, so the bird is less likely to die due to over or under feeding. They are also one of the more vicious raptors to handle, never really losing their call of the wild or fully taming. The buzzard like most large raptors is an impressive sight to see flying wild, sadly it is also unable to defend itself in flight, as a result, it is open to attack from any birds smaller than it.

The buzzard has excellent eyesight, it can often be seen sitting on the top of telegraph poles or dead trees searching the ground for prey.

The buzzard's medicine is similar to that of the eagle and the hawk, its graceful flight inspires us to look up to the heavens, seeking higher visions, dreaming of flight, mentally dancing the thermal spiral dance of life, as we always aim to fly higher, whilst ignoring the irritations and distractions of life.

The Buzzard also reminds us that patience and focus are needed to reach our goals, it is more sensible to focus our energy on what we know is best for us, rather than try anything and everything that comes along, then when all is in place, to strike decisively.

Wild Cat
The wild cat is very similar to the domestic cat in all but its attitude. These slightly larger relatives of our domestic cat live in isolated pockets of Scotland and Europe.

The cat has always been viewed as a special animal by our ancestors. In some cultures like Egypt, they were viewed as god-like beings. They have always been closely associated with the witch, as their familiar. The cat has a natural aloofness and even the domestic variety tends to give us the impression that they are in charge and that they tolerate our presence.

The Scottish wild cat is a lethal predator, living in wooded areas with open ground around, they spend a lot of their time in the trees and are extremely agile, not developing that fat layer our domestic cats do. They will hunt animals up to the size of a lamb and eat carrion.

The cat has a heightened sense of awareness, often reacting quite actively to things we can't see. It is believed they are naturally psychic and spend half their time asleep.

The wild cat's medicine is as a protective companion in the Otherworlds, they sleep so much, half their lives are spent there anyway. They are also very good at indicating when the supernatural has entered our space, also whether to be worried about it or not. A wild cat as a power animal may well scratch you on your first encounter, simply to let you know it is not the domestic variety.

Crow

The crow is a common carrion bird in Britain, not to be confused with the raven. The smaller crow, has a black iridescent plumage and a long pointed beak, a small number are often in the company of rooks, which are smaller still and have white, flaky skin at the base of their beaks. The crow is a very intelligent bird, it hangs out in small groups and watches what is going on around it, learning from the mistakes and successes of others, they then share this information with the other crows. They have an arrogant sort of attitude, their walk looks like the Nazi march, legs stiff and high, which looks quite amusing.

The feathers of the crow are iridescent, black to look at initially, as you move them in the light you will see a multitude of different colours contained within them. This speaks of their medicine power which is 'shapeshifting', this power doesn't mean they literally change shape, but that they consciously change themselves, adapting to each moment, learning from the past, acting on what they have learnt, in the present and moving consciously towards their goals of the future. They know how to release the pain and mistakes of the past and focus on the now; changing their life direction when necessary, to reach their goals. Working to an older set of Sacred laws, than the cultural ones we are conditioned with, they are not held back by past mistakes, regrets or the illusions which surround us, cutting through the web of invisible red tape, which affects us all, controlling our actions and inactions.

Crow simply does what it knows will work and what feels right, taking into account the consequences of its actions or inactions. It is seen as an oracular bird, knowing the past, present and future, this gave it a fearful reputation. The truth is not always as we choose to perceive it and that can often hurt.

Deer

Deer have always been held in high regard by our ancestors, especially the mature stags or harts, with their impressive antlers. Cernunnos and Herne have always been depicted with antlers, usually with seven tines (the branches on the antlers) indicating that they are fully grown and mature, at their peak of life, the first cave painting of a Shaman was shown with antlers (see chapter heading).

Note: When reading books about the Native American totems and power animals, the elk depicts the stag or hart energy, the deer depicts the hind energy.

The Stag or Herne/Cernunnos appears frequently throughout Celtic mythology, often as the white hart, which is believed to be a 'messenger from the gods'. This is an image the Mongolians share in their Spirit Lord of the Forest, 'Orboli Sagaan Noyon' (Prince White Deer) provider of the game animals and natural harvests.

The Stag is in many ways two animals. During the summer months, he is the gentle soul, seeking the brotherhood of his fellow harts, every bit as sensitive and fleeting as the hinds. Then during the fall (this is the original English name for autumn) a transformation occurs within him, his antlers are grown and he distances himself from the other harts, gathering together harems of the gentle hinds for his breeding pleasure, displaying his sexual prowess and fertility. Any other stag is an enemy to be faced down, scared off or defeated. He defends his harem from every unwanted advance from other stags, exerting immense stamina and strength; in every way depicting the Celtic warrior/bard's dual nature. Showing the duality of the year, in the dark months of winter, filled with death and hardship for our ancestors, he is the warrior stag.

Then comes the spring the antlers are shed, peace, light and new life reign a bountiful land of plenty and he becomes the bardic hart.

The hind also features strongly in Celtic mythology. In a more feminine role. Usually she is depicted as the beautiful maiden, a shapeshifter, who can turn into a woman or a deer. She leads the hero to the land of the Sidhe and gives birth to magikal, gifted half faery children, the heroes of the future. Her dual nature speaks of the day and night, of the conscious and subconscious mind, in the light of day she is a hind, but her Sidhe blood allows her to transform into a beautiful maiden as the moon rises.

The hind's gifts are sensitivity, grace, beauty and swiftness of mind and body. Both the stag/hart and hind share shapeshifting as their medicine, both express the duality of nature and life, the stag is every bit the archetypical Celtic warrior/bard, the hind every bit his counterpart the magikal faery princess.

Dog

We all know and love the loyal dog, descended from the wolf. The dog has been with us as a companion and protector for centuries. Originally wolf cubs were raised from young by our ancestors to guard and protect our homes. They have served other uses though, the Native Americans used them as beasts of burden for years before the horse was introduced to them by the Spanish. They were also eaten by many cultures, including the Native Americans, though usually this was only done as part of an important ritual.

Our Celtic and Norse ancestors used hounds for hunting, many of the famous heroes of legend owned nearly as famous hounds. There are also famous supernatural hounds, like the two-headed hell hound Garm, which guards the gates of Hades, or the white bodied and red eared hounds of the underworld called 'Cwm Annwn' who accompany Arawn on the Wild Hunt, judging and riding down the guilty.

Hounds were also believed to be healers, due to their saliva. Today people take dogs to hospitals as petting dogs which make patients feel better and reduces stress levels.

The supernatural image still exists even today in the form of black hounds which when seen usually indicate the death of a loved one such as Black Shock of Norfolk and Suffolk.

The medicine of the hound though is mainly in their loyalty, protective qualities and reassurance. When everything is going to hell, you can always rely on your dog to still love you.

Dolphin

The dolphin like the whale is a cetacean an ocean living warm-blooded mammal. The dolphin started in the ocean, as did all life, developed into a wolf-like creature, then for some reason, returned to the ocean, evolving into the smiling, gentle, playful creature we know and love. The smile is not a smile as we know it, their mouths are simply designed like that, they still smile whilst being slaughtered for food by the Japanese. But despite this they do exhibit very trusting playful natures, they are highly intelligent, possibly in some ways more so than us, and they are also well known for saving drowning people.

Dolphins live in large schools, led by a matriarch and take it in turns to nurse the young, care for the sick, helping the injured to the surface to breath, they also talk to each other in a highly complex series of clicks and whistles, each dolphin having its own unique series of these, which could be classed as a name, it is also believed that they meditate, by staying upright and near motionless in the water. They also appear to practice sex for the fun of it, mating all year round, but only reproducing once a year. In many ways they are very similar to us, but seem to have lost their aggressive nature, but they are still capable of violence in defence of their school from sharks.

The medicine of the dolphin is one of community, of sharing, caring and lightening the load, of intelligence, freedom, innocence, trust and playfulness. They are also very healing, simply being in their presence will lighten the mood of the most depressed.

Eagle

The eagle is generally renowned as the 'King of the Birds'. The inspiration for the Native American 'Thunderbird', the mythical giant birds whose wings create the thunder and whose lightning impregnates the Earth and makes her pregnant with life. The Eagle mates for life and performs an impressive

aerial courtship display, which involves the two Eagles locking talons and plunging towards the ground, only separating at the last moment before they impact, before once again soaring upwards.

The eagle is an impressive creature to watch soaring through the sky, able to travel huge distances without effort, when in a thermal. Britain has golden eagles, and the larger sea eagle, living wild in Scotland; a pair of golden eagles also live in the Lake District. You will be lucky to see them though, as golden eagle's territorial range is 75 miles.

Eagles live a long life, in captivity their lifespan is similar to ours, but shorter in the wild. They live in eyries a large nest often inhabited by eagles for hundreds of years over several generations. These are repaired and built on each breeding season and occasionally become so big and heavy that the tree supporting it collapses under the weight.

Eagles have been flown in falconry for many centuries, mainly by kings, though they do not make the easiest bird to train. In Mongolia golden eagles are used to hunt wolves; although unable to actually overpower a full-grown wolf, they are trained and capable of gripping its snout in their talons, so that the wolf is held in place, ready for the hunter to shoot it.

As said earlier, the eagle is renowned as the 'King of birds'. However in Celtic mythology it is the wren, the smallest bird, that is the king; this is the result of a competition between all the birds to find out who was to be their king. It was decided that whoever could fly the highest would rule. The eagle easily outsoared the rest of the birds and was confident it was he who would be crowned king; when the tiny wren, who had been hiding on the eagle's back suddenly took flight and flew a few inches higher than the eagle, so winning the competition. The eagle is the King of the birds if you don't count cheating, though like the buzzard, it is subject to the humiliation of attack from every bird smaller than itself. It is still able to fly the highest, closest to the sun and as such is often identified with the Celtic and Norse sun gods.

The eagle has incredibly powerful talons, chainmail is needed to handle one, a large ripping beak and amazingly powerful eyesight, 10 times better than ours; the stare of an eagle is quite intimidating.

The eagle is believed to be another of the natural Shaman's power animals shared by all, in Mongolia it was the eagle which created the first Shaman. Eagle's Medicine is of the spirit, it flies closest to the sun and heaven, closest to the gods. The Native Americans believe he is the messenger which delivers their prayers to the Great Spirit. The eagle also has the medicine of visions, due to his incredible eyesight and powerful stare. Eagles Feathers are marks of bravery in Native American traditions as well as symbols for having passed various trials of life. Eagle's feathers are medicine gifts which are earned, through dedication and hard work. The Celts and Norse also held eagles' feathers as highly prized possessions, as do most cultures, but none so much as the Native Americans.

Fox

The red fox with its striking bushy tail and dog-like appearance lives as commonly in town now as it does in the countryside. The fox eats small rodents and other prey up to lamb size, as well as carrion, fruit and food from dustbins. The dog fox stays near the vixen when she has cubs, acting as the devoted father, he feeds both the vixen and 3-8 cubs, often going without himself. When the cubs are established and able to travel and hunt, the dog will go his own way, leaving the vixen to train them, although he still visits on occasion. The same foxes may breed together often, but don't ever really live together.

The fox's den or earth is easy to distinguish from a badger's as it will be littered with remains, the fox not being the world's tidiest animal. The vixen emits horrible screams in the winter months, which sound like a woman shouting 'Help'.

The fox's medicine is of camouflage and cunning, the fox has the ability to merge effortlessly into the background, simply by looking so much like it belongs, its red colouring helps it to merge with undergrowth and brick walls. The fox's cunning intelligence allows it to rid itself of fleas, picking up a stick and slowly submerging into water, the fleas climb higher looking for dry ground. When they are on the stick and the fox is submerged, the stick is dropped and away float the fleas. When being hunted the fox will use lots of tricks to try and evade the hounds, running along walls, crossing streams, doubling back on itself, travelling through strong-smelling plants, it has even been known to jump into passing trailers.

Hare

Although the hare looks like a rabbit it is very different, larger, colouring-wise it tends to be more brown than grey, depending on the species. It does not live in burrows or groups, a small scrape called a 'form' is sufficient in bad weather. Their young are raised in tufts of grass, which serve as a nest, they simply stay very still when danger looms, while the  parents cause a distraction. The hare is mainly nocturnal, travelling far and wide during full moons. This earned it associations with the Goddess Eostre, from where our Easter is derived and the hare gave rise to the Easter Bunny, as this is when the hare is most prominent. The hare is not timid like the rabbit, which can be seen in the male's 'boxing' behaviour, for the right to breed. The hare is also very fast, opting for a flat out run, rather than the twisting and turning of a rabbit.

The hare's medicine is that of Otherworldly guide, like the rabbit in *Alice in Wonderland*. Its instincts and sixth sense (or intuition due to its association with the moon) allow it to know when to stay still, when to bolt and when to fight, which also earn it the status of a tactician.

Hawk

The hawk (sparrow hawk, goshawk) has long rounded tail feathers and short rounded wings ending in slightly flared primary feathers. These differences from the buzzard and eagle mean these raptors are capable of hunting other birds, so you will not see these birds get mobbed by smaller birds. The hawk is a popular falconry bird, used for centuries for catching flying prey and ground prey.

242

This medium-sized raptor, like all birds of prey, has excellent eyesight and due to its size also uses the air thermals to gain altitude. This is also where it derives its medicine, flying high, scouring the ground beneath it, it sees all, its penetrating 'kekkekkek' calls often indicates things coming, other than its potential prey. As such it is viewed as a seer, able to see events ahead; its cry forewarns the attuned to be on the look-out for 'something new' in their lives. This medicine also allows the hawk to see the big picture, rather than just what is currently visible, allowing it to make a more informed decision about the opportunities presenting themselves.

Hedgehog
The hedgehog is a common visitor in most gardens, known as the gardener's friend as it loves to eat big fat juicy slugs, which is of obvious benefit to the plants around it. The hedgehog hibernates during the winter months, often curled up in a ball of leaves, sometimes in an empty flower pot or similar. They are most active at twilight, when their noisy snorts can be heard as they stumble around the garden in search of insects to eat.

The hedgehog sow produces a litter of 2-9 pink soft-spined young in the late spring or early summer; occasionally a second litter is produced if the weather permits or the first litter is lost. Hedgehog's eyesight is not good at distance, but their sense of smell and touch is superb.

Hedgehogs have few natural predators, their spines make them immune to snake bites and most other predators, only the badger is able to unroll and eat them. The hedgehog will usually roll up into a tight spiky ball when scared, but they are capable of lifting themselves up, revealing surprisingly long legs and a short tail and scuttling off at a rapid trot.

There are several 'Old Wives Tales' about them, saying they roll on windfall apples and carry them off, apples won't stick to their spines; and that they need their fleas and ticks to live. This is not true as the hedgehogs taken to Australia, have no fleas or ticks and are very happy.

The hedgehog was celebrated on Imbolc, February 2nd, by the Romans as part of their spring celebrations;. It has also been known as the 'warrior of 100 spears' by the Anglo Saxons, as it is fairly fearless and rarely runs away from a fight. They are also quite trusting, innocent creatures and quite playful.

The hedgehog's medicine acts as protective guardian of the inner child, innocence and trust, surrounding this soft vulnerable side of our natures with a wall of impenetrable spears. They are also good as dreamtime guides, they spend much of their time hibernating as the bear does, making them excellent guides through the subconscious dream world and Underworld of Shamanic journeys. They are a little like walking dream catchers.

Horse

The horse is probably one of the most impor-  tant animals our ancestors tamed. They have been used as beasts of burden, opened up communication, and they also indicated great wealth. All nomadic cultures immediately recognised their potential; they have been domesticated and bred since.

In Mongolia it is said the children learn to ride before they can walk. The Native Americans, descended from these same Mongolians, took to horses like a duck to water, increasing their hunting range and skills ten-fold.

The Celts were famous for their horses, the Iceni tribe of Norfolk, especially, the Norse also saw the horse as a gift from the gods; Odin's 8 - legged horse Sleipnir was symbolic of the year and cycle of life. The white horse chalk drawings at various places around Britain, most famously at Uffington, attest to their great importance.

The horse goddess Epona was worshipped far and wide and horse cults were common, the horse whisperers is one such cult still in existence today. The Horse was considered sacred to the Celts, who introduced it to Europe from the east, where the Celts originated. A taboo existed about eating its flesh or harming them. The horse symbolised the land to our ancestors, there was even a symbolic mating between a new king and a white mare, to indicate that the two were the same. If the king failed in his duties, so did the land, the king would then be replaced. The Horse also made the warrior a truly formidable opponent; the historical King Arthur, was believed to be a Celtic warlord who raised a cavalry army, which enabled him to travel rapidly, defeating the Saxon foot soldiers by horse power.

The Shaman's Drum is also known as the Shaman's Horse, the sacred steed which carries the Shaman on his otherworldly journeys. The horse's medicine is balanced power, both earthly and otherworldly.

Jay

The jay, like the magpie, is a member of the crow family, they share all of the crow's traits, but have some more of their own. The jay is a beautiful coloured bird, with brown, white and black feathers, added to this are some exquisite bright blue feathers on its wings. The jay stands out, it is a very confident almost arrogant bird, it often takes over other birds nests and is very territorial. In the forest it is the look out, if a deer stalker comes across a jay whilst hunting, he may as well give up and move elsewhere, the deer know to heed the jay's noisy clamouring and move on.

The jay is also responsible for growing many Oak trees, it often gathers and buries acorns, presumably as a food store, but these acorns are rarely dug up and grow. Jays are very clever and can be taught to speak.

The jay's medicine is as a forest guardian or conservationist, looking out for his neighbours and ensuring the forest will always be there by planting more trees.

Kestrel/Falcon

The kestrel is a member of the falcon family and the only raptor I am aware of which is capable of hovering, which they often do along roadsides. They are very small raptors who feed mainly on field mice. The male's blue white and brown in colour, the females are brown and white.

The kestrel is rarely used in falconry, as keeping it a healthy weight is very difficult. Kestrels like all raptors do not drink water, it would kill them, instead they derive all the water they need from their prey. Another famous falcon shares its name with a famous wizard/sorcerer/seer and Shaman called Merlin.

Falcons are the fastest species of raptor in the world, a peregrine falcon has been clocked at over 130 miles an hour in a stoop. They are also mainly a species of bird-hunting raptors, so not only do you not see them get mobbed, you will be lucky to see another bird in the air when they are present.

The medicine of the falcon is mastery of the air. The falcon family has the only raptor capable of sustained hovering and the fastest raptor, they are all capable of taking down almost any other bird. The falcon's medicine speaks of planning establishing yourself in the right area, patience in waiting for the right conditions to present themselves in life's situations and then taking decisive action, swooping in for the kill.

Ladybird

The Ladybird, Ladybug or Bishy Barnaby, is a well-known and loved beetle, it is a voracious predator of aphids, despite its pleasant appearance. The ladybird is named after the Virgin Mary, its red colouring is said to represent the blood shed by Christ on the Cross. I feel this is a Christianised story and that the original would be more like, the ladybird represents the goddess, in a fertility form and the colouring represents the menstrual blood of women.

The ladybird, like the butterfly, has the medicine of transformation. The ladybird also transforms through four stages, egg, larvae, which is also a voracious predator of aphids, looking more like lobster than a ladybird in this stage, then it enters its pupa stage prior to emerging as a ladybird. The ladybird is also much loved by gardeners as it eats dozens of aphids (greenfly) a day. The ladybird is a story of change from ugly duckling to beautiful swan. The ladybird gathers in large numbers during the winter months and hibernates in a mass of bodies, their combined body heat keeping them warm. When they emerge in the spring they breed and in a very hot year, such as in 1976, they can reach almost plague numbers.

The ladybird's medicine is very much connected with the Triple Goddess, being transformation, menstruation, fertility, conservation and the sub-conscious of the dream world.

Lynx

The Lynx was once common all over Europe, including Britain, but it is now extinct in many areas. There are still small populations in Iberia, Scandinavia and parts of eastern and south-eastern Europe. There are progra-mmes to reintroduce it into its former areas of habitat in Switzerland, Germany and other parts of central Europe. One of the factors  affecting the lynx is habitat loss, caused by the cultivation of early strawberries. So if you want to assist the lynx, don't buy early strawberries from Europe.

The lynx is a dog-sized cat, characterised by its short tail, long legs and distinctive ear tufts. It spends most of its time on its own, only coming together to breed. A single litter of 3 or 4 kittens is born in the summer, these stay with the mother for a year, mainly in and around a hollow lair until they are old enough to start hunting.

The lynx is known for its 'knowing' smile, like the Cheshire Cat of *Alice in Wonderland*. The lynx is traditionally associated with 'secrets', about knowing things about others, that maybe they wouldn't want you to know, their fears, lies, regrets and self deceptions; the lynx knows where all the skeletons are buried.

The lynx is also reputed to be the 'Knower' of the lost magikal systems and lore of our ancestors, which can be accessed via the stillness of meditation. The biggest problem with the lynx is getting it to instruct or talk to you, the lynx says very little; but it may lead you, if you will follow. Be warned, the lynx's medicine comes at a price, in showing you its truth, it will also show you the things you don't really want to see about yourself, introducing you to your shadow self, as well as showing you the things you have forgotten about yourself, helping you to reawaken any forgotten talents.

Mouse
The mouse is a small rodent, with big ears and a long tail, they are common inside and outside. The field mouse lives among the stalks of the wheat and barley crops, their nest is a cricket ball sized construction of stems. They produce several litters of up to 6 per year and feed primarily on seeds; they are also the prey of many predators.

The medicine of mouse is paying attention to detail, the mouse lives in a small world, where most things are bigger than it is, so to it the small things are important, like the seeds it eats and stores. It is a very nervous little creature, paying attention to every slight sound, smell and movement, as so many other creatures prey on it, it has to be. Mouse always says 'read the small print' before you commit yourself.

Otter
The otter is very much a creature of two worlds, earth and water. The otter is a wonderfully playful character, who glides through the water, and moves in an interesting lollop on the land. Its holt is accessed below the

water level and is usually a simple tunnel leading up into a single room. The otter lives mainly on fish and eels, leaving signs of its activities on the riverbank, in the form of fish scales and spraints. These also serve to mark its territory, a dog otter will often have a territory of 35 miles of riverbank. They reproduce all year, with a litter of 2 kittens being the norm. Otters are doting parents, spending hours playing with their young, as they learn the ways of the world, curiosity is also a strong otter trait. Otters were recently very scarce in our waterways, due to pollution and hunting, but they are now far more frequent thanks to reintroduction programmes.

The medicine of otter is its playfulness. It enjoys life, its antics will often make you laugh; laughter is a good cure for many ills and that is also why the otter's skin is often turned into medicine bags for medicine women. The otter's energy is very feminine in its nature. It is about shared joy, pleasure and playfulness for pleasure's sake, not for power games or reward.

Owl

There are many species of owl, some are huge, like the eagle owl, some are very small like the little owl. All owls are raptors of the night, their feathers are unique, designed with soft edges so that they fly almost silently. They also have the ability to look almost all-round, their eyes are excellent for night vision, designed to absorb as much light as possible, their main sense is their hearing, their faces are designed like twin radar dishes, to absorb as much light and sound as possible. They mainly live on rodents and small mammals (depending on their size). Many owls are endangered due to loss of habitat. The most famous of these is probably the near-white barn owl, which lives in barns, many of which have been converted to houses today.

The tawny owl is probably the most common owl in Britain, though there are barn owls, little owls and a few rare eagle owls living wild. They are difficult to train for falconry, as they are nocturnal, but are regularly used.

The owl is another of the shared power animals of Shamen. The owl is known as the night eagle and is the best guide through the dark. We all have a shadow side we often prefer to ignore, Owl sees this and teaches us to accept and learn from it. This dis-empowers our fears and allows us to see our true selves, balanced with our light sides. The owl is sometimes associated with evil or ill omens, this is due to this fear of the shadows, the owl is more commonly known for its wisdom, its powers are of clairvoyance and clairaudience, of being able to see beyond the darkness into the truth.

Rabbit
The rabbit, made famous by Richard Adams' *'Watership Down'*, is a common sight in Britain, although not a native of the country, having been brought over by the Romans as a food source. Rabbits live in large groups in complex underground burrows called warrens. Rabbits are famous for their reproductive rate; a pair of rabbits will produce 3 litters of 4-7 kittens per year, which in turn become sexually mature at 3 months, which means that 2 rabbits can produce between 144 - 441 rabbits in one year. This is just as well because virtually every predator eats them. Myxamatosis was introduced to the rabbit population several decades ago to try and control their numbers, as we no longer have enough suitable predators to keep their numbers in check, the rabbit is very resilient though and many rabbits now survive this awful disease having become immune to it.

The rabbit's medicine is fertility and fear, the rabbit was harvested like a crop for many years, being kept in large fenced off areas, feeding many people and animals. The rabbit has always got to be aware of potential predators; they are highly timid creatures, with nearly all-round vision and other acute senses. They sit still and low watching the fox approach, only bolting when they have no other option. Their medicine teaches us it is okay to accept our fears, fear is a necessary emotion, upon which our survival instincts are based. They also teach us that our fears need to be faced and overcome at times, being ungrounded or irrational, otherwise the rabbit will starve and there will be no future generations.

Rat

The rat has always had a bad press, as a dirty, disease spreading creature, often featuring in horror films. I have kept several rats and find them fascinating and intelligent creatures, very agile and they are constantly cleaning themselves, I've always felt that most people don't like them due to their worm-like, near bare tails. Their sizes are usually exaggerated, they grow to about 50cm in length, half of this is the tail and can weigh up to 500 grams, half a bag of sugar. They are prolific breeders, far worse than the rabbit, producing 5 litters of up to 12 young per year, these are sexually mature at 3 months, so a pair of rats is capable of producing 3600 rats in one year. They are preyed on by all predators, their numbers have boomed as we are so messy. If we weren't such a wasteful society, leaving food lying around everywhere, they wouldn't be so common. Rats are one of nature's dustmen, they clear up the mess. They live in complex under-ground burrows in the wild, often in large numbers, this is ruled by a dominant pair and they eat most things. Sewers make good homes for them, as they are full of rubbish, mainly dry and rats are excellent swimmers.

The Black Death of the Dark Ages, was started by the fleas on the now rare black rat, the most common rat is the brown. In China, there are barter rats, they don't steal, they exchange stones for the grain they eat.

The rat's medicine is waste control, they spend all their time cleaning up after us. They warn us by their numbers, not to be so wasteful, to remember there are others in the world who are starving. Wild rats care for and look after their injured, ensuring they don't starve.

Raven

The raven is a large black carrion bird, to look at similar to the crow, whom it shares many traits with, but bigger with a larger beak. Due to its colour and main food source it is often associated with ill omens and negativity. This is not true, the raven is a very intelligent bird, capable of being trained to speak and always, like its cousin the crow, working things out, solving problems and learning. They are one of the best parents in the bird world, whereas most birds simply feed the strongest of their young, allowing the runts to die, the raven ensures all their chicks survive. They feed the biggest to start with, the runt gets ignored for a while. Then the healthy chicks get ignored and they focus on feeding the runt, so that it grows as big as the others, ensuring all survive.

They are strongly associated with magik; Odin the chief Norse god owned two Ravens, Muninn (Memory) and Hugin (Thought), who flew all around Midgard, reporting back anything that would be of interest to Odin. They are also kept at the Tower of London, to ensure our country is kept free of invasion by enemies.

The raven's medicine is as a messenger from the gods, its iridescent feathers speak of the same shapeshifting qualities as the crow, raven is also known for carrying the energy, raised for absent healing, to the person in need of it and as a guardian of the circle, due to its protective maternal qualities.

Robin

The robin redbreast is a well-known small bird, most often associated with Christmas cards. This small bird is a local resident of most gardens, the robin is a highly territorial songbird, it will violently defend its home from other robins and sometimes other bigger birds, during the mating season. The nest, in a hollow sometimes in the ground, lined by moss and raise 5 or 6 eggs.

The robin gets its red breast in Irish folklore by killing the wren 'the little king' (see eagle) with his bow and arrow (which may also associate the robin with Robin Hood); at Winter Solstice the wren governs the last year, associating the wren with the Holly King of Wicca, the role of Oak King is played by the robin, who governs the new year.

The medicine of the robin is renewal and protection, the robin demonstrates his courage by attacking the other robins and bigger birds, defending his home for the birth of his new young; in the folklore the old year is also banished to make way for the new year and the spring, by his actions.

Salmon

The salmon is an amazing fish, it lives to  an old age for a fish, starting in a fresh water lake, it grows to adulthood in these fresh waters, then it travels out to sea, where it can live for up to 7 years. At about the age of 10 years it becomes overwhelmed by the urge to spawn. All the salmon spawned in the same lake have a compulsion to return to that same lake, regardless of distance, obstacles or any other considerations. They stop eating and swim back to where their lives began, they swim upriver, against the current, leaping up 12 foot waterfalls, past bears, eagles, otters and all other predators. The few that complete this journey, then spawn and die, their cycle of life completed, back where it started.

The salmon occurs again and again in Celtic folklore, their medicine speaks of longevity, wisdom and determination. The Salmon of Assaroe was reputed to be as old as time and the Celtic hero Fionn Mac Cumhail acquired his wisdom by eating a salmon which had swum in a pool below the 9 Hazels of Wisdom, eating their hazelnuts. The salmon tells us that there are times when it is necessary to be totally single-minded to achieve our goals.

Seal

Grey Seals make up the largest breeding colony of seals residing off the British coast. They are the largest of the European species, with the male bulls growing up to 3 metres in length and weighing up to 200kg; the female cows average about 2 metres in length. The grey seals breed in the autumn in small colonies, mostly on rocky outcrops and small islands. Their pups are white at birth, but after about 10 days they begin to moult and acquire the grey coat of adults.

Grey seals are highly vocal, especially the cows, which make a high pitched hooting when they are on the breeding beaches. Grey seals usually sleep out of the water on the rocks, but they are also known to sleep upright in the water with just their heads showing.

The combination of basking on rocks, sleeping upright in the water and the high pitched hooting, helped to create the legend of the mermaids, beautiful half fish/half women, who lure sailors and their ships to the rocks and their ruin according to legend. These beautiful creatures with their long eyelashes and big brown eyes, look very friendly. Their clumsy movement on the land, is in sharp contrast to their graceful movements in the water.

The medicine of the seal is enchantment gained by their association with sailors' deception or self delusion, seeing them as mermaids; these friendly looking animals also hid their sharp dog-like bite, which has caught several people unaware, especially in the defence of their pups. The seal warns us that unless we keep our feet firmly on the ground, we often deceive ourselves, seeing what we want to see, rather than what is really there, which is occasionally even better than we expected.

Shark

The shark has a reputation as a terrifying predator, especially since the film *'Jaws'* was released. They are thought of as mindless eating machines, swimming through the ocean depths eating all in their path. This is not completely true, the shark comes in many forms, some of the largest the whale and basking shark are baling feeders, like many of the whales, filtering the tiny plankton to sustain them. It is true that they are terrifying predators, the shark is one of the Earth's oldest inhabitants, having existed almost unchanged since the dinosaurs. Their senses are excellent, able to smell blood from up to two miles away, swim at a very fast pace and hear over huge distances. They can feel struggling movements from a long way off, their eyes are their last sense used. Their teeth are constantly being replaced, their tough hides are formed from tiny teeth-like scales and it is not known how long they can live.

What is not so well-known, is that they are immune to many of our worst illnesses so are being studied as a result. The great white shark, nearly became extinct as a result of hunting, the blue shark, a potential killer, lives about 50 miles off our coast. Most shark attacks are a case of mistaken identity, they mainly hunt seals, so lilos and surf boards get attacked. Shark attacks usually occur in only three feett of water and once in a while a shark will rescue a drowning sailor.

The shark's main role is similar to that of the rat on land, they keep the ocean clean. The shark's medicine is as a guide to the darkest depths of our subconscious mind, they are a mystery to us and can help us to explore those parts of ourselves that are also a mystery to us and a little frightening, helping us to have the courage to look into the jaws of truth.

Spider
The Spider is member of the arachnid family, made up of two groups; the wolf spiders and the globe spiders. Wolf spiders are the hunters, they don't make webs, they hunt for prey, often able to leap and move rapidly. The globe or bulbous spider is the web builder, they sit in wait in their near invisible ambush, for their careless prey to come to them.

Spiders scare many people, especially house spiders as they are big, black, ugly and run at you. There are no native poisonous spiders in Britain, few spiders in the world are truly dangerous to man. The American Black Widow and the Australian Red Back, are probably the most dangerous, even tarantulas usually only have a bite equivalent to that of a bee sting. The best way to avoid the scary house spider charging at you, is to move, they are rarely even aware of you, you are so large, they are simply heading for the shadow you are casting, feeling vulnerable and exposed in the light.

The spider sits at the centre of their wyrd web spinning the threads of life, which seems very similar to the world-wide web of the internet, it is certainly weird enough. The spider encouraged Robert the Bruce to continue in his struggle to free Scotland. It is an essential part of the world's ecology, controlling the insect and fly numbers.

Spider's medicine is about weaving the webs of our life, our wheel of life, the spider is also reputed to have weaved the first alphabet, giving us the written language, to record and save things, like the spider stores silk-wrapped food in its pantry. The spider is also about having the strength to see our life paths through and not to let the things which are beyond our control fester and infect us, distracting us. The spider's web is one of the strongest materials known to man, of its size. It is also antiseptic in its nature and has been used to dress wounds for centuries. The spider sits at the centre of the web, its strands linked to the many areas of its life, she is constantly aware of what is happening around her and responds quickly to the tremors of life, reaping rewards or making necessary repairs. She reminds us not to take on more than we can successfully balance.

Squirrel

The red squirrel is the native squirrel of Britain, though this has been largely reduced in numbers by the introduction of the larger American grey squirrel. The red and grey squirrels share many of their habits, both have a similar diet of shoots, nuts, berries, fungi, insects and bird eggs. They both

produce 2 litters of 3-7 young per year, which become mature at 2 months and independent at a year. They build several untidy dreys (nests) of twigs and branches, sometimes in hollow trees.

The red squirrel is more of a specialist than the grey, preferring coniferous woodland, whereas the grey is happy in all woodland. The red spends most of its time in the trees, but the grey is just as happy on the ground. As a result the red has been largely eaten out of house and home, which has resulted in a population decline. However there are areas where the red squirrel is still regularly seen, such as Thetford Forest. Squirrels don't really hibernate they simply stay inside their dreys during the winter.

The squirrel is a playful creature, playing chase and hide and seek, throwing nuts at passers-by. They are famous for storing nuts and acorns for the winter months, they do this in large quantities, but often forget where they have buried them; as a result many trees are planted by them each year.

The medicine of the squirrel is that of preparation and trust, they are very trusting creatures and certainly in towns can often be fed by hand, trusting the Earth to provide for them, but just in case, they also save their nuts for a rainy day, in so doing reminding us we should also put a little something aside for our own rainy days.

Swan

The swan is a large graceful white water bird, which looks a little ungainly in flight. Their diet consists of aquatic plants; their long powerful necks allow them to feed from river bottoms, without having to dive. Swans mate for life, laying 5-8 eggs during their breeding season in April-May. Their nests are large, made of sedge and reeds, their cygnets have messy brown fluff rather than the white adult feathers, earning them the 'Ugly Duckling' imagery, but this soon passes to reveal the swan beneath.

The swan is a regular player in Celtic mythology, often associated with the Ulster hero Cuchulainn and stories such as 'The Dream of Angus Og' and 'The Fate of the Children'.

In these Celtic legends the swan is often an otherworldly beautiful maiden, who spends half the year as a woman and half as a swan, or they have been transformed into the swan as the result of a curse. The swan in these legends is also often involved in ill-fated affairs of the heart, the lonely forlorn swan is a sad sight, in nature and in legend.

The medicine of the swan is of spiritual and emotional transformation, from the egg, through the ugly duckling stage to the beautiful pure and graceful swan. The swan's medicine also speaks of the sadness of ill-fated love, making it a good confidante for the broken-hearted, once again speaking of the transformation from emotional ugly ducking to graceful confident Swan.

Toad / Frog

British common toads are easily distinguished from frogs, their skin is rough and warty; frog's skin is smooth. They are also usually less colourful, with browns predominating, their pupils are also horizontal and their hind legs are rather weak, only allowing them to hop, rather than jump. Frogs breed in early spring, March usually, whereas toads breed a little later in April. Both frogs and toads produce 'spawn' and the tadpoles of frogs and toads are difficult to distinguish from each other. Toads sing loudly at breeding season, frogs remain silent.

When the tadpoles of both species have matured they leave the water and head into the undergrowth, the frog will usually remain close to the spawning pond, returning to the water from time to time, the toad however only returns the following breeding season, spending the majority of its time in woodland. Some toads, such as the natterjack toad are very rare, having the same legal protection as the crested newt. We are lucky to have a breeding colony of these in Norfolk.

The toad's medicine is visionary transformation and is strongly linked to Shamanism; the cane toad of South America is licked to induce Shamanic visions via its skin toxins, which are designed as a defence from predators. The toad also undergoes a series of transformations, just as the developing Shaman does, starting in the water it evolves into an earthier form. Returning to where it started to produce future generations; just as the Shaman is aware that the circular, or spiral path, they are travelling will lead back to the beginning, or a similar stage in their life.

The toad is also linked with witchcraft, being used to remove warts by rubbing with a toad, or more interestingly as the provider of a magikal bone. A dead toad is buried in an anthill, to clean the carcass down to the bones; then on a full moon, the bones are taken to a small stream or fjord of running water, the gods are then asked to make the magikal bone known. The bones are placed into the running water, most of them will wash away downstream, but the magikal one will travel upstream briefly. This magikal bone is then retrieved and used in the manner of a tiny wand, being kept on its owner in a small red cloth bag at all times.

The frog's medicine is similar to that of the toad, purifying transformation, the frog remains close to the water, despite the very similar transformation, its medicine is used to cleanse and purify. South American Shamen are often seen spitting a spray of water over their clients; this is done whilst calling upon the power of the frog to cleanse and purify the client's energy systems and aura, it is a similar idea to the more air orientated smudging process of other Shamanic cultures and can also be used to clear spaces of negative energy.

Wasp

The wasp or 'sky tiger' as I call it, has long been disliked by modern man. It is similar in many ways to the bee, there are a variety of different species, some living singularly, some in colonies, organised in similar ways to beehives.

The wasp has the ability to sting many times, this is especially true in the autumn when it becomes drowsy and aggressive, shortly before hibernating or dying off. They usually live in nests of a spherical form and made of a paper-like substance, these are very complex, incorporating up to 4 floors and hundreds of cells where the wasp pupae are developing, in the autumn these nests can contain up to 3,000 individuals.

The wasp is another gardener's friend like the ladybird. It is responsible for killing off thousands of other insects and caterpillars each year, to feed its young on. The adult wasp prefers flower nectar and fruit juices, helping in the pollination of flora, like the bee.

The best way to kill off wasps is to introduce the hover fly, which is able to infiltrate the wasp's nest and eat the young wasps.

The wasp's medicine is that of respect and purpose, they are only aggressive when provoked and defending themselves, sometimes you will find one blocking your way, it hovers and moves when you do, making it difficult to pass without injury to either it or yourself, it demands your attention and your respect, despite its small size. It knows it has a purpose in life, it knows it is important. Wasp reminds us all, that we are also worthy of respect and have a purpose in life, even if it is currently eluding us.

Weasel

The weasel is a strange elongated animal, similar in its look, energy and medicine to a stoat, mink, polecat (ferret) or pine marten. Weasels are small, males are only 26 cm in length (including the tail) and weighing only 130 grams; the females are even smaller, sometimes only weighing 45 grams. The stoat is the easiest to mistake it with, this is larger and has a black tip on its tail, even in its white winter coat (which both species share), when it is known as an ermine. The weasel produces 2 litters of 5 kittens per year, the stoat only one litter; both species make a variety of hissing, spitting and screaming noises. The weasel is a ferocious predator, often taking on animals much larger than itself, such as the rabbit. Its low, long body makes it perfect for cornering prey in their own burrows. The weasel is also quite wasteful, eating only the brains and drinking the blood of its prey, this means the rest of the carcass is often wasted as only the weasel can reach it.

The medicine of the weasel is its fearless reactions, it is no good at the chase, but lightning fast at striking, it also knows little fear, when confronted with a larger predator it is just as likely to strike, often surprising its opponent making it back off, long enough to escape. The weasel reminds us that at times it is important to react to a situation quickly and without fear, regardless of our feelings, especially in an emergency, reacting first, solving the problem and then allowing our emotions to be expressed.

Whale

There are several different species of whales, they, like the dolphin, are a part of the cetacean family, they form two distinct groups 'toothed' and 'baleen' whales.

Toothed whales have teeth and eat fish and squid, they include the orca or 'killer whale', a large dolphin-like whale, smaller than most other whales, these swim in a pod of about 30 individuals, they are a distinctive black and white in colour and have a very large fin on their back. The orca is the wolf of the ocean, they hunt in packs, often attacking other larger whales, they are even known to drive these towards whaling ships, as they will get to eat the waste, after it is processed.

Baleen whales eat plankton, sieving the tiny creatures from the water with large bone-like plates, instead of teeth, they include the largest mammal on the planet in their group, the 'blue whale' growing up to 30 metres in length.

The humpback whale, has one of the most complex languages of all the whales, their songs are famous and very beautiful to listen too.

The whale's medicine is as a record keeper, it is believed that the whale was placed here by the people of the Dog Star, Sirius, to record what happens on our planet. This was used as a plot for '*Star Trek 4: the voyage home*', which raises an interesting point, it is strange to think that on a planet which is 70% covered in water, that the ego of the human land dweller, believes their mere 30% of the world's surface holds the most important species on the planet, namely them; this doesn't really make a lot of sense to me. Despite its huge barnacle-encrusted mass, the whale's skin is highly sensitive to touch, they are also very gentle around people swimming with them. They are truly awe inspiring creatures, who we almost made extinct, with hunting. Sadly they are still hunted today, but they are still not fully understood, their language may yet cause us to re-evaluate our role. The whale provides us with the guide to the sub-conscious and ancient wisdom stored deep within our genes.

Wolf

The wolf is the fourth of the power animals traditionally shared by all Shamans. The wolf was a British native species until the 12th Century in Scotland when the last was killed, near to the source of the River Findhorn in Scotland. Wolves were very common in Europe for many years, but have been persecuted ruthlessly by our ancestors, who drastically reduced their numbers. There are still several packs in Europe, but mostly they are found in Siberia and Canada. The wolf has suffered at our hands, yet it is also the wolf's descendants who ended up as man's best friend the Dog.

The wolf has several reintroduction programmes running for it in Europe and a trial was held to reintroduce it to the Inverness area of Scotland. Sadly this was opposed by the local residents, who were still scared of the big bad wolf image.

In reality the wolf is a very shy animal, who goes out of its way to avoid man, having learnt from our treatment of them in the past. The wolf lives and hunts in a pack, ruled by an alpha male and female, these are the only wolves allowed to breed in this pack, a strong pecking order is also in effect when it comes to food. The cubs are born once a year in a litter of 3-4, the pack is usually formed from the alpha pair and two years worth of litters, averaging about eight members. The cubs are raised by the whole pack and fed by them all also. The wolf is famous for its howl, associated with the full moon, this also serves as a powerful message to other packs to stay clear as well as a homing beacon for pack members on the hunt.

The wolf is the deer's natural predator, which is why there are so many deer in Britain. In Celtic folklore the wolf is usually seen as the baddie, due to the Celt's high regard for livestock. In Norse mythology Odin owns two wolves and they are held in higher regard. The Native Americans view them as brothers, wearing their skins allowed them to get close enough to the buffalo to hunt them, prior to the introduction of horses. They were also held in high regard by the Romans, at least as fierce warriors. The wolf has also provided a lot of legends about the werewolf, the wolf is often used to represent the inner beast of man, locked in a constant battle between the civilised man and the barbarian, or the good and evil in us.

The medicine of the wolf is as a pathfinder and individual. The pathfinder is the teacher, the wolf teaches us to pass on our skills and talents to the future generations. The wolf also teaches us to respect the family and social groups we run with, but to remember to remain an individual within the group, able to shapeshift into a leader, leaving the pack and starting their own, when the time is right.

Animal Medicine and Physical Encounters

Totems and power animals are believed to derive their medicine not only from the individual animal itself, but also from a sort of universal consciousness, which is shared by all the members of that particular animal species like a sort of instinctive or genetic consciousness or memory. When you have an unusual encounter with one of that species' physical counterparts, you are experiencing the spirit of that species. It is as if the physical animal is channelling that spirit or being possessed by it. The physical animal may, as a result, act in an unusually friendly way for a time, then suddenly revert back to its normal everyday consciousness and become for no discernable reason very wary of you and run off. This is very similar to the process mediums and other psychics experience when channelling spirits. Sometimes they have no memory of what transpired or more often it will have felt hazy and dream-like.

8

THE SPIRIT WORLD

The Shaman's Spirit Helpers

Sidhe & Nature Spirits

Powerful Lakota Spirits

Powerful Siberian & Mongolian Spirits

Other Spiritual Guides and Guardians

Angels / Guardian Angels

Archangels

The Shaman's Spirit Helpers

It is said in Tungenese tribes that the spirits call you to be a Shaman and you ignore them at your peril, reluctant Shamen are often reported to die as a result of refusing to follow their vocation. This is a Tungenese belief; it is very unlikely that anyone will die as a result of refusing to follow a Shamanic path. In the modern Western world, our culture is very different to the tribal society that formed these beliefs many centuries ago.

All people have spirit guides, whether they are spiritually inclined or not, whether they believe or not. Our spirits know they are real and play an important role in our lives, we don't need to believe in them, they believe in us; we live a temporary material life, not them. The Norse called these guardian spirits Hamingjur, every man, woman and child had at least one; they were responsible for improving your luck; scraps of food and splashes of mead were dropped on the floor for them. This is a very common belief the world over, which is still regularly practiced by the Mongolian and Siberian people to name just a few. Modern-day Pagans also perform similar rituals at the festivals, although we don't tend to drop food and drink on the floor anymore, at least not inside. A bowl would be placed separately for them, it is also common to burn Incense in their honour. The Native Americans salute them with un-inhaled puffs of smoke and tobacco offerings.

It's interesting, that no matter how non-religious any culture in the world is, there is always recognition of ghosts and ancestral spirits within its culture.

A belief in Shamanism means there is always a belief in the spirit world, or at least an interest; just as there is always a recognition, awe and appreciation, of the sacredness of the natural world around us. Shamanism is a system that does not require you to have any blind faith, it is a belief system that unfolds to you and which proves to you that you should believe.

The spirit helpers you will encounter as a result of your interest in Shamanism will present themselves in a form you are comfortable with and you will understand, especially to start with. This does not mean this is their natural chosen form, sometimes it is, sometimes it isn't. Your spirit helper may take on many forms in their time with you; they will also attract other spirit helpers, as will your actions; it's surprising how often you may need some information and suddenly it's there, with little effort from you. You will notice things like this especially when healing, it is also quite common for other spirits to help you in situations you have been called to, often they are only present during your time there, when they are needed in other words. Sometimes you will gather a whole entourage of spirit helpers, they can take all shapes and forms. I mainly seem to have animal guides, though they are not all animals, many of these turn up in physical form, when their spirits are about, though I rarely see anything, its more of a feeling, when they are about. I tend to find I can see, when I need to, the rest of the time I don't. Necessity is a great provider of the needed assistance.

Many psychic people say they have a Native American guide; this is because part of their chosen role is to act in this capacity, after they leave this world. There is always one spirit guide or helper with you throughout your life, the same one. I assume they need to learn similar lessons to you from a different perspective, they must benefit from this commitment in some fashion. Often you have a male and female guide, these will present themselves on the right and left hand sides of you respectively. You may experience an amorous spirit, these are believed to be very powerful helper spirits, though can be a little frustrating to deal with.

Sometimes spirits will simply be close to you, sometimes they will enter you, this is fairly common during healing. It is important to remember if they do this, it is because you have allowed them to, you are always in charge and can retake control of your body at will. Our helpers or guides may be related to us, distant ancestors; they are less commonly recent relations, although it does happen; this is not always a healthy state and can indicate that the deceased loved one is unable to move on, as you are unable to let go, which can hinder their spiritual progress.

Though our recently deceased relatives will often hang around for a while to ensure we are okay. In some cultures (e.g. Mongolia) it is taboo to even mention their names as it is feared their spirit will become stuck in a limbo type state and that this will also damage the health of the living relative they are attached to, by draining their energy. Personally I can see this being a very difficult period for those trying to mourn the loss of their loved one.

Many spirit helpers and guides will come and go throughout your life, they are like friends in this life, some are always there, some are new, some drift away for various reasons and sometimes they come back.

Sidhe & Nature Spirits

To the Shaman, the natural world is filled with spirits, more than there are humans; not only the spirits of the ancestors, but also the spirits of nature. The Suld soul of humans resides in nature after death, so the natural world is full of these, not to mention the spirits of the plants, trees, rocks, animals, rivers, hills, lakes, springs, mountains, etc, etc. Collectively these are called nature spirits, they are present in all the Other Worlds, which is just as well as the one world would be very crowded. It's also just as well we can't see them all, all the time; can you imagine what a quiet, peaceful walk in the woods would be like; worse than any city at rush hour.

There are many types of nature spirit, I would suggest a separate study of them as there is not room here; I have only seen a few, so do not count myself as an expert in this field. I simply remain conscious of where I am and that others live here and have a greater right to be here than me, when walking through the woods; I always greet them with a flamboyant bow and state my reasons for being there; I also leave an offering for the things I take, usually tobacco, although it may be more accurate to say, the things that choose to accompany me.

We have all read fairy tales as children, but the fair folk, are not always like in the children's books. The Sidhe (pronounced She) is the traditional Celtic name for the fairy folk, and include such things as elves, dryads (tree spirits), nymphs (associated with fresh water), sylphs (associated with the air), gnomes (associated with the Earth), salamanders (associated with fire), willow o'the wisps (associated with marshes), traditional fairies (associated with flowers), dwarves (associated with stone), piskies or pixies (associated with fungi and the earth), knockers (associated with underground chambers, mines, etc). All of these nature spirits are reasonably friendly, none are hostile if you are respectful of them or where they live, they are like humans, treat them the same way, or better; they are a lot rarer to see. They may approach you, though not always visibly, think of them as spirits, they will become visible if they choose; they can be as curious of you, as you are of them. That said, they are very childlike in their attitudes, sometimes mischievous and playful, it depends on the type you encounter. This can be scary if you are not used to it, sometimes it is, even if you are. The Sidhe should always be treated with respect, they are magikal in nature and can cause trouble if you are unruly in their home.

A good book to read on the subject is '*Women who run with the Wolves*' by Clarissa Pinkola Estes; it is written from a female perspective, but is essentially a book about the more original fairy tales; which can be quite scary. Disney do not give an accurate portrayal of the fair folk; they can be very sensual, cunning and scary at times. Celtic mythology is full of heroes being lured into the fairy mounds, being unable to return home and worse. I will describe some of the Norse fairy folk as an example:

Dwarves are important in Norse traditions, four of them hold up the sky; they are called Nordhri (North), Austri (East), Sudhri (South) and Westri (West).They are described as small powerful men who create magikal items for the gods. They are ruled by Modsgnir, whose second in command is Durin. They live deep underground as the sun turns them to stone, their homeland is called Nidavellir. They have long fangs and claws for burrowing through the ground.

Alfar is the name given to the elves, of which there are 2 types:

Dark Alfar these live underground near the Dwarves at their homeland of Svartalfheim. These Alfar can turn at will into wolves with eagle's wings; they are not good or bad, simply neutral, much like humans, though they do avoid our company. They are experts in dark magic and are able to change size at will, they can appear very small or man-sized. They use elf shot, this is a magikal bow and arrow; the arrows whistle through the air, as tiny objects, they feel like a sting when they hit; they are poisonous and travel through the bloodstream to the heart, which takes 13 hours, once there they become full-sized arrows, which kill the victim. They also steal human babies, replacing them with changelings, who are soulless copies of the original baby. As they grow they do whatever they please with no regard of others, until recognized and killed. Nice, heh!

Light Alfar these, like their dark cousins, are also neutral in their nature, but tend to be a lot nicer. They are also highly skilled in the occult, but tend to use it to make magikal tools; their homeland is Alfheim (elf home) in Asgard; they were considered to be the real faery folk of legends. They could also change size at will, remain invisible if they choose and also used elf shot. They possessed butterfly-like wings at will. The Norse left offerings of cakes and milk out for them at night.

A natural hag stone, a stone with a natural hole through it, was considered a powerful ward (protection) against both dark and light alfar.

Kobolds these are helpful little hearth spirits, who live in people's homes and do chores in exchange for a warm place to sleep and food. They look like little mice-headed, furry men.

This doesn't mention, wraiths, banshees, giants, trolls, ogres, etc. As you can see some of the traditional faery folk are quite scary characters, not very Hans Christian Anderson.

Nature itself was seen as full of a variety of powerful spirits, differing from the nature spirits, sidhe and elementals (earth, air, fire and water). Although you are in a wood, full of different nature spirits, there was often a spirit of the place, the wood itself, this would have been classed as a Landvaetti (powerful land spirit). These were considered to be friendly; an angry one may cause earthquakes etc. They guarded the homes of the Norse and were left offerings in caves, carnes and hillocks. Such places were considered to be powerful places and were often named after gods and became places of worship, examples include:

Hof - house
Horgr - mound shrine/carne
Ve - sanctuary/open space
Lundr - grove
Akr - cultivated ground
Berg - rock
Ass - ridge
Ey - island
Haugr - mound

It is common practice among Shamen to find the head tree (usually the biggest, sometimes the most interesting looking) upon entering a wood and greet it. Tell it your intentions or business and ask for its blessings in your endeavours, leaving offerings, prior to going about your business. Assuming it says it's okay, sometimes it isn't. This is the same with visiting a stone circle; each stone is greeted as an individual, prior to entering the circle itself.

The Powerful Lakota Spirits

The Lakota have much in common with the other Native American tribes in their view of the universe, to them there are the Creator and 16 powerful spirits which are like the Creator's thoughts, together they form the Creator, these are ranking in order of importance:

Wakan Tanka is the Creator, sometimes called Tunkashila (Grandfather), he is all that is, was and shall be; he is not perfect, nothing is, but nothing else comes closer.

Wakan Akantu (the Highest Spirits)

Wi (Great Life Giver), is the Sun, without who there is no life.
Taku (The Power That Moves Everything), is motion, distributes Wi's Power; this is the power to grow and evolve.

271

Maka (All Mother), this is the Earth, mother of us all, she creates all we need, but we need to care for her also, sometimes called Unchi Maka (Grandmother).

Inyan (Rock), sometimes called Tunka, only the rocks and Wakan Tanka are immortal, the rocks contain the wisdom of all ages.

Wakan Kolaya (Spirit Friends)

Hanhepi Wi (Night Sun), this is the Wife of Wi, the moon, she is the supernatural in all women.

Tate (The Wind), he is Wi's brother and is associated with the Northern Lights, he is the Father of the Four Winds of the Four Directions. He controls the seasons and watches over the ghost trail, which leads to the spirit land.

Unk (Father of all Evil), he is contention and passion, he is the negative aspect of the thunder being, it is he who makes man kill, etc.

Wakinyan (Thunder Being/Thunder Bird), he is thunder and lightning, he creates Electrical energy; he eats his children and they become smaller versions of himself. Dreaming of him creates a Heyoka, a contrary, back to front person.

Wakan Kuya (Lesser Mysteries)

Tatanka (Buffalo Spirit), that which reaches highest, that which excels; not just a buffalo, the giver of food, health and life.

Tob Tob (Bear Spirit), also called Mato, not just a bear spirit. The wisest spirit of them all, he created the animals, teaches the Shaman, heals wounds, stands for love and bravery.

Wani (The 4 Direction Wind), he makes the weather and energizes things; he represents the Powers of the 4 Directions (Circle) and is a messenger for those more powerful than he.

Yumni Wi (The Sea Goddess), she represents the power of the feminine and maintains balance in the world. She is also the goddess of love, sports and games.

Wakanlapi (Like Something Sacred)

These are the 4 Souls of Everything, like the 3 Souls mentioned earlier:

Niya (the Spirit), the personification of Life, sometimes called the Breath of Life; he lives in us all, leaving upon death, he is the guardian spirit who talks to humans and gives a newborn its first breath.

Nagi (a Presence or Ghost), he is what we think of as a ghost, one of the 4 Souls, he is our shadow, always present, immortal, he knows what has been and what shall be and goes with us into the spirit world upon death.

Sichun (the Intellect), embodies our knowledge and gives us the power to guard against evil, but this power has both a positive and negative side to it, as does everything.

Yumni (the Whirlwind), this is all that is immaterial, the unborn orphan, the swirling winds, poltergeists, potential unused, spare energy, impish messenger of the supernatural.

These are the main spirits of the Native American (Lakota) traditions; there are 444 Native American tribes, each has variations within its belief system, different names etc, but they all have a similar idea. There are many other spirits, as the Wakan Akantu and the Wakan Kolaya are also able to create beings; some are positive, some are negative.

Powerful Mongolian & Siberian Spirits

The Mongolian and Siberian Shamanic traditions are very similar in many ways to the Native American tradition; this is not surprising as the Native Americans largely come from the same group and share common ancestry; the Mongolian Life Cycle or Circle of Life is based on the Water Cycle.

Tenger Etseg (Father Heaven) is the universe, the Creator and Sustainer of Balance, the weather is seen as a direct manifestation of his disposition; lightning-struck areas are seen as either Tenger's displeasure or an indication of a spiritual power, he resides in the Upper World, although he is all things. The sun (Fire) and moon (Water) are his eyes, although they are also seen as 2 sisters.

273

Gazar Eej (Mother Earth) is the wife of Tenger Etseg; she is the planet itself and mother of all who live upon it.

Umai (the Womb Goddess) is the daughter of Tenger Etseg and Gazar Eej; she is a fertility goddess who sends Ami souls from the Upper World into babies being born.

Golomto Eej (Spirit of Fire) is another of their daughters, she was begotten by flint and iron, she is seen as the re-enactment of the original union between Heaven and Earth; fire is central to all rituals and life, reminding us of the light of Father Heaven and the nurturing nature of Mother Earth.

Tenger

These are the most powerful Upper World spirits, who belong to 4 groupings associated with the 4 Directions. Don't confuse them with Tenger Etseg.

Erleg Khan (Son of Heaven) is the son of Heaven and Earth, he is Master Spirit of the Underworld, judge of the Sun's souls, determiner of future incarnations.

Atai Ulaan Tenger, Chief Spirit of the 44 Eastern Tenger; he represents the destructive aspect of the Universe, he can also kill Suns souls if they were very evil during their lifetime; he is invoked from the East. The Eastern Tenger created the eagle, chaos, animals we are forbidden to eat and the disease spirits.

Ulgen Khan (High Heaven), another Son of Heaven and Earth, he is Erleg's younger brother, he sent mankind fire and the first Shaman.

Han Hormasta Tenger, Chief of the 55 Western Tenger and the Upper World; he is invoked from the West. The Western Tenger created man, order, dogs and all the food animals.

Uha Loson Khan, is the Lord of the Lus Water Spirits, he is invoked from the South.

Huherdei Mergen Tenger or Tatai Tenger, is the controller of violent weather, lightning and tornadoes, he is invoked from the North.

Khan Sogto Tenger, Head of the 77 Tenger of the Northern Skies, his arrows are lightning and he rides through the heavens in a chariot drawn by winged horse.

Aligan Sagaan Tenger, the Leader of the 99 Tenger of the Southern Skies.

Ubgen Yuruul Tenger, the eldest and most mysterious of the male deities; forefather to all of the Tenger; responsible for making the number 3 one of the basic principles of shamanic and magikal practice; not very active in man's affairs presently.

Esege Malaan Tenger, the highest ranking Male Tenger, regarded as responsible for the appearance of mankind.

Shargai Noyon Tenger descended to Earth to live in the Sayan Mountains in order to establish the present order of Siberian Shamanism.

Buuluur Sagaan Tenger, the Shamanic protector and spiritual father of the Tenger and Shamans and Elders; the Great Shaman of the Heavens.

Golto Sagaan Tenger (White Tenger of the Gol), Gol means the centre of existence, represented by the World Tree and Fire. He is the patron of all religions and helper of all religious leaders, regardless of their tradition. He is the bringer of the 8 Wisdoms of the World and leader of the 1,000 benevolent Burhan (Nature) Spirits, who assist in magikal work.

Mnazan Gurme Toodei, Ancestress of the Western Tenger, possessor of the greatest power and knowledge of all Tenger.

Mayas Hara Toodei, Ancestress of the Eastern Tenger.

The Ancestors

The Ancestors are very important to the Mongolians and Siberians; and are invoked daily with Mother Earth and Father Heaven. They are not always literal ancestors, Blue Wolf, Red Deer, Prince Father Bull and Father Bear are all important ancestors, despite being in animal form.

There are a great many other spirits also in this tradition, some good, some not.

Other Spiritual Guides and Guardians

We have already looked at the powerful spirits, our ancestors, the Sidhe (fairy folk) have also been mentioned; we have also mentioned the spirits of magikal tools, the Ezen's; now many of the totems and power animals have been added to this list, remember this is not a complete list. However the list of spiritual beings which populate the Shamanic universe does not end there.

In Animism, from which Shamanism is derived, it must be remembered that all things are viewed as having a contactable consciousness. This means that the world which surrounds us is full of spiritual beings, which take many different forms.

The trees all have their own individual spirits, called dryads, but they would also share a universal spirit for that species of tree, in much the same way as the animals do. The same could be said for all flora and fauna, including the human species. The mineral kingdom is the same, we are all aware that crystals are a bit special and have many qualities associated with them, but ordinary stones also share special qualities. Many Shamen from different cultures have what are collectively called 'Power Objects', these are often in the form of stones with special powers the Shaman is able to tap into, often for locating lost things or healing. Meteorites and other space rocks are especially considered to have these special qualities.

In Mongolia and Siberia it is believed that meteorites (Tektite or Moldavite) transport new Udhas to the world (Udhas are the main helper spirits of Shamen, they choose, instruct and initiate the new Shaman into the Shamanic Path). It is believed that if a 'non Shaman' steeps the meteorite in liquor and then drinks it, the Udha Spirit can enter the person and enable them to become a 'true Shaman'.

In many other cultures this process is taken a step further and many forms of tribal art, such as African and Aboriginal, include the insertion of small quartz pebbles and similar into the Shaman's skin, resulting in raised patterns on the skin; or the swallowing of small quartz pebbles and other objects. The idea is the same, to take the essence of that object into you, to absorb and become at one with it.

So the world is full of potential power objects and helper spirits, including some less obvious ones, a good example of this is your car. There are also other more well-known spiritual beings which you can contact and will be able to help you in your Shamanic and healing work.

Angels

Angels are usually associated with Christianity, but they are older than this, Angels are basically a more modern term for Guardian Spirits or Guardian Angels, as they are more usually called today. There are two main types of Angels, Guardian Angels and Archangels:

Guardian Angels

We all have Guardian Angels, though we don't all call them that, often they are called luck or coincidence. Guardian Angels, Guardian Spirits or Hamingjur's (Norse guardian spirits), are basically spirits that look out for our well-being from the spirit world. Sometimes we call them our higher selves, but this is not really correct. They are more likely to be the spirits of those we have known who have passed over, parents, grand parents, brothers, sisters, husbands, wives, children, friends and ancestors.

All the people we have shared our lives with, remain connected to us. They drop in from time to time to keep an eye on us, they have their own lives in the spirit realms, in many ways they are still in a similar relationship with us, as when they were alive. These are often called guides or helpers; they are not necessarily genetically connected to us, though they have probably been very close to us at some point during our various incarnations. They will usually have skills and experience of a similar type to those we are developing during our present lives and will have walked a very similar path to us, maybe even with us.

In spiritual and Shamanic work they will help us to develop our skills, act as channels for energy, teach those other spirits wanting our attention how best to communicate with us, arrange circumstances, with the help of other people's Guardian Spirits, so we are in the right place at the right time for whatever reason. They are our unseen friends and family, they try and do what they can to assist us. Sometimes they may make mistakes, at least from our point of view, but they will usually have a clearer view of the big picture than we do, as a result they will act in accordance with what is best for us, which isn't always the same as what we think it is. It may be that they are like spiritual working partners; next time around, we may be their guardian spirits, whilst they manifest as physical beings.

There will also be a true Guardian Spirit or true Guardian Angel who has chosen to watch over us as part of their role in the spirit realm, these guardians are usually spiritual beings, who spend all their time as spiritual entities, rather than manifesting as physical beings. It may be more accurate to describe them as the pure spiritual aspect of ourselves which doesn't manifest. They are not us; we take on various forms, circumstances, families, cultures and personalities depending on how we are formed from our three souls (which change from incarnation to incarnation) and what we are here to learn during our current incarnation. They are nearer to our true self than we are, we are more like a reflection of that true self, or one of their spiritual children.

Archangels

There are several Archangels, the best known are Michael, Gabriel, Raphael and Uriel. Archangels are similar to the Pagan gods in their powers, each one being responsible for certain aspects or realms of life. Archangels do not normally get personally involved with us, but instead send other angels who work for them, to listen to and resolve our problems. These Archangels will have a greater understanding of the 'big picture' than will our own Guardian Angels and will act in accordance with the truth of that, rather than our own individual whims; these in turn will probably advise and work through our own Guardian Angels.

Archangels, like true angels, are non sexual beings, they do not reproduce, so are neither male nor female in their energy, but a balance of the two. They do seem to appear as masculine forms in most cases, though this is probably largely to do with the patriarchal belief system with which they are most strongly associated. It is far more likely that this level of spiritual being will manifest in a form which we will most easily recognise, so when a Christian may see the Archangel Michael appear in a vision, a Pagan may see the god Lugh. The Archangels are connected with the Elements and the Star Signs they are governed by:

Michael - Fire - South - Aries, Leo, Sagittarius

Gabriel - Water - West - Cancer, Scorpio, Pisces

Raphael - Air - East - Gemini, Libra, Aquarius

Uriel - Earth - North - Taurus, Virgo, Capricorn

Archangel Michael

Michael is the angel of courage, strength and protection; he is a warrior and his symbols are the sword and deep blue cloak, he will be able to assist you with physical and psychic protection, faith, developing leadership skills, focus and the will to achieve your goals successfully.

Archangel Gabriel

Gabriel is the angel of harmony, beauty, purification and guidance: his symbol is the chalice and the colour green. he will be able to assist you with hope, guidance, intuition, love, purity, order and the discipline to be able to move forward in your life, especially when you feel stuck.

Archangel Raphael

Raphael is the angel of healing, abundance, creativity, truth and vision; his symbols are the wand or staff and the colour white or yellow. He will be able to assist you with healing, nurturing, empathy, compassion, creativity and psychic development helping you to become more connected with the universal consciousness.

Archangel Uriel

Uriel is the angel of peace, wisdom, transformation and forgiveness; his symbol is the shield and the colours red, purple and gold. He will be able to help you with developing forgiveness, peace of mind and heart, overcoming fears, learning new skills, knowledge and wisdom and in developing a desire to be of spiritual service to others.

The angels can be of help to you even if you do not consider yourself a Christian; the energies they represent are far older than any religions.

9
GODS & GODDESSES

Celtic & Norse Gods & Goddesses

Celtic and Norse Gods and Goddesses

Given below are the brief details of the Norse (indicated with 'N') and Celtic (indicated with 'C') gods and goddesses and their 19 spheres of influence. These realms of influence are rough guides to the sort of help you may be able to receive from these deities; the realms are categorized into subjects which you are likely to encounter in Shamanic/Animistic practice:

Shamanism

(C) **Cernunnos, Herne** or **Green Man**; this is probably the oldest and best known Shaman God, he is the antlered figure in a meditation posture, on the Gundestrup Cauldron, surrounded by animals, often depicted with a goat-horned serpent (representing the power of the land/nature) in one hand and a torc (representing the power of society/leadership) in the other, he is also on the cover of this book. He is sometimes shown as having a red deer stag's head, sometimes shown as made of leaves; he represents the balance and union of man and nature. He is said to sit at the base of the World Tree, which was an oak to the Celts. In cave paintings from the Stone Age he is known as the sorcerer. He is the best god to contact for all Shamanic work, he is the male equivalent of Mother Earth.

The Sorcerer

Cernunnos

(N) Odin, Woden, Wotan, Allfather; Odin is the Norse Shaman God, he has over 100 names; he also appears in as many guises. He is the chief of the Norse gods as well as the god of war, shamanism, poetry, wisdom, dead warriors, hanged men and runes. He is a cunning god, who doesn't always tell the complete truth. He will trick you into doing something good for you or others, even if you didn't intend to. He lives in Valhalla (Hall of the Slain) and owns another called Valaskjalf (Shelf of the Slain). He sees all, with the help of his two ravens Hugin (Thought) and Muninn (Memory), who fly through the three worlds and report back to him.He is always seeking after knowledge, especially if it can prevent Ragnarok.

Odin often appears to man, usually in a wide-brimmed hat pulled over one eye, which was sacrificed for a drink from the Fountain of Wisdom, and wearing a blue mantle. He sacrificed himself to himself, when he hung on the World Tree for nine days and nights, without food or water and with a spear piercing his side, in order to discover the runes. He has many treasures as well as his power animals the ravens, he has two wolves Geri (Greedy) and Freki (Voracious); he also possesses the Mead of Poetry, Sleipnir the eight-legged horse, Gungnir a magikal Spear that never misses and returns to your hand, Draupnir a solid gold arm band, which reproduces eight of itself every ninth night, which fall to Earth. Wednesday is named after him and he also controls half the Valkyries, associated with the ash.

(N) Freya, Gullveig, Heid, is the twin sister of Frey, daughter of Njord. She is the Goddess of Fertility, love, passion, beauty and Death. Odin made her the Goddess of Death in punishment for sleeping with four dwarves to secure the Brisingamen Necklace, which is the magikal equivalent of the Jormungand the Midgard Serpent, an enormous serpent who encircles the world with his tail in his mouth; bringing shame to herself and her family. As a result she now controls half the Valkyries, powerful warrioresses who travel the battlefields collecting the heroic slain to form Odin's Warrior Army and feast at Valhalla. Her hall is Sessrumnir (Rich in Seats) on the plain of Folkvangar (Field of Folk).

Freya belongs to the Vanir, but she and her twin brother live as hostages with the Aesir; a traditional Norse method for maintaining peaceful relations with a former enemy. She is often Odin's mistress, much loved by all, she cries tears of solid gold. She is a Goddess of all Magikal Arts, including Shamanism, Witchcraft, healing and prophecy. She also owns many magikal treasures, a box containing her magikal secrets, a pair of slippers which make her invisible, a chariot pulled by two giant cats Bygul (Bee gold or Honey) and Trjegul (Tree gold or Amber). A magikal boar Hildskjalf (Battle Pig), lethal and fast; a magikal cloak of falcon's skin, which enables her to shapeshift into a falcon. She foretells the future of all babies and is sometimes thought to have Friday named after her. Married to the Sun God Odur, who got bored of this static life and wandered off, greatly distressing Freya, who could love no other, she searched high and low for him and eventually found and returned with him.

(N) Volund
(C) Weyland
(C) Goibnui, Gofannon

Healing

(C) Bride, Brigit, Brighid, St. Brigit, Goddess of fosterage, healing, fertility, midwives, doctors, learning, inspiration, smithcraft, arts and crafts. She is so well liked the Christian Church even made her a saint, whereas Pagan deities are usually made into demons. She has many healing wells named after her and is a strong protectress and teacher. Her symbol is the eternal flame, which was a real fire, maintained in Kildare for centuries by Pagan priestesses and Christian nuns alike. She is celebrated at the Festival of Imbolc on 2nd February; the Romans also celebrated the Festival of the Hedgehog on this day and connected her to their Goddess Juno (Queen of Heaven), so I feel they are her power animal.

(N) Frigga, Frigg, Jorth, Mother Goddess of caring, nurturing, healing, fertility, faithfulness, nature, occult knowledge, midwives, child-birth and farseeing. She is Odin's wife and the only other god permitted to sit on

Odin's throne, from which he can see all things. Her hall is called Fensalir (Water Halls), she is associated with the elm tree and water; she looks especially favourably on women and children. She often disobeys Odin's orders and advises mankind via one of her handmaidens, she is more trustworthy than her husband. She lends her name to the female act of masturbation and Friday is named after her. She is the mother of Baldur.

(N) Eir, Goddess of Healing and one of Freya's handmaidens.

(C) Nodens, God of Healing, his magikal hounds are believed to be able to cure the sick.

(C) Cliodhna, Goddess of Beauty and Healing; She owns three magikal birds who sing to the sick, lulling them into sleep and curing them in the process.

(C) Airmid, Goddess of Healing, she is responsible for medicinal plants and herbalism; she is also the guardian of a spring which brings the dead back to life.

(C) Dian Cecht, God of Healing, ruled the waters that restored life to the old and dying gods, when Nuada (Celtic Hero) lost his hand in battle, Dian Cecht made him a silver one to replace it.

(N) Freya
(N) Odin

Nature (Land)

(N) Nerthus is an Earth Mother Goddess of antiquity; she is one of the original Vanir, however Nerthus, is more often seen as Freya and Frey together in one form; a nine yearly festival held at Uppsala was in her honour, as a single embodiment of the twins.

(N) Frey, is the twin brother of Freya and like his sister is also well loved by all. Frey is a god of fertility, peace and plenty. Ground dedicated to him is sacred and it is illegal to bear arms or fight upon it. He also owned many treasures, including Skidbladnir, a magikal ship that always had a favourable wind, was big enough to carry all the gods and could be folded up and put in your pocket; a chariot pulled by a golden boar, made by the dwarves, called Gullinbursti (Golden Bristled), whose bristles were solid gold. Gullinbursti could run as fast as a horse and could be slaughtered every night to feed the gods and be well and healthy the next morning.

(N) Sif, is a Goddess of fertility, beauty, fruitfulness and plenty. She has long golden hair and is Thor's wife and the mother of Magni, Thor's young son, who despite being 4 is already stronger than Thor.

(N) Skadi, she was originally a Giantess whose family was killed by Odin when he stole the Mead of Poetry; As compensation she was allowed to marry any god she wished, but she could only choose by looking at their feet; she chose the most beautiful ones, hoping they were Baldur's, but they turned out to be Njord's. They were married, but it didn't work out, she loved the mountains and Njord loved the ocean, eventually they decided to live separately and she became the goddess of hunting and skiing.

(C) Blodeuwedd, she was created from flowers by the magicians Gwydion and Math as a wife for a Celtic god Lleu llaw Gyffes (Lugh), who was unable to marry a woman, due to a curse. She fell in love with another man and was turned into an owl as punishment; she is a Goddess of the Wilds and Nature, of the boundaries of the Otherworlds and wrongful persecution.

(C) Rhiannon, Rigantona, the daughter of the King of the Underworld, wrongfully accused of killing her own child; she was later vindicated. She is the Goddess of Horses and the Sacred Land; in Celtic times a new king had to copulate with a mare, as a sign of his pledge to look after the land. She also looks after those wrongfully accused, over-burdened with responsibility and women who have suffered miscarriage.

(C) Tigernonos, Teyrnon, he is the husband of Rhiannon, another god of the sacred land and of shepherds, he is also good for primal wisdom, empowerment and guidance.

(C) Belenus, Bel, Bile, God of Light and the Sun, also sheep and cattle welfare, fertility, his Bel fires are central to the celebrations of all the Pagan (country dweller) festivals especially Beltaine 1st May.

(C) Dagda, Dagde, DaGodevas, is a Father God and God of the Earth, the male version of Mother Earth; he is a formidable warrior and skilled craftsman, his club can restore life as well as kill. His symbols are a bottomless Cauldron of Plenty and a harp which rules the seasons.

(C) Danu, Anu, Don, the Universal Mother and mother of Dagda.

(C) Epona, Goddess of horses, mules, cavalry men, fertility and the land. Her symbols are the horse, of which there was a Celtic cult, as the horse was as important to the Celts as it is to the Mongolians, and the Horn of Cornucopia.

(N) Odin
(N) Freya
(N) Frigga
(N) Thor

Nature (Sea)

(N) Njord, the God of fertility, sea, wind, waves, fish and chief god of the Vanir; father of Freya and Frey; lives in a underwater hall called Noatun (anchorage).

(C) Dylan, God of the Sea, brother of Lleu; he is reputed to have slipped into the sea at birth to avoid his mother's curses.

(N) Aegir, God of the Sea, his hall is under the sea near the Island of Hlesey; his moods are changeable, like the ocean. He is married to Ran and they have nine daughters who move the waves and bring drowned sailors to his hall.

(N) Ran, Goddess of the Sea, wife of Aegir, owns a fishing net, which always catches fish.

(C) Manannan, Manawyddan

Protection

(N) Thor, Odin's eldest son, God of the Common Man, Thunder, Lightning, Law and Order, Things (Law Courts), Keeper of Oaths, Agriculture, Rain, Fair Weather and Protection. He is very strong and powerful, often has clashes with the Midgard Serpent, occasionally pulling it partially out of the water. He battled old age and almost won. He owns two halls Bilskirnir (lightning) and Thrudvangar (might), as well as several treasures, Mjollnir (lightning) a short handled war hammer that never misses, returns to hand and strikes with the power of a lightning bolt; a girdle of might, iron gauntlets which allow him to use any weapon, an iron staff which grows as large or small as wanted and is pulled through the heavens on a chariot drawn by two goats Tanngnost (tooth grinder) and Tanngrisni (tooth gnasher); associated with the oak tree.

(C) Taranis, God of Life and Lightning, his symbols are the Wheel and the Lightning bolt; Celtic version of Thor.

(C) Teutates, God of War, Fertility and Wealth, he was a Chief god of the Celts and human sacrifices were often made to him, similar to Odin.

(N) Tiw, Tyr, another of Odin's sons; god of courage, honour, bravery, law and order, Things and Oaths; similar to Thor. He is known as 'one handed', as he sacrificed his hand, to gain the trust of Fenris Wolf, an enormous wolf monster which was wreaking chaos; the other gods then bound Fenris with unbreakable cord, to keep it under control; as a result Fenris bit off Tiw's hand. He owns a magikal sword that fought of its own free will, though he is reputed to have lost it, due to a Frost Giantess's unrequited love.

(N) Heimdall, God of Protection and Warning, son of Aegir and Ran, he guards the Bifrost Rainbow Bridge, has a magikal sword and the sight of an eagle.

(N) Honir, God of Bravery, although a bit dim-witted, exchanged as one of the hostages for Freya and Frey, which led to problems for Mimir, the second hostage.

(N) Odin
(N) Frey
(N) Freya
(N) Frigga

(C) Arawn, God of the Underworld of Annwn, he leads the Wild Hunt, which strays into our world at Samhain; he is a powerful protector who patrols places which are unsafe for travellers and grants access to ancestral wisdom.

(C) Bran, God of Boundaries, Inspiration, Guardianship, Protector of Travellers and Patron of Storytellers. He is associated with the raven, his head is supposed to be buried in the Tower of London, beneath White Hill, to serve as protection against invasion, which is also why the ravens are there.

(C) Lugh, Llew, Lleu, the God of Light, Sun, Warmth, Inspiration; Patron of Poets, Artists and all talented people; he is reputed to be 'Master of all Trades, Jack of None'. He is also a great warrior, known as 'skillful hand'; he is celebrated on the festival of Lughnasadh, August 1st; married to Blodeuwedd, he is the brother of Dylan. Arianrhod, his mother, cursed him, with no name, would not allow him to bear arms or marry.

(C) Macha, a Goddess of Battle, she is associated with a mirror maze, as a sign of carrying the soul beyond life, she is apparently not very friendly to mankind, but will help in times of great need; strangely, thought of as being an earlier version of Bride, or another aspect of her.

(C) Belatu-Cadros, God of War and the destruction of enemies, his name means 'fair shining one'. Probably, another name for Bel.

(C) Gwydion, God of Warriors and Magicians, brother to Arianrhod, father of Lugh and Dylan.

(C) Cernunnos

Creativity

(N) Volund, God of Inventions, Craftsmanship, Blacksmiths and Rebirth.

(N) Bragi, God of Poetry, Eloquence, Songs, Music, Wisdom and Skalds (Bards); he is the son of Odin and Frigga and the husband of Idunn. He greets the new arrivals to Asgard, by singing of their deeds, before they settle into Gimli the hall of Odin's Chosen. Source of the word bragging.

(N) Bil, Goddess of Weaving, Thread, Spells and Magic.

(N) Loki, is the sworn brother and friend of Odin; he is not a God, he is a Fire Giant; he could be classed as the God of Trickery and Deceit; he starts off as a practical joker, who causes lots of problems, but as he ages he becomes more and more wicked. It is Loki who brings about Ragnarok and the fall of the gods, he is married to Sigyn, but has an affair with a giantess who gives birth to the monsters Fenris Wolf, Jormungand and Hel, Queen of the Dead. He is here because as well as being an important part of Norse mythology, he was a good inventor; he invented the first fishing net.

(C) Goibnui, Gofannon, God of Blacksmiths and Patron of Craftspeople, Metal Workers and Weapon Smiths. His job was to shape the souls and swords of warriors.

(C) Weyland, God of Blacksmiths, Farriers and Rebirth he shod the horses of the gods, he also conducts Shamanic initiations, in which the would-be Shaman's spirit is ripped apart and then re-smelted and shaped by Weyland's hammer, into a form better suited to the rigours of Shamanism.

(C) Manawyddan, Manannan, God of the Sea; Patron of Druids and Craftsmen. He had the gift of prophecy and was skillful and procreative.

(C) Belisama, Goddess of Light, Fire, Forging and Craft; wife of Belenus.
(N) Odin
(N) Freya
(N) Sif
(C) Lugh
(C) Bran
(C) Bride
(C) Dagda
(C) Arianrhod

Wisdom & Knowledge

(C) Ceridwen is best known as the Dark (Hidden) Goddess; her name means witch/sorcerer; she is the brewer and keeper of the Cauldron of Knowledge and Inspiration, the initiator of Taliesin, the Shaman and poet, forerunner of Merlin. She is both a creator and initiator, she is known as the 'Old One'. She is in charge of rebirth and growth through change and she knows what needs to be known. She is associated with the wolf and the hazelnut.

(N) Mimir, God of Wisdom and Guardian of the Fountain of Knowledge; he is more of a head than a god, when the Aesir sent the dim-witted god Honir, as a hostage in exchange for the Vanir hostages Frey and Freya, the

Vanir were so insulted and annoyed that when Mimir arrived they beheaded him and sent his head back to Odin; Odin brought the head to life and set it as Guardian of the Fountain of Knowledge, lest his great wisdom be lost.

(C) Ogma, Ogmios, God of Scholars and Eloquence; he invented the secret Druidic tree alphabet known as the Ogham, which also worked as a sign language on the hands; these teachings held his audience in awe it is implied, as he is said to have gold chains hanging from his tongue which he fixed to his followers' ears.

(N) Odin
(N) Freya
(N) Tiw
(N) Bragi
(N) Frey
(N) Nerthus
(N) Baldur
(N) Frigga
(C) Bride
(C) Gwydion
(C) Math
(C) Manawyddan
(C) Cernunnos
(C) Tigernonos

Blessings

(N) Baldur, God of Light, Sun, Purity, Beauty, Wisdom, Gentleness, Kindness and Honest Judgment; the most beloved of all the gods. Son of Odin and Frigga, he lived in a hall called Breidablik (broad splendour), he was troubled by dreams of his death, so his mother, Frigga, set about ensuring it would never happen. She went to ask all living things not to harm her son; this they all gladly agreed, so loved was he. Only the mistletoe was overlooked, seemingly so harmless. It became a favourite sport of the gods to hurl things at Baldur, who was now impervious to harm. However Loki discovered this weakness and fashioned a dart from the mistletoe, this he gave to Hodur the Blind, God of the Blind and Hermits, who never got to play this new game, he guided Hodur's hand and the dart struck and killed Baldur.

Hermod, God of Honour and Lost Causes, was sent to Nifleheim to retrieve Baldur, but Hel said he could only return if all living things cried for his loss. Once more Frigga set out and all things willingly cried for his loss, except for a wicked old giantess (Loki in disguise). So Baldur had to stay in Hel's Court.

When Loki was discovered as the culprit, he was then bound over sharp rocks by Narvis's (Loki's son) entrails and a serpent was set to drip venom into his eyes forever. This was one of the signs of the coming of Ragnarok.

(N) **Freya**
(N) **Frey**
(N) **Odin**
(N) **Frigga**
(N) **Thor**
(N) **Njord**
(N) **Nerthus**
(N) **Gefion**
(C) **Bride**
(C) **Lugh**
(C) **Ceridwen**
(C) **Bran**
(C) **Bel**
(C) **Dagda**

Abundance

(C) **Rosmerta**, Goddess of Fertility and Wealth; her symbols are a staff with two snakes carved on it and the Horn of Cornucopia.

(C) **Boann**, the Goddess of Bounty and Fertility, her symbol is the sacred white cow. She is the wife of Nechtan, a water deity. Apparently she had an affair with the Dagda though and a son was born; to prevent accusations they arranged for the Sun to stop for nine months, so that their son was conceived and born on the same day.

(N) **Frey**
(N) **Freya**
(N) **Nerthus**
(N) **Njord**
(N) **Odin**
(N) **Aegir**
(N) **Ran**
(N) **Frigga**
(N) **Baldur**
(N) **Sif**
(N) **Gefion**
(C) **Dagda**
(C) **Epona**
(C) **Rhiannon**
(C) **Bel**
(C) **Teutates**

Divination

(C) **Arianrhod**, Goddess of the Moon and Destiny, daughter of Don, sister of Gwydion, given the position of a foot holder for Math, so a Virgin, although she did give birth to Lugh and Dylan when raped by Math's nephews, she cursed Lugh when he was born as revenge on men, Dylan escaped into the sea. Her symbol is the Silver Wheel.

(N) Vor, Goddess of Divination, she knows all secrets and all futures.

(N) Freya
(N) Odin
(N) Frigga
(C) Ogma
(C) Gwydion
(C) Manawyddan

Dreams

(N) Nott
(N) Odin
(N) Freya
(C) Ceridwen
(N) Baldur
(N) Frigga
(C) Cernunnos
(N) Njord
(C) Arianrhod
(C) Arawn

Love & Sex

(N) Sigyn, Goddess of Forgiveness, Love and Loyalty. Loki's unfortunate wife; throughout Loki's punishment, Sigyn stayed by his side, catching the serpent's venom in a bowl; whenever she had to empty it, the venom fell in Loki's eyes making him convulse with pain and the ground shake.

(N) Sjofn, Goddess of Passion, Sex and Lust. What can you say?

(N) Lofn, Goddess of Illicit Affairs.

(N) Eostre, Goddess of Spring, Dancing and Fertility. Easter is named after her, her symbols are the hare (Easter Bunny) and the serpent's egg (Easter Egg).

(N) Nanna, Goddess of Love and Devotion; wife of Baldur, she died of a broken heart when he died.

(C) Bres, God of Fertility and Agriculture.

(C) Aine, Goddess of Love and Fertility; later she became the Irish Fairy Queen.

(C) Branwen, Goddess of Love and Beauty. After the death of her brother Bran, due to a war caused by her husband the Irish King Matholwch, she died of a broken heart.

(N) Frey
(N) Freya
(N) Sif
(N) All the Vanir
(C) Teutates
(C) Rosmerta
(C) Boann
(C) Danu

Shapeshifting

(C) Math, eminent Magician and Lord of North Wales; brother of Don, the Welsh Mother Goddess. He could only rule when his feet were in the lap of a virgin, except when at war. When he returned from battle and discovered Arianrhod raped by his nephews he turned them into a stag and hind, then a boar and sow and finally a wolf and she wolf, presumably they were all on heat.

(N) Freya
(N) Odin
(N) Frigga
(C) Cernunnos
(C) Blodeuwedd

Justice

(N) **Forsetti**, the son of Baldur and Nanna, he is the God of Justice.

(N) **Syn**, Goddess of Justice, invoked by defendants at trials.

(N) **Var**, Goddess of Oaths and Punishment of Oath Breakers.

(N) Thor
(N) Tiw
(N) Baldur
(N) Frigga
(N) Freya
(N) Hermod
(C) Blodeuwedd
(C) Rhiannon
(C) Taranis
(C) Arianrhod
(C) Math

Journeys & Travel

(N) Odin
(N) Freya
(N) Frigga
(N) Skadi
(N) Njord

(N) Aegir
(C) Blodeuwedd
(C) Arawn
(C) Cernunnos
(C) Rhiannon
(C) Epona
(C) Bran

(C) **Sucellus**, God of Agriculture and Forests, he also ferries the dead to the afterlife; his symbols are the hammer and a dog.

Peace

(N) Baldur
(N) Hodur
(N) Mimir
(N) Forsetti
(N) Freya
(N) Frey
(N) Honir
(N) Sigyn
(N) Thor
(N) Nerthus

(N) **Nott**, Goddess of Night, Inspiration, Peace and Rest. She married Annar (Water) and gave birth to Jord, Thor's Mother. She also married Delling (red elf of Dawn) and had a son called Dagr (Day).

Empowerment

(N) Thor
(N) Odin
(N) Tiw

298

(N) Freya
(N) Frey
(N) Volund
(N) Frigga
(C) Ceridwen
(C) Weyland
(C) Tigernonos
(C) Taranis

Magik

(N) Freya
(N) Odin
(N) Frigga
(N) Volund
(N) Thor
(C) Gwydion
(C) Math
(C) Arianrhod
(C) Ceridwen
(C) Ogma

Change

(N) **Magni**, Thor's young son, who replaces him after Ragnarok.

(N) **Modi**, another of Thor's sons, who helps Magni after Ragnarok.

(N) **Vidir**, Odin's son who replaces him after Ragnarok.

(N) **Vali**, another of Odin's sons who helps Vidir after Ragnarok.

(N) **Honir**

(N) Baldur
(N) Hodur
(N) Nanna
(C) Ceridwen

Elementals

Air: KARI
(N) Thor
(N) Odin
(N) Freya
(N) Tiw
(N) Heimdall

Water: HIER
(N) Aegir
(N) Njord
(N) Ran
(N) Mimir
(C) Dylan

Fire: LODUR
(N) Baldur
(N) Loki
(N) Volund
(C) Weyland
(N) Freya

Earth: YMIR
(N) Nerthus
(N) Frey
(N) Freya
(N) Nanna
(N) Sif
(N) Frigga
(C) Epona
(C) Rhiannon
(C) Blodeuwedd
(C) Tigernonos

These Gods and Goddesses are not limited to these realms, they all have many tasks and responsibilities. There are also many other gods and Goddesses of other cultures, who perform the same functions; there are also other gods and goddesses whose names and roles have sadly been lost over the years. These gods and goddesses are also not ranked in any particular order of hierarchy.

10

SHAMANIC JOURNEYS

Altered States of Consciousness

In a normal state of consciousness your mind and body act in harmony together, working at quite a quick rate, this is called a Beta state of consciousness. However when you are practicing meditation and other forms of altered consciousness, your mind switches to an Alpha, Theta or Delta state of consciousness. These levels of consciousness are far more relaxed than the Beta state; Alpha equates to gentle relaxation or light sleep; Theta is a deeper state of relaxation than this, more like a deep sleep; Delta is a very deep state of relaxation, more like hibernation.

Alpha states are usually fairly easy to reach, while remaining conscious and aware. With regular practice of meditation techniques, this state of mind puts you in contact with your subconscious. Theta states are harder to reach, while remaining conscious and aware, taking daily practice for months, often years. This is the state of mind which allows for astral projection/Shamanic journeys and very deep levels of meditation, putting you in contact with your super-consciousness or higher self.

The Delta state of consciousness, while remaining aware; is usually only attained by Yogi's and Buddhist monks etc, who have devoted their lives to attaining higher states of consciousness via meditation. It is this state of consciousness which allows them to be buried alive for days on end; it is a state of suspended animation or hibernation. This state of mind allows you to reach the universal consciousness. It is possible to reach this level for short periods during sleep and very deep meditation, but only people who have dedicated themselves to this level of commitment are able to reach this level at will.

During meditation and healing you are liable to be in an Alpha state of consciousness. If you allow spirits/spiritual beings to possess you, often called channelling, you will alternate between Alpha and Delta states of consciousness. Whatever state of consciousness you are in, you should remain fully aware and in control of what is happening.

As a result of shifts in consciousness, it is essential to ground yourself properly after meditation and healing work. This is even more important if you are new to this type of work, as it can be a bit disorientating to begin with; it is a little like being drunk, your body is a little out of sync with your mind; as a result you will find your body awkward to manoeuvre and you will feel clumsy. In time and with regular practice, it becomes easier to move at will through these different states of mind.

Deep relaxation exercises are about conscious transformation. The aim of these relaxation exercises are to put your mind in an active, aware, Alpha state of consciousness, whilst putting your body into more of a Delta State, similar to deep sleep. As this is the state of consciousness the Shamanic Journey requires, also known as a Delta state of Consciousness, or as Michael Harner ('*The Way of the Shaman*') calls it, an SSC (Shamanic State of Consciousness). This may take a long time to achieve, whilst remaining awake, many people may never attain this level, but even if you do not, trying to achieve it will still bring a number of benefits to you. Having said that, it is possible to journey in a Theta state of consciousness. This is the state of consciousness you are in when you are in deep sleep, an example of journeying whilst sleeping would be lucid dreaming, this is a state of mind it is possible to reach, when you are in deep sleep, dreaming, yet aware you are asleep and dreaming, thus able to consciously take control of your dreams, rather than simply being in them. You are though, only likely to travel to the Underworld in a lucid dream state.

Grounding

The term 'Grounding' is the process you use to return to your normal state of consciousness after meditation, giving or receiving healing. This is a very important process and must be done at the end of any Spiritual Practices. When you meditating or healing, you are in an altered state of consciousness; this is due to your relaxed state and altered oxygen intake. This is a little like being slightly drunk. It can make you a little clumsier than usual, you may also feel heavier. This is because your spirit has been functioning as a bridge outside of your body and has not fully returned yet;

it takes a little while for the two to become co-ordinated again. The sensation itself is quite pleasant, but be very careful not to do anything needing lots of concentration or manual dexterity for a while.

The easiest way to ground yourself is to do something very mundane and normal: brush your teeth, comb your hair, wash your face, have a cup of tea, vacuum the floor, wash up, etc.

Protection

Sometimes after a deep meditation, journey or powerful healing, it can be very difficult to return to your normal state of consciousness, especially if you were channelling another entity. Sometimes they don't want to let go. If this happens they are attempting to possess you, this may take the form of trickery, such as letting you feel it is a good experience for you, so it is essential to remain in control. Never surrender completely to another entity. If these spiritual beings are truly there to assist you, then they know the rules and never try to fully manifest within you, if they do not leave when you want them to, you must not panic, simply allow them to continue the experience, see where it takes you, sometimes there is simply more for them to offer you than you were expecting; but as soon as it becomes scary or uncomfortable for you, then you must expel them.

To do this you must regain control, remember it is your body and your spirit is the only one that has the right to fully interact with you. It can be a difficult process, but you will win, it is simply a matter of willpower. This sort of situation should not occur if you have protected yourself properly prior to the situation in which you allowed the entity access to you, i.e. healing work, meditation, etc.

Before attempting any magikal workings, it is essential to cast a circle of protection about yourself and the others involved. There are also other methods of protecting yourself of a more individual nature, these include wearing amulets, medicine bundles, charms and other empowered magikal items, which you believe will protect you. This sort of possession experience is rare though, I have only experienced it once and I was in a weakened state myself to begin with; I still don't believe it really meant to harm me, it was simply teaching me something I needed to know, but it didn't feel like that at the time. Basically it is better to be safe, than sorry.

Shamanism is a primeval belief system, as such it is from a time when life was a lot harder and wilder than it is today. It is not a fluffy white light New Age energy, it is a lot tougher than that, it does not require you to walk about trying to be a perfect white light being of pure energy, it requires you to be REAL. You are a human being, as such you are full of what we consider negative emotions, fear, anger, ego, vanity, jealousy, etc. You are not expected to walk about expressing these feelings at all times, that would simply make you a spoilt child, but it does expect you to master these emotions and to know when to let them out and when not to, as well as to take personal responsibility for your actions and inactions.

I've always felt that Aslan from the '*Lion, the Witch and the Wardrobe*' books by C S Lewis, or Gandalf from the '*Lord of the Rings*' by J R R Tolkien are good examples of Shamen. Both of these characters are good spiritual powerful beings, but they are not perfect and they are fully prepared to express their darker, lethal aspects, as well as their more vulnerable aspects, when the need arises.

Relaxation Exercises

In today's fast-paced world it can be difficult to find time to allow yourself to relax, or having found the time, being able to relax without feeling guilty about it. Relaxation for most of us is flopping down in front of the TV and putting your feet up, or having a drink at the pub. This is not the sort of relaxation I am talking about, I am talking about conscious relaxation techniques, think about chilling out in the bath, with soft candle light, relaxing music, pleasant smells and you are nearer to the relaxation I am talking about.

Relaxation is a skill which you need to learn. Like all the Shamanic techniques, it is about letting go of your normal state of consciousness, of letting go of yourself and all the responsibilities of your material life. Relaxation exercises are necessary as they help the body to release the chemicals and knots stored within its nervous system which are created by the stress of everyday life, wear and tear, as well as more traumatic incidents from our lives. These forms of deep relaxation exercises are about conscious transformation, as opposed to simply crashing on the sofa with a good film and a beer, which may make you feel temporarily better, but will not produce any long term health benefits. It takes a lot of energy to suppress emotions and traumatic shock, within our systems, so when this energy is released, it also allows us to use that spare energy for additional activities.

Physical exercise is good for releasing a lot of toxins, tension and chemicals from our systems, if done correctly; though the best forms of physical exercise also stimulate our minds, such as martial arts, Qi Gong and yoga. The aim of these relaxation exercises are to keep your mind in an active, aware, beta or alpha state of consciousness, whilst putting your body into more of a delta state, similar to deep sleep, a delta state of consciousness. In order to achieve this consciousness, it will be necessary to practice regularly, at least an hour a day, through differing stages of relaxation exercises:

Qi Gong Exercises

There are many forms of Qi Gong exercises, look in the local press for classes, they are often based on ancient Chinese martial arts exercises, or work patterns, such as these ones. They are physical exercises of a gentle, stretching nature, which have the benefit of promoting the development of strength, suppleness and additional ki or chi. Given here are a set of exercises called 'The 8 Strands of the Silk Brocade' or 'Silk Weaver's exercises'. They are designed to be non-strenuous, breathing and stretching exercises. They stretch the meridians, strengthen internal organs and develop ki. They consist of 8 exercises; each of which should be performed

8 times, facing the East. This gives a total of 64 exercises which relate it to the 64 Hexagrams of the 'I Ching' or 'Book of Changes'.

Silk Weavers' Exercises

In all exercises, keep your tongue on the roof of your mouth, breathe in through your nose and out through your mouth. Breathe in on the relaxed motion and out on the stretching motion. Ladies especially, remember to breathe deeply, means to breathe down to the abdomen, not the chest. If you have been pregnant, you will have been shallow breathing from the chest; often women forget to go back to normal breathing, which must be done consciously.

1) Two Hands Push Heaven

Standing with your knees slightly bent and feet shoulders width apart; back straight, arms hanging relaxed in front of you; this is called a Bear stance. Bring your hands up in front of you in a cupped fashion, palms up, as you breathe in deeply through your nose. When your hands are level with your collarbone, rotate your hands so the palms are face down and exhale as you push your arms up in front of you and over your head, so your palms now face upwards. Continue to breathe out and push upwards until you have finished exhaling. Now lower your arms back to their starting position, as you inhale. Repeat this exercise 8 times, focusing on the breath and stretch.

2) Separating Heaven and Earth

Standing in a bear stance do the same as in exercise one until your hands are at your collarbone. Push your right hand up as in the previous exercise and your left hand down behind your left leg; breath out as you push. When you have finished exhaling bring your hands back together in front of you as you inhale. Now repeat this exercise on the opposite

307

sides; left hand up, right hand down. Eyes look upwards. Each exercise is
in 2 parts, so this is 16 movements, not 8.

3) Wise Owl Looks Round

This is a very simple exercise; standing in a bear
stance, breathe in deeply. Now exhale as you turn
Slowly at the waist to look over your left shoulder and
down at the heel of your right foot. Inhale as you return
to the front and repeat this exercise on the opposite
side. This exercise is in 2 parts, equalling 16 movements.

4) Scooping Water

In a bear stance, breathe in deeply as you raise your hands to a horizontal
cupped position level with your heart, palms up. Now exhale as you bend
forward at the waist, keep your legs straight if possible. When you are bent
over, scoop the water from the stream and raise up again, as you inhale.
Repeat this exercise 8 times.

5) Relaxed Punching

This exercise is done in a horse-riding stance; Imagine you are riding a big
fat horse, legs wide apart, bent at the knees, back straight and feet facing

forwards. Make fists at your sides, thumbs outside the fingers and facing upwards. Take a deep breath, now exhale and punch slowly and gently, upwards and forwards, keep your elbow bent slightly. Use the gap between the knuckles, nearest to the thumb as a sight and GLARE through this gap. Now inhale as you withdraw the fist; repeat this on the opposite side, 16 punches in total.

6) Searching the Heavens

In a horse stance, place your hands on your thighs to give you some extra support. Breathe in deeply and looking upwards to your right, breathe out as you move from the waist only in a circular motion from right to left, finishing with you looking upwards on the left side. Now breathe in deeply and repeat this exercise so you return to your starting point. This is in 2 parts and forms 16 movements.

7) Zen Archery from Horseback

In a horse stance, take a deep breathe and raise your hands so they are in a prayer position level with your heart. Now as you exhale imagine you are firing a bow and arrow to your left, put your hands and arms in an appropriate position; with the Index finger on the left hand pointing straight up. Now return to your starting position as you

inhale. Look to your right and repeat the exercise on that side. Fire 16 arrows, 8 on each side.

8) Eagle Landing
In an Eagle stance, feet nearly touching at the heels and turned out slightly, knees slightly bent, back straight. Inhale deeply as you rise up on your toes, now exhale as you bounce down to the ground, use 3 bounce's to land. Repeat this 8 times.

These 'Qi Gong' exercises are called the 'Silk Weavers' exercises' or the '8 Strands of the Silk Brocade' because they were the exercises performed each morning and evening after work, by the silk weavers of China. 'Qi' is another name for 'Ki' or 'Chi'. These exercises should be done once a day, you may alter the order other than 1) and 8), to make it easier; with practice you should be able to enter a light meditative state as you do them.

Progressive Mental Relaxation Exercises

Having mastered the Qi Gong Exercises, the next step is to move on to Progressive Mental or Inner Relaxation Exercises. This involves sitting in a comfortable position with your back well supported and entering a light meditative state of consciousness (Alpha / Beta); from this state you can begin to influence or take conscious control of your body system.

Step 1
To do this first prepare the environment in which you are going to meditate:

1) Play some soft soothing instrumental music, block out the light, light some candles and some pleasant incense, make sure you won't be disturbed, ensure you are in a comfortable sitting position, with your back well supported.

310

2) Close your eyes, rest your hands in a comfortable open position, then take a deep breath though your nose into your tantien (navel) area, (this may take some practice if you are a woman who has had children), so that you stomach inflates. Place your tongue on the roof of your mouth as this connects all your meridians. Hold this in breath for a moment, then exhale from your mouth so that you empty your lungs; again hold this for a moment, then inhale again deeply through your nose into your tantien.

3) Focus only on your breath, in, hold, out, hold, in, etc; forget all other things, nothing else matters in this moment, just your breath. If any other thoughts enter your mind during this process, simply acknowledge them and them and then return to your breathing.

4) This is called the '4 Fold Breathe' technique, it is a good idea to simply practice this exercise on its own until you are no longer getting other thoughts distracting you while you breathe. You may also find that you have fallen asleep to begin with; this is quite common, eventually, with practice and conscious effort you will remain awake.

Step 2
1) Repeat what you are doing in Step 1, until you have reached that point where you are focused, only on your breathing pattern, yet awake and un distracted.

2) Now, as you breathe in, visualise the air as white light, which fills your entire body with a warm tingly sensation as you breathe it in and absorb it; as you breathe out visualise your breath carrying all of your body's tension and stress with it, feel your shoulders slump down.

3) Continue doing this exercise until you feel comfortable with it.

Step 3
1) Repeat the previous steps until you are at point where you are comfortable and full of warm tingling white light.

2) Now as you inhale feel a gentle breeze across the top of your head, moving a couple of hairs, visualise this as golden light.

3) As you inhale, this golden light moves down from the top of your head into your face, as it does so it relaxes your scalp and face, feel the tension dissolving in the golden light, all the deeply buried stress and tension of your life, is melting away, to be replaced by peace.

4) Allow this to continue in this manner, down through your neck, shoulders, biceps, elbows, forearms, hands, chest, abdomen, hips, groin, thighs, knees, calves and finally your feet; now allow this golden light to leave your feet and enter the Earth, where this purifying energy will be recycled.

5) If you feel some areas of your body are tenser than others, simply allow the golden light to linger there longer, there is no rush.

Step 4
1) Repeat Steps 1-3.

2) As the golden light travels down your body, relaxing you further, become aware of your chakras. Focus on these coloured whirlpools of energy, see any dark blemishes contained within them, as the golden light travels through them, see the blemishes vanish, leaving a pure-hued whirlpool of colour, White at the crown, purple at the third eye, turquoise at the throat, green at the heart, yellow at the solar plexus, orange at the sacral and red at the base.

3) Again allow the Golden Light to leave through your feet into the Earth.

Step 5
1) Repeat Steps 1 - 4.

2) As the golden light of the Heavens leaves your feet, become aware of roots stretching down from your feet, deep into the Earth, drawing up

energy from the Earth Mother. See this energy rising up through your roots and into your feet. From here it travels slowly up your legs and through your body chakras, as it does become aware of your body as it is turning into a tree trunk, as the Earth's sap rises through your system become aware of your arms stretching up to the Heavens, covered with strong supple branches and shimmering leaves of every colour, as the silver light fills them and then continues upwards towards the Sun, until it is beyond your sight.

3) Now the golden light descends into your body again, travelling down through your leaves, into your chakras, into your body and turning back to your human self once more, as it leaves through your feet.

Step 6
1) Repeat Steps 1 - 5.

2) As the golden light leaves your body allow the silver sap light to travel up through your system again, turning you once more into the world tree. This time as the golden light reaches out to you from above, draw the silver sap light up your roots also, so that you are now experiencing the both the golden light travelling down through your system into the Earth and the silver light travelling up through your system and into the Heavens.

3) Be aware of how it feels when they meet in your heart chakra, try and hold that feeling for a while.

4) Allow the silver and golden light to do this process once more, turning you back into your human form.

Step 7
1) Repeat Steps 1 - 6.
2) Allow the Silver and Golden Light to travel through you once more until they reach your heart chakra and meet, while you are in human form.
3) Now simply focus on that feeling for as long as possible and become aware of any other images, feelings, tastes, smells, sounds, that come to

you. Allow yourself to travel without constraints, knowing that you are perfectly safe and balanced within your centre.

Step 8

1) Repeat Steps 1 - 7.

2) At this point you will probably be meditating, you may even be journeying. Simply remain aware of where you are, you may find yourself sitting at the base of a tree, if so look around you, take in the landscape before you, allow your senses to experience it as fully as you can.

Steps 1-6 of these relaxation exercises are designed to allow you to enter an altered state of consciousness this will initially be an Alpha/Beta state, whilst providing you with enough instructions to maintain a conscious mental state, which with practice will prevent you from falling asleep. From Step 7, you are being guided to open up to a more receptive meditative state, with practice you should be capable of reaching a Theta state and with more practice a Delta State.

Meditation

Meditation is different for everyone, some people take to it like a duck to water, some people are very reluctant to relinquish complete conscious control, especially if they have suffered with recurring nightmares. Meditation can take place at many levels of consciousness, in many ways it is a self-induced state of trance, similar to the state a hypnotist would put you into, a highly receptive state of mind. From this receptive state of mind you are likely to experience a variety of experiences, such as a sensation of dissolving into nothingness, it is a state which allows you access to your subconscious. As a result, you will find you are likely to have experiences which are related to your normal state of consciousness, i.e. if you spend a lot of your spare time reading about spiritual subjects you will probably have a very spiritual experience, which will be coloured by the way in which you perceive your spirituality, or belief system; a Christian might see angels, whereas a Pagan might see fairies. As a result it is important to remember that what you allow into your mind will be reflected back at you, when I first started serious meditation, I got rid of my TV as it was likely to influence my subconscious, just as it does in dreams, this allowed me more conscious control of what I experienced. It is also important to begin your mediation at roughly the same time each day, this trains your mind to prepare itself on a subconscious level for the meditation also if possible practice meditation each day.

If you are undergoing a severely stressful period, meditation will allow you to access a completely new reality, without any of that stress which is related to your normal reality. However, it is also likely that this stress will present itself within your meditation, it may take the form of something that will scare you, but within this state you will be able to interact with the stress in what you would perceive as a physical form. As a result of this you may be able to talk to it, ask it what it is teaching you about yourself or life, you may even befriend it, changing the experience from a negative one, to one which presents more opportunities to grow, or you may find you have to fight it and defeat it. Whatever happens, you will alter your perception and feelings towards this stress, when in your normal state of waking consciousness.

Meditation can take a variety of forms. The method I have been describing would be classed as free-form, this method allows your imagination to free range. Other forms would include mantra meditation, when you meditate on a group of words or sounds, such as 'OM', or another form of Meditation would focus on a object such as a crystal, exploring it fully, allowing all your senses to become involved with the experience, another method would involve focusing on a set of movements in your mind, such as visualising a Tai Chi Form/Kata; try them all, you may find one type suits you better than another.

When you have been meditating for a while, you will realise how all things are connected, you will be in a position in which, you will be able to directly observe, the connection between the microcosm and the macrocosm. As you continue to meditate, you will find you have built

315

another world for yourself, where you can retreat to find peace, or to look at a problem from a different angle, you may even discover that other beings live in this inner world, who you can inter-react with, seeking advice, they will probably be characters or animals with whom you feel a bond or who have inspired you.

Shamanism is in many ways a form of psychology, but instead of being, in the worst cases, full of long-winded technical terms and science, looking very clinical, with a belittling attitude, populated with self righteous pompous experts (who somehow, often look like they need more help, than you do) who confirm you are different to everyone else, abnormal or damaged; it is created from your childhood dreams, imagination, fantasy, innocence, beauty, hopes, fears and unconditional love; working in a way which also allows you access to your subconscious, but in a fascinating and fun way, which also allows you to implement positive change to your inner workings and ultimately your perception and outer world.

This doesn't mean if you are undergoing psychological treatment, you should stop it and start meditating instead, but it would probably allow you to increase your healing process, relax, alter your perception and discuss deeper issues with your psychologist, by discussing your meditation experiences with them. As children, we often resolved our inner questions and problems through play, fantasy and imagination; Shamanism, meditation and journeying allow us to do this again.

As part of your Shamanic development I would strongly suggest a study of the mind, looking into psychology and counselling, do some introductory courses, read some books and keep a journal. Meditation is the key to all spiritual development.

The Inner Landscape

As you continue to meditate, you will probably begin to develop an inner landscape, if you do not naturally, then during a meditation, think about where you would really like to be, what sort of landscape would you find most inspiring, relaxing and safe, what sort of trees would there be in it, would there be water, hills, mountains, flowers, animals, etc. As you continue to visit this landscape, you will often find that you arrive at the same place each time you travel there. Many Shamanic traditions talk about a tunnel, leading to this Underworld, from a natural hole in this world; this is simply a trigger for your imagination, it is not necessary. I simply follow the purple pulsing lights I see in my mind and eventually find myself in my own Inner Landscape, although these lights could be perceived as a tunnel; or as a root system leading up or down.

In Shamanism, this otherworldly landscape is often portrayed as being outside you. I do not believe this is the case, I believe it is a represent-ation of your subconscious, your underworld. If it is a separate reality, then you reach it by going within, not by going outside of yourself, although as the microcosm and macrocosm are connected, then you will eventually travel outside of yourself, however you will still be perceiving from within. I have had several out of body experiences, as a result I am aware that it is possible to exist outside of your own body, within this world; these could be classed as astral projections or as journeys to the Middle World, our normal world.

The Underworld is closely connected with our Subconscious levels, the reality is all these levels merge, we are our own World Tree. As a result we can travel upwards into the upper worlds or downwards into the under-world, simply by travelling within. We always remain connected to our physical body though, some people talk of a silver life line, which connects us to it; I can not say I have seen this, but it makes a good analogy of the process. In Shamanism, the drum's beat is usually the link between the worlds, which we follow out of and back to our body. This is why the drum is often referred to as the Shaman's Horse. In some cultures though the drum is not used in Shamanic training until much later in the process; a staff is used instead, often this has bells on it and is banged on the floor to create a beat, though this is not always necessary either and some Shamen have to learn to journey without the aid of a drum or any other tools.

Having found yourself within your inner landscape or otherworld, you will need to explore it. This involves testing your senses:

Can you smell this world? What can you smell?

Does it seem real to you? Can you feel it?

Can you hear anything? What?

Can you taste the water or fruit?

Movement within this world is via thought, simply see yourself there, it is a little like meditating, within a meditation.

This inner landscape will become more real as you visit it more often. You will also find you can look over the landscape by transforming into a bird and flying over it. This will lead you to discover new areas, which you can explore by seeing yourself at them. Each of the areas within your inner landscape, you will realise, will have a different feel to them. One area may teach you lessons with the northern quarter, having an elemental feel to it, or maybe an animal or guide lives there you can talk to, who is an expert in healing or something else. It is up to you to discover where you are and what this area will teach you. It is also up to you to bring these lessons back with you to your outer world of your normal waking consciousness.

You will find your Inner Landscape grows as you do, you will suddenly discover an entrance to some new area of it. In this inner landscape you are neither, outside of yourself or inside of yourself; other spiritual beings or different aspects of yourself, can visit you here and talk to you, though they may need to be invited. You may also discover at some point, that you are more drawn to the natural world outside of yourself, wanting to visit local woods and landscapes in your normal state of consciousness, the inner landscape and the outer landscape of the Middle World are closely connected, each will lead to the other. Though both are the same, they are also different, each having their own rules, it is necessary to learn the rules of all of the worlds, Shamanism is not about avoidance of the normal world we live in. Many people on their spiritual quests make that mistake. I have made it myself in the past; if you continue to only really live in your inner world, only having inner adventures and experiences, you will end up a total space cadet and that is not Shamanism.

Although it may be perfectly normal to have a conversation with a grizzly bear in your inner landscape, I would strongly advise against trying to do the same in the outer world. It is important to learn to take responsibility for your life, it is down to you to make your dreams come true, the inner world will help you to see these dreams, to inspire you, but you must make them a reality in this world, the middle mundane material world in which you can't fly like an eagle, talk to a bear, or any of the other amazing things you can do in your inner world. But what you can do, is learn falconry, or how to hang-glide, or fly a plane, or become a zoo keeper, or a conservationist. All of these are equally wonderful adventures and will provide you with a host of experiences, often even better than your inner world experiences.

Another important thing to do is to practice meditation in the wilds, find yourself a spot in your garden, in the park or out in the woods, where you can relax enough to meditate with nature. When doing this sort of thing, the wildlife will not view you as an immediate threat, as you are being very quiet and not moving much, as a result animals may come nearer, than they normally would. Your inner landscape will always remain with you, for whenever you choose to visit it.

Pathworking

Pathworkings, also known as guided meditation or visualisation, are what they sound like. Basically a pathworking involves a journey to an area in which the main events of the meditation will take place. After these events, or experiences, the same journey is repeated, to return to normal consciousness. Usually one person will lead (vocalise) the pathworking, while a group of other people share (listen) the same experience, but from their own unique perspectives. Pathworking is a little like telling or listening to a story.

The person leading the pathworking can either be in an altered consciousness themselves, if they are able to talk freely while in an altered state, or in a normal state of consciousness. It is important to remember, if you are leading a pathworking, to check if the other people in the group have any phobias, which may be triggered by this pathworking, i.e. a fear of the water, snakes, heights, etc, then to adjust the pathworking accordingly. The pathworking should be relaxing, interesting and have positive effects on those involved, you don't want people to have fits or panic attacks as a result. Shamanic journeys are a form of pathworking, as they usually involve not someone relating a journey to them, but simply a very well known journey, which the Shaman involved relates to him or her self. The Shaman will normally have well-trodden paths to reach the otherworlds, ones they will recognise as the way to the Under World or Upper World, etc.

The journey is serving the same purpose in both cases, as a form of preparation for the events ahead, a period in which to gather the support of their power animals, totems, guides and helpers etc, as well as their own inner resources on the way there and to give thanks to their helpers on the way back, while preparing themselves to re-enter a normal state of consciousness.

The events of a pathworking are usually shared with each other, after the pathworking has ended, as are most forms of group meditation. A good pathworking will usually allow a period of time for the people involved to do their own thing, i.e. a pathworking may involve 'a walk through some woods, where they will come to a clearing where their power animal is waiting to greet them, they will then be encouraged to spend some time (non guided meditation) getting to know this power animal, then they will bid the power animal farewell and return along the same woodland path'. Another important thing to remember when leading a pathworking is to make the experience as real as possible for those involved, encourage them to use their inner senses, describe the 'smell of the wet leaves and the sound they make as you walk on them' etc. Don't give too much detail though, don't tell them what sort of leaves they are, allow them to fill in their own gaps, as some things have deeper meaning to one person, than to another.

Shamanic Journeys

Shamanic journeys as I have already mentioned are basically forms of pathworking. They usually involve certain similar aspects in most cultures, i.e. 'a journey through the World Tree, to the appropriate Otherworld, on route the Shaman will meet with their spiritual allies, a discussion of what the journey is for will ensue, a course of action will be decided upon, the Shaman and their allies will then go and do whatever it is that needs to be done. Having completed the task, the Shaman and their allies will discuss what happened, what was to be learnt from the experience, then a thanks and farewell is bid to the allies and the Shaman will return home again, via the same World Tree route or root'.

While this is happening the Shaman will have either been playing their drum themselves or had an assistant who played the drum for them. The drum will have had several rhythms played upon it, a slightly faster one for the journey to the Otherworld, similar to a horse galloping, then a slow steady beat after a period, like a heartbeat, while they are in the Otherworld, doing whatever it is that needs doing. Prior to the journey the Shaman would have discussed with their drumming assistant, how long would need to be spent in the Otherworld, once this time was reached, the drummer would beat their drum rapidly 3 or 4 times to warn the Shaman, that it was time for them to return to the Middle World. The drummer would then beat the drum, like a galloping horse again, as the Shaman journeyed back and until the Shaman showed signs of coming out of their trance. If the Shaman is playing their own drum, then the rhythms will probably vary quite erratically, depending upon what is happening to the Shaman, whilst in the Otherworld.

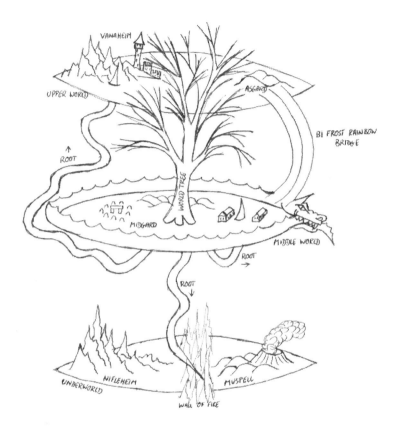

The World Tree is a map of the universe, a path, which the Shaman can travel to get to the Otherworlds.

In some cultures the Shaman will dance themselves into a trance. The principle is the same, using rhythm to influence the heart beat and the mental state. The Shaman will sometimes ride an animal to the Otherworlds, often a reindeer or horse, sometimes they will transform into a power animal and travel there in that form, sometimes a spring or other water course is the route followed to the Otherworld, sometimes the

Shaman will actually climb a tree to reach the Upper World, or a form of ladder. In India a rope is often used, sometimes the entrance is a cave or an animal hole. The method in which most Shamen travel is basically dependent upon their training, culture, tradition, environment and what works best for them.

In Norse traditions the Shamanic journey is called a 'Seidr'; the Norse Shaman is called a 'Vitki', this involves the use of a raised platform upon which the Shaman will sit, whilst they journey. Around the platform, the Shaman will have physical and spiritual allies posted, as well as magikal protection, to guard the Shaman's body from harm. It is their job, to ensure the Shaman's body isn't possessed and the Shaman has a body to come back to.

Shamanic journeys can begin in many ways, as many modern stories prove. In the *Narnia Chronicles* by C.S. Lewis, the children enter Narnia through a magic wardrobe, this wardrobe was made from an apple tree, the apple from which the tree was grown came from Narnia. 'A wood between the worlds' is also mentioned in the *'Magician's Nephew'*, where there are pools of water, each leading to different worlds. In Lewis Carroll's *'Alice in Wonderland'* the Shamanic journey starts down a rabbit hole, later Alice visits the Underworld I'd imagine via a mirror, or 'looking glass'. In the *'Wizard of Oz'*, Dorothy gets to Oz via a tornado, then returns via a pair of ruby slippers. All of these and many other famous stories are classic Shamanic journeys.

States of Ecstasy

Ecstatic states are often associated with Shamanic traditions, these are induced by various means, in different cultures, many of these methods are very similar. An ecstatic state means a state of excitement, a state of euphoria, this is brought about by the Shaman's spirit allies entering their body, in a sense possessing the Shaman. Wicca also employs a similar ritual, called 'Drawing Down the Moon', in this ritual the god or goddess are invited to enter the Witch's body; Voodoo also uses a similar method, with possession by spirits or gods being common place in their rituals. This experience generates a great high, leaving you in a state of exhaustion, but glowing, in many ways it is similar to how you may feel after a very good, very long, sexual encounter; although a better description would be how you felt in a first love situation; however, I can see this state as becoming quite addictive in nature, which is rarely a good thing.

In some cultures this state of ecstasy is induced by sexual practices. Wicca sometimes uses this method, as do Tantric cultures. In other cultures it is induced by the use of some form of drug. Yhe most common Western ones are magic mushrooms and fly agaric, although flying ointment has been used which contains belladonna and henbane. Most of these can generate a heightened sensory awareness combined with flying sensations. Often in Siberian and Scandinavian traditions, fly agaric is ingested by drinking reindeer urine, as the reindeer love eating the fungi. In American traditions, cannabis, coca leaves, peyote and other more bizarre methods are used, such as licking a cane toad, or millipede.

Drug induced states of ecstasy are highly dangerous practices and I do not recommend them. It is also important to remember that, in many cultures the drug induced ecstatic high is usually only used by either inexperienced Shamen, in that area of their work, or as a training step, to allow initial experience of the Otherworlds. It is possible to reach the same sort of state of receptiveness via far safer means, such as deep meditation or very vigorous dance, no doubt that is why some of today's dance music is called trance and why the drug called 'Ecstasy' is very popular, much of today's dance music is based on a highly Shamanic rhythms.

Practice of the safer methods, especially meditation is what I would recommend, it will take longer and more dedication than the quick fix route, but it is more permanent, safer and can eventually be entered at will.

Channelling

Channelling is becoming quite commonplace in the New Age movement; there are channelled gurus and many channelled books. Sadly there are very few real channels for spirits, most are fakes who simply talk in a funny voice, with a suspect accent and somehow make lots of money.

I have had very little experience of channelling personally and it is only during healing that it is likely to happen to me, then the spirit doesn't take complete control, it simply holds the reins for a while. I get the feeling the sensation is awkward for them, they don't want to talk, simply do what they are there for and leave, sometimes even getting irritated if asked questions; responses are brief and to the point. I don't consider myself a channel for spirits, simply a channel for healing energy, occasionally that takes a spirit's form.

I've seen many people who claimed to be channelling spirits or higher beings, most are rather pitiful. Talking in a funny accent and breathing heavily doesn't mean you are channelling. Many so-called 'channels' are simply trying to make money out of it, some have mental conditions, such as schizophrenia and don't realise it. For example someone who is channelling a Chinese spirit or a Native American spirit, will be easily able to respond in their native language if greeted in it, they will also know about their culture.

A real channel will alter in an almost physical manner, looking and sounding different when a spirit has entered them, it is also likely to be the same spirit each time. They will probably also be a recognised medium, who has proved themselves in this field, they are also likely to remember what happened. I have only seen what I would call channelling once. On that occasion the channel wasn't so much physically altered, as looked as though they were involved in a form of reversed ventriloquism; the spirit was hovering slightly above the channel and spoke in the spirit's voice, their appearance was white and transparent, yet colours were also perceived, it was the spirit of someone I knew, so it was difficult to fake.

The 'Mudang' are Thai Shamen, who are famous for channelling spirits, many of them are highly childish in nature, often needing elaborate costumes to feel important. The rituals to channel these spirits also seem to need a lot of money, this always makes me suspicious. Voodoo is another tradition which involves a lot of channelled spirits, though it is referred to as possession, the currency involved in their rituals is usually blood; this seems far more credible to me, even if it does creep me out.

Channelling is a part of the Shamanic tradition, though that doesn't always mean it involves some form of all-knowing spirit, addressing an audience, through the Shaman; more often it would be more like a flash of inspiration. In this context I have experience of both as a healer, it was in this manner that I discovered the meridians and tsubos in people, before I had heard of them. It was also in this manner that I was taught how to make many of the magikal tools I make and their meanings.

So I suggest, when confronted by someone channelling a spirit, especially a really famous one, be sceptical and have lots of salt at hand, don't be afraid to challenge or question them. A real spirit will respect this, especially a famous and enlightened one. This advice is also valid for mediums, sadly most people who go to a medium, have recently lost someone dear to them and are in desperate need of comforting and reassurance from those they have lost. A real medium will always pass on specific information, which only you and your loved one would know, silly nicknames or events, etc, to prove who they are, before passing on a message to you.

Soul Retrieval

In Shamanic cultures the human soul is believed to be in 3 parts or separate souls, not as one spirit as we often perceive it in the civilised world; each of these plays a different function and exists differently after death. A common belief in a wide ranging selection of Shamanic cultures is that we all have at least 3 souls; a soul is a smaller part of a spirit. In Siberia and Mongolia these are known as:

Suld

Ami

Suns

The **Suld** soul, resides in nature after death; it is the most individualistic aspect of the 3 souls. It only lives in a human body once, it carries no past life experiences, so learns as it travels through life, developing the characteristics which distinguish one person from another. Charisma and dignity are believed to be signs of a strong Suld soul. The Suld soul hangs around the deceased body for a while after death, before returning to nature to reside as a nature spirit. The Suld soul only lives on this plane of existence. The Suld resides at the crown of the head, if the Suld is forced out of the body, the person will die very soon.

The **Ami** soul is very bird like in its nature. Upon death it returns to the World Tree to nest in the form of a bird. The Ami soul is related to our genetic make-up and reincarnates among our family group and descendants. It is closely related to the ability to breathe, which also links it to what the Japanese call Original Ki, which is the Ki passed to us via our Parents' joining. The Ami can be temporarily displaced during illness, although it will not leave permanently until death.

The **Suns** soul, like the Suld soul contributes to the formation of someone's personality, but carries the collected experiences of past lives within it. A Suns soul is an inhabitant of the underworld upon death, where it resides until reincarnated again, though this may not be within the same bloodline. It is the Suns soul which returns as a ghost to visit family and friends; the Suns soul may be scared out of the body due to trauma, illness, etc.

The Suns and Ami souls oscillate in balance through the chakra system, on opposite sides of our central axis; when you become excited these souls speed up, causing the heart to beat faster and creating a feeling of high energy or tension; if these two souls are thrown off balance for any length of time the person will become ill or mentally confused. It is these two souls that a Shaman sometimes travels to retrieve in a soul retrieval journey. In modern Western thinking, we would probably consider the Suld as the personality, the Ami as the higher self and the Suns as the spirit. It is believed in Shamanic cultures that following trauma, illness, shock, emotional incidents one of these three souls can become lost, it literally runs away in fear. When this happens, the soul will often return after the event has passed; if this is the case, all is well. However, sometimes the soul that has fled becomes lost, or is kidnapped by another chaotic spirit of some sort. If this is the case the client can become seriously ill; in this event a Shaman will undertake a soul retrieval. During this the Shaman travels in spirit form to wherever the soul is to literally bring it home. If the soul is being held against its will, the Shaman may have to fight to get it back, which can be quite dangerous. When the soul is safely returned to its body, the client will usually make a rapid recovery.

A soul retrieval is basically a Shamanic journey, it is usually not necessary to resort to this method of healing though, in the modern civilised world. This healing method is more commonly used in the less developed world, especially in isolated locations.

Obviously in our culture it is essential that any client who needs (as opposed to feels they need) a soul retrieval should be sent to seek profess-ional medical advice from their doctor. In the less developed world a soul retrieval is usually only performed as a last resort, the patient may well be unconscious and have been carried many miles by their family to see the Shaman. In this situation with an obviously very ill patient on his hands, the Shaman will resort to whatever means are necessary and possible to attempt to heal the patient.

The Shaman will probably have already treated the patient in the past, but for some reason, the patient has failed to recover, slipping deeper into their illness, in the worse case scenarios into coma or death. Shamen do not always succeed in healing their patients, often being the only medical assistance available, they can only do the best they can with what is possible, their knowledge and resources available. Modern Shamen in the civilised world are unlikely to encounter these sorts of situations. As a result, soul retrievals are performed for clients who feel they have lost something of themselves, who are depressed, confused or feel they have lost the will to live. A good Shaman will strongly advise a client who is in such a bad state, to discuss these feelings with their doctor or a psychologist.

Clients in need of a soul retrieval will have recently experienced some form of strong trauma, at least for them. It is important to remember that people experience trauma from their own unique perception and state of normality. What is very traumatic for one person, may seem like a minor hiccup to someone else, so try not to be to judgmental. Trauma will often be brought about by big life changes. This could be as simple as losing their job or it could be that they have been diagnosed as seriously ill or maybe their partner has left them, or died.

All of these are potential sources of soul loss; the client will have been seriously emotionally disturbed as a result of the situation. It is most likely that if the client has lost one of their souls, then it will only be temporary and it will come back to them, in time, of its own accord. The souls are strongly connected to the body they occupy in life and may even experience a form of home sickness, if separated for too long; this tends to make them return if possible. The Suns soul is the most likely one to be shocked out of the client, returning to its home in the Underworld. The Ami may also be shocked out of the client, but this will rarely travel far away, being so strongly connected to the family blood line, it will probably go no further than a relative.

A Soul Retrieval usually consists of:

1) The Shaman begins to help the client and tune into their energy, by asking what the client feels is the root of their current problem, listening attentively to the client's response.
2) Placing the Client into a light mediation, by taking them on a simple pathworking, leaving them somewhere they feel very relaxed and

comfortable; reassuring them that you will come back for them when you have finished the healing.

3) The Shaman now performs a Shamanic journey to retrieve the missing soul.

The soul itself can take many forms, often it will be an animal, but it could take the form of a rock, crystal, plant, object or even the client as a younger version. The soul will often find the Shaman and ask to be taken back, having simply gotten lost or suffered slight amnesia.

The Shaman will have to rely upon their allies and instincts as to whether this is the soul of their client or another soul presenting itself as the client's missing soul. Sometimes the soul has been captured by a stronger spirit and is being held to ransom, in this case the Shaman will have to enter negotiations for the soul's return, offering to burn incense or offer food and drink as a reward for finding the soul, if this does not work, it must be taken by force.

In Mongolia and Siberia, a Shaman who dies on a journey or whilst engaged in soul retrieval, is believed to have been defeated by a stronger spirit opponent.

Battles fought whilst on a journey are like dream fights, limited only by your imagination, as in many ways you are travelling to the client's subconscious self to retrieve the soul. It is in many ways a battle of wills, between the Shaman's and their client's imagination, often being more symbolic than actual. In Arthurian Legends, the Knights of the Round Table are sent out to find the Holy Grail, so that it can cure King Arthur, who in turn will heal the land. This is a form of soul retrieval, the knights are the Shamen, the Grail Quest is the Shamanic journey and Arthur's (the patient's) missing soul is represented as the Holy Grail.

In the '*Wizard of Oz*', the Tin Man is searching for his missing heart, being represented by a pocket watch, the Scarecrow is seeking his brain, being represented by a college diploma and the Cowardly Lion is seeking his courage, represented by a medal. All these are missing souls, which are symbolically returned to them by the wizard (Shaman). These are examples of soul retrieval whilst on Shamanic journeys, although very different to look at, they are essentially the same story.

4) Once the Shaman has found the missing soul, it is held close to the Shaman, or placed in the Shaman's drum or other suitable safe container for the journey back.

5) Once the Shaman has returned to the client, the soul is immediately returned to the client by placing the soul's form on the client's heart, whilst still in a Shamanic Journey state of consciousness. When that is done the Soul will have been returned to the client.

6) The Shaman will now return to their normal state of consciousness and as a symbolic gesture of the Journey, to ground the returned soul and to make the Journey reality, the Shaman will now do the same thing physically, by blowing the soul back into the client's heart, or gently placing the container in which the soul journeyed back with the Shaman on the client's heart.

7) The Shaman should now collect the client from their meditation (they will probably have fallen asleep) and ground them.

8) The client should now be asked what they experienced in their meditation and how they are feeling. A good soul retrieval will have been reflected in the client's meditation and dreams in some way. You can tell the client a brief version of what you experienced on your journey, if asked, pointing out the relevant connections with their experiences.

Given below is a diagram of this basic soul retrieval method, work in a clockwise direction:

Soul Retrieval Journey

Listen to Client

Ground Client

Take Client on
a Pathworking

Earth the Journey
(End Journey)

Begin Shamanic
Journey

Return Client's
Soul

Find Client's Soul

Store Client's Soul for Return

11
ENERGY HEALING

Learning to be a Healer

All good energy healing systems are easy to learn and allow the healing energy, or Ki, to flow through the healer and not from them. As a result it is not necessary to spend years trying to develop a state of near-spiritual perfection in order to channel the energies involved. When I've been asked about being a healer in the past I've always said 'You don't learn how to heal, you learn how to become a channel through which healing energies can flow'. To put it very simply I don't consider myself to be a healer, I think of myself more as a healing tool.

In my mind everyone is capable of being a healer. If you are able to express concern for others, feel empathy or love for others you are capable of being a healer. When someone we know is in tears and upset, we don't just sit there, we hold them; this is a powerful healing technique; we are reassuring them they are not alone and it is okay to feel what they are feeling, it's okay to be themselves. When your child grazes their knee, we kiss it better, or when we hurt ourselves we rub it better. These things can't logically make any difference to the injury, yet we all do them and somehow they help. This is all healing in its simplest form.

How Healing Works

The body is an incredible self-contained unit, which instantly activates its own chemical laboratories and medical staff as soon as we are injured. All that is required is enough surplus energy or fuel to initiate and maintain this process and a feeling of security. To look at healing in a scientific manner for a moment, what a healer is doing is twofold:

1) Supplying additional external energy often in the form of heat, to the injured person.

2) Putting the injured person into a highly relaxed and safe state, allowing the injured person's own internal healing mechanisms to draw on additional energy to increase the natural healing process.

The first step is explained scientifically in that one of the main uses for our bodies' fuel (food, water, oxygen) is to produce heat and to maintain a constant body temperature. When a healer touches or holds an injured person, they are supplying additional external heat to that person's body. This means additional energy normally used to generate internal heat is freed to assist with the healing processes in operation within their body.

It is also interesting to note that external heat energy, can be transferred as there are no such things as solid objects. All things are formed from the same energy. Everything is formed from protons, electrons and neutrons or stardust as it is also said. The difference between what we perceive as solid objects, fluids and gases is the distance between which these protons, etc, move in relation to each other, within their gravitational field.

The second step is explained as a matter of evolution and psychology. Our basic human body structure has changed very little over thousands of years. We contain dormant organs and largely dormant psychological responses and instincts; leftovers from our animal origins. As a result of injury the body is, to a degree, thrown back into a survival instinct mode. In this mode stresses are put into effect which mean the 'body' is worried about wild animals picking up on its blood scent and it being eaten. This is a dangerous situation for the body, especially if it is alone.

As a healer you are, in effect, assuring the injured person's 'body mind' that it is not alone and that you will keep watch for any danger, so it doesn't have to. This frees the body to relax and allow the adrenaline, generated by the injured body to fuel additional relaxation chemicals and increase the body's natural healing processes. So in short, the healer is supplying warmth and reassurance to their client, allowing them to channel additional energy to aid in their recovery. That was the scientific explanation of how healing works. But as anyone who has done healing knows there is a bit more to it than that.

In healing it is assumed that as everything is formed of energy. It is possible to channel additional external energy from the universe around us, into ourselves; then focus it and direct it out of our hands, to aid in the healing of a specific injury, in another person. In short, you act as a lightning rod.

As I said earlier, the healer does not so much learn how to heal, as learns how to conduct/channel excess universal energy through their body, into another person's body, so that the client's internal healing systems can redirect this energy, in the way that is of most benefit to them. It is not truly even necessary to believe in the existence of a god, etc, for this to work. Though I personally believe this does assist the process.

I often describe myself as a screwdriver, a simple tool, which does little until it is needed; then it is picked up and used. So my job, as I see it, is to be as effective a tool as possible, so if I am a screwdriver, I try and be an electric one, with multi-changeable heads, multi-directional rotation, multiple speed settings, cordless, solar powered and have a lifetime guarantee. This will allow the universal energies (Ki, Chi, Prana, angels, gods, fairies, elementals, electricity, the force, etc) to flow through me with as little resistance as possible, whilst still remaining aware and in control.

A belief system which allows you to channel the energies of more evolved, powerful and wiser spiritual beings; does help to make the whole process easier and increases the amount of energy available to you. This is especially true when your hands are not in physical contact with the client as in the case of auric healing or absent healing. In order to heal, all you need to do is relax your client; set an appropriate mood, using candles, incense, soft music, etc; sit them in a comfortable chair in front of you, ask them to close their eyes and focus on their breathing. Then place you hands on their shoulders and ask for help in healing this person, relax and allow the energy to flow, intention is the most important thing.

Healing terms or holistic healing terms, an illness or dis-ease be it physical, mental, emotional or spiritual in nature is first perceived by our systems as an energy within our spiritual consciousness, this then slowly filters down through our aura into our chakras and into our body, where it manifests as a physical symptom of some type. So healing the aura, etc, helps to remove the problem before it reaches us. That said, healing doesn't always work as occasionally the dis-ease or illness is a part of our growth as individuals. In this case no amount of healing will help it as it is something we need to experience. The same can be true of this if a client feels, often on a sub-conscious level; that their illness gets them the attention they want, on these occasions it is being used as a sort of psychological crutch. Often the actual illness has already gone and what remains is psychosomatic, but it will not be given up until the client is ready to move on in their life, this is often termed as a 'victim consciousness'.

Given below is an overly simplified and dramatic example of how a 'Dis-ease' can manifest in a physical illness:

Possible Dis-ease Manifestation Example

"When our client was very young he was abused physically by a relative for a brief period, when he complained no-one believed him, in fact he was punished for making it up. The abuse ended when the relative passed away in an accident. As our client grew up he forgot about this experience as best he could, though it had deeply scarred him psychologically and damaged his relationship with his parents. As he grew up, he was nervous and had trouble relating to and trusting people. It also made him feel self conscious and unimportant.

His system had dealt with the experience in the only way available to it and as result this wound had not healed well; like a broken bone which wasn't set and had healed badly; causing great arthritic pain in later life. As the years passed, he grew up and had children, then a similar experience happened to his child, he reacted the same way his parents had. This was because it was all too painful for him to bear as a result of his own un addressed experiences. But as time passed this incident began to eat away at him, first on a subconscious level, later on a more conscious one. The negative energy, from his own experience, which was being fed by his child's experience; (which he subconsciously dealt with by falling out with the child's abuser over another issue) until one day, he began to experience a pain in his stomach. When he went to his doctor he was told he had cancer. This is how the negative energy, which had been eating away at him all his life, had manifested itself."

In this example the dis-ease occurs on a holistic level, filtering through the client's whole system affecting his every decision; cancer is only given as an example of a serious illness or disease. Healing is often a good prevent-ative medicine as it teaches you to be aware of yourself and your body. In Chinese traditional medicine in the past the doctors were paid when their patients were well, not when they were ill.

Healing Energies

When we talk about healing energies we are usually talking about what the Japanese call 'Ki', the Chinese call it 'Chi', the Indians call it 'Prana', Spiritual Healers call it 'universal energy' or 'unconditional love'. All of these energies are one and the same; they may be slightly different vibrations of it, as light is always light, whatever colour/vibration/ frequency it is.

In healing it is important to remember we are talking not just about physical illness, we are talking about holistic healing, covering mind, emotions, body and spirit. Often we are dealing with the root cause of the symptoms, which are being presented to us, a lack of self respect may lead to depression, but we will probably be healing the cause of the client's lack of self respect; this will help to Heal the whole person. We will be healing the client's 'Dis-ease'.

Healing is a very big subject; it incorporates all of the most well-known complementary therapies, orthodox medicine, religious practices, psychology and the paranormal. As a result this will only serve as a basic introduction and will focus on the more Shamanic techniques and spiritual healing. With regular practice, the techniques I will show you will help you to become an accomplished healer. You will have to decide how much you wish to look into this subject, what courses you wish to explore and how far you wish to go.

Ki Energy

Ki Energy is divided into two types, Yin (female, cold, empty, etc) and Yang (male, hot, full, etc). These are considered as complementary opposites, however in health terms in Oriental therapies such as Shiatsu, Acupuncture and Reiki, the Ki is perceived in the body in 5 types:

Although the Ki of the body is one energy, it is traditionally distinguished, according to function, into five types:

339

a) Organ Ki – associated with the proper characteristic functioning of the solid and hollow organs (Zang Fu).

b) Meridian or Nourishing Ki – the refined part of the 'True Qi' which circulates mainly in the meridians, some flows with the blood in the vessels.

c) Protective Ki – the coarser part of the 'True Ki'; circulates outside the Meridians, in the chest and abdomen and between the muscles and skin. The most Yang type of Ki, resists external perverse energy (Climatic factors) and regulates the pores and sweat. It has a rough quality, classically described as 'fierce and bold', the body outer defence system.

d) Chest Ki / True Ki – the precursor of 'True Ki', formed from the fusion of 'Grain Ki' and 'Cosmic Ki' (clean air) in the lungs. It activates and regulates the heart and lungs, respiration and circulation of the vessels; the upper sea of Ki known as 'Essential Ki'.

e) Original Ki – the active, dynamic, transformative component of Kidney essence, which derives from pre- natal or 'Ancestral Ki', supplemented by surplus reserves of 'True Ki'. Original Ki itself acts as a catalyst in the transformations of energy from food and air (i.e. the production of 'True Ki'). It regulates development and growth throughout life and is associated with sexual energy and reproductive power. It circulates the whole body and activates the 'Triple Heater'.

As mentioned before, Ki is divided into the 2 concepts of Yin and Yang, this provides a basis upon which to work in Shiatsu, allowing the Ki energy to be viewed as flowing through the body in a balanced manner, or a Yin (empty) manner, or Yang (full or over full manner); this provides us with a means to diagnose medical problems and treat them.

The 5 Elements or Phases

This was further expanded in the 4th Century to include the 5 Elements or 5 Phases as they are also known; this system allows us to refine the basic diagnose and treatment further. In this system, Yin is viewed in a Destructive or Insulting Cycle, Yang in a Creative Cycle; these concepts are then applied to the 5 Phases concepts of:

Wood – expansion and growth
Fire – Upward movement and climatic activity, a maximal state
Metal – contraction and declining state
Water – downward movement, stillness and rest, maximal decline
Earth – the centre, a pivot for change and a moderating influence in transitions, neutrality

In addition to these Creation and Destruction Cycles a Controlling Cycle was added and the 5 Elements were viewed as this:

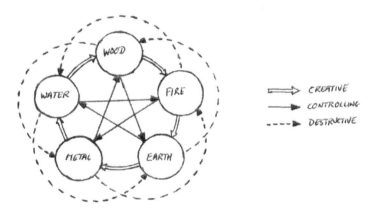

The Creative cycle shows that Wood (fuel) produces Fire; Fire produces Earth (ashes); Earth produces Metal (ore); Metal produces Water (condensation); Water (rain) produces Wood.

The Destructive cycle shows that Wood conquers Earth (covering it); Earth conquers Water (damming it); Water conquers Fire (dowsing it); Fire conquers Metal (melting it); Metal conquers Wood (cutting it). These 5 elements are then linked with the solid and hollow organs of the body:

Wood – Liver and Gall Bladder
Fire – Heart and Small Intestine
Metal – Lungs and Large Intestine
Water – Kidneys and Bladder
Earth – Spleen and Stomach

The solid organs are said to 'store and not drain'; the hollow organs are said to 'drain and not store'. These organs are connected via the Meridian and Tsubo system so that we get:

Kidney Meridian stimulates Liver but sedates Heart
Liver Meridian stimulates Heart but sedates Spleen
Heart Meridian stimulates Spleen but sedates Lung
Spleen Meridian stimulates Lung but sedates Kidney
Lung Meridian stimulates Kidney but sedates Liver

The 'Mother – Son Law' is also applied to this, this states that the Ki flows through the Meridians in a set sequence (Controlling Cycle):

Lung - Large Intestine - Stomach - Spleen - Heart - Small Intestine - Bladder - Kidneys - Heart Protector- Triple Heater - Gall Bladder - Liver

Eastern Philosophy

The Meridians and Tsubos, are thought to have been discovered as the result of battles. The Samurai warriors realised, as a result of their wounds received in battle, that other long-term health problems they had, would clear up or improve.

342

Eventually these areas and wounds were studied and collected in a healing system and the Meridians and Tsubos were discovered. From there Acupuncture, Acupressure and Shiatsu originated. There is evidence that the curative properties of many of these pressure points were known about long before the Samurai discovered them. The late Stone Age / early Copper Age, frozen mummy, known as the Oetzi Ice Man, found in Italy, has tattoos on his body which relate to arthritis relief Tsubo's; It is also known that he suffered from this complaint. There are 14 Meridians throughout the body; these are named after the Internal Organs they relate to. These in turn are governed by Yin and Yang Ki energy:

Yin and Yang are the Eastern equivalent of light (Yang) and dark (Yin), or good and evil. There is one MAJOR difference though; they are not considered to be in opposition to each other, rather they are complementary opposites. All things can be categorised into either Yin or Yang energy:

Yin is Feminine in nature and is associated with things such as night, moon, cold, passivity, earth, in, front, matter, low, down, negative and heaviness.

Yang is Masculine in nature and associated with things such as day, sun, hot, active, heaven, out, back, spirit, high, up, positive and lightness.

There is no truly pure Yin or Yang thing, even the Yin and Yang symbols contain a little dot or seed of their opposite. All things are formed from a combination of both Yin and Yang energy. In Eastern Philosophy there is no good or evil, as it is seen in the West, this is because this philosophy is based on the observations of Nature. There are many things to be cautious of in nature, things which can cause harm to you, but there is no evil. Nature is about survival and although that can appear harsh, it is not evil. A person who is excessively Yin or Yang in nature, would be considered off balance and prone to illness associated with the excessive energy.

In the Yin/Yang symbol, or Taiji to give it its proper name; you can see that each half contains within it the energy of its opposite; it is also considered that something, which is excessively Yin or Yang, will transform into its opposite. The Eastern Philosophy teaches the only constant is change. The Taiji symbol is not considered to be a static one but rather one that is constantly rotating, via transformation. So the same symbol can also look like this:

YANG

YIN

Think of it like a waterwheel, spinning as it fills and empties. Neither Yin or Yang is considered better than the other both are considered essential to life. The Meridians are considered either primarily Yin or Yang, although they contain aspects of both within them. In addition to this distinction between energy governing the Meridians and everything else; the

344

Meridians and everything else was said to be ruled by the 5 Elements; These Elements exist in a Creative / Destructive Cycle with each other (as mentioned earlier):

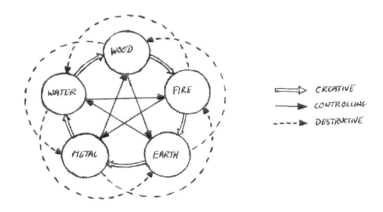

These 5 Elements are known as the '5 Phases'. The Basic Associations given for these 5 Phases or Elements are given below:

WOOD

Meridians: Liver (Yin) and Gall Bladder (Yang).
Meridian Function: Liver – control, planning, Detoxification.
Gall Bladder – Decision making, distribution.
Season: Spring
Transformation: Birth
Emotions: Positive – Humour; Negative – Anger
Capacity: Planning
Activity: Starting
Mental Capacity: Planning, Asserting and Controlling
Colour: Blue and Green
Western Element: Air (East)

FIRE

Primary Meridians: Heart (Yin) and Small Intestine (Yang)
Secondary Meridians: Heart Controller (Yin) and Triple Heater (Yang)
Meridian Function: Heart – Emotional/ Spiritual Centre; Small Intestine –
Assimilation: Heart Governor – Circulation; Triple Heater – Protection.
Season: Summer
Transformation: Growth
Emotions: Positive – Joy; Negative – Hysteria
Capacity: Spiritual Awareness
Activity: Peak
Mental Capacity: Sensitivity and Love
Colour: Red
Western Element: Spirit (Centre)

EARTH

Meridians: Spleen (Yin) and Stomach (Yang)
Meridian Function: Spleen – Digestion, transformation; Stomach –
  Nourishment
Season: Late Summer
Transformation: Ripening
Emotions: Positive – Sympathy; Negative – Self Pity
Capacity: Ideas and Opinions
Activity: Decreasing
Mental Capacity: Concentration and Analysis
Colour: Yellow
Western Element: Earth (North)

METAL

Meridians: Lungs (Yin) and Large Intestine (Yang)
Meridian Function: Lungs – Vitality, intake of Ki (from air); Large
  Intestine – Elimination
Season: Autumn
Transformation: Decay
Emotions: Positive – Positivity; Negative – Grief, Melancholy

Capacity: Elimination
Activity: Balance (Activity / Rest)
Mental Capacity: Taking in / Letting go
Colour: White
Western Element: Water (West)

WATER

Meridians: Kidneys (Yin) and Bladder (Yang)
Meridian Function: Kidneys – Impetus; Bladder – Purification
Season: Winter
Transformation: Storing
Emotions: Positive – Courage; Negative – Fear
Capacity: Ambition and Willpower
Activity: Rest
Mental Capacity: Willpower and Endurance
Colour: Blue and Black
Western Element: Fire (South)

These lists of correspondences of the 5 Traditional Eastern Elements only scratch the surface of this subject. I have also included a rough guide to the 5 Western Elements of Earth, Air, Fire, Water and Spirit, which are used in magikal practices.

As you can see they do not relate exactly; this is because the Eastern associations would be governed by a different Western Element. The elemental associations are used in all magikal and healing practices the world over, they do not always correspond to the same directional quarters though. This is because these are only a rough spiritual map of the cosmos, usually depicted as a circle, hence the directions and all the elements reside in each of the quarters. Both systems work well though providing a good framework of associations.

You will also notice that some of the meridians do not exist in modern medicine, this because it is a very old system and because the physical associations have slightly differing functions as well. There also another 2 Meridians known as the Central Meridians, they run down the centre of the body front Conception Meridian (Yin) and back Governing Vessel Meridian (Yang); these Meridians relate more to the Chakra System (we will look at this shortly). Given over the next few pages are diagrams illustrating the Meridians and Tsubos:

The Meridians

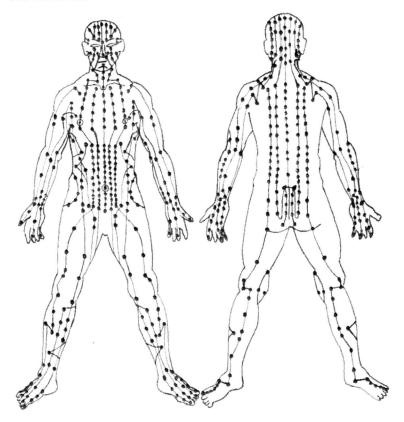

BASIC SHIATSU POINTS - FRONT

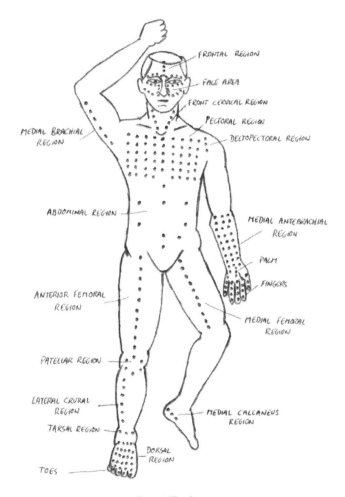

FRONTAL REGION

FACE AREA

FRONT CERVICAL REGION

PECTORAL REGION

MEDIAL BRACHIAL REGION

DELTOPECTORAL REGION

ABDOMINAL REGION

MEDIAL ANTEBRACHIAL REGION

PALM

FINGERS

ANTERIOR FEMORAL REGION

MEDIAL FEMORAL REGION

PATELLAR REGION

LATERAL CRURAL REGION

TARSAL REGION

MEDIAL CALCANEUS REGION

TOES

DORSAL REGION

Front Tsubos

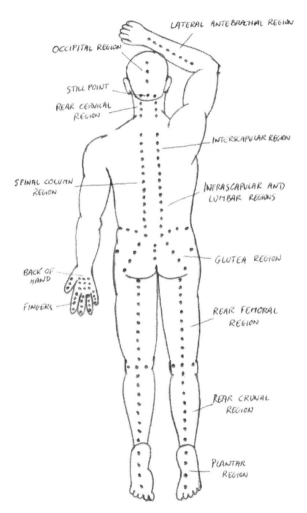

Rear Tsubos

BASIC SHIATSU POINTS - SIDE

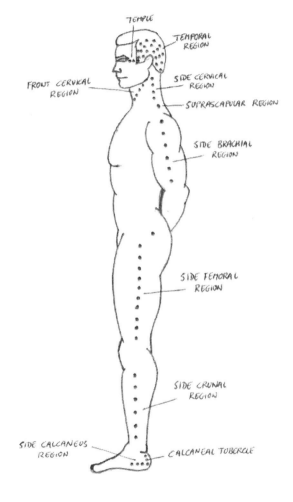

TEMPLE

TEMPORAL REGION

FRONT CERVICAL REGION

SIDE CERVICAL REGION

SUPRASCAPULAR REGION

SIDE BRACHIAL REGION

SIDE FEMORAL REGION

SIDE CRURAL REGION

SIDE CALCANEUS REGION

CALCANEAL TUBERCLE

Side Tsubos

Auric Healing

In spiritual traditions it is considered that we (and all things) exist on many different levels, at many different frequencies of vibration during our lifetime. Our bodies generate an energy field, which relates to what we consider our personal space; this is known as our aura. As can be seen from the illustration the body's aura is closely related to the main energy centres or chakras, having 7 layers of corresponding colours. This is a view the scientific community is also beginning to accept with its study into dimensions beyond the usual 3. The aura can also be seen using Killian photography. Also with practice looking just past the person's body with a defocused stare using a plain background. Not all healers see auras etc; this is entering into more psychic levels. The chakras and aura are commonly seen as being constructed of a spectrum of colours much like the rainbow. The aura is usually hazy to look at and the chakras look like coloured whirlpools.

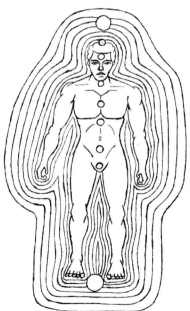

The aura and chakras

Given below are the colours most commonly associated with the chakras and aura layers of a healthy person, the order is top – bottom for both:

Crown Chakra – Auric Layer furthest from body- White
Brow Chakra – Aura – Purple
Throat Chakra – Aura – Blue (Turquoise)
Heart Chakra – Aura – Green
Solar Plexus – Aura – Yellow
Sacral Chakra (Tantien) – Aura – Orange
Base Chakra – Auric Layer Closest to Body – Red

These chakras and auric layers can be seen like the different levels of consciousness within our beings. Each one relating to specific levels of thought and feeling; e.g. it is often said that 'men only think with their dicks'; another way of expressing this would be that 'men only think with their base chakra'. However someone like Buddha would be considered to only think with their crown chakra.

All these levels of consciousness have their purpose and vital roles to play in life, overall when all are used in their proper ways you will have a well balanced individual. Creating balance is one of the most important roles of a healer or any spiritually inclined person. It is a healer's duty to remain in and improve upon their state of balance in order to function effectively as a healer, it is also important for them to re- establish a state of balance within their clients and to encourage them to improve on their state of balance.

Illness and disease, be it physical, mental, emotional or spiritual; is perceived as the client being in a state of 'dis-ease' with themselves and their circumstances. This leads to a state of 'unbalance', when they become more susceptible to other illness. Spare universal energy is viewed as having different levels of vibration, some positive some negative; but in many ways it is like electricity, it is neutral. It is our intent which defines its use. It can be used for good or ill. Healing energy is viewed as one of the highest forms of energy.

Sometimes it can be difficult to accept all this, most of us only believe in what we can see or feel. Healing involves taking a leap of faith, as often we can not see or feel anything; especially if we are new to it. Spiritual energy and energy work needs to be viewed like the wind, we can't see it, but we can see its effects and feel it on our face. In auric healing, which is often done in combination with hands on healing, we are working within the client's aura. As a healer you will be aware that you are standing within your client's aura in order to do the healing, just as they are sitting within your aura. This means you are doing aura healing even when you are not concentrating on it.

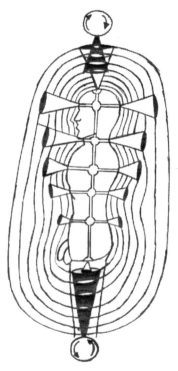

Chakra routes front and rear

The aura of a person is viewed as a large protective bubble which surrounds everyone and at the same time connects everyone and everything. It acts much like a filter, trapping any negative energy within it, which is directed at us, or trapping any, that is directed from us. It also does the same for positive energy. The aura is believed to be constructed in a similar way to a feather, which is why the Native Americans use feathers to clean the aura in their smudging ceremonies. As our auras act as filters they need cleaning regularly, retuning and occasionally repairing. It is this which you do when you are working on an aura.

Aura Smudging

This technique is most commonly associated with the Native American Indians, however the Native Americans originated in Mongolia. Smudging is a technique which has been used by Shamen the world over for centuries, it is safe, effective and simple to learn. As already said, the Amerindians originated in the East on the Russian Steppes and Mongolian plains. The technique involves the use of incense which is a wholly Eastern tradition, it is used to purify the aura of any negative energy which may be trapped in it.

A sage wand is traditionally used to smudge; this is available in many New Age Shops. Dried sage from the supermarket is just as good and very cheap. The sage is often mixed with other herbs to add additional benefits to the process, these include juniper, pine, sweet grass, cedar and lavender. The herbs themselves are believed to drive away negative entities or energies and bless the person being Smudged.

If you are using dried herbs, it is advisable to use a charcoal block (also easily available) to burn them on and a fireproof dish or shell. Make sure you get your client's permission prior to smudging them, also explain what you are doing and why. Having gained their permission, light the smudge wand, (or the charcoal block, wait until it begins to glow before adding the dried herbs).

Ask your client to stand up with their arms stretched out to the sides and legs a little open. Now starting about 6 inches away from the crown, move the smouldering smudge mix though your client's aura. Start at the top, move down the front of the body, including the legs and feet and up the back, to the head again. Then the process is repeated, from the head, move down the right-hand side of the body, going around the arms, down to the feet, across and up the left-hand side, ending at the head again. As you perform the smudging pray that the client's energy system is balanced and cleansed.

Traditionally a raptor's (bird of prey's) feather or wing is used to waft the smudge smoke around the aura. This is because raptors are viewed as sacred beings which fly closest to the sun and God; also because the aura is formed like a feather and so it acts like a comb to straighten out the auric fibres. If you do not have a raptor's feather any large feather will do.

If you are concerned about the smudge mixes which can be a little messy, you may use joss sticks. The general idea is that the smoke carries your prayers to the heavens and the sweet smoke repels and also sedates the negative entities or energies, as it does with insects and makes it easier to remove them.

Energy Projection and Absent Healing

When you are doing healing (especially absent healing) this is what you are basically doing, projecting energy. Energy projection is a combination of knowledge and willpower, or mind over matter. First, it is essential to remember you are made of energy, everything is made of energy. In fact that's all there is, if you are looking for God, think about what that word means (omnipotent, omnipresent, omnisentient, creative spiritual being), think about what I just said and the answer is staring you in the face, especially if you are looking in the mirror!

Energy can not be stopped it simply spreads out, dissipates into infinity, so is there life after death, if all is made of energy? Work it out for yourself!

356

Everything there is, was and shall be, is already there simply vibrating at different rates. So once you have realised that, which can be as simple or as complex as you choose to make it; then you should realise that energy projection is a very natural process via which everything moves. Then all you need to do is to decide how you are going to visualise the energy and what purpose it will serve.

Light and colours are very useful media for this. It is easier and more powerful if you use the well-established symbols which the majority of people use, as this is already implanted in the human super-consciousness. The super-consciousness is like the human race's higher self.

To empower these symbols it is necessary to use strong emotion, guided by rational thought. The emotions are the powerhouse of our being. This is why there is so much poltergeist activity around teenagers or pubescent teenagers and mentally ill people. Then all you need to do is direct this energy, using a link or connection, e.g. hair, photo, visualisation, etc. It is not necessary to visualise the energy on its journey as it will naturally travel via the most direct and efficient route since this is its nature, much like electricity travels via the route of least resistance.

Basic Colour Therapy

Given below are the most commonly used colour meanings, which relate to the colours of the rainbow and the chakras, this also relates them to the whole colour spectrum. Colours will appear as you are doing healing work and meditation, so these meanings will give you a basic guide.

White – Crown Chakra, Brain and Pineal Gland; **Positive emotion** - Peace and Harmony; **Negative emotion** – Inferiority complex, Martyr Syndrome.

Purple – Brow Chakra, Pituitary Gland, Eyes, Nose and Ears; **Positive emotion** – Trust, Innocence; **Negative emotion** – Fears, Phobias, Self Doubt, Inability to trust one's own intuition.

Blue – Throat Chakra, Thyroid and Parathyroid metabolism; **Positive emotion** - Communication, Openness; **Negative emotion** - Inability to express oneself, unmotivated.

Green – Heart Chakra, Heart, Lungs and Blood Pressure; **Positive emotion** - Compassion, Sympathy, Unconditional Love; **Negative emotion** – Insecure, Needy Love, feelings of persecution.

Yellow – Solar Plexus Chakra, Nervous System, Liver, Pancreas; **Positive emotion** – Self Esteem, Confidence; **Negative emotion** – Jealousy, Envy, Fear, Obsessive, Emotional immaturity.

Orange – Sacral Chakra, Adrenals, Kidneys, flow of body fluids; **Positive emotion** – Creativity, Sexual and Emotional expression; **Negative emotion** – Shyness, Daydreamer, unable to cope with reality.

Red – Base Chakra, Tanden, Coccyx, Gonads; **Positive emotion** – Courage, Honour, Responsible; **Negative emotion** – Irresponsible, Ruthless, Bad Tempered, Stubborn.

White is all colours and is always seen as a positive sign in the aura or chakras.

Black is an absence of light, not colour, it is usually seen as a negative sign in the aura or chakras.

This is only very basic colour therapy; I would suggest you read a good book on the subject. There are many things associated with these colours, which may be used as visualisations for the client to focus on during healing, e.g. water – blue, trees – green, etc. they will help to stimulate the appropriate chakras.

Chakras and Meridians

In addition to the 7 (9) Major Chakras observed in healing, there are additional chakras you may come across, another 23 are commonly observed. These chakras are not essential in healing, the main chakra system takes these extra ones into account and represents a more compressed form. There are also 23 minor chakras; these are located mainly at your joints and many are used for giving healing. The major chakras can also be used in this manner:

Many of these are essential to healers, especially the ones in the palms. Personally I also find I often use the ones in the wrists and elbows a lot. I often feel the minor chakras are confused with the Tsubos on the body's meridian paths. These could also be classed as minor chakras, as they basically perform the same function as energy centres. There are approximately 650 Tsubos on the body which run along 14 Meridian Paths, roughly in alignment with the Nervous System:

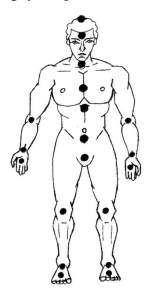

The 23 minor chakras

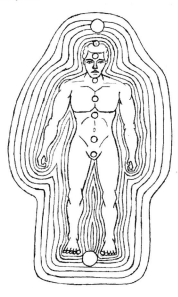

The 9 major chakras

359

Shiatsu

Shiatsu is a form of Japanese healing combining healing energy, in the form of Ki, with acupressure techniques. Acupressure involves applying directed weight to pressure points (Tsubos) on the body's meridian system, which runs closely with the bodies nervous system, to restore and balance the Ki energy flow through our systems. Given below are the basic techniques for applying Shiatsu techniques, plus some safe exercises to try on yourself or family and friends:

The 3 Tonifiers

Given here are 3Tsubo Points Stomach 36 (St.36) and Spleen 6 (Sp.6); these are Tonification Points, they are stimulating in a general 'pick me up' sort of way:

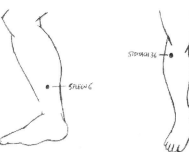

Spleen 6   **Stomach 36**

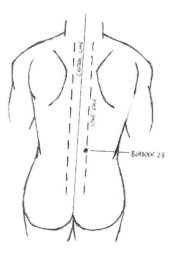

Bladder 23 (and Yu points)

The Yu Points and Shiatsu Techniques

The Yu Points or Tsubos are the Shiatsu Points which relate to the internal organs. It is possible to give a short Shiatsu treatment to the whole Meridian System simply by working on these points. use the same method as for the Tonifiers.

The basic method for using Shiatsu is 4 fold:
1) Palm Heel Massage
2) Applied Pressure Technique
3) Palm Heel Massage
4) Energy Brush

Palm Heel Massage
The palm heel is the raised area of your palm, nearest the wrist. The technique is simply a basic massage, moving the muscles in a stretching movement. Its purpose is preparation.

Applied Pressure Technique
When using pressure techniques as used in Shiatsu or acupressure it is important to remember that no physical excursion should be used. The applied pressure is from body weight only. The techniques used are finger and thumb tips.

Energy Brush
This simply refers to brushing any excess energy, generated during the treatment, off your client and into the Earth.

The Still Point Spinal Alignment
This is a powerful technique, which when performed correctly can stop a migraine, headaches, relieve neck and lower back pain, align the jaw, help to release emotional tension, has sedative qualities and has been known to be as effective as a full chiropractic treatment. If done incorrectly, nothing happens; so it is a safe technique.

Whilst in Reiki Chiryo Position '1', use your index fingers to locate Tsubos '10' on the Bladder Meridian. These are located on the back of the upper neck, on both sides of the spinal column, where the bony structure of the head meets the neck, close to the hairline.

The Tsubos are two tiny depressions in the neck muscle under the skin. Ask your client to tell you when they feel something like a pinprick in their brain, accompanied by a slightly spaced-out sensation. It is not painful unless the client is highly stressed out or has a damaged neck, so check first. There are several other Tsubos in this area, which have a similar effect, Bladder 10 is the closest to the spine. When you have located these points, apply gentle pressure and watch the client's breathing. This technique balances the spinal fluid pulse (17 beats per minute). When the balance occurs the heartbeat, pulse rate and breathing become momentarily synchronised.

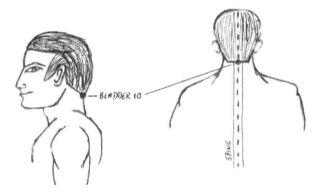

You will know when the still point synchronization is reached, it may take a couple of moments or minutes, the client will usually sigh deeply and their breathing will still. When this happens apply slightly more pressure to the points and pull back/down on the points about 2cm. If you do this too early the technique won't work, wait until it happens again. You may feel the neck move slightly, the traction should be gentle, don't use any force; hold that position.

362

After a short while you will feel a slight pulse in your two fingertips, when you feel it in both, release the pressure and remove your hands. The technique is complete. It will probably take some practice to get it right, you can try it on yourself. Now finish off the Reiki treatment and be sure to ground your client afterwards, as the effects will leave them a little spaced-out for about 30 minutes.

Note: Shiatsu Techniques use the same pressure points that are used in the Martial Arts to great effect; DO NOT experiment with additional pressure points, unless you are, or you are under supervision of, someone who is properly trained in Shiatsu.

Reiki

Reiki (pronounced Ray – Key) is made up of 2 Japanese words:

REI – Meaning Universal Wisdom
KI- Meaning Life or Universal Energy

Reiki basically means universal life energy guided by universal wisdom. The Reiki system of natural healing was partly re-discovered from the Buddhist *Sutras* (ancient holy texts) by Dr. Mikao Usui in 1850, who also filled in the gaps to make a complete working healing system.

Ki is an ancient word, which the Japanese use to express a concept, which has many names in all cultures worldwide. To the Chinese it is Chi, to the Hindus it is Prana, to many it is spirit. It is closely connected to the breath. Everything has Ki, if it is alive, it has Ki. Or everything is formed from Ki and everything is alive.

Reiki is not a part of any particular religion or set of beliefs; it is constantly evolving and will enhance and complement any belief system you may have. Ki is the same energy used, generated and stored in the martial arts, yoga and healing. You can call it what you like, but it is basically the energy of life.

Reiki is a simple method, which allows you to consciously channel this Ki energy through you in order to heal yourself and others. Reiki is a simple method of spiritual intuitive healing or laying-on of hands, probably adapted from an ancient traditional Japanese healing system, called Te a te. Reiki is taught using a standard Oriental teaching method known as a Kata or Form, called a Chiryo in Reiki. This Chiryo (the full Reiki treatment hand positions) will allow you to learn effectively how to give a whole body treatment, which will ensure you treat what needs treating.

How Reiki Works

Reiki is considered to be an intelligent form of healing energy, which is directed by spiritual beings known as Reiki guides. Reiki is a pure energy and is unaffected by the healer's own state, although the clearer/more balanced the healer is the more effective the Reiki will be. The amount of Reiki which flows through the healer will vary depending on what is needed and whether the client is resisting the healing or not. Never give Reiki to someone without asking the client's permission.

Reiki, like all healing, doesn't always work. If you don't feel the Reiki energy is flowing, but you haven't had this sort of problem before, then simply go continue the hands on treatment as normal.

A person can be experiencing ill health for a number of reasons, some of these may be karmic. It is also often the case that you feel you have done very little and the client has experienced wonderful healing, this is why I say go through the treatment anyway.

When Reiki is flowing well it is most apparent in the healer's hands. Reiki most often manifests as extreme heat through the hands; although there are other sensations which may also manifest, it is different for everyone. Reiki manifests in a manner which is needed at that time, however the effects of a full treatment can be more powerful than at first perceived. Always allow clients to get up in their own time and offer them a glass of water afterwards.

364

The effects of a full Reiki Treatment will last approximately 2 – 3 days as it takes time for it to filter through the client's energy system. Simply tell the client the effects are ongoing and to take it easy on themselves for a few days. Never try to force Reiki energy out, you will only start to draw on your own energy, the treatment will not be as effective and you will be worn out. Always use the path of least resistance.

After giving a Reiki treatment you will have also received Reiki yourself, so take time to ground yourself, before doing anything important.

Healing Treatment Preparation

When you are about to give a Reiki Chiryo, or any other form of healing, there are a number of things you must do in preparation:

Room Preparation – Prior to your client's arrival, it is important to ensure that the room in which the treatment is to be given is conducive to relaxation e.g. soft lighting, gentle relaxing music (preferably no vocals, you could offer your client a choice), a non-cluttered, clean environment. The client will need somewhere to lie down which is comfortable and which you can get around easily. Traditional Japanese medicine is usually practised on the floor or a futon, although a massage couch may be easier for you to work on.

Healer Preparation – Personal hygiene is essential. Always ensure you are clean prior to giving a treatment (especially if you smoke, ensure you are not smelling of it). Ensure any plasters being worn are fresh, check your nails are not too long. It is a good idea to remove any metal items from yourself and the client, as shocks can occasionally occur. Wash your hands before and after each treatment, as you work on the eyes and feet during it; ensure you are in a relaxed state, calm your mind and forget all your worldly concerns. Give yourself a token wash prior to the treatment, even if you are clean. This allows you time to relax and go into healing mode. I always go to the toilet, then wash my hands, allow cold water to run over them, then I dab a little on my forehead and crown, followed by a sip of water. This is a trigger to my subconscious to prepare to heal; I am also cleaning myself physically on an external and internal level, as well as spiritually.

Client Preparation – Talk to your client, check you have their correct details for your records. Explain what is involved in the treatment (If they haven't had a treatment before), tell them what they may experience, ask for their permission to give the treatment. Never touch the groin (or breasts if your client is female), ask them if there are any areas that are highly sensitive and they want you to avoid. Ask them if they have any medical conditions or specific problems. Do not make a diagnosis, unless you are professionally qualified to do so. Ask your client if they are comfortable to close their eyes, place their tongue on the roof of the mouth and forget all their problems and just focus on their breathing.

The Full Reiki Treatment (Hand Positions)

Given on the next pages are the hand positions for a full Reiki treatment in numerical order (begin on the top right) and the approximate time periods for each position. These times apply only to inexperienced healers, I suggest experienced healers use their intuition to guide them on the time periods needed. As will new healers as their experience increases.

The hand positions used to give Reiki involve the two hands being in contact or close proximity at all times, this is believed to increase the energy flow during healing. Ensure at least one hand remains in contact with the client throughout the treatment, even if you are moving and not involved in actual healing; this is for reassurance. Your hands should be resting lightly on your client, do not apply any pressure.

When you reach positions 31 and 32, which are the same as positions 15 and 16, cup the foot between your 2 hands, front and back. Brush any excess energy from the feet into the ground, this helps to ground your client.

At the end of the treatment place one hand at the base of the spine and the other at the top of the spine. Visualise a brilliant white light surrounding your client and balancing all their energies. When you have done this, gently rub your client's back to help bring them back to their normal awareness and tell them you have finished. Offer your client a glass of water and have one yourself. Ask them how they feel and tell them to stand up carefully when they feel ready to. Keep an eye on them as they may be more affected than they realise. I suggest you keep written records of your clients, this should contain relevant contact details, relevant medical information and a progress report. Read and update these records when you see the client.

The Benefits of the Hand Positions

Given below are the basic benefits of the Hand Positions used in a Chiryo:

1) Bindu Chakra – Brain, Upper Spinal Cord. Balance and coordination helps to reduce stress, fear, irritation and shock. (1 minute)

2) Crown Chakra – Ears, Pineal Gland, Hypothalamus. Balances Left and Right Brain Hemispheres - Helps in control of headaches, worry, depression, hyperactivity, fear and memory retention. (1 minute)

3) Brow Centre Chakra – Eyes, Sinuses, Nose, Mouth, Teeth, Mucus Membranes, Pituitary Gland and Thalamus. Head - Helps concentration and enhances Intuition. (30 seconds)

4) Throat and Heart Chakras – Chest, Heart, Lungs, Pectoral Muscles, Thymus Gland, Immune System, Trachea, Thyroid and Parathyroid. Throat and Chest – Reduces anger, jealousy, emotional release, increases expressiveness, unconditional love and increases acceptance. (1 minute)

5) & 6) Solar Plexus Chakra – Liver, Spleen, Gall Bladder, Duoenum, Intestine, Kidneys, Pancreas and Adrenals. Mid Section – Assists in detoxification of the Blood Systems and Energy circulation. 930 seconds0

7) Sacral Chakra (Tantien) – Transverse Colon, Ascending and Descending Colon, Small Intestine, Bladder. Stomach Region – Relieves cramps, flatulence, fluid retention and increases confidence. (30 seconds)

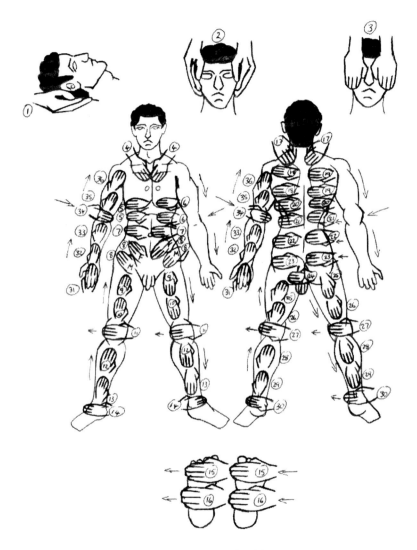

Front and Rear Positions

8) Base Chakra – Intestines, Bladder, Ovaries, Uterus, Prostate, Urethra, Lymph and Gonads. Groin Region – Helps skin problems, PMT, Migraines, Constipation and Diarrhoea. (30 seconds)

15) & 16) Root Chakra – Feet. Stimulates Reflexology points on the feet, increases balance and grounding. (30 seconds)

17a) Rear Heart Chakra – Nervous System, Upper Back and Shoulder Blades. Top of the Spine – Reduces tension, stress and sense of burdens. (1 minute)

19) & 20) Rear Solar Plexus Chakra – Kidneys, Adrenals, Middle back. Mid Back – Relieves mood swings, fear and phobias. (1 minute)

21) - 24) Rear Base Chakra – Coccyx, Rectum, Spinal Nerves and Sciatic Nerve. Lower Back – Helps in release of past energies, balancing and grounding. (1 minute)

9) – 14) & 25) – 30) – Legs Front and Back – Helps flexibility, releases tension and stress. (30 seconds)

When not to use Reiki or Other Healing

Reiki is a powerful and safe form of natural healing. However there are situations when extra care should be taken:

1) Do not use Reiki directly on any broken bone prior to it being set; it may increase the healing process and make it harder to reset them correctly.

2) Never knowingly transmit Reiki energy directly into a cancerous area as it may energise the tumour. Instead work around the area and visualise the tumour becoming de-energised and shrinking.

3) If your client is undergoing chemotherapy only give them Reiki a maximum of twice per week, to ensure its effects are not diminished.

4) Treating someone who is under the influence of alcohol may sober them up quicker and bring on a hangover.

5) Never give Reiki when you have been drinking alcohol or taking recreational drugs.

6) If your client is on medication for a long term ailment, advise them to have their GP check their doses, as they may diminish in time.

7) If in doubt about how to conduct a treatment, ask for divine guidance and intend the energy to work for the client's highest good.

8) Do not diagnose unless qualified to do so.

9) Suggest your clients also seek professional medical advice for their ailments, especially if serious.

Note: Remember Reiki and all Healing is a Complementary Therapy, NOT an alternative to Allopathic Medicine, Professional Medical Advice or First Aid.

Reiki Attunements

Reiki differs from other forms of healing instruction, in that it usually involves a form of Initiation Ritual, called an attunement. An attunement works in a way Reiki sounds like; a Ray – Key. The attunements performed at each level of Reiki, basically act as keys to allow you access to higher and purer energy levels and sources. During these attunements Reiki symbols are placed within your energy system via your chakras. These symbols act as a key or pass to allow you access to the Reiki energy and guides. They also act as a beacon, attracting people to you in need of Reiki Healing.

In addition to this they rearrange your own energy system; this has the effect of purifying and balancing it, this will also improve your healing abilities.

In Reiki, the attunement ritual looks a little like someone blowing into your head, waving their hands about and tapping you, while you pray. It is an Internal Process, in which the Reiki Master redirects their Ki energy from its natural path and forces it out through their hands into your Energy System, while also asking for assistance from the Reiki Guides and placing the Reiki Symbols into your energy system. The Attunement is only the start of the process, which lasts for the next 21 days, as the Reiki energy filters slowly through your chakras.

Attunement can be a very powerful experience; it has a wide range of effects on people, though is rarely the same for any two people. I've heard of mass Reiki attunements being given, with up to 7 people being attuned at the same time; like a production line, it makes me wonder if they are asked 'do you want fries with that?'. This, to my mind, cheapens the experience and detracts from its sacredness. All attunements given by me will be on a 'one to one' basis in privacy.

I believe the Reiki attunements will have the most profound effects on people who are new to healing, but it also improves the energy of experienced healers, most notably via excessive heat in their hands. Once you have been attuned to the Reiki energies, they will be with you for life, even if you reject the energy. It will still be there at a later date should you choose to access it again.

At Level One, Reiki mainly focuses on the hand positions of the Reiki treatments, the history and other relevant information.

At Level Two (Practitioner), you will be taught some of the Reiki symbols and how to use them, absent healing and more relevant Information.

At Level Three (Master), you will taught the remaining Reiki symbols and their uses as well as how to do attunements, you will also be qualified to teach Reiki.

Note: As in all healing, intention is the key, this means it is not essential to have undergone an Attunement in order to use the Reiki hand positions for healing purposes, if you can already do healing, simply use them; if you have never tried before, try the hand positions, you may be surprised by the results.

Attunement Energy Shifts

This is sometimes known as the 'Healing Crisis'; healers are usually people who have experienced a lot of pain of some type in their past, which is why they are often referred to as a 'Wounded Healer'. It is this that gives them the empathy needed to be a healer. This past pain is always with you no matter how well you have dealt with it in the past. It is your past, you lived it. As a result of the attunement process and its ongoing effects on your entire energy system, it is likely that you will experience some form of re-emergence of these old wounds.

The attunements act as a form of de-tox of all your negative energies. Do not resist this process; seek any help you believe you may need to deal with this crisis; e.g. counselling, if you still have strong issues you need to resolve.

The attunement process lasts for approximately 21 days after an attunement, as it takes 3 days to work through each chakra. It is very common to catch a cold or similar after an attunement. The best way to deal with this process is to go through it and out the other side. Experience whatever it is that is resurfacing and deal with it as you feel is appropriate. The pain of the past, the negative energies we have encountered, have had an effect on our lives, whether we like it or not. The re-emergence of this during this period, allows us to look at what has gone before, with the eyes and rationale of an adult, not a child. It allows us to turn this negative energy, into positive energy, to turn it into a source of power from which we can draw energy and experience; rather than something we feel dis empowered by and cower at, in the presence of. To turn us from victim, to master of ourselves.

All Healers go through an experience like this, in truth it is ongoing. An old saying says to "Heal others, first Heal thyself". During this period it is important to drink lots of fresh water, avoid excessive alcohol, caffeine, meat and other heavy or impure products, such as E numbers and GM foods. The symptoms generated by this experience are a very positive sign of deep healing on all levels and at the end of this process you will feel more energised and positive. Be aware that you may be more sensitive than usual during this period, so adjust your reactions to others appropriately, don't overreact.

Clients suffering from acute symptoms or pain may find their symptoms worsen for a couple of days, for similar reasons, following a treatment, so warn them of this possibility. It takes pain 3 days to pass through the physical body into the finer energy body and dissipate. Following each attunement it is important to assist the process by giving yourself self healing sessions daily. Reiki is unusual in that it is excellent for giving self healing sessions.

Below are the hand positions for giving yourself Reiki. If any of these positions are extremely uncomfortable to use, feel free to modify them to suit your needs.

Reiki Self Healing (hand positions)

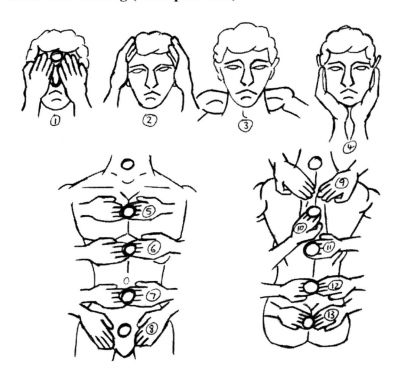

Note: If you have never practised healing before, try these hand positions on yourself, before trying them on anyone else, it will help to develop your confidence in your healing abilities.

Healing and Crystals

It is possible to use crystals with energy healing. In healing practices, crystals act as an amplifier and focus, multiplying the energy sent through them and focusing it on a small area via its point; similar to sunlight through a magnifying glass. I would suggest if you want to experiment with using crystals with healing that you use a clear quartz crystal, as this is a good multi -purpose crystal, which is easy to programme.

To Programme a Crystal:

1) Attune the crystal to your energy; hold the crystal in one hand point down over your other palm. Move the crystal about 3" away from your palm and rotate it clockwise. When you feel a little resistance, the crystal is attuned to your energy system.

2) Hold the crystal between your hands in a prayer position, level with your heart and ask the crystal to assist you with your healing. You will probably feel a reaction to this request in your heart chakra.

3) Always thank the crystal after using it.

4) Cleanse the crystal after each healing session; to do this place it in running water, a stream is best, but a tap will do if necessary; or place the crystal in a glass of spring water and add some sea salt to it. Leave this on a windowsill during the full moon for at least a night. Rinse the crystal with spring water and leave in the sun to dry.

When you want to buy a crystal shard, before entering the shop ask to be guided to the right crystal for your purposes. It will simply feel right and probably be the first one you are attracted to. It's not so much a matter of you picking a crystal, as of the crystal picking you. The best way to get a crystal is to be given it or to find it. Several of the crystals I use look a bit old and battered, but I found them on tin mine slag heaps, whilst living in Cornwall and they work very well.

Crystals have different properties, making some more appropriate for different ailments than others; I haven't got the space to go into all of them, so I suggest you buy a good book on crystals, minerals and their properties. Given below is the basic crystal healing kit, quartz is easily programmed to different functions, so is probably the most useful crystal.

7 X Chakra coloured crystals of your choice (tumbled ones are fine)
1 Large generator quartz crystal
6 Quartz shards (smoky is good, as well as clear)
1 Double terminated (points at both ends) quartz shard

In addition to these crystals the following crystals are good for a lot of common problems:

Rose Quartz (asthma, aching bones, burns, promotion of love, Multiple Sclerosis, scars)
Spinel (Creativity, delusions, fear of lightning, stress)
Amethyst (alcoholism, blood clots, cancer, diseases, emotional pain, fear, infections, joint inflammation, peace, spiritual growth)
Turquoise (ESP, headaches, strengthening the heart, hysteria, malaria, nightmares, popularity, throat problems)
Aquamarine (eyesight, fear, feet problems, grief, peace, phobias, spleen problems, stomach upsets, thyroid problems, varicose veins)
Aventurine (anger, brain damage, nervous system, confidence, fear, gastric ulcer, sore throat)
Tourmaline (bladder problems, blood cleanser, low blood pressure, ear problems, drunkenness, envy, food poisoning, healthy hair, indigestion, laryngitis, lethargy, melancholy, memory, MS, pain, sciatica, loss of smell, throat problems, tonsillitis, ulcers, weakness)

Chrysocolla (PMT, skin pigmentation, healthy hair)

Lapis Lazuli (breathlessness, bruises, Chakra blocks, depression, envy, fractures, hysteria, inner growth, intuition, joint inflammation, dispel negativity, counteract negativity, nervousness, pain, shingles, stomach pains, thyroid, vomiting)

Jade (benevolence, bladder problems, clarity, coldness, endocrine system, nervousness, serenity, tranquillity, high blood pressure)

Haematite (backache, headaches, faithfulness, joint inflammation, neck tension, nightmares, weakness)

Carnelian (anger, bone marrow, cell rejuvenation, compassion, physical decay, frustration, lethargy, malignancy, pancreas, unblock spinal energy point)

There are many different crystals and minerals, with many different properties. This is only a selection of useful ones, with a number of uses.

Clearing the Chakras with Crystals

Firstly prepare the room and yourself; prepare the 7 quartz crystals, ensure they are cleansed and charged. Place a bowl of spring water with sea salt in it in the treatment room for cleansing the crystals after use. The client needs to be prepared also, tell them what you are going to do and what they may feel, the treatment now begins:

1) Ask the client to lie down and close their eyes; their head should be in the north and their feet in the south, to align them with the planet's electro-magnetic flow.

2) Ask the client to focus on their breath and to breathe deeply into their abdomen, to forget all other worries and just focus on their breath. Synchronise your breath with the client's, to help attune your energies.

3) As you are holding the 7 crystals, ask for help with healing the client from the crystals and whatever gods, spirits, angels, etc you feel comfortable with.

4) Place the crystals around the client with their points aimed at the client in the following formation:

a) Place a Crystal between and below the Clients feet.
b) Place a Crystal on either side of both knees.
c) Place a Crystal above the Clients head.
d) Place a Crystal on either side of the elbows.
e) You have now formed 2 interlinking triangles, the Downwards pointing one represents the Water Element, the upwards pointing one represents the Fire Element; together they form the 6 pointed Star of David.

5) Now holding the generator crystal point downwards in your hand furthest away from the client, start at the client's crown and walk clockwise around the client 3 - 4 times, with the crystal held at least a foot away from you. You are casting a circle or sphere of protection and containment.

6) Now holding the crystal lengthwise brush the energy up the client's body from the feet to the crown.

7) Ask the client to roll over onto their front and repeat the brush from crown to feet.

8) Ask the client to roll back onto their back.

9) Now using the generator crystal point downwards, work down the client's body, starting at the crown and finishing at the base chakra. At each chakra rotate the crystal 7 times, whilst you focus on clearing away any negative energy, visualise the chakra you are working on being bathed in brilliant white light. As you finish the motions see it as a vibrant clean and bright colour appropriate to that chakra.

For this example I will assume the client is male so the crystal is rotated in a clockwise direction around the crown chakra, anti-clockwise around the brow, clockwise around the throat, anti-clockwise around the heart, clockwise around the solar plexus, anti-clockwise around the sacral and clockwise around the base chakra. In a female client the directions are reversed, starting and ending anti-clockwise.

10) To finish walk anti-clockwise around the client with the generator crystal, uncasting the circle/sphere you cast earlier and giving thanks for the help you received.

11) The treatment is now over, thank the crystals, gather them up and place them in the bowl of water. Gently awaken the client, tell them to get up when they feel able; take them to another room, offer them a drink and discuss the treatment. Ensure they are properly grounded before you let them leave. Remember to wash your hands after the treatment.

You could also use appropriately coloured small tumbled crystals placed on the chakras during the treatment, if you wish. If the client has any specific problems you could recommend they buy a crystal which will help with it, to carry with them.

Herbalism

I am not trained in herbalism, so will just give some introductory information; but I can say it is an enormous subject upon which all our modern medicines are based. It largely involves the use of infusions/tisanes (teas), decoctions (50/50 water and herbs, a strong tea), poultices (freshly harvested herbs applied to the damaged skin with lint and plaster) and compresses (a larger version of a poultice using bandages).

Herbalism can be as easy or as hard as you like, if you wish to gather wild herbs, then you must learn plant identification, as many look very similar, some are good for you, some are lethal; it is easier to visit a shop which sells herbs; then you know you are getting the right thing. There are also herbal teas available from most supermarkets.

Shamanism in all cultures has used herbs to cure illness and other problems for centuries, this is a large part of this subject; as is gathering wild food to eat; many of which are herbs. Incenses and smudge mixes are also made from herbs. Given below is a simple list of infusions which can be taken for some common ailments, many of these should be easy to get access to:

Acid Indigestion - Meadowsweet, Mint

Acne - Burdock

Antiseptic - clean Spiders web can be used to dress wounds

Arthritis - Dandelion, Agrimony, Nettle

Asthma - Meadowsweet

Backache - add Hawthorn leaves to tea

Bruises - Lady's Mantle, Comfrey

Chestiness - Marshmallow, Horsetail

Colds - Yarrow

Coughs - Comfrey, Mullein

Dandruff - Burdock, Chamomile (rub into scalp)

Diarrhoea - Meadowsweet

Flatulence - Mint, Chamomile

Headaches - Chamomile

Hiccups - Mint

Insomnia - Chamomile

Intestinal Tonic - Marshmallow, Meadowsweet

Nausea - Mint, Lemon verbena

Stings (not Bee) - Dock Leaves rubbed into area

Rheumatism - Dandelion, Horsetail, Agrimony, Burdock, Chickweed, Rue, Comfrey, Meadowsweet

Spots - Burdock

Obviously this is a very simple list, but it's as good a place as any to start; most of these are available at the supermarket, as ready-made teas. More clues about herbalism are to be found in the chapter on 'The Natural World'.

Recommended Herbal Reading

'*The Wild Flower Key*' - Francis Rose
'*Food for Free*' - Richard Mabey
'*A Modern Herbal*' - Mrs. M. Grieve
'*Complete Herbal*' - Culpeper
'*Herbs for Cooking and Health*' - Collins Gems
'*Guide to Herbal Remedies*' - Brockhampton Reference
'*A Cook on the Wild Side*' - Hugh Fearnley-Whittingstall
'*Foods that Harm, Foods that Heal*' - Readers Digest

Extraction Techniques

This form of healing is required when an energy intrusion was diagnosed as being the client's problem. The idea was simply to remove this intrusion, to extract it. What was this energy intrusion though?

In Shamanic cultures, spirits were believed to influence everything; not just the spirits of people, but the spirits of animals, trees, rocks, lakes, mountains, etc, etc. As a result there was a constant sort of plea bargaining system in effect. For example if the hunter wanted to catch a bear to eat or for the skin, it was necessary for him to work with the Shaman, to contact the spirit of the bear, to convince it to allow itself to be caught for the greater good; this was done by promising to honour the bear's spirit in a traditional or individual manner, such as offerings of alcohol, at a certain time, on a regular basis, to bury part of the animal, like a seed, so that it can re-grow, burying the animal's remains in an honoured way, like a human, etc, etc.

An energy intrusion, was believed to be caused by the hunter not keeping up their side of the bargain. As a result the bear spirit had come back to haunt the hunter, or make him sick. If the Shaman diagnosed this as the problem, then the Shaman would have to arrange a higher priced form of compensation to the bear spirit, as a result of the hunter's deception. The energy intrusion would then have to be removed from the client.

Another form of energy intrusion, which was common was that the client had offended the Shaman or another Shaman in some way. As a result the Shaman had made the client sick; a similar process was entered into to extract and placitate the energies involved. Occasionally the client may have completely unbeknown to them violated some taboo and been attacked by guardian spirits for this reason; or have picked up a chaotic and benign spirit who was wandering around looking to cause trouble. In this situation, the Shaman would simply extract the energy and banish it.

A Shaman would know if an energy intrusion was the problem or not, partly as a result of experience, partly through diagnosis. Diagnosis is often done using a rattle; the client lies down and the Shaman slowly shakes the rattle over the client's body length. He is looking for a change in pitch, it is said the rattle's sound will dull, when it is in the close proximity of an energy intrusion.

Having located the Intrusion, the Shaman will attempt to establish what its cause is. Is it a spirit which needs placating? Or is it simply a leech-like energy which has attached itself to the client and is feeding on him. This is established by the Shaman summoning his guides and using a combination of skills; the Mongolian Shaman would throw their drumstick into the air and interpret the way it falls, in relation to a Yes or No question asked. Or the Shaman may meditate, or enter a trance, to attempt to contact the energy and establish its intent. Once this has been established and the client has agreed to abide by any agreements made with the intrusive spirit, the Shaman will begin to extract the intrusive energy form. This is often done using a stone with which the Shaman has formed a conscious link, the stone has temporarily agreed to contain the Intrusive Energy or sometimes permanently contain it. This stone is placed in the Shaman's mouth, its job is to prevent the intrusive energy entering the Shaman. A Shaman may have a special stone, used just for this purpose, a power or medicine object. A special jug or other form of earthenware container which is only used for this purpose, usually with a lid on it, so it can be shut, is used for this purpose. This may contain a liquid, such as liquor, or salt water.

The Shaman then enters a healing consciousness or trance and asks for the intrusive energy to show itself. This often takes the form of a black snake or worm-like creature, sometimes it resembles a spider. When the Shaman can see this he will often place his mouth over it and suck it out of the client, it will then be forced by the Shaman's helper spirits, which have entered his body, into the stone which has agreed to contain this intrusive energy.

The Shaman then leans over the jug and lets the stone fall into it, before sealing it in with the lid. This serves a number of purposes, firstly it seals the intrusive energy into a safe place, away from the client. Secondly it reinforces the client's impression that the energy has gone as the audible thud of the stone is heard entering the jug, especially as the client would not have been told about the stone in the Shaman's mouth.

The Shaman will now dispose of the spirit contained in the stone safely; this may involve entering a journey to the underworld and taking the spirit there, sometimes spirits don't know how to get there on their own and need to use this sort of method, to enlist a Shaman's help, to get where they are supposed to be. Or the stone may be left somewhere in nature to allow the energy to disperse naturally, having asked the Earth Mother to deal with this energy and cleanse this stone of all ill effects.

Intrusive energies are come across quite commonly during healing. Usually they are simply strong emotions, with no real form, which have become stuck in the client's aura, simply as a result of walking round town, etc. These types do not need such intense effort to remove; they are usually simply pulled or brushed off with a fan, feather or hand. I normally simply visualise a white vortex of swirling light behind me, then throw them into it, knowing they will be dispersed harmlessly.

A similar process can also be used, with the help of your spirit guides and helpers, to remove intrusive energies which have taken on the form of a snake, etc. Snakes are the form they take when I see them. I then use the spirit of a raptor, working through me, usually a buzzard in my case, to remove them prior to throwing them into the vortex of light. This makes sense to me as they are one of their natural predators in the wild. This doesn't mean I have a low opinion of snakes, I feel I work with the adder particularly. This means to me a snake spirit has chosen to contain the intrusive energy and present itself to me; then a natural ecological scenario is enacted with the buzzard catching the snake. This natural act also indicates to me, that little else is needed to be done to placate any intrusive spirits. I always thank the spirits who have helped me though.

Grounding

Do not forget to properly ground your client after any form of healing. Full details are given in the chapter on 'Shamanic Journeys'.

First Aid

Although it is not currently essential to be a trained First Aider as a healer, this may well soon be law. I would very strongly advise you do at least a basic one day 'Emergency Aid Course' in First Aid; there's nothing worse than being a healer at an accident and not knowing basic First Aid, it will really bring you down to earth with a bump. It is essential to follow these rules in First Aid:

Get an Ambulance; do this first
D - Danger; check to see if there is any to you or the patient
R - Response; try and get a response from the patient
A - Airways; check to see if the patient's airway is blocked
B - Breathing; check to see if the patient is breathing
C - Circulation; check to see if the patient has a pulse

Basic Anatomy and Physiology

You do not need to be an expert on anatomy and physiology to practise Reiki or other forms of energy healing. It may be necessary to gain a qualification in it to get insurance, although this is not always the case. As a healer though it makes sense to have a basic understanding of how the body works and where the organs etc are. For this reason I include a few diagrams of the body's anatomy. I also suggest you invest in a copy of: *'Anatomy Colouring Book'* by Wynn Kapit and Lawrence Elson.

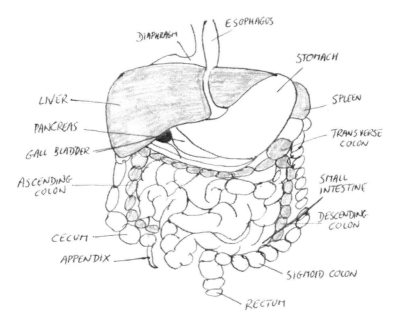

Internal Organs

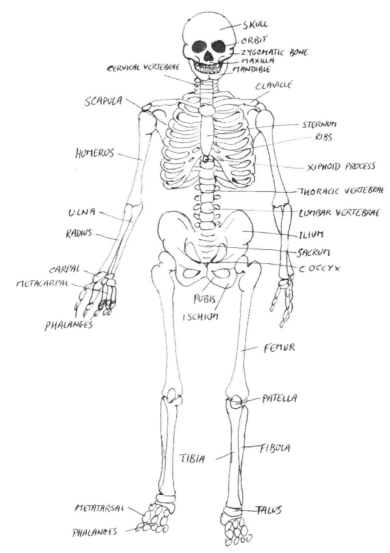

Skeleton

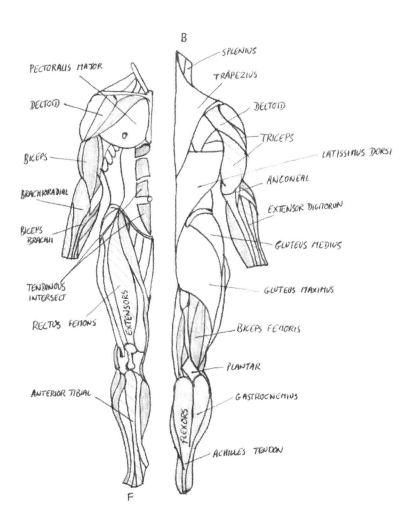

B

PECTORALIS MAJOR

SPLENIUS

TRAPEZIUS

DELTOID

DELTOID

TRICEPS

BICEPS

LATISSIMUS DORSI

BRACHIORADIAL

ANCONEAL

BICEPS
BRACHII

EXTENSOR DIGITORUM

GLUTEUS MEDIUS

TENDINOUS
INTERSECT

GLUTEUS MAXIMUS

EXTENSORS

RECTUS FEMONS

BICEPS FEMORIS

PLANTAR

ANTERIOR TIBIAL

GASTROCNEMIUS

FLEXORS

ACHILLES TENDON

F

Muscles Front   **Muscles Back**

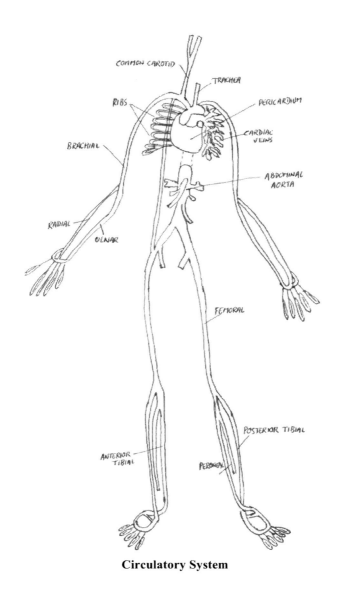

Circulatory System

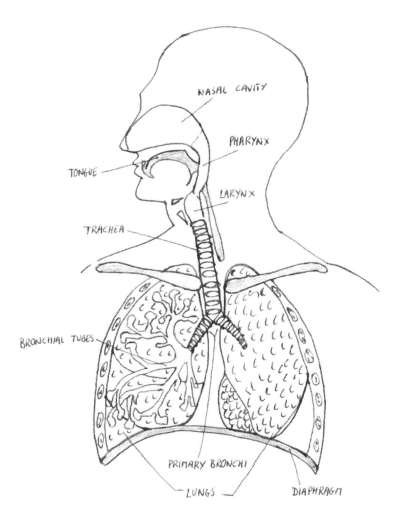

Respiratory System

12
DIVINATION

Divination Systems

One of the many roles a Shaman is often expected to perform is that of 'Fortune Teller'. There are hundreds of different types of divination systems; I suggest you become proficient in at least one of them, which one is up to you. I shall talk briefly about some of these divination systems and about predicting the future in general, then I shall give more details about a very Shamanic divination system, 'The Bones' and introduce you to an adaptable divination system based on the epic poet 'The Words of the High One' (Odin) from the Norse 'Elder Edda', which can be used with the Runes or the Celtic Ogham.

Many of these systems are very old and little is really known about how they work, the Celtic Ogham or Tree Alphabet for example. Some are well known and a lot has been written about them, such as the Norse runes, astrology and the tarot cards. The runes will be the divination system I will mainly discuss in this chapter, as it is Norse in origin and one of my favourite systems.

The Role of the Fortune Teller

Before we look at any divination systems it is important to look at the whole idea of predicting the future. Is it actually possible to predict the future? The future is a time period which is yet to occur, it may refer to seconds, minutes, hours, days, weeks, months or years ahead. It is obviously easier to predict what is likely to happen a few minutes ahead in time than it is 10 years ahead, but even that is not easy.

Time works in a circle, or more accurately a cycle or spiral, we are each to some extent trapped within a cycle of events, initially of our own making, our life plans; those things we wish to do during the course of our lives, the actions we need to take to allow them to happen. For example, if you wish to become a nurse, you can either sit around and dream about becoming one and leave it at that, hoping somehow that will come to pass. Or you can dream about becoming a nurse, study biology and other related sciences at school to your best ability, then move on to a nursing degree at

390

university, from there into employment as a nurse. Obviously the first example is very unlikely to achieve any results, but the second will, providing you pass the appropriate exams and don't change your mind about being a nurse will allow you to realise that dream.

Sadly there are many people who seem to believe that the first example is a valid option. It doesn't take a fortune teller to predict that they will be disappointed. In a similar situation, many people dream of winning the lottery, this is only likely to happen if you actually buy a lottery ticket, even then the odds are hugely stacked against you, although there is as much chance of it happening to you as there is of it happening to someone else. However in this scenario there is the random chance or luck effect, the virtually unpredictable events, that life presents us with. We are never totally in control of our lives, other people and other events will influence any future events. However we have more control over our lives and choices than anyone else does, even if we choose not to see that or put our own needs on temporary hold whilst we do something which will be of more benefit to someone else, such as when we become parents.

In the case of the nurse, she may well decide to do all the training, pass all her exams, then fall in love, become pregnant and never actually practise nursing, or she may be on route to her first day's work as a nurse and die in a traffic accident, or she may win the lottery and decide not to bother nursing.

The future is and isn't predictable; most events in our lives are influenced to some extent by outside forces beyond our control. The future is affected by our choices and the choices of others, some people believe all our lives are under the control of the 3 Norns, the Fates and Destiny, if this is the case, then free will doesn't exist, we are simply pawns in the game of life. It is more realistic to believe there are certain events in our lives that we are destined to experience and that free will is how we choose to react to them. Fortune telling and divination systems are in many ways misleading in how they work, they are largely unable to predict the future with any certainty; all they can do is produce a possible outcome.

Psychology plays a large role in fortune telling, the best known systems themselves are largely based on this, highlighting personality traits that are both beneficial and hindrances to our goals in life. People who spend a lot of time and money consulting fortune tellers are basically saying "tell me what to do, because I can't think for myself". There are many people like these in the world, the New Age therapists and gurus thrive on them, but they can only advise; ultimately people must make their own choices.

There are times in all our lives when we can feel like this, when events feel like they are spiralling faster and faster beyond our control. At these times a fortune teller may be able to help you to see a way forward, but that is really all they can do. The future is not set; we influence it via our choices, via our actions and inactions.

In many ways the role of the fortune teller is not as someone who can see into the future, but as someone who can see into the past and present and the person, in many ways actually acting as a guidance counsellor, the divination system used is simply the tool being used to access and initiate the resulting conversation. That doesn't mean the divination system doesn't work, it acts on a subconscious level, with runes or cards being drawn which are random, but which are psychologically relevant to everyone and can be interpreted in many ways and on many levels.

The fortune teller is a neutral aspect, who from their emotionally detached standpoint, may well be able to see what the client is too close to and emotionally involved with, to be able to see for themselves. People in general are creatures of habit, we generally go through life following our usual routines, until a spanner is thrown into the works and we are forced to react differently. We become accustomed to our stress levels and even when these are uncomfortable and distress us, we are reluctant to let them go, because it feels like something is missing from our lives or something is wrong; we will even go to the state of subconsciously sabotaging ourselves when this stress level is removed. This is common in the case of alcoholics and other forms of drug addiction.

392

The alcoholic knows that s/he has to stop drinking as it is having a negative effect on their life. They know that they are damaging their health, causing distress to their family and friends and making some very bad life decisions. Their usual reaction to these sort of thoughts is to have another drink though - avoidance tactics. Sadly, many alcoholics were raised by alcoholic parents, in other words this is a learnt coping mechanism, for when things go wrong in life.

At Alcoholics Anonymous (AA) and Narcotics Anonymous (NA), it is well known that people with these sorts of problems, generally have to 'hit rock bottom', before they can find the strength to pull themselves up out of the gutter. This could take many forms, some have to be near fatal, some are less drastic, depending on how far down the path of alcohol dependency they are. They will also realise they need support from others, who have been where they are. If they are parents themselves, they may well have to watch their own children turning to alcohol before they see their own problem staring back at them.

Sadly many people (seriously) trying to give up, unlike the many celebrities that frequent detox clinics regularly, will often 'slip' in their attempts to give up, often this is because all they try to do is give up the alcohol and ignore the root of their problems. They still need to deal with the problems that drove them to drink in the first place and often need to change large chunks of their lives in order to do so. This may mean finding new friends, especially if their old friends were old drinking buddies. The cure for these sorts of problems can often be almost as hard as the problem itself, but ultimately it is worth it. But it will mean re-assessing your own normal stress levels, both consciously and subconsciously.

This sort of reaction to a change in our normal stress levels, can affect everyone to some extent, due to a change in our normal routines and our own subconscious roles we play. Common things which will leave us feeling a bit lost are losing our job, the children leaving home, extended illness, accidents, bereavement or divorce, often these can be connected, with one leading to another.

The good fortune teller will be able to pick up on these sort of clues and advise the client accordingly, or at least recommend they see a good counsellor. The fortune teller is in a position which allows them access to the deeper levels of the client, with the conversation often involving aspects of life the client wouldn't normally stop to consider, breaking away from the normal automated routines we follow.

When it comes to predicting the future, the best any divination system can do is to look at the client's past choices, look at their present choices and make an educated guess at their future choices; based on them continuing in a similar pattern of choices. The client should always be advised that the future is NOT set and if they don't like what they are hearing, they can alter their future by making different choices in the present.

In the case of the Shaman, fortune telling is simply one of the tools used to find out what the real problem is. The Shaman knows that people don't usually go to a fortune teller in the normal course of events. The client will, most likely, therefore be either simply 'curious' or 'seeking help' of some sort. If the later is true, then the Shaman's healing role should come into play, in an appropriate manner.

Astrology

Astrology is an ancient divination system, based on the movement of this galaxy's planets in relation to each other and to what time and where you were born. This creates 12 main personality types, which are known as our star signs (more accurately our sun signs). The science behind astrology is quite complex and would take a whole course to teach, although in this day and age it is possible to simply buy a computer programme, which does this work for you.

We are all aware of our daily horoscopes, which say what we are likely to experience during each day. These are only based on our sun sign, so are rarely accurate, as this would imply that all Leos, Geminis, Virgos, etc, are exactly the same; obviously this is not the case, just as there are more than

12 personalities in the world, so anyone who spends the day in a panic because their daily horoscope says they are in for trouble or that they will win the lottery is a fool.

A personal horoscope will be based on the movement of all the planets when you were born and observed from where you were born. It will then make a prediction of how you are likely to develop as a personality and the sort of experiences you are likely to have during your life. This is obviously far more in-depth than the daily newspaper horoscopes, which are only really meant to be a bit of fun. The personal horoscope is also quite accurate in its predictions, not totally, but it is usually worth getting one to look at.

Astrology was once considered a science, but now due to the science of astronomy we are aware of the existence of many millions of other planets, stars and galaxies. For astrology to truly work, it would make sense that the movement of all of these should also be taken into account, as they all subtly influence each other, which is currently impossible. Astrology is a fascinating Subject and well worth looking into more deeply.

Tarot

The Tarot is an old divination system, which originally used playing cards to predict the future, the tarot as we know them today has existed at least since the medieval age. The Tarot is a story based on the Fool's progress through life to enlightenment; this is symbolic of our own journeys through life from our naïve beginnings to hopefully worldly wisdom. The Tarot is a pack of two parts, the Minor Arcana, which is divided into the four elemental suites of Earth, Air, Fire and Water. These are represented by their associated Magikal Tools:

Earth = Pentacles - Diamonds - Material and Physical Aspects
Fire = Wands - Clubs - Will Power and Actions
Air = Swords - Spades - Intellectual and Spiritual Aspects
Water = Chalices - Hearts - Feelings and Relationships

The Tarot cards are also closely associated with the everyday playing cards, as their associations show, also having 56 cards in number.

The Major Arcana is made up of 22 cards which are not related to the playing cards and represent the soul's journey through life from innocence to enlightenment; they deal with aspects and influences on our life; such as people, concepts, qualities, cycles, change and transition.

The Fool is the only Major Arcana card present in the ordinary playing cards. The Tarot are available in most New Age shops, they are usually connected with a well known myth, legend or culture, such as the Legend of King Arthur. This gives them an additional example of a well-known life journey, which most of us can relate to or at least recognise. There are many hundreds of different Tarot packs available, most come with a book of interpretation. The best Tarot pack to buy is the one that is most attractive to you; you should like the way the cards look and should understand and be familiar with the legend the cards have been associated with.

The Tarot can be interpreted on various levels and are a very good psychological tool for accessing the deeper aspects of yourself. The tarot like all good divination systems, should be used for guidance only, to help you to see what is at the root of your current situation, which in turn allows you to take the appropriate course of action to change yourself, your perception and your situation, if necessary.Tarot readings are not set in stone; they simply look at your past reactions to similar situations, your current actions in relation to the situation and the likely outcome as a result of these considerations. They do this by looking at your psychological makeup and highlighting those aspects relevant to the situation, which allows you to alter your course of action, to reach the most desirable outcome for all concerned.

All divination systems are easier to read for other people, as they require you to be detached from the situation; at least enough to be able to read the cards accurately, rather than seeing what you want to see in them, so when reading them for yourself, you need to do so, with a cold eye. The Tarot are a good system to learn, there is not the space here to give full details of how to read them, but I strongly advise you to buy a pack and learn how to use them.

Ogham Alphabet

The Ogham are the Celtic Tree Alphabet, they are used as a writing system and are now available as a divination system; it is only fairly recently that they have been available in this manner and I am not sure how accurate the information is about them in this capacity. They have already been looked at when looking at the tree identification section, the best book available on the subject I am aware of is Robert Graves '*The White Goddess*', this also shows them as a sign language using the creases of the hand and fingers to represent the letters; I only present them here as an alphabet, as this is the capacity in which I use them.

The Ogham alphabet is not a full one, with several letters in our alphabet missing, yet with additional groups of vowel letters. I personally add these additional letters using appropriate symbols, to lengthen the Ogham alphabet. I leave it up to you to decide whether you choose to do this or not; my reasoning to do this is simply practicality; I believe if the Druids had continued to exist and evolve in an unbroken lineage then they would have evolved their knowledge and tools to relate to the language we use today, as I've already said they were a practising a practical religion, their roles are filled today by teachers, scientists, judges, doctors and lawyers.

Original Ogham

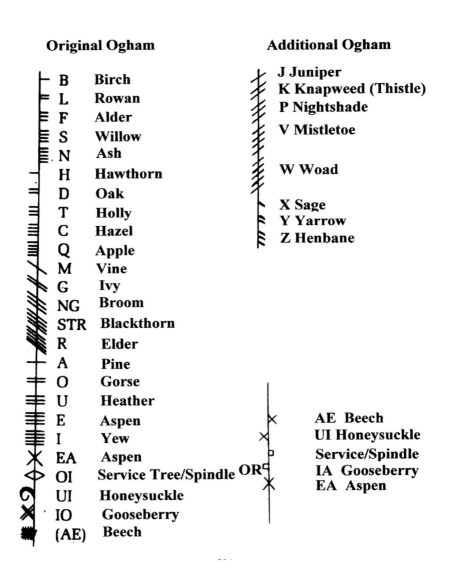

B	Birch	
L	Rowan	
F	Alder	
S	Willow	
N	Ash	
H	Hawthorn	
D	Oak	
T	Holly	
C	Hazel	
Q	Apple	
M	Vine	
G	Ivy	
NG	Broom	
STR	Blackthorn	
R	Elder	
A	Pine	
O	Gorse	
U	Heather	
E	Aspen	
I	Yew	
EA	Aspen	
OI	Service Tree/Spindle	OR
UI	Honeysuckle	
IO	Gooseberry	
(AE)	Beech	

Additional Ogham

J Juniper
K Knapweed (Thistle)
P Nightshade

V Mistletoe

W Woad

X Sage
Y Yarrow
Z Henbane

AE Beech
UI Honeysuckle
Service/Spindle
IA Gooseberry
EA Aspen

The Ogham are an interesting Celtic system, which I am sure will continue to evolve as a divination system and well worth further study.

The Meanings of the Ogham

I will give you some indications of the interpretations of the Ogham, these are not complete and further study of them is recommended:

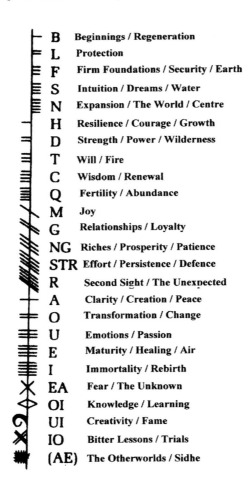

B	Beginnings / Regeneration
L	Protection
F	Firm Foundations / Security / Earth
S	Intuition / Dreams / Water
N	Expansion / The World / Centre
H	Resilience / Courage / Growth
D	Strength / Power / Wilderness
T	Will / Fire
C	Wisdom / Renewal
Q	Fertility / Abundance
M	Joy
G	Relationships / Loyalty
NG	Riches / Prosperity / Patience
STR	Effort / Persistence / Defence
R	Second Sight / The Unexpected
A	Clarity / Creation / Peace
O	Transformation / Change
U	Emotions / Passion
E	Maturity / Healing / Air
I	Immortality / Rebirth
EA	Fear / The Unknown
OI	Knowledge / Learning
UI	Creativity / Fame
IO	Bitter Lessons / Trials
(AE)	The Otherworlds / Sidhe

The Bones

The Bones are a popular divination system used in many countries, they are 4 sheep, goat or deer anklebones, roughly rectangular in shape, used like dice (dice could be used instead, with only 4 faces being read). They are all shaken in the hands and then thrown on a casting cloth. The Bones have 4 faces and 2 ends, the 2 ends known as boar are not interpreted, if a Bone lands on its end, it is simply thrown again. The remaining 4 sides are:

Sheep - rounded, humplike side
(Rein) Deer - indented side
Goat - Has an 'S' like swirl on it
Horse - Like Goat, but the 'S' shape is not as obvious

The Bones are asked a question and then thrown like dice, the resulting combinations are interpreted as:

4 Horses = Yes /excellent result, good luck and success
4 Goats = your desires will be fulfilled with little effort
4 Sheep = your desires will be fulfilled eventually
4 Deer = your desires can be achieved, but with a lot of effort
3 Horses & 1 Goat = quick successful result
3 Horses & 1 Sheep = there will be no problems
3 Horses & 1 Deer = you will achieve most of what you desire
2 Horses & 1 Goat & 1 Sheep = you will be pleased by the results
2 Horses & 1 Sheep & 1 Deer = with luck a good result
2 Horses & 1 Goat & 1 Deer = your plans will bear fruit soon
2 Horses & 2 Goats = success
2 Horses & 2 Sheep = work will be problem free
2 Horses & 2 Deer = your plans are working against each other, success is
   achievable, but will not satisfy you
1 Horse & 3 Goats = success eventually
1 Horse & 3 Sheep = success is in your own hands
1 Horse & 3 Goats = minor problem
1 Horse & 2 Goats & 1 Sheep = expect hard negotiations
1 Horse & 1 Goat & 2 Sheep = your plans are opposed

1 Horse & 1 Goat & 2 Deer = slow healing
1 Horse & 2 Sheep & 1 Deer = you should experience no problems in life
1 Horse & 2 Goats & 1 Deer = expect good news
1 of Each = prosperity
2 Goats & 1 Sheep & 1 Deer = you are unlikely to succeed
2 Goats & 2 Sheep = ill health
2 Goats & 2 Deer = no problems
1 Goat & 2 Sheep & 1 Deer = a few small obstacles to be overcome
1 Goat & 1 Sheep & 2 Deer = your plans will work better in a different place
1 Goat & 3 Sheep = you need no advice
1 Goat & 3 Deer = failure likely, bad luck
3 Sheep & 1 Deer = it will probably work successfully
2 Sheep & 2 Deer = your plans will succeed
1 Sheep & 3 Deer = No / failure

The Runes

The Runes are an ancient Norse divination system and magikal alphabet, believed to be discovered by Odin, when he sacrificed himself to himself. There are a number of different runic alphabets, varying from tribe to tribe, depending on their dialect, given below are 3 versions of the runic alphabets:

Anglo Saxon Runes

Futhork Runes

These are just 2 examples of the runic alphabet, the Elder Futhork is the oldest, the newest is found in JRR Tolkien's '*Lord of the Rings*'; in addition to these written alphabets, there are also the Predictive runes:

Fudarc Runes

I shall give a brief description of each of the Fudarc runes interpretations, for their upright and reversed meanings; though further study of these is recommended, I will then give a divination method for them, using different Interpretations based on the Norse Poem or Edda, 'The Words of the High One (Odin)'; this system can also be used to read the Ogham.

The most usual method for casting the runes is in the pattern known as Thor's Cross or Hammer; this uses 5 Runes, giving them the following meanings in relation to the 5 Runes drawn from a bag, containing a set of shaken Runes

Thor's Cross Rune Spread

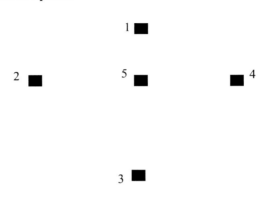

Position 1 - Circumstances surrounding the enquiry, the general nature of the enquiry.
Position 2 - Problems or Obstacles in relation to the desired outcome.
Position 3 - Beneficial Circumstances assisting in reaching the desired outcome.
Position 4 - Short Term effects of your actions towards reaching your goal.
Position 5 - Long Term effects of actions taken towards reaching your goal.

Meanings of the Runes

 Feoh - Upright: Wealth, Success, Money, Financial Status. Reversed: Bankruptcy, Failure, Financial Loss.

The Feoh rune's meaning is Cattle; the Norse and many ancient cultures associated wealth and status with livestock. So the meanings associated

403

with this rune are associated with financial matters. On a more spiritual level this rune is associated with the spiritual gifts we all possess, or personal power (medicine) and encourages us to let them to shine, for the benefit of self and others.

 Ur - Upright: Good Fortune, Promotion, Good Health.
Reversed: Bad Luck, Missed Opportunities, Illness.

Ur meaning auroch or wild ox, refers to the cattle of feoh and was symbolic of masculine yang energy. Ur refers to fitness, strength and stamina; it speaks of the challenges of life and the need for the physical or inner power to face and overcome these challenges and obstacles. On a spiritual level this rune speaks of a person who is aware of the spiritual side of life and seeks to develop and face life's challenges from this angle.

 Thurisaz - Upright: Protection, Important Choices, Guidance, Good News.
Reversed: Warning, Avoid Rash Decisions, Inaction better than wrong action, Bad News.

Thurisaz meaning Thorn, this rune is symbolised by a thorn, such as on a rose, hawthorn or blackthorn; these hedgerow plants and trees were grown to act as defensive barriers around livestock and villages, to keep out the wild animals and enemies. The thorn also refers to Thor's hammer Mjollnir, used to defend the common man and closely related to the law and justice. This rune implies that you are being protected and guided and that an important decision is soon to be made which will have lasting effects. Spiritually this rune speaks of the minor discomforts of life that must sometimes be endured, it is important not to make a mountain out of a mole hill, these challenges are tests of character, to see if you are ready to progress on your spiritual path.

Ansur - Upright: Wisdom or Guidance from an Elder or Knowledgeable Person, Communication, Learning. Reversed: Bad Advice, Rumours and Lies.

Ansur meaning Wisdom or oral tradition, refers to wisdom or knowledge transmitted via an oral tradition. This is the rune sacred to Odin, it speaks of good communication skills and the need to say what is actually meant. It may indicate a period of learning, when you may start a formal college or university course, or it may speak of an apprenticeship of some sort. It may simply refer to asking for advice from someone you would consider wise. It can also warn of bad advice, smooth talkers and people trying to sell you 'get rich quick' schemes, or similar. Spiritually this rune may tell you to look into the oral arts of a bardic nature, song and poetry, or it may be that you have been given wisdom from an unexpected source, such as a child.

 Rad - Upright: Good Travel, Day Trip, Business Trip, Holiday. Reversed: Bad Travel, Difficult Journey, Unwanted Trip, Delays.

Rad meaning Wheel, refers to movement, this may be a short day trip to the woods, or a round the world cruise; whatever the journey it will open your eyes to new sights and maybe new friends. Or it may refer to an unwanted trip, such as to visit sick friends or attend a funeral. Spiritually Rad speaks of the wheel of life and the journey we are all embarked upon for wisdom and development; it may indicate that it is necessary to make some sort of movement in your development, such as mixing with others of a like mind at a local moot or a workshop.

 Cen - Upright: Spiritual Enlightenment, Inspiration, Creativity, Guidance from Spirit World. Reversed: Loss of Possessions, Losing Face or Reputation.

Cen meaning Torch, talks of fire, of the state of ecstasy of being inflamed with inspiration, of a overwhelming urge to create, be it a new life or a painting, it speaks of spiritual enlightenment and revelations; eureka moments. It also speaks of passion and the opportunity to start new relationships, Cen offers new opportunities for change. It can also speak of the destructive power of fire, of loss; learning that enlightenment isn't the goal in life, simply a step towards it; as an old proverb goes, 'before enlightenment, chopping wood, carrying water; after enlightenment, chopping wood, carrying water'. It can also speak of the dying embers of passion of long term relationships dying out, separation or divorce, or even redundancy from work. Spiritually Cen speaks of enlightenment, inspiration and change.

 Gyfu - Upright Only: A Gift of Love or Talent ,Personal Power.

Gyfu meaning a Gift, a gift is something we all like to give and receive, but in the Norse tradition, the giving of a gift required a gift to be returned. The gift can be of a divine nature, a natural talent or power you possess; but if used unwisely this can also be taken away, permanently or temporarily. Likewise it is important to be careful to give gifts to others for the right reasons, not as a bribe, or in the thought of getting something in return. Gifts are a form of sacrifice, of the energy required to make, or earn the money, plus the process of choosing the right gift, it is not simply an object, there is thought and feeling behind it. Spiritually Gyfu speaks of the ability to both give and receive gifts and that the receiving of a gift, be it an object or talent, may require more in return than we bargained for, as the old adage goes 'be careful what you ask for, you just might get it'.

 Wyn - Upright: Joy and Happiness, Personal Achievements, Goals reached.
Reversed: Sadness, Grief and Loss.

Wyn meaning Joy, Wyn is a rune which promises that things are about to improve for the better. This could take many forms, but is often the result of your own achievements and recognition from others. It can also mean that there is a lot of effort needed and the journey ahead of you is an uphill struggle. Wyn is said to have the ability to grant our deepest wish, but sometimes this does not manifest as we envisioned it; maybe that beautiful girl you have been fantasising over at a distance, turns her attention to you and you realise she is a transvestite. The promise of the Wyn rune, can be similar to the rose tinted glasses worn by many spiritual people; Wyn reversed can also crush these glasses underfoot. Spiritually this rune, teaches that often we need to see the darker side of life, before we can truly appreciate what we already possess, that life is about learning, growth and our development as spiritual beings, these lessons are not always pleasant, but sometimes they are.

 Hagel - Upright: Challenges, Obstacles, Delays.
Reversed: Natural Disasters, Circumstances beyond our
Control.

Hagel meaning Hail, Hagel is probably best summed up with the old adage of 'the best laid plans of mice and men'. Even the best-laid plans don't always go to plan, that business trip may be suddenly cancelled due to bankruptcy or severe weather conditions, delayed flights etc. This may seem to be a disaster at the time, but it may turn out to be in your best interests in the long run, the business trip may have cost you a more valuable and reliable client, or you may get compensation for the delayed flight, etc. If reversed the Hagel rune may be warning you not to make solid long term plans, things can change in a moment, it is always a good idea not to put all your eggs in one basket, so have a fallback plan; it's better to have one and not need it, than to not have one. Spiritually the Hagel rune tells us we are not as in control of our destinies as we would sometimes like to think, if the universe has a different use for us, we will have little choice than to follow where it leads.

Nyd - Upright: Fate, Destiny, Needs Met.
Reversed: Use extreme Caution, especially with new ventures.

Nyd meaning Need, our needs are often met, though what we consider our needs to be and what the universe considers them to be, are not always the same thing. Destiny and the Norns have their roles to play in our lives, things do not always go to plan, we must learn to be flexible like the willow, bending in the harsh winds, or else we will snap. Sometimes we need to learn the lesson of failure, to know when to give up and cut our loses, or to alter our plans. Sometimes inaction is the best action to take, just wait and see. Spiritually Nyd teaches us that we should be motivated by need, rather than greed. It is our greed which is destroying the world we live on, the only world we can live on, our short sightedness, haste and greed will cost us all dearly if we are not careful.

Is - Upright Only: Matters Frozen, Patience, Inaction, Limbo.

Is meaning Ice, Ice is one of the two basic elements which formed the Norse world in their creation myths, the other being fire. Ice is normally fluid, flowing water, frozen in place; the meaning of this rune is that new activities should be put on hold for a while, so that the different elements of your activities have a chance to move into place and catch up with each other, before further progress is made. It is always important to rest, when you need to. It can also indicate the 'cooling off' of a normally passionate relationship, meaning a couple may spend some time apart, to reassess where their relationship is going and if they want to follow. Spiritually ice is yin, as fire is yang; to the Norse these were the building blocks of life, actions taken (fire), awaiting responses to the actions (ice), followed by appropriate follow up actions, this creates balance.

Jara - Upright Only: Harvest, 'As we sow, so shall we reap', Karma.

Jara meaning Harvest; Jara speaks of harvesting the rewards of our labours from the previous months. Harvests are joyful times, seeing the results of our work, but they are also busy times, in which a lot of work lies ahead to store these fruits before they spoil. If for example you have just qualified in a college course, you now have to find work using these new qualifications to make them worthwhile and to create future harvests. Spiritually Jara speaks of Karma, both positive and negative, of the rewards of our good deeds and the backlash of our not-so-good deeds. Everything is subject to cause and effect, so your actions and inactions should reflect this.

 Eoh - Upright Only: Natural Endings, Winter, Night, Death

Eoh meaning Yew Tree; the yew is planted in graveyards all over the Britain, or graveyards were built around the yew trees. The yew is one of the longest lived trees in the world, reaching ages of more than 2,000 years, it almost seems immortal, but everything is subject to the laws of change, which includes death and decay. The yew often appears to die its trunk begins to rot and death looks certain, then it transforms/ changes one of its main roots into a new trunk and continues to grow. When we leave home or education we are subject to the power of the Eoh rune, we have finished what we started, undergoing a form of death or transition from our normal state of affairs and now we change and grow into a new role. Spiritually the Eoh rune speaks to us of these cycles of change, cycles of death and rebirth.

 Peorth - Upright: The Unknown, Gambling, Choices, Risks. Reversed: Secrets, Ill Choices, Gambling, Risks.

Peorth meaning Dice Cup; life is full of the unknown, the future consequences of our actions and inactions, as well as what fate has in store for us. The Peorth rune is about this energy, it says it is sometimes necessary to take a risk, to take a gamble, to make a choice. Ultimately it is our choices which have the greatest influences on our life, but we do not always know what the outcome of these choices or gambles will be, some work out for us, some don't. When you are stuck in a catch 22 situation, you may as well make a choice, you have no other options. In its reversed position, Peorth warns us that sometimes our past choices come back to haunt us, sometimes the things we would sooner stayed buried are discovered and have effects on our present and future choices. Spiritually Peorth says you can't always leave things to fate, at some point you must take responsibility for your life and your choices, your actions and in-actions. Only this way will you ever reach any of your goals, if you are desperate and down to your last quid, you may as well take a gamble and try to win some more, but it is your choice how you choose to gamble. If you are unable to make a choice between two courses of action, you may as well flip a coin, but it is better to simply choose. Flipping a coin will only disempower you, leaving things to fate, making a choice empowers you; either way you may make the right or wrong choice.

 Elhaz - Upright: Protection, Blessed, Banishing Negative Energy.
Reversed: Vulnerability, Caution Needed, Negative Energy.

Elhaz meaning Elk; this rune speaks of being blessed and protected in your actions, it is the symbol of the guardian or higher self looking out for us. It is as if a large stag with a full rack of antlers is walking beside you, guarding you and scaring off negative energies and influences. This doesn't mean you should be reckless, a certain amount of caution is always needed, but at times things just seem to be on a roll, everything goes as planned and the world seems to be your oyster. In a reversed position this rune warns that the stag who is guarding you is in rut and is in danger of impaling you on those antlers, extreme caution is advised, avoid any known conmen or smooth talkers, be cautious of new acquaintances and think your actions over twice, if in doubt, don't. Spiritually this rune advises us to stay on our chosen path and stick to our principles; tricksters can take many forms and try to trick us into making the wrong decisions, or going against what we know is right.

410

Sigel - Upright Only: Good Fortune, Success, Good Health, Wise Decisions.

Sigel meaning Sun; this Rune represents the sun, the sun in most cultures is masculine in its energy, but in Norse culture it is feminine. The sun is where all life draws its energy from; hence this is a very positive rune. Spiritually Sigel speaks of the soul (in Mongolia the sun is one of the 3 Souls); the sun is the most powerful life giver in our galaxy, yet it is also subject to laws which govern it; it has a cycle in which it lives and will eventually die as a part of this cycle; just as we all do.

 Tyr - Upright: Masculine Warrior Energy, Courage, Sexuality, Potential, Victory.
Reversed: Fear, Cowardice, Blinded by Lust, Failure.

Tyr meaning Tiw; Tiw is the son of Odin and Norse God of Courage and Bravery. He sacrificed his own hand to bind the Fenris Wolf; Tiw exemplifies the Norse hero, he is a potent symbol of masculine energy, who uses his skills and knowledge to the benefit of others. But he also lost his magikal sword, causing his downfall in the Battle of Ragnarok by being tricked into giving it away to a giantess he blindly lusted after. This is the reversed meaning of the rune, the negative side of the idealistic image of masculine energy, the warrior who boasts of the great victories he will win, but when it comes to the crunch, turns coward and flees, costing his people dearly. Spiritually, Tyr speaks of the warrior who is there to defend his people from harm and wrongs; but also warns to keep your head. The best victories in life are won by using your skills and your wisdom. True warriors only fight when there is real need, they are not bar-room brawlers and are aware of the real enemy. Fears are the enemy within and must be overcome, if we are reach our true potential.

Beorc - Upright Only: New Beginnings, Spring, Birth, Fertility, Feminine Energy, Sexuality, Motherhood.

Beorc meaning Birch; the birch tree is the first tree to spread to new land, to start new or expand existing forests. So it is associated with beginnings, of all types; be they business, relationships, ideas or births. An interesting time is ahead. Spiritually this rune speaks of feminine energy and the sexual powers of the woman, the strength and total dedication of the mother, the ability to start afresh from apparently barren ground. Women have never needed to compete with men, their strength is their ability to wrap men around their little fingers, with a flutter of their eyelashes, the ability to bear the rigours and pain of childbirth, the stamina to raise a child against all odds and the power to create new life. This rune also warns not to abuse this power.

 Ehwaz - Upright: Travel, Progress, Movement. Reversed: Restlessness, Travel Difficulties, Stagnation.

Ehwaz meaning a Horse; this rune speaks of the Horse and Rider working together, moving forward together in harmony, also of the energy of our lives moving in such a manner, benefiting not only ourselves, but also those we care about, it may refer to actual travel of some sort, such as a holiday or moving house. Reversed this rune talks of our lack of movement, warning us we are stagnating like a still pool of water; we may be feeling we need to move, but have become stuck in a routine or rut, we need to make changes. It may also speak of missed flights, car problems and difficult journeys. Spiritually this rune speaks of our need to feel we are making progress in life, to explore new things and places, to make changes in our life, otherwise our free Spirits will stagnate.

 Mannaz - Upright: Family, Friendships, Humanity. Reversed: Isolation, Loners, Enemies.

Mannaz meaning Man (Human); This rune is about our relationships with others and ourselves. It talks of the help available to us from our families, friends, clans and groups, from the others in the human tribe. It talks of how new contacts will enlarge our world view and opportunities within it, of the fun of sharing and our duties to help others. In a reversed position, it talks of the isolation one can feel within that tribe, alone in a crowd, feeling like an outsider. This can mean you are mixing with people you don't really get on with, who you have outgrown, or that you are lacking confidence and need to try and fit in better. The isolation can be as mean as snubbing you or that you have simply chosen to withdraw into your own space, we should all be our own best friend. It can also speak of trouble from our enemies or people, who have it in for us. Spiritually this rune speaks of humanity, of the great potential and positive aspects of this race and of the negative aspects of it, jealousy and cruelty, etc. It speaks of the balance of the light and dark halves of all humans, we all have parts of ourselves we would sooner not show. It also speaks of our need to find new people, people who we fit in with and share common bonds of respect and appreciation; this can sometimes mean distancing ourselves from our old families or friends as we grow.

 Lagu - Upright: Crossing Water, The Subconscious, Instinct, Intuition, Psychic Development, Creative Inspiration.
Reversed: Confusion, Self Delusion, Space Cadet Syndrome, Paranoia, Mental and Emotional Problems, Life Crises.

Lagu meaning Water; water flows, it evaporates, is turned into rain and falls from the sky, it nourishes life. It is also strongly influenced by the moon, it is connected to the female menstrual cycle. It is a symbol of the subconscious and psychic development, of intuition, instinct and creativity; these are the inner water crossings, it can also relate to journeys across water, be them rivers or oceans. Reversed this rune points towards mental and emotional imbalance, the self delusion of the space cadet, believing the world is full of love and light and that nothing can hurt you; to avoidance of our emotional problems, wishing things away, instant enlightenment, the miracle cure. Brainwashing ourselves into believing all will be okay, without needing to do anything about it, when we know deep down we need to take some sort of action or seek help. It can also point to self doubt and stagnation, to a block in our creative expression. Spiritually Lagu speaks of spiritual development; this often happens when we most need it, when we feel powerless and don't know which way to turn. This can give us a major rush, sometimes we may feel we are going insane, it is important to question what you are experiencing, but it can be damaging to block it out, especially if drugs or alcohol are needed to do so. Sometimes our perception of the spiritual path, simply doesn't seem worth the hassle. The bills still need to be paid and life goes on, this can be why this is occurring, things are stagnating and movement is needed, sometimes any movement is better than none. Often this can take a truly chaotic form such as divorce, or job loss, just when things seem they can't get worse, they do. Then a focus is needed to give us direction, this may involve seeing a counsellor or joining a self help group, it involves stopping and looking at where you are, in relation to where you want to be, like a ship lost and adrift at sea, it is time to make changes to your course, before you set off again.

 Ing - Upright Only: Inspiration, Quiet Reflection, Seed, Fertility, Creativity, Withdrawal from Life.

Ing meaning the Inner Flame; this rune speaks of a time when your life is given a natural break; when you have successfully finished what you were doing and have a chance to unwind and look at what you want to do next. It is like a seed in the ground, waiting for the sun to germinate it, you are free to explore those creative outlets, to withdraw from the world for a moment and prepare to burst forth from the soil again, often growing differently and in new directions; it also speaks of birth of children and new ventures, of spring. Spiritually this is a very liberating rune it gives you a sense of peace and completion. It is the eye of the storm, a quietmoment to reflect in your life before moving forwards into the chaos of life again. It is an opportunity to try new things or start all those things that have been put on hold, it may be temporary though, so should be used wisely.

Daeg - Upright Only: The Dawn, Light at the End of the Tunnel, Success, Prosperity, Good Fortune.

Daeg meaning Dawn or Day; this rune speaks of the coming of the light, the start of new adventures; it is a very positive rune. It speaks of the light at the end of the tunnel, a time when all will go your way; that all your hard work is beginning to pay off. Spiritually this rune promises good times ahead, allowing you the vision to see things for what they are, that scary shape at night, is simply a bush in the light of day. You realise that without the night there can be no days or new dawns, that the world is a mixture of essential complementary opposites; that without the bad times, the good times would be meaningless. A time when even the bad things in your life, can be seen for what they truly were and appreciated; they also played their part in leading you here.

 Odal - Upright: Property, Wealth, Possessions,
Reversed: Legal Matters, Financial Problems, Risk of loss.

Othel meaning Homestead; this rune speaks of material wealth, the fruits of your labour, the resources you have acquired throughout your life's journey. It speaks not only of enjoying these things, but of taking care of these things, of looking to the future and being prepared for it, of writing wills and making plans for the future, investing this wealth. Reversed this rune warns there may be financial trouble ahead, that those get rich quick schemes didn't work out, or that acquiring money has cost you too much, you are wealthy, but sad and alone; 'Money can't buy you love', as someone once sang. Spiritually this rune speaks of the transience of material wealth, it says its good to have, but the things you can't buy like love and happiness, are greater possessions in the long run. This doesn't mean that you should be a happy, loved tramp (unless you want to be), simply that you need balance in all things; we all need enough for our needs, be that money, free time, love, happiness or whatever. You can't take money with you when you die, but your memories you can, make sure they are good ones.

Blank Wyrd - Upright Only: Destiny, Fate.

Wyrd meaning The Way; this rune is the blank one in the rune set, it is an indicator that this reading or the next rune you pull from the bag is an important one, connected with your destiny and fate in Life, it says 'PAY ATTENTION'.

'The Words of the High One'; Casting Method

The next part of this section on runes can be used with the Runes (or the Ogham) to gain a reading. It is based on using 25 runes and a casting method as opposed to a drawing method. A cloth with 5 rings on it is needed as shown below, these are named after the 5 Norse elements of Earth *(Ymir)*, Air *(Kari)*, Fire *(Lodur)*, Water *(Hier)* and Spirit *(Ond)*.

5 Runes are then drawn from the rune bag and cast onto the cloth, their meanings are then read, depending on which circle they land in. Their meanings are related the 125 verses of the *Norse Edda* (Poem) 'The Words of the High One (Odin)'. These are given below with a number beside each verse and a key is given, to let you know which verse to read. In this method the runes all have 5 meanings, depending on where they fall. They should be read from the outside in, using the same Interpretations as the Thor's Cross Spread, if needed.

The Edda itself is a poem of lots of practical advice, though it can be a bit cryptic at times and needs to be thought of in relation to the modern world. The previous Rune Meanings are not needed using this method, so the Ogham could be used or any other 25 Symbol Stones.

'The Words of the High One'
From 'The Elder Edda' translated by O. Bray

1) " Young and alone on a long road, once I lost my way;
    Rich I felt when I found another, man rejoices in man.

2) A kind word need not cost much, the price of praise can be cheap;
   With half a loaf and an empty cup, I found myself a friend.

3) Two wooden stakes stood on the plain, on them I hung my clothes;
   Draped in linen, they looked well born, but naked I was a no body.

4) Too early to many homes I came, too late, it seemed, to some;
   The ale was finished or else un-brewed, the unpopular can not please.
   Some would invite me to visit their homes, but none thought I needed a meal;
   As though I had just eaten a whole joint, just before with a friend, who had two.

5) The man who stands at a strange threshold, should be cautious before he cross it, glance this way and that;
   Who knows beforehand what foe may sit, awaiting him in the hall?
   Greetings to the host, the guest has arrived, in which seat shall he sit?
   Rash is he, who at unknown doors, relies on his luck.

6) Fire is needed by the newcomer, whose knees are frozen numb;
   Meat and clean linen a man needs, who has fared across the fells.

7) Water too, that he may wash before eating, hand cloths and a hearty welcome;
   Courteous words, then courteous silence, that he may tell his tale.

8) Who travels widely needs his wits about him, the stupid should stay at home;
   The ignorant man is often laughed at, when he sits at meat with the Sage.

9) Of his knowledge, a man should never boast, rather be sparing of speech, when to his house a wiser comes;

Seldom do those who are silent make mistakes, mother wit is ever a faithful friend.

10) A guest should be cautious, when he comes to the table, and sit in
   wary silence, his ears attentive, his eyes alert;
   So he protects himself.

11) Fortunate is he, who is favoured in his lifetime, with praise and words
   of wisdom;
   Evil counsel is often given, by those of evil hearts.

12) Blessed is he, who in his lifetime, is awarded with praise and wit,
   for ill counsel is often given by mortal men to each other.

13) Better gear than good sense, a traveller can not carry,
   Better than riches for the wretched man, far from his home.

14) Better gear than good sense, a traveller can not carry,
   A more tedious burden, than too much drink,
   A traveller can not carry.

15) Less good than belief would have it, is mead for the sons of men;
   A man knows less, the more he drinks, he becomes a befuddled fool.

16) 'I Forget', is the name men give the Heron, who hovers over the feast;
   Fettered I was in his feathers that night, when a guest in 'Gunnlods
   Court'. (Guardian of Inspiration)

17) Drunk I got, dead drunk, when Fjalar the Wise (Odin) was with me,
   Best is the banquet, one looks back on after,
   and remembers all that happened.

18) Silence becomes the son of a Prince, to be silent, but brave in battle;
   It befits a man to be merry and glad, until the day of his death.

19) The coward believes he will live forever, if he holds back in the battle, but in old age he shall have no peace, though spears have spared his limbs.

20) When he meets friends, the fool gapes, is shy and sheepish at first, then he sips his mead and immediately all know what an oaf he is.

21) He who has seen and suffered much, and knows the ways of the world, he who has travelled, can tell what Spirit governs the men he meets.

22) Drink your mead, but in moderation, talk sense or be silent;
No man is called discourteous who goes to bed at an early hour.

23) A gluttonous man who guzzles away, brings sorrow on himself;
at the table of the wise, he is taunted often, mocked for his bloated belly.

24) The herd knows its homing time, and leaves the grazing ground;
But the glutton never knows how much, his belly is able to hold.

25) An ill tempered, unhappy man, ridicules all he hears;
makes fun of others, refusing always to see the faults in himself.

26) Foolish is he, who frets at night, and lies awake to worry;
A weary man when morning comes, he finds all as bad as before.

27) The fool thinks that those who laugh at him, are all his friends;
When he comes to the 'Thing' (Counsel Meeting of many Tribes) and calls for support, few spokesmen he finds.

28) The fool who fancies he is full of wisdom, while he sits by his hearth at home, quickly finds when questioned by others, that he knows nothing at all.

29) The ignorant booby had best be silent, when he moves among other
men, no one will know what a nit wit he is, until he begins to talk;
No one knows less what a nit wit he is, than the man who talks too
much.

30) To ask well, to answer rightly, are the marks of a wise man;
Men must speak of men's deeds, what happens may not be hidden.

31) Wise is he not, who is never silent, mouthing meaningless words;
A glib tongue that goes on chattering, sings to its own harm.

32) A man among friends, should not mock another, many believe the man;
Who is not questioned to know much, and so he escapes their scorn.

33) An early meal a man should take, before he visits friends, lest when
he gets there, he go hungry, afraid to ask for food.

34) The fastest friends may fall out, when they sit at the banquet board;
it is, and shall be, a shameful thing, when guest quarrels with guest.

35) The wise guest has his way of dealing, with those who taunt him at
the table;
He smiles through the meal, not seeming to hear, the twaddle talked
by his foes.

36) The tactful guest, will take his leave early, not linger long;
He starts to stink, who outstays his welcome, in a hall that is not
his own.

37) A small hut of ones own is better, a man is his master at home;
A couple of goats and a corded roof, still are better than begging.

38) A small hut of one's own is better, a man is his master at home;
His heart bleeds for the beggar, who must ask at each meal for a bone.

39) A Wayfarer should not walk unarmed, but have his weapons to hand;
He knows not when he may need a Spear, or what menace, meet on the road.

40) No man is so generous, he will jib at accepting a gift, in return for a gift;
No man so rich, that it really gives him pain, to be repaid.

41) Once he has won wealth enough, a man should not crave for more;
What he saves for friends, foes may take; hopes are often liars.

42) With presents friends should please each other, with a Shield or a costly Coat;
Mutual giving, makes for friendship, so long as life goes well.

43) A man should be loyal through life, to friends, to them and to friends of theirs;
But never shall a man make offer, of friendship to his foes.

44) A man should be loyal through life to friends, and return gift, for gift, laugh when they laugh;
But with lies, repay a false friend who lies.

45) If you find a friend you fully trust, and wish for his good will,
exchange thoughts, exchange gifts, go often to his house.

46) If you deal with another you don't trust, but wish for his good will,
be fair in speech, but false in thought and give him lie, for lie.

47) Even with one you ill trust, and doubt what he means to do,
false words, with fair smiles, may get you the gifts you desire.

48) To a false friend, the footpath winds, though his house, be on the highway;

To a sure friend, there is a short cut, though he live a long way off.

49) Hotter than fire amongst false hearts, burns friendship for five days,
but suddenly slackens when the sixth day dawns;
Feeble their friendship then.

50) The generous and bold, have the best lives, are seldom beset by cares,
but the base man sees bogies everywhere, and the miser pines for
presents.

51) The young Fir that falls and rots, having neither needles or bark,
so is the fate of the friendless man;
Why should he live for long?

52) Little a sand grain, little a dew drop, little the minds of men;
All men are not equal in wisdom, the half wise are everywhere.

53) It is best for man to be middle wise, not over cunning or clever;
The fairest life is led by those, who are deft at all they do.

54) It is best for man to be middle wise, not over cunning or clever;
No man is able to know his future, so let him sleep in peace.

55) It is best for man to be middle wise, not over cunning or clever;
The learned man, whose Lore is deep, is seldom happy at heart.

56) Brand kindles brand, till they burn out, flame is quickened by flame;
One man from another is known by his speech, the simpleton by his
silence.

57) Early shall he rise, who has designs on another's land or life;
His prey escapes the prone Wolf, the sleeper is seldom victorious.

58) Early shall he rise, who rules few servants, and set to work at once;
   Much is lost by the late sleeper, wealth is won by the swift.

59) A man should know, how many logs and strips of bark from the Birch
   to stock in autumn, that he may have enough wood for his winter
   fires.

60) Washed and fed, one may fare to the 'Thing', though ones clothes be
   the worse for wear;
   None need be ashamed of his shoes or hose, nor of the Horse, he owns.

61) As the Eagle who comes to the ocean shore, sniffs and hangs his head,
   dumbfounded is he who finds at the 'Thing', no supporters to plead his
   case.

62) It is safe to tell a secret to one, risky to tell it to two,
   to tell it to three, is thoughtless folly, everyone shall know.

63) Often words uttered to another, have reaped an ill harvest;
   Two beat one, the tongue is heads bane, pockets of fur, hide fists.

64) Moderate at council, should a man be, not brutal and overbearing;
   Among the bold, the bully will find, others as bold as he.

65) These things are thought the best;
   Fire, the sight of the Sun,
   Good health, with the gift to keep it,
   and a life, that avoids vice.

66) Not all sick men, are utterly wretched;
   some are blessed with sons, some with friends, some with riches,
   some with worthy works.

67) The halter can manage a horse, the handless a flock, the deaf can be a
doughty fighter, to be blind is better than to burn on a pyre;
There is nothing the dead can do.

68) It is always better to be alive, the living can keep a cow;
Fire I saw, warming a wealthy man, with a corpse at his door.

69) A son is a blessing, though born late, to a father no longer alive;
Stones would seldom stand by the highway, if sons did not set them
there.

70) He welcomes the night, who has enough provisions;
Short are the sails of a ship, dangerous the dark in autumn,
the wind may veer within five days, and many times in a month.

71) The nit wit does not know that gold, makes apes of many men;
One is rich, one is poor, there is no blame for that.

72) Cattle die, kindred die, every man is mortal;
But the good name, never dies, of one who has lived well.

73) Fields and flocks, had fit young sons, who now carry begging bowls;
Wealth may vanish in the wink of an eye, gold is the falsest of friends

74) In the fool who acquires cattle and lands, or wins a woman's love,
his wisdom wanes with the waxing pride, he sinks from sense to
conceit.

75) Now is answered what you ask of the Runes, graven by the Gods,
Made by the All Father (Odin), sent by the powerful Sage;
"It is best for man, to remain silent".

76) For these things give thanks at nightfall:
The day gone, a guttered torch, a sword tested, the troth of a maiden,
ice crossed, ale drunk.

77) Hew wood in Wind Time, in fine weathers sail, tell in the night time
tales to House Girls, far too many eyes are opened by day:
From a Ship expect speed, from a Shield cover, keenness from a
Sword, but a kiss from a Girl.

78) Drink ale by the hearth, over ice glide, buy a stained sword, buy a
starving mare to fatten at home;
and fatten the watch dog.

79) Trust not an acre early sown, nor praise a son to soon;
Weather rules the acre, wit the son, both are exposed to peril.

80) A snapping Bow, a burning flame, a grinning Wolf, a grunting Boar,
a raucous Crow, a rootless tree, a breaking wave, a boiling kettle,
a flying arrow, an ebbing tide, a coiled Adder, the ice of a night,
a brides bed talk, a Broad Sword, a Bears play, a Princes children,
a Witches welcome, the wit of a slave, a sick Calf, a corpse still
fresh, a brothers killer encountered upon the highway, a house half
burned, a racing stallion who has a wrenched leg;
All are never safe; Let no man trust them.

81) No man should trust a Maidens words, nor what a woman speaks;
Spun on a wheel were women's hearts, in their breasts was implanted
Caprice.

82) To Love a woman whose ways are false, is like sledding over slippery
ice, with unshod horses out of control, badly trained 2 year olds,
or drifting rudderless on a rough sea, or catching a Reindeer with a
crippled hand on a thawing hillside;
Think not to do it.

83) Naked may I speak now for I know both;
Men are treacherous too.
Fairest we speak, when falsest we think;
Many a Maid is deceived.

84) Gallantly shall he speak and gifts bring, who wishes for a woman's love;
Praise the features of the fair girl, who courts well will conquer.

85) Never reproach another for his Love;
It happens often enough, that beauty ensnares with desire the wise, while the foolish, remain unmoved.

86) Never reproach the plight of another, for it happens to many men;
Strong desire may stupefy Heroes and dull the wits of the Wise.

87) The mind alone knows what is near the heart, each is his own judge;
The worst sickness for a Wise man, is to crave what he can not have.

88) So I learned, when I sat in the Reeds, hoping to have my desire;
Lovely was the flesh of that fair girl, but nothing I hoped for happened.

89) I saw on a bed 'Billing's Daughter' (unattainable beauty / unrequited Love), Sun white, asleep;
No greater delight I longed for then, than to lie in her lovely arms.

90) "Come Odin, after nightfall, if you wish for a meeting with me;
All would be lost if anyone saw us and learned that we were Lovers".

91) Afire with longing, I left her then, deceived by her soft words;
I thought my wooing had won the Maid, that I would have my way.

92) After nightfall, I hurried back, but the Warriors were awake, lights were burning, blazing torches;
So false proved the path.

93) Towards Daybreak, back I came, the Guards were sound asleep;
I found then that the fair woman, had tied a Bitch (watch dog) to her bed.

94) Many a girl, when one gets to know her, proves to be fickle and false;
That treacherous Maiden, taught me a lesson, the crafty woman,
covered me with shame, that was all I got from her.

****

95) *Let a man with his guests be glad and merry, modest a man should be,*
but talk well, if he intends to be wise and expects praise from men;
'Fimbul Fambi' (stuttering sound made by an actor, who has forgotten
his lines) is the fool called, unable to open his mouth.

96) *Fruitless my errand, had I been silent when I came to 'Suttungs Court'*
(Giant who owned the Draught of Inspiration);
With spirited words, I spoke to my profit, in the hall of the aged
Giant.

97) *'Rati' (Odin's Rock Giant servant) had gnawed a narrow passage,*
chewed a channel through stone, a path around the roads of Giants;
I was like to lose my head.

98) *'Gunnlod' sat me in the golden seat, poured me the precious mead;*
Ill reward, she had from me for that, for her proud and passionate
heart, her brooding foreboding spirit.

99) *What I won from her, I have well used;*
I have waxed in wisdom since I came back, bringing to Asgard
'Odrerir' (the Mead of Inspiration), the sacred draught.

100) *Hardly would I have come home alive from the Garth (Hell Hound)*
of the grim Troll, had 'Gunnlod' not helped me, the good woman,
who wrapped her arms around me.

101) *The following day the Frost Giants came, walked into 'Har's'*
(God of Wisdom) Hall, to ask for Har's advice;
"Had 'Bolwerk'" (Odin's false name he gave, meaning 'Evil Doer'),

they asked, "come back to his friends? or have he been slain by
'Suttung'?"

102) "Odin", they said, "Swore an oath on his Ring";
  "Who from now on will trust him?"
  By fraud, at the feast, he befuddled 'Suttung' and brought grief to
  'Gunnlod'.

It is time to sing in the Seat of the Wise, of what at 'Urd's Well'(a Norn)
I saw in silence, saw and thought on.
Long I listened to men, Runes heard spoken, Counsels revealed, at 'Har's'
Hall, in 'Har's' Hall;
There I heard this.

'Loddfafnir' (All Father, Odin) listen to my counsel;
You will fare well, if you follow it, it will help you much, if you heed it.

                    ****

103) Never rise at night, unless you need to spy, or ease yourself
   in the Outhouse.

104) Shun a woman, wise in Magik, her bed and her embraces;
   If she cast a Spell (Love Spell), you will care no longer to meet and
   speak with men, desire no food, desire no pleasure, in sorrow fall
   asleep.

105) Never seduce another's wife, never make her your mistress.

106) If you must journey to the mountains and firths,
   take food and fodder with you.

107) Never open your heart to an evil man, when fortune does not favour
   you;

From an evil man, if you make him your friend, you will get evil for good.

108) I saw a warrior wounded fatally, by the words of an evil woman;
Her 'Cunning Tongue' caused his death, though what she alleged was a lie.

109) If you know a friend you can fully trust, go often to his house;
Grass and Brambles grow quickly, upon the un-trodden path.

110) With a good man it is good to talk, make him fast your friend;
But waste not words on a witless oaf, nor sit with a senseless ape.

111) Cherish those near you, never be the first to break with a friend;
Care eats him who can no longer open his heart to another.

112) An evil man, if you make him your friend, will give you evil for good;
A good man, if you make him your friend, will praise you in every place

113) Affection is mutual when men can open, all their heart to each other;
He whose words are always fair, is untrue and not to be trusted.

114) Bandy no speech with a bad man;
Often the better is beaten, in word fight or the worse.

115) Be not a Cobbler, nor a Carver of shafts, except it be for yourself;
If a shoe fit ill or a shaft be crooked, the maker gets curses and kicks.

116) If aware that another is wicked, say so;
Make no truce or treaty with foes.

117) Never share in the shameful gotten;
But allow yourself what is lawful.

118) Never lift your eyes and look up in battle, lest the Heroes enchant you, who can change Warriors, suddenly into Hogs.

119) With a good woman, if you wish to enjoy, her words and her good will, pledge her fairly and be faithful to it;
Enjoy the good you are given.

120) Be not over wary, but wary enough;
first, of the foaming ale, second, of a woman wed to another,
third, of the tricks of thieves.

121) Mock not the Traveller met on the road, nor maliciously laugh at the Guest;
Scoff not at Guests, nor to the gate chase them, but relieve the lonely and wretched.

122) The sitters in the Hall seldom know, the kin of the new comer;
The best man is marred by faults, the worst is not without worth.

123) Never laugh at the old, when they offer counsel, often their words are wise;
From the shrivelled skin, from scraggy things, that hide among the furs and move amid the guts;
Clear words often come.

124) Heavy the beam above the door;
Hang a Horse Shoe on it, against ill luck, lest it should suddenly crash and crush your Guests.

125) Medicines exist against many evils;
Earth against Drunkenness, Heather against Worms, Oak against Costiveness, Corn against Sorcery, Spurred Rye against Rupture, Runes against Bales, the Moon against Feuds, Fire against Sickness, and Earth makes harmless the Floods."

This poem or Edda is split into several sections, some recount some of Odin's adventures under a variety of guises, but all of them deal with Wisdom and Common Sense.

The Key to 'The Words of the High One'

Given below is the Key to the Interpretations of the 'Words of the High One' Edda. The verses in the Edda are all numbered, so when you cast the runes, consult the elemental circle Spread lay out to determine where the runes have landed, then simply cross reference the rune with the appropriate element in the elemental circle spread, to determine which verse to read:

Rune	Ymir	Kari	Lodur	Hier	Ond
Feoh	1	26	51	76	101
Ur	2	27	52	77	102
Thurisaz	3	28	53	78	103
Ansur	4	29	54	79	104
Rad	5	30	55	80	105
Cen	6	31	56	81	106
Gyfu	7	32	57	82	107
Wyn	8	33	58	83	108
Hagel	9	34	59	84	109
Nyd	10	35	60	85	110
Is	11	36	61	86	111
Jara	12	37	62	87	112
Eoh	13	38	63	88	113
Peorth	14	39	64	89	114
Elhaz	15	40	65	90	115
Sigel	16	41	66	91	116
Tyr	17	42	67	92	117
Beorc	18	43	68	93	118
Ehwaz	19	44	69	94	119
Mannaz	20	45	70	95	120

Lagu	21	46	71	96	121
Ing	22	47	72	97	122
Daeg	23	48	73	98	123
Odal	24	49	74	99	124
Wyrd	25	50	75	100	125

Elemental Circle Spread

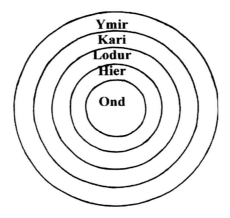

'The Words of the High One' Divination System may prove to be of most use as a simple question and answer system, using only 3 runes instead of 5, applying simple Past, Present and Future meanings to the runes drawn. The Past Rune will be the one cast furthest away from you, the Future Rune will be the next furthest away and the Present Rune will be the one nearest to you. This is not a fixed system; you may easily recognise which runes apply to these positions, simply by reading them and remembering.

13
PERSONAL POWER & MAGIK

Magikal Energy

Casting Spells

Personal Power / Medicine

Magikal Energy

Spells and magik, these are methods also used by Shamen from various cultures; they are a part of the animism belief system, working in a similar way to healing and other energy work. As mentioned in earlier sections, the universe is formed from raw energy, science calls these protons, electrons and neutrons, all things are formed from them, the distance at which they vibrate from each other defines whether something is perceived of as a solid, liquid, gas, spirit, energy, etc.

These protons, etc are left over matter from the Big Bang when the universe was created, they are literally star dust and all things are made from them. They are also energy, much of it is unused energy or energy which we can create ourselves. All things live on energy, in ecology the food chains and webs are the simplest forms of energy exchange models used, all life depends on energy to exist. We convert light, air, food and drink into raw energy we call life force, via our internal organs, this is used up by exerting the body's muscles.

The brain is another of the body's muscles; we are aware that we use only a fraction of the brain's potential and that we still don't fully understand how the brain functions, or what it is capable of. The animistic belief systems are based largely on exploring that untapped potential of the brain. This is why it is essential to look into psychology and other related subjects such as counselling when looking into these forms of belief systems. Shamanism was the earliest form of psychological exploration.

Healing is a form of magik; it involves rituals, movements, invocations (prayers), generation of energy and use of energy. In the martial arts and yoga, Chi, Ki or Prana energy is often talked about, as these forms of exercise are designed to generate this energy, which is then directed through the body for various uses. In the martial arts it is used to generate protection from blows or to add power to your strikes, to preserve or destroy. In the healing arts this same energy is used to heal, if you study the Oriental healing arts, such as Acupuncture, Acupressure, Te a Te, Reiki, Qi Gong or Shiatsu, you will hear the same words used to describe this Life Force as you will in the martial arts. They are also described as being yin (passive) or yang (active) in their nature. This refers to our perception of the energy, not the energy itself, the energy itself is neutral in nature.

In magik you hear of black magik and white magik being practised; this is exactly the same as the concept of Yin and Yang Chi energy used in the martial arts, it is used to destroy (black) or preserve (white). Interestingly the colours for Yin and Yang terms for this process are reversed in our Western image of black and white magik. In the Eastern concepts, destroy would be considered yang in its energy and white in colour; preserve would be considered yin in its energy and black in colour. This is because the energy itself in these colour definitions would be classed as grey or neutral.

In the colour spectrum all colours or lights are contained in the colour white, black is the absence of light and so the absence of colour. In heat absorption, black attracts heat energy, white repels it. So the energy used in magik, healing, martial arts, etc, is basically neutral in its origin, being formed of equal quantities of yin and yang energy, placing it in the central region of the colour spectrum, eg greens and yellows. The Shaman, Sorcerer, Witch, Magician, etc, is the one who defines what use the energy is put to.

The Shaman's nature (psychological make-up) unbalances this neutral energy, by over focusing on either the light or dark aspects of it. The idealistic nature of it, reflected in the top part of the colour spectrum, e.g. blues, purples, white. Or the base nature of it, reflected in the lower part of the colour spectrum, e.g. orange, reds, black. This also relates to the chakra system and aura, from which you can see we are made of all the colours of the spectrum in balance. The Shaman, etc, will have the main Influences on the type of energy that is attracted to them; by the basic nature of the Shaman themselves and the subconscious aspects of their being.

In the case of a Shaman who is unbalanced (be it emotionally, mentally, physically or spiritually), for example a Shaman who is largely unhappy, greedy, power hungry, in need of recognition, fame, success, money, etc and prepared to use almost any means possible to achieve this, e.g. all publicity is good publicity; is liable to attract the baser energies, the potentially more negative energies to himself. Whereas a Shaman who is unbalanced in the opposite direction; who is on a crusade to right the wrongs of the world, to battle evil, to help and heal others, who wants to be seen to be doing good in the world, who is also probably largely unhappy, poor and unnoticed, lonely, sad and in need of love; is liable to attract the idealistic energies, the potentially positive energies to himself.

I would class the first type of Shaman as a Black Shaman, be it consciously or unconsciously; the second type I would class as a space cadet; or plastic/white Shaman as they are often called, generally coming from a New Age background.

I once met a plastic Shaman who described himself as 'a Shaman from a different planet, in the future' (??).

Imbalance in the Shaman is caused by a number of things, including 'unfinished business' as a counsellor would name it; the emotional pain of the past, the negative behaviour patterns they have learnt, be them playing the victim or playing the bully, both are damaged, they have simply chosen the role, which they feel benefits them the most, sympathy or fear, be it consciously or subconsciously. The Shaman is often referred to as the wounded healer, this is because they are often attracted to this form of work as a result of trying to heal their own hurts.

The Black Shaman will get fed up with the whinging twits he finds himself surrounded by and decide that he isn't in as bad a state as they are, then decide to see how much influence he can have over them, bullying them, in the nicest way possible (at first) into seeing things his way.   The White Shaman will put their own needs for healing on hold, as it is less painful to help to heal the others around them, than to focus on healing themselves, plus they will get more attention this way, than by simply playing the victim, thus playing the saviour role, although their healing will not work very well as they have neglected their own needs. An old Greek proverb states 'physician, heal thyself'.

The Balanced Shaman ('Grey' for sake of colour definition) is the one, who has probably played both of these roles to some degree; then experienced something that reminded them that they still have their own 'unfinished business' and focused on healing themselves, reaching a level of healing where their own inner pain, their wound, just doesn't matter anymore, it is no longer ruling them, this leaves them free to decide their direction in life. Which may well have nothing to do with Shamanism, or they may decide to continue on that path, or more often than not, they will simply take an extended break from it, before being offered the choice to go back to it or not, which may not be quite the same as it was before, combining other aspects of life, often very practical ones, with the spiritual side. This also applies to other forms of Pagan practice, we often hear of

Black or White Witches for example. The balanced Shaman is then able to see that the grass is as green, on both sides of the fence, upon which he sits; leaving him free to use all energy in a more balanced manner.

A prayer springs to mind at this point:

"Lord grant me the power to change the things I can, the courage to accept the things I can't and the wisdom to know the difference".

This may all seem a long way from the title of this section, dealing more with personal power/medicine than with magik and spells, but these things are all connected. The whole process is part of one circle, or cycle of life.

The point is the trainee Shaman should be careful of using magik or spells until they are balanced in themselves. It is harder to recognise this than you may think, the cycle contains many tricks and deceptions to make you believe you are balanced all the time. In some ways you are, but deep down you know whether this is really the case, truth is a hard lesson and usually a painful one. You will know whether you have done all the work on yourself you need to, or not. Then when you have, as the old saying goes:

"Before enlightenment, chopping wood, carrying water; after enlightenment, chopping wood, carrying water".

A new cycle begins. In the martial arts, the black belt is considered the point, where you actually start to learn the martial arts, not the final point. In Mongolia the Shaman is considered to be in training for 15 years. Ultimately the Shaman is on a path, to find their own, state of balance; that is the real magik. I once heard a wise Witch say 'All real Magik only changes yourself'. This is often the case.

Casting Spells

Spells are cast by all types of Pagans; Witches/Wicca tends to be feminine in its energy, focusing mainly on the Earth and Lunar energies.

Druidry is masculine in its energy focusing mainly on the Earth and solar energies, the Gothi of Norse/Nordic traditions tend to be masculine in their energy focusing mainly on the elements, they also use solar and lunar energies but they are reversed in their sexual energy, with the moon being male and the sun being female. You can make the process as easy or as complicated as you wish.

Casting spells is a bit like baking a cake, there are a number of different ingredients added, depending on the sort of cake you want. These are prepared and mixed together and then they are baked. Sometimes, just like cakes, they don't work out right, they can be undercooked or overcooked. The ingredients of the spell include things like appropriate herbs for the spell, coloured candles, incenses, water, salt, ribbons or cord of appropriate colours, crystals, fruit, paper, symbols, etc. These ingredients are in addition to, or instead of, any you would normally use when performing a magikal ritual.

The preparation involves deciding when you think the spell will be most effective to cast, this will include things like the moon's cycle. A waxing moon is good for attracting things to you, a waning moon is good for repelling things away from you or another. There are tables and books of correspondences available in many New Age shops, to help you to decide when is the best time to cast your spell; these take into account the movement of the planets and are based on astrology, looking for favourable astrological energies which can work in favour of your type of spell. There are several types of spell commonly cast:

Blessing Spells, such as healing or guidance in exams, etc.

Wishing or Attraction Spells, to help you find love or a job, etc.

Protection, to keep negative influences away from you or another.

Binding Spells, to prevent another from harming themselves or another.

Offensive Spells or Curses, used to cause harm or scare another.

The offensive spells or curses are what is commonly classed as black magic, but many of these spells can also be used in a negative manner. It is important to be careful what you ask for and to phrase it correctly, as you may get exactly what you asked for and that may not have been what you really wanted. Curses and offensive spells should always be used as a last resort; it is better to punch someone in the face, than to cast an offensive spell in my opinion. Wiccans follow a creed or code of practice, which simply states:

"An it Harm none, do as thou Will"

What this means is 'as long as it doesn't hurt anyone else, do what you like'. This is an impossible rule to follow, simply by existing we cause harm to the world around us, we eat meat, which means animals have to die, we upset other people, etc, its life. A better way to think of it is 'Try not to cause any more harm to others, than is absolutely necessary'. Wiccans also often believe in a 'Threefold Law', this states that:

'Everything you do; returns to you 3 times over'.

Things may not be as simple as this, but it is worth bearing in mind. In short it means if you steal £10 from someone, you will have at least £30 stolen from you in some manner. This is called karma, or cause and effect, everything we do is witnessed, even if only by ourselves, these things have a habit of coming back to haunt us at a later, inconvenient time, in the case of negative karma.

The ingredients for the spells can be bought in ready-made packs, from some New Age shops today; I wouldn't recommend you use them. There are many books available about casting spells, which give you ideas for the sort of things you may want to use, or better still allow your feelings to guide you. For example a love spell would use things associated with love, such as pink candles and ribbons, roses, rose quartz, love poems, locks of hair (only in the case of a willing subject, but if they are willing, why are you bothering to cast a love spell on them?) love tokens, etc.

In things like love spells and other spells it is important to remember that if you want to attract a lover, it is better not to be specific, for example don't try and attract someone who is already involved with someone else, that will lead to bad karma. Ask instead for the 'right person' for you and for you to be the 'right person' for them. These words would be included in the Invocation or love spell itself, this usually take the form of a simple rhyme which is easy to remember.

If you are using more people than just yourself to cast the spell, the preparation is even more important, each person must know what they are doing and when. One reason a witches' coven meets is to raise extra power, this is done by having a number of people, traditionally 13, dancing in a circle with the same intent in mind, working together as one, chanting the spell; it makes it more powerful or power-full.

A magikal circle should always be cast prior to doing a spell or magikal activity, this is usually done in the same way each time, asking for the assistance of your normal guardians.

When a spell is being cast an additional invocation is made after this, to ask for the assistance and blessings of an appropriate deity. In the case of a love spell a fertility goddess would probably be invoked; this invocation (recipe) would included things like the reasons why they are being asked for help and for whom the spell is being cast, this should be worded carefully as mentioned earlier, in a form of poem.

The ingredients of the spell are used in the manner considered appropriate for the spell, when the deity's presence is felt, or when the group feels is the best time, if using specific tables and correspondences this can often be timed to the minute.

While the spell is being cast (ingredients mixed), the candles burnt, ribbons tied, etc, by those performing the spell, the rest of the group will be dancing in a circle around the outside, chanting a simple and sympathetic love rhyme, to raise energy (bake the cake).

The one who the spell is for (cook), should take the leading role here, if they are a part of the group. Sometimes if they are not, it is appropriate to invite them to witness it, sometimes it is not; but usually they will have been told when it will be happening and have been advised to be doing something appropriate themselves, e.g. meditating on love or similar.

When the spell is finished the group working on it and those dancing, should all end at the same time, so a signal is necessary. The spell is cast when the circle is cut (with a ritual knife or sword) and the energy rushes out on its mission. This is how it is done in a group, however Shamen more often than not are not in a group, being part of a more solitary belief system; they are not alone in this. Many witches are classed as hedge witches or solitaries, as are any Pagans not part of a working group.

So how does the solitary Shaman raise the energy needed to cast an effective Spell?

Traditionally in a very similar manner, by dancing and chanting. Yhis can take the form of traditional tribal dances and songs, or more spontaneous movements, such as animal imitations and chanting; sometimes this takes the form of nonsensical gibberish, or 'speaking in tongues', which may or may not mean something, as it is often in another language, or at least sounds and feels like it. It is also important to remember the Shaman is never truly alone, their group is simply made up of spirits of various forms; these Spirits play their part in the spellcasting as well.

Other than this, the intention and the ingredients of the spell, the ritual, invocation and casting of the spell are very similar, though it will probably be more simplified and take a more primitive form, rather than the poetry, there may simply be requests or instructions. This is because only half the ritual is visible to the onlooker, other parts are held in the otherworlds. Plus the Shaman would have to make the ritual more simple, because in this world they are acting alone.

The main form of energy generated is emotional in nature, half the time that is all that is needed, simply very strong emotions. People often subconsciously cast spells, even if they know nothing about magik; simply directing a very strong emotional energy, with an Intention, will often have effects.

In all the animism belief systems a lot of emphasis is placed on the ritual, or the performance, which is much like a play, with actors, storyline, props and costumes. But these are not the spell, they are simply the trimmings. Basically all that is needed to cast a simple form of spell is:

Need
Knowledge
Intention
Strong Emotion
Will Power
Focus

There is one more very important Ingredient needed for a Spell to have any chance of working:

Opportunity

Without this, a spell, no matter how good it was, will have very little chance of manifesting. This means if, for example, you are casting a love spell, unless you put your glad rags on, fix your hair, put on your make up, etc, and go to places where you are liable to meet an appropriate new lover, you will not find one; this doesn't mean go down the pub once, you have to put some effort into it, just like you did the spell, you must also give it some time.

It is pointless going to places you wouldn't feel comfortable, an appropriate or right lover is going to have to have things in common with you, if it stands any chance of working. A college course is a good example of how you might meet the right lover. Spells are a back-up, they help to boost your confidence, making you more likely to succeed. After all you wouldn't expect to win the lottery unless you actually bought a lottery ticket, would you?

Coincidence is the space that spells use to manifest; once you have been following this path for a while, you will begin to realise there really is no such thing as coincidence, it is all cause and effect, energy released returning to you. Spells are used all the time by many people, every day, most commonly they are called 'prayers'. However most prayers are rattled off when you are knackered, just before you fall asleep, in a "da de da de da" manner, this will have little effect. Yet if you pray, in the same way you would cast a spell, there is every chance it will generate results, especially if you give it the opportunity.

Personal Power/Medicine

The Native Americans often talk about medicine in their traditions; this does not refer to cough mixture or pain killers, they are talking about personal power. Personal power has already been mentioned a few times through out the Sections, it is essentially your natural gifts, those things you find easy or seem to pick up with little problem you seem to have a natural flair for them. It also refers to your personality and what you would consider to be your natural virtues, those aspects of yourself which are dear to you.

Medicine or personal power can relate to many things, though they do have to be proven. The personal medicine of the Native Americans is normally most visible in their war paint and shields, at least the ideas or symbols for it are expressed there; most of us only see these in films, I don't know how accurate these images are in this context, but the imagery is how these aspects are presented. They are also present in the other arts of Shamanic cultures, in cave paintings, on drums, in patterns on cloth, in pottery designs, jewellery, ritual scarring, tattoos, etc.

Many of these symbols, colours, patterns have similar meanings in different cultures, but this not always the case. In many ways this is truly a personal expression. It's a bit like wearing a badge which says who you are, what you do for a living, what you are interested in, what your dreams and ambitions are, what your religion is, etc.

But as I've already said, these are usually proven; a Native American wouldn't wear make up that marked them as a seer if they weren't, they would only look foolish when people asked them to interpret their dreams, as well as calling into doubt their other medicines. Personal power or personal medicine can take many forms, it is not limited to what would be normally considered 'spiritual matters', though I hope you are beginning to realise that everything is connected, so ultimately everything is spiritual.

Your personal medicine may be that you are good with engines, you may have a natural talent for healing cars; or you may be an artist, a computer whiz; many of the skills we have today, didn't even exist when our ancestors laid the foundations of Shamanic belief. What tends to happen quite often is that the more modern skills are related to more ancient ones; so a mechanic would probably be painted as a chariot maker or a blacksmith, but there would be nothing wrong with a mechanic painting a spanner on his face as part of his so-called 'war paint', in fact it would also mark you as honest, which is a very important medicine.

How your medicine is proven is more important, one person saying you are a good healer wouldn't prove you were, though it may indicate you would be good at it and perhaps should get some training. A car mechanic would usually have some form of diploma to prove they were trained in it, but some people only do it as a hobby and wouldn't necessarily have a diploma; but I guess if they can mend your car, when it doesn't work, you could assume they have proven their skill. An artist is likely to have painted some form of painting, though art can be subject to interpretation. A proven artist would have probably sold some of their paintings, or at least could if they chose to.

Ultimately it is better to know you are proven in that medicine and to turn up at a Native American ceremony or similar with one small line painted on your face, than to lie about what you are good at; you would receive more respect for that, than for a face full of nonsense. Even better, would probably be to ask for their guidance in what your 'medicine paint' should look like, by relating your skills to them.

Another symbol of your personal medicine is the 'medicine shield'. This may have all sorts of symbols painted on it, often only its owner and close relatives may even know what the symbols mean. But often they are associated with their power animals, which are also strong indications of your personal power or medicine. The sort of paints used were often made from natural ochres and plant dyes, such as blue woad in the case of the Celts. Given below are some examples of what different colours are used to represent to Native Americans, though these may vary from tribe to tribe:

Yellow Lines above the eyes = Seer

A totally Black face = Mourning

Blackened eye sockets = Truthful, Good Advisor

Red line down the nose = Leader

Red line down forehead and down chin = Protector of the Weak

White = Wisdom has altered their perception

Red Symbol = Hereditary Skills

The medicine colours used are also related to the 4 directions, a new medicine would be painted in the colour of the direction the person was facing when they learnt it. The Native American direction colours are different to our's, most often being:

East - Yellow
South - Red
West - Black
North - White

Though occasionally, as in the case of 'Black Elk' and 'Lame Deer', they are:

East - Red
South - Yellow
West - Black
North - White

The various meanings of these directions are given in Section 2. Eagles' feathers are another indication of medicine; eagle/raptor feathers are similar to certificates to the Native Americans and mean they have passed certain rites of passage and had certain spiritual experiences.

Final Word

That is the end of this book; once more I must say this book won't make you a Shaman, but you can be sure you have a good foundation on which to build, should the spirits call you to be one. You will also have a good working knowledge of Animism/Paganism. This book, like all real learning, is only the beginning of your journey, which is why I called it a foundation. It will provide you with good foundations on which to build and learn more. You will also only get out of this book what you put into it, reading alone doesn't make you an expert. Now you must use this knowledge and new skills to develop your path, as well as adding to them new knowledge and skills, remember the best teacher you will ever have is:

'The One Inside Of You'

"Walk your Talk Gently, in Truth, Balance and Harmony"

Adam Bear 2008

446

Bibliography

Flight of the Seventh Moon by Lynn Andrews, RKP, 1984

Black Elk - the sacred ways of the Lakota by Black Elk, Wallace & Lyon, Harper & Row, 1990

Black Elk Speaks by John G Nerhardt, Washington Square Press, 1959

Journey to Ixtlan, by Carlos Castaneda, Penguin, 1974

A Separate Reality by Carlos Castaneda, Penguin, 1970

The Teachings of Don Juan by Carlos Castaneda, Penguin, 1970

Lame Deer - Seeker of Visions by John Fire Lame Deer & Richard Erdoes, Washington Square Press, 1972

Gift of Power - the life and teachings of a Lakota Medicine Man by Archie Fire Lame Deer & Richard Erdoes, Bear & Company Publishing, 1992

Shamanism by Mircea Eliade, Arcana, 1989

The Shamans Path by Gary Doore, Shambhala Publications, 1988

The Way of the Shaman by Michael Harner, Bantam Books, 1982

Earth Medicine by Kenneth Meadows, Element Books, 1989

Shamanic Experience by Kenneth Meadows, Element Books, 1991

The Medicine Way by Kenneth Meadows, Element Books, 1990

Shamanism - Rituals for Spirit Journeying and creating Sacred Space by Will Adcock, Hermes House, 2000

Kumalak - Mirror of Destiny by Didier Blau, Simon & Schuster, 1999

Riding Windhorses by Sarangerel, Destiny Books, 2000

Chosen by the Spirits by Sarangerel, Destiny Books, 2001

Entering the Circle by Olga Kharitidi, Thorsons, 1997

Master of Lucid Dreams by Olga Kharitidi, M.D., Hampton Roads Publishing Company, Inc, 2001

Celtic Totem Animals by John Matthews, Gothic Image Publications, 2002

The Celtic Shaman by John Matthews, Element Books,

Taliesin: Shamanism and the Bardic Mysteries in Britain and Ireland by John Matthews

The Clan of the Cave Bear by Jean M Auel, Coronet Books, 1980

The Valley of the Horses by Jean M Auel, Coronet Books, 1982

The Mammoth Hunters by Jean M Auel, Coronet Books, 1985

The Plains of Passage by Jean M Auel, Coronet Books, 1990

The Shelters of Stone by Jean M Auel, Coronet Books, 2002

The Ceremonial Circle by Sedonia Cahill & Joshua Halpern, Mandala, 1991

Circles and Standing Stones by Evan Hadingham, Abacus, 1978

Pagan Cornwall: Land of the Goddess by Cheryl Straffon, Meyn Mamvro, 1993

Ancient Sites in West Penwith by Cheryl Straffon, Meyn Mamvro, 1992

The Sun and the Serpent by Hamish Miller and Paul Broadhurst, Pendragon, 1989
Secret Shrines by Paul Broadhurst, Pendragon, 1988
Animal Energies by Gary Buffalo Horn Man & Sherry Firedancer, Dancing Otter Publishing, 1992
Sacred Path Cards by Jamie Sams, Harper Collins, 1990
Medicine Cards by Jamie Sams & David Carson, Bear & Co, 1988
The Shamanic Wheel of the Year by Alawn Tickhill, Pagan Products Publications, 1987
Mysteries of the Runes by Michael Howard, Capall Bann, 1994
The Druid Tradition by Philip Carr-Gomm, Element, 1991
The Book of Druidry by Ross Nichols, Aquarian Press, 1990
The Druids by Stuart Piggott, Thames & Hudson, 1985
Earthlights Revelation by Paul Devereux, Blandford, 1989
The Druids by TD Kendrick, Cass, 1927
Complete Herbal by Culpeper, Wordsworth Reference, 1995
A Modern Herbal by Mrs. M Grieve, Penguin, 1980
Herbs for Cooking and Health by Christine Grey-Wilson, Collins Gems, 1987
Trees by Alastair Fitter & David More, Collins Gems, 1980
Wild Animals by John A Burton, Collins Gems, 1980
The Wild Flower Key by Francis Rose, Frederick Warne, 1981
Animal Tracks by Miroslav Bouchner, Blitz Editions, 1998
Plants & Animals by Jan Toman & Jiri Felix, Blitz Editions, 1990
Animals Tracks and Signs by Alfred Leutscher, Usborne, 1979
Food for Free by Richard Mabey, Collins, 1972
Mushrooms of Britain and Europe by Paul Sterry, New Holland, 1995
The Making of Mankind by Richard E Leakey, Book Club Associates, 1981
Living Britain by Peter Crawford, BBC, 1999
Healing Remedies by C Norman Shealey M.D., Ph.D., Element, 1998
British Trees by Archie Miles, Ted Smart, 1999
Wiccan Wisdom Keepers by Sally Griffyn, A Godsfield Book, 2002
The Illustrated Guide to Witchcraft by Tony & Aileen Grist, A Godsfield Book, 2000
Runes by Andy Baggott, Hermes House, 2002
Spells, Charms, Talismans & Amulets by Pamela Ball, Arcturus, 2001
The Pictish Guide by Elizabeth Sutherland, Werner Soderstrom OY, 1997
Dictionary of Beliefs and Religions by Rosemary Goring, Wordsworth Reference, 1995
People of the Lake by Richard E Leakey, Discus, 1978
Grasses by C E Hubbard, Penguin Books, 1984
The SAS Survival Handbook by Peter Darman, Parragon, 1997
Wicca; the Old Religion in the New Age by Vivianne Crowley, Thorsons, 1996
Witchcraft: A Tradition Renewed by Evan John Jones & Doreen Valiente, Robert Hale, 1990
Eight Sabbats for Witches by Janet & Stewart Farrar, Robert Hale, 1984
The Witches' Way by Janet & Stewart Farrar, Robert Hale, 1984

What Witches Do by Janet & Stewart Farrar, Robert Hale, 1983

Spells and how they Work by Janet & Stewart Farrar, Robert Hale, 1985

The Witches' God by Janet & Stewart Farrar, Robert Hale, 1982

The Witches' Goddess by Janet & Stewart Farrar, Robert Hale, 1982

The White Goddess by Robert Graves, Faber & Faber, 1961

The Celtic Tree Oracle by Liz & Colin Murray, Rider, 1989

The Tree: The complete Book of Saxon Witchcraft by Raymond Buckland, Samuel Weiser, 1974

An ABC of Witchcraft by Doreen Valiente, Robert Hale, 1973

Natural Magic by Doreen Valiente, Robert Hale, 1975

Witchcraft for Tomorrow by Doreen Valiente, Robert Hale, 1978

Natural Magic by Marian Green, Element Books, 1989

The Path through the Labyrinth by Marian Green, Element Books, 1988

North American Indian: Myths & Legends by Lewis Spence, Senate, 1994

The Norsemen: Myths & Legends by H A Guerber, Senate, 1994

Celtic: Myths & Legends by T W Rolleston, Senate, 1994

Ecology by Odum, Holt-Saunders International Editions, 1979

Ecology: Individuals, Populations & Communities by Begon, Harper & Townsend, Blackwell Scientific Publications, 1990

Green Plants: their Origin and Diversity by Peter R Bell, Cambridge Press, 1992

An Introduction to Behavioural Ecology by J R Krebs & N B Davies, Blackwell Science, 1993

Psychology: the Science of Mind & Behaviour by Richard D Gross, Hodder & Stoughton, 1992

Client Centred Therapy by Carl R Rogers, Boston, 1951

On Becoming a Person by Carl R Rogers, Boston, 1961

Gestalt Therapy by F S Perls, Bantam, 1969

Zen Shiatsu by Shizuto Masunaga with Wataru Ohashi, Japan Publications Inc, 1977

Shiatsu by Susanne Franzen, Hermes House, 2002

Crystals and Crystal Healing by Simon Lilly, Hermes House, 2002

The Original Reiki Handbook of Dr. Mikao Usui by Dr. Mikao Usui & Frank Arjava Petter, Lotus Press, 1998

The Lord of the Rings by JRR Tolkien, Unwin Paperbacks, 1989

Legend: The Arthurian Tarot by Anna-Marie Ferguson, Llewellyn Publications, 1995

Resources

Shamanic Links, Adam Bear, shamanic.links@ntlworld.com Shamanic Links Forum: http://s1.zetaboards.com/Shamanic_Links/index/

For Courses in Shamanism / Animism, Reiki, Magikal Tool Making; also Hand Crafted Magikal Tools made to order and Healing.

The Order of Bards, Ovates & Druids, PO Box 1333, Lewes, E. Sussex, BN7 1DX.
For Correspondence Courses in Druidry.

Galdraheim, Alawn Tickhill, 35, Wilson Avenue, Deal, Kent, CT14 9NL.
For Courses in Shamanism / Wicca and Hand Crafted Magikal Tools.

Sacred Hoop & Pathways, Nick Wood, Anghorfa, Abercych, Boncath, Pembrokeshire, West Wales, SA37 0EZ.
For Sacred Hoop Magazine, Hand Crafted Magikal Tolls and Courses in Shamanism.

Sacred Trust, Simon Buxton & Naomi Lewis, Wyld Hive House, St. Marys Place, Penzance Cornwall, TR18 4EE.
For Shamanic Courses and Healing and Organic B & B.

John & Caitlin Matthews, BCM Hallowquest, London, WC1N 3 XX.
For Courses in Celtic Shamanism.

Eagles Wing Centre, Leo Rutherford, BM Box 7475, London, WC1N 3XX.
For Courses in Shamanism.

Odinshof, Pete Jennings, BCM Tercel, London, WC1N 3XX.
For Courses in the Norse Tradition.

Odinic Rite, BCM Runic, London, WC1N 3XX.
For Courses in the Norse Tradition.
Dragon, 39, Amersham Road, London, SE14 6QQ.
Eco Pagan Organisation.

Invisible College, Marian Green, SAE to PO Box 42, Bath, BA1 1ZN.
For Courses on Witchcraft.

British Druid Order, P.O.Box 635, Halifax, HX2 6WX
For Druid Events.

Wicca Study Group, Vivianne & Chris Crowley, BM Deosil, London
WC1N 3XX.
For Courses on Wicca.

Pagan Federation, BM Box 7097, London, WC1N 3XX.
For Pagan Information.

Kantara, Julie Gillott, Ancestral Spirits, 23, St. James Street, Kings Lynn,
Norfolk.
For Hand Crafted Magikal Tools and Courses in Shamanism.

Kenneth Meadows, BM Box 8602, London, WC1N 3XX.
For Courses in Contemporary Shamanism.

FREE DETAILED CATALOGUE

Capall Bann is owned and run by people actively involved in many of the areas in which we publish. A detailed illustrated catalogue is available on request, SAE or International Postal Coupon appreciated. **Titles can be ordered direct from Capall Bann, post free in the UK** (cheque or PO with order) or from good bookshops and specialist outlets.

A Breath Behind Time, Terri Hector
A Soul is Born by Eleyna Williamson
Angels and Goddesses - Celtic Christianity & Paganism, M. Howard
The Art of Conversation With the Genius Loci, Barry Patterson
Arthur - The Legend Unveiled, C Johnson & E Lung
Astrology The Inner Eye - A Guide in Everyday Language, E Smith
Auguries and Omens - The Magical Lore of Birds, Yvonne Aburrow
Asyniur - Women's Mysteries in the Northern Tradition, S McGrath
Beginnings - Geomancy, Builder's Rites & Electional Astrology in the
        European Tradition, Nigel Pennick
Between Earth and Sky, Julia Day
The Book of Seidr, Runic John
Caer Sidhe - Celtic Astrology and Astronomy, Michael Bayley
Call of the Horned Piper, Nigel Jackson
Can't Sleep, Won't Sleep, Linda Louisa Dell
Carnival of the Animals, Gregor Lamb
Cat's Company, Ann Walker
Celebrating Nature, Gordon MacLellan
Celtic Faery Shamanism, Catrin James
Celtic Faery Shamanism - The Wisdom of the Otherworld, Catrin James
Celtic Lore & Druidic Ritual, Rhiannon Ryall
Celtic Sacrifice - Pre Christian Ritual & Religion, Marion Pearce
Celtic Saints and the Glastonbury Zodiac, Mary Caine
Circle and the Square, Jack Gale
Come Back To Life, Jenny Smedley
Company of Heaven, Jan McDonald
Compleat Vampyre - The Vampyre Shaman, Nigel Jackson
Cottage Witchcraft, Jan McDonald
Creating Form From the Mist - The Wisdom of Women in Celtic Myth and
        Culture, Lynne Sinclair-Wood
Crystal Clear - A Guide to Quartz Crystal, Jennifer Dent
Crystal Doorways, Simon & Sue Lilly

In Search of Pagan Gods, Teresa Moorey
Intuitive Journey, Ann Walker Isis - African Queen, Akkadia Ford
Journey Home, The, Chris Thomas
Kecks, Keddles & Kesh - Celtic Lang & The Cog Almanac, Bayley
Language of the Psycards, Berenice
Legend of Robin Hood, The, Richard Rutherford-Moore
Lid Off the Cauldron, Patricia Crowther
Light From the Shadows - Modern Traditional Witchcraft, Gwyn
Living Tarot, Ann Walker
Lore of the Sacred Horse, Marion Davies
Lost Lands & Sunken Cities (2nd ed.), Nigel Pennick
Lyblác, Anglo Saxon Witchcraft by Wulfeage
The Magic and Mystery of Trees, Teresa Moorey
Magic For the Next 1,000 Years, Jack Gale
Magic of Herbs - A Complete Home Herbal, Rhiannon Ryall
Magical Guardians - Exploring the Spirit and Nature of Trees, Philip Heselton
Magical History of the Horse, Janet Farrar & Virginia Russell
Magical Lore of Animals, Yvonne Aburrow
Magical Lore of Cats, Marion Davies
Magical Lore of Herbs, Marion Davies
Magick Without Peers, Ariadne Rainbird & David Rankine
Masks of Misrule - Horned God & His Cult in Europe, Nigel Jackson
Medicine For The Coming Age, Lisa Sand MD
Medium Rare - Reminiscences of a Clairvoyant, Muriel Renard
Menopausal Woman on the Run, Jaki da Costa
Mind Massage - 60 Creative Visualisations, Marlene Maundrill
Mirrors of Magic - Evoking the Spirit of the Dewponds, P Heselton
The Moon and You, Teresa Moorey
Moon Mysteries, Jan Brodie
Mysteries of the Runes, Michael Howard
Mystic Life of Animals, Ann Walker
The Mystical and Magical World of FAerie, Ralph Harvey
New Celtic Oracle The, Nigel Pennick & Nigel Jackson
Oracle of Geomancy, Nigel Pennick
Pagan Feasts - Seasonal Food for the 8 Festivals, Franklin & Phillips
Paganism For Teens, Jess Wynne
Patchwork of Magic - Living in a Pagan World, Julia Day
Pathworking - A Practical Book of Guided Meditations, Pete Jennings
Personal Power, Anna Franklin
Pickingill Papers - The Origins of Gardnerian Wicca, Bill Liddell
Pillars of Tubal Cain, Nigel Jackson
Places of Pilgrimage and Healing, Adrian Cooper
Planet Earth - The Universe's Experiment, Chris Thomas
Practical Divining, Richard Foord
Practical Meditation, Steve Hounsome
Practical Spirituality, Steve Hounsome

Psychic Self Defence - Real Solutions, Jan Brodie
Real Fairies, David Tame
Reality - How It Works & Why It Mostly Doesn't, Rik Dent
Romany Tapestry, Michael Houghton
Runic Astrology, Nigel Pennick
Sacred Animals, Gordon MacLellan
Sacred Celtic Animals, Marion Davies, Ill. Simon Rouse
Sacred Dorset - On the Path of the Dragon, Peter Knight
Sacred Grove - The Mysteries of the Forest, Yvonne Aburrow
Sacred Geometry, Nigel Pennick
Sacred Nature, Ancient Wisdom & Modern Meanings, A Cooper
Sacred Ring - Pagan Origins of British Folk Festivals, M. Howard
Season of Sorcery - On Becoming a Wisewoman, Poppy Palin
Seasonal Magic - Diary of a Village Witch, Paddy Slade
Secret Places of the Goddess, Philip Heselton
Secret Signs & Sigils, Nigel Pennick
The Secrets of East Anglian Magic, Nigel Pennick
A Seeker's Guide To Past Lives, Paul Williamson
Seeking Pagan Gods, Teresa Moorey
A Seer's Guide To Crystal Divination, Gale Halloran
Self Enlightenment, Mayan O'Brien
Soul Resurgence, Poppy Palin
Spirits of the Air, Jaq D Hawkins
Spirits of the Water, Jaq D Hawkins
Spirits of the Fire, Jaq D Hawkins
Spirits of the Aether, Jaq D Hawkins
Spirits of the Earth, Jaq D Hawkins
Stony Gaze, Investigating Celtic Heads John Billingsley
Stumbling Through the Undergrowth , Mark Kirwan-Heyhoe
Subterranean Kingdom, The, revised 2nd ed, Nigel Pennick
Symbols of Ancient Gods, Rhiannon Ryall
Talking to the Earth, Gordon MacLellan
Talking With Nature, Julie Hood
Taming the Wolf - Full Moon Meditations, Steve Hounsome
Teachings of the Wisewomen, Rhiannon Ryall
The Other Kingdoms Speak, Helena Hawley
Transformation of Housework, Ben Bushill
Tree: Essence of Healing, Simon & Sue Lilly
Tree: Essence, Spirit & Teacher, Simon & Sue Lilly
Tree Seer, Simon & Sue Lilly
Torch and the Spear, Patrick Regan
Understanding Chaos Magic, Jaq D Hawkins
Understanding Second Sight, Dilys Gater
Understanding Spirit Guides, Dilys Gater
Understanding Star Children, Dilys Gater
The Urban Shaman, Dilys Gater

Vortex - The End of History, Mary Russell
Warp and Weft - In Search of the I-Ching, William de Fancourt
Warriors at the Edge of Time, Jan Fry
Water Witches, Tony Steele
Way of the Magus, Michael Howard
Weaving a Web of Magic, Rhiannon Ryall
West Country Wicca, Rhiannon Ryall
What's Your Poison? vol 1, Tina Tarrant
Wheel of the Year, Teresa Moorey & Jane Brideson
Wildwitch - The Craft of the Natural Psychic, Poppy Palin
Wildwood King , Philip Kane
A Wisewoman's Book of Tea Leaf Reading, Pat Barki
The Witching Path, Moira Stirland
The Witch's Kitchen, Val Thomas
The Witches' Heart, Eileen Smith
Treading the Mill - Practical CraftWorking in Modern Traditional Witchcraft by Nigel Pearson
Witches of Oz, Matthew & Julia Philips
Witchcraft Myth Magic Mystery and... Not Forgetting Fairies, Ralph Harvey
Wondrous Land - The Faery Faith of Ireland by Dr Kay Mullin
Working With Crystals, Shirley o'Donoghue
Working With Natural Energy, Shirley o'Donoghue
Working With the Merlin, Geoff Hughes
Your Talking Pet, Ann Walker
The Zodiac Experience, Patricia Crowther

FREE detailed catalogue
Contact: Capall Bann Publishing, Auton Farm, Milverton, Somerset, TA4 1NE